Great Riding Holidays

A global guide to holidays on horseback

BY JOHN RULER AND ARTHUR SACKS

Edited by Sheva Stoloff

First Editon

A publication of THE COMPLEAT TRAVELLER

The information in this book is subject to change. The authors and the publishers make no claim as to the absolute accuracy of all information. Errors and omissions may occur. Please call or write to places listed to verify and update information or look for our web site at: www.ridingholidays.com

Published by
The Compleat Traveller
2425 Edge Hill Road
Huntingdon Valley, PA 19006
USA

Copyright © 1999 by The Compleat Traveller

ISBN: 0-9653558-2-9
ISSN: 1520-7889

First Edition: December, 1998
Printed by Creative Printing, LTD, Hong Kong
Front Cover design by Richard Schiff/Guilford Graphics International, Toms River, NJ
Book design and type formatting by Bernard Schleifer
Map graphics: Guilford Graphics International

Cover photos:
Front: Ts'yl'os Park Lodge - photo by Mike Woodworth
Back: Corbett's Trails and Times, Kumaon Region, India

Distributed to the trade by: Portfolio Books, London, UK as *Great Riding Vacations*

DEDICATIONS

To my wife Janet for so often playing second fiddle to a bunch of horses.
My daughter Jenny for encouraging me to continue riding.
My grand-daughter Polly, who at age of two, is already passionately fond
of her rocking-horse which she rides in style.
Betty Ferrand who dedicated so much time and effort through Calvary
Tours to encouraging the growth of worthwhile riding holidays.

—JOHN RULER

To my 3 fastriders, daughter Kelly and sons Aron and Joshua,
and to Sheva Stoloff "the gurl of my dreams."

—ARTHUR SACKS

ACKNOWLEDGMENTS

John Ruler would like to thank the following UK sources for their help in compiling this guide: The British Horse Society; the Association of British Riding Schools; the riding and trekking associations of Scotland and Wales and their Irish counterparts; numerous tourist offices worldwide, the African Horse Safari Association; various air and shipping lines, along with the specialist riding holiday companies—for their support and interest, And, above all, the horses who made it all possible. In particular, Marquesa, Monty, Rosie and Komati—for making some rides more memorable than others.

Arthur Sacks would like to thank his ex-wife, always loved, Muffie Geissler, Horse Whisperer supreme, who taught me all about horses and I have never been the same since. Thanks to all the people in the horse riding holiday industry who know that riding vacations are the soul food of life. To all the people who helped, Bayard Fox, Olwen Law, Ryan Schmidt, Anne Mariage, Susan Eakins, Nelly Gelich, Vivian Ashley, Susy Morris of Creative Printing, a publisher's dream, Bernie Schleifer and Gertrude, who spin paper into gold. Finally, I thank my friends, who endured the egocentric process of writing a book, Herby and Sharon, Diane and Phil, Richie and Betsy, Jack and Jane, Karen and Chief Five Strands & tribe.

CONTENTS

SELECTION OF DESTINATIONS FEATURED   8

ABOUT THE AUTHORS   9

AUTHORS' GUIDE: HOW TO USE THIS BOOK   10

INTRODUCTION TO GREAT RIDING HOLIDAYS
   by John Ruler   12

AFRICA   16

Out of Africa by John Ruler   17
Africa by Bayard Fox   20

BOTSWANA
African Horseback Safaris   26

KENYA
Horseback Safaris on Lewa Downs   28
Offbeat Safaris Africa Limited   30
Safaris Unlimited Africa Ltd.   34

MOROCCO
Southern Oasis & High Atlas Valley   38

MALAWI
Nyika Horse Safari   40

NAMIBIA
Namib Desert Trails   42

SOUTH AFRICA
Equus Horse Safaris   44
Horizon Horse Adventures at Triple B   46

ZIMBABWE
Carew Safaris-Mavuradonna Wilderness   48

ASIA   50

India by John Ruler   51
India by Billa Edwards   52

Riding in India by Inder Jit Singh   54
Mongolia by Arthur Sacks and Anne
   Mariage   56
Mongolia: Land of the Horse by Cynthia
   Davidson   57

BHUTAN/NEPAL
Horse Riding in Bhutan/Chitwan National
   Park in Nepal   60

INDIA
Corbett's Trails and Times   62
The Aravalli Hills   64
Hadoti Ride   66
Riding with Nihangs and into the
   Himalaya   68
Pushkar Fair Ride   72
Shalivan Stables   74

MONGOLIA
Altai and Arkhangai Trips   78

NEPAL
The Valley of the Mustang Ride   80

PAKISTAN
The Pakistani Journeys   84

TURKEY
The Cappadocia Tour   86

AUSTRALIA   90

Australia by Nelly Gelich   91

NEW SOUTH WALES
Brush Gully Guest House   94
Kelly's Bushranging Adventures   96
Khancoban Trail Rides   98

Millamolong Station   100
The 2000 Olympic Rides   102
Pub Crawls on Horseback   106

QUEENSLAND
Clip Clop Horse Treks   108
Horse Trek Australia   110

N E W   Z E A L A N D   114

New Zealand *by Rob Stanley*   *115*

NORTH ISLAND
North River Treks   118
Pakiri Beach Horse Rides   120
Te Urewara Adventures of New Zealand   122

SOUTH ISLAND
Hurunui Horse Treks   124
New Zealand Backcountry Saddle
   Expeditions   128

E U R O P E   130

Austria *by John Ruler*   131
France *by John Ruler*   132
Germany and the Benelux Countries
   by John Ruler   134
Hungary *by John Ruler*   136
Iceland: A Personal View *by John Ruler*   137
Italy *by John Ruler*   139
Poland *by John Ruler*   141
Portugal *by John Ruler*   142
The Russian Horse Tradition *by*
   Anne Mariage   144
Scandinavia: Denmark, Sweden, Norway
   and Finland *by John Ruler*   146
Slovenia *by John Ruler*   148
Spain *by John Ruler*   149
Switzerland *by John Ruler*   152
United Kingdom and Ireland
   by John Ruler   154

AUSTRIA
Castles Ride   158
Explorers' Ride   160
South Bohemia Ride   162

FINLAND
Finnair Riding Tours   164

FRANCE
Le Moulin du Chemin   174
Mudinina Horse Trekking Centre   176
Pyrenees Mountain Ride   178
The Heart of Provence   180

ICELAND
Icelandic Riding Tours   182

IRELAND
Allie Cross Equestrian Centre   192
Connemara/Coast Trails   194
Drumgooland House and Equestrian
   Centre   198
El Rancho Horse Holidays, Ltd.   200
Eric Pele: "The Art of Horsepersonship"
   at Brookvale Farm   204
Horse Holiday Farm   206

ITALY
Malvarina Trail Ride   210
The Heart of Tuscany Ride   212

PORTUGAL
Alcainca Dressage Program   214
Blue Coast/Mira Atlantic/Trail to the
   End of the World   216

RUSSIA
The Russian Adventure   218

SPAIN
Andaluz Adventure   220
Cabalgar Rutas Alternativas   224
Finca el Moro—Riding the Borders of
   Extremadura   226
Sierra Nevada: The Contraviesa and
   Alpujarra Rides   228

SWEDEN
Haurida Skogs Hast Safari   230

United Kingdom
ENGLAND
Albion Rides   232
D & P Equestrian Enterprises   234

SCOTLAND
Argyll Trail Riding   236
Hayfield Riding Centre   238

WALES
Ellesmere Riding Centre   240
Rhiwiau Riding Centre   242

NORTH AMERICA   244

Riding in North America *by Arthur Sacks and Russell True (The American Southwest)*   245

Canada
ALBERTA
Holiday on Horseback/Warner Guiding
   and Outfitting   252

BRITISH COLUMBIA
Big Bar Guest Ranch   254
Cascade Ride—From the 49th to Paradise   256
Douglas Lake Ranch Cattle Drive   258
Three Bars Guest and Cattle Ranch   260
Ts'yl-os Park Lodge and Wilderness Trips   262

QUEBEC
Gaspe Peninsula Ride   266

Mexico
The Banana Ride   268
La Sierra Cavalcade and Monarch
   Butterfly Sanctuary   270

United States
ARIZONA
Grapevine Canyon Ranch   272
White Stallion Ranch   276

CALIFORNIA
Adventures on Horseback   280
McGee Creek Pack Station   282
Ricochet Ridge Ranch   284

COLORADO
Bar Lazy J   286
Drowsy Water Ranch   288
Rawah Guest Ranch   290
Sylvan Dale Guest Ranch   292
Wilderness Trails Ranch   294
Wit's End   298

IDAHO
Small Cattle   306

MAINE
Speckled Mountain Ranch   308

MONTANA
Flynn Ranch Vacations   310
Hargrave Cattle Ranch   312
Lazy K Bar Ranch   314
Lonesome Spur Guest Ranch   316
Montana Equestrian Tours   318

NEW MEXICO
Double E Guest Ranch   320
Hartley Ranch   322
N Bar Ranch   324

NEW YORK
Bark Eater Inn   328

VERMONT
Vermont Icelandic Horse Farm   332

WEST VIRGINIA
Swift Level   334

WYOMING
Bitterroot Ranch   340
High Island Ranch   344
Lazy L & B Ranch   346
Lazy L & B's Bear Basin Wilderness Camp
350 Lozier's Box "R" Ranch   352
Renegade Rides   354
Vee Bar Guest Ranch   358
Western Encounter   362

SOUTH AND CENTRAL AMERICA/CARIBBEAN   366

South and Central America and the
   Caribbean *by Arthur Sacks*   367

DOMINICAN REPUBLIC
Casa de Campo   368

ARGENTINA
Estancia Huechahue Trek   370

CHILE
The Patagonia Experience   372
Torres del Paine   374

ECUADOR
Andean Mountain Ride   376

WHO CAN HELP   378
INDEX OF RIDES   382

SELECTION OF
DESTINATIONS FEATURED

Many of the best riding holidays in the world are mentioned in the general articles and/or featured in our full color presentation. Most of them have been visited by either John Ruler or Artie Sacks and found worthwhile. Many of the rides were included on that basis alone. Others were included because they have stood the test of time, offering quality riding opportunities that have been well received by riders for over a decade. Several were included because of their unique features and/or exotic location, some are first time rides and, thus, have not "passed judgment" with riders...yet.

We sent out about 300 individual invitations to appear in our book, and over 70% of the places we invited, accepted. We also encouraged equestrian and other specialist travel agencies to participate. We wholeheartedly endorse the efforts of these agencies to promote the best riding opportunities available. When an agency chose to "sponsor" a riding destination it is so noted, and while other agencies might also feature that ride, we limited it to one, in order to avoid needless repetition. Accordingly, those of you who favor using agencies should note that your favorite agency may feature a given ride, even if they are not listed in the description of the ride itself.

We charged a modest fee for featured color presentations so as to enable us to produce a higher quality book than might otherwise be attempted. Ours has historically been a relatively small market sport, and books written on the subject are often restricted by budgetary considerations. To date, the most colorful stuff has been produced by the equestrian agencies. We hope to break that trend and become an important source of information and a forum for announcing the great diversity of riding opportunities available around the world, thereby allowing the equestrian travel agencies to concentrate on producing quality riding holidays. We hope that you find this book worthy of one life's great pleasures—riding holidays.

It is our hope that you enjoy this book, that reading it makes you want to mount up and ride away. It matters not whether you are rescuing calves, mustering sheep, finding the nerve to edge your pony onwards and upwards over a steep and narrow mountain trail, or dismounting at a French inn and handing your reins to a waiting caretaker, so that you can get ready to enjoy a good glass of wine at the local café or vineyard and a gourmet meal. Riding is a joy. Horses are wonderful creatures and we are fortunate to share the earth with them. So let's get on with it! "Yes, thank-you. I enjoyed my ride today."

ABOUT THE AUTHORS

JOHN RULER has been a travel writer, specialising in horse riding holidays, since 1970—having only taken up the sport two years previously, after feeling a fool in front of his horse riding wife. She has since given up. John has not, but continues to combine worldwide travels with riding. During this time he has learnt the rudiments of polo in Argentina, ridden at the equestrian center in Moscow in the company of a World War II colonel, celebrated his 60th birthday on a cattle drive in Montana, and galloped 2 miles to get a local train in Australia in order to catch his connecting flight back home. Asked if he is a good rider, he replies that he has coped with the differing styles of some 600 horses from the British Isles and Ireland to New Zealand, from France to Poland, and from Denmark to Iceland. He has also ridden in Rajasthan, India, and in Botswana and South Africa. This, he feels, has brought him closer to the average holiday rider—someone who is competent enough to enjoy seeing the world from the back of horse in a non-competitive way.

John contributes to both the equestrian press, including *Horse & Hound*, consumer magazines and, occasionally, to national and regional newspapers, including *The Daily Telegraph*. In 1989 he wrote *The Alternative Holiday Guide to Horse-Riding In Europe*, a few rare copies of which can still be found. He has his own photo library, which he uses to illustrate his work. John is currently planning riding visits to Namibia, Malawi and Slovenia, as well as a return to Scotland.

ARTIE SACKS has been a college professor, a renovator, a horse farm owner and manager, and, for the last 6 years, writer and publisher. His interest in publishing has led to the creation of the first cyber-magazine where the focus will be on riding holidays, soon to be seen on the web at **www.ridingholidays.com.** His travel plans this year include ranches and rides in Colorado, Wyoming, Montana, and New Mexico as well as plans to visit Iceland, Finland, Ireland and the UK. Next year the travelling agenda will double, with trips to India, Australia, New Zealand, Africa, and Canada. He hopes you will visit with him on the web.

AUTHORS' GUIDE:
HOW TO USE THIS BOOK

Prices:
We decided to list specific prices rather than use a system of symbols, for example, 2 saddles, 3 saddles, which indicate price ranges. Instead, to the extent possible, we listed exact rates, at least for 1998 and, sometimes the projected prices for 1999, but never the prices for 2000. In all cases prices are shown in British pounds and US dollars. This is true for all of our rides, even those in Canada, New Zealand and Australia, which also use the dollar sign for their national dominations. **PLEASE NOTE: Prices listed are provided only as a guide to costs.** Up to date information and specific details should be obtained from the agencies or destinations listed in book.

Telephone/Fax/E mail:
It is no secret that the international telephone systems are in turmoil and subject to constant flux, the result of changing technology. The development and wide-spread use of mobile telephones, pagers, beepers, modems, and who knows what the next 5 years will bring, has produced overcrowded telephone lines. Although every country posts changes in their international codes, changes in regional and city codes may sometimes be difficult to obtain. Persistance and downright hostility may be the only way at times to deal with this phenomenon. We have tried to list numbers conveniently for our UK and US readers. If we have not suceeded in reducing the confusion, we apologize and recommend that you contact your telephone company's customer service department or long distance operators for updated information.

Airplanes, Trains, Buses and Private Vehicles:
We have listed the nearest international airports with regularity, although sometimes it may get a bit confusing. For example, if 3 airports serve the same location and are located in 3 different countries, it may require some research to determine the most convenient one. We have been less diligent in providing car routes, train stops, etc. However, any difficulty in this regard should be eliminated by contacting the destinations or the agencies directly. Where possible, we tried to indicate if free transfers are part of the package but, once again, the data may be somewhat incomplete.

Language:

Although all of the writing in the book was subject to the capable direction of our editor, Sheva Stoloff, we have been purposely inconsistent and—depending on your continental position—remiss, by leaving in peculiar Americanisms and English spelling and writing styles (e.g., center – centre; program – programme; instruction – tuition; and, of course, civilization – civilisation). We fear that the globilization of the world will diminish the differences and we will all suffer a loss. In the meantime, "you say potato, we say potaato, you say tomato, we say tomaato," to paraphrase a popular American song, sung by Louis Armstrong among others, says it all. On the other hand, we did try to avoid confusion. We suggest you learn to live with the differences, consider it a charming foretaste of your next exotic riding adventure.

General Notes:

Wherever possible we have tried to either make a reference to or list places we feel have something pleasant to offer riding holiday enthusiasts. We have offered you a myriad of ways of to get additional information from national tourist boards, regional and national equestrian organizations books, and equestrian travel services.

While we stand behind all the places we have included, we do not believe that they will all prove ideal riding holiday places for every class of rider or traveler. Some offer 4 star comfort, others basic outdoor camping. There are also camping trips that provide greater comfort and service than many inns and hotels. Some are family oriented and can accommodate all skill levels, while others require fit and experienced riders. In all cases we have tried to indicate what is on offer and for whom.

Any mistakes and omissions are to be blamed solely on our staff. That we have included specific references to rides not featured in this book if we felt they deserved the mention reflects the authors' concern with offering you a good resource that is as complete as possible.

Arthur Sacks and John Ruler
August, 1998

INTRODUCTION
TO GREAT HORSE RIDING HOLIDAYS
by John Ruler

Selection

FIRST, MAKE SURE THAT YOU CAN RIDE. Sound silly? You would be surprised how many times so-called riders have turned up at stables worldwide who have either never sat on a horse, let alone ridden one, or have been on a 1 hour nose-to-tail ride and think they know it all. Others may have ridden at one time, or so irregularly it really doesn't count—yet expect to tackle daily rides of generally up to 6 hours. So do make sure you can at least, walk, trot (post) and canter (lope) on a horse. If not, take lessons and get some practice in, then match the holiday accordingly. In other words, be honest when you book—it is no use being macho if your riding ability is simply not up to the requisite standard. You will only ruin your holiday if you cannot keep up and frustrate your fellow riders as well. Some companies may even insist that you switch to a more suitable ride. You should be reasonably fit and not too overweight—many places restrict riders to those under 13 stone. If on medication, make sure you are well supplied, and check with your doctor over any uncertainties. Altitude, for instance, affects some, so does extreme heat or cold. A sudden change of environment, is stressful anyway, let alone when sitting in the saddle.

If possible allow a day to settle in before setting off on a long ride. Good centers will devote the first day to matching horse to rider and limit the number of riding hours. Experience shows that, by the third day, riders should feel completely at ease. If not, speak up! A lot of mishaps can be blamed on bravado. Age need not be a barrier. As long as the spirit is willing and the skills still there, there is no reason why you should not enjoy riding holidays well into your late sixties or even seventies. Just be sensible. Remember, too, that a change of tack can take some adjustment. While the Western saddle might be considered armchair comfort over its English counterpart, sitting long-legged does not always come easy, nor does neck-reining or resisting the automatic urge to use both hands. Horses accustomed to a hackamore, a single rein bitless bridle, react quite strongly as you will quickly discover! Cavalry style saddles, often specially made locally, are used in many countries. Spain's sturdy Vaquero version, complete with a thick sheepskin seat, is extremely comfortable once you get used to the bucket-size stirrups. Don't be too disappointed if the tack does not always match-up to what you have at home. What matters most is that it is reliable and the horse is not suffering. Sadly, this is too often the case at top tourist spots where the majority of rides are inevitably geared towards novices and not genuine riders.

If you have doubts, seek reassurance from equestrian approval organizations. In some countries these simply do not exist or restrictions are placed on membership. Some centers which are perfectly sound see little point in joining every existing equestrian organization, but any agency or holiday center worth their salt should be happy to discuss these points with you. Climate and scenery are also deciding factors. It is no using tackling Africa's Namib Desert if you prefer something a little lusher, even perhaps a bit cooler. By the same token, Iceland could be a no-no if a chill wind or gusts of rain will ruin a ride for you, however spectacular the surroundings. Be prepared, either way, to face getting wet, sweaty, and even bitten by mosquitoes (see separate section on clothing).

With this in mind, see what location suits you best, check what level of skill is required for riding and the pace set. The latter is largely dictated by the type of terrain covered. You can hardly canter up a mountain, nor should you expect a slow walk along a long tempting stretch of sand. Regional descriptions given in this guide, provide a good indication of the local topography. Some rides are said to be suitable for "improvers" or beginners. A better bet might be to sample one of the excellent tuitional holidays, especially in the UK and Ireland. Even on rides taken at gentler pace, you will still need experience to cope with some 6 hours daily in the saddle. Intermediate and competent riders have the most options. Both should be capable of covering plenty of ground daily, perhaps at a fast trot, and be able to canter as well. It is best to be comfortable at a faster pace for that extra confidence when it comes to dealing with a spirited horse in a tight situation. Only you can judge in which category you belong. Finally, consider the accommodations. Creature comforts take on added importance after a long day in the saddle. Accommodations can vary from rugged camping, basic but comfortable log cabins and school rooms, to local inns, guest houses and top-notch hotels. Food likewise is dependant on location, and almost always reflects the flavour of the region. The same is true of the horses. For example the frequent use of sure-footed Andalucians in Spain or Highland ponies in Scotland.

A lot rests with the type of holiday taken. Basically it is a straight choice between a center based holiday, where you ride out daily and return to home-base each night, and rides which follow a set route, staying at different places most nights. You could also choose either a straight riding holiday, or a pack trip into the wilderness, with equipment carried by pack animals. Cattle drives are increasingly popular, not only in North America, but also in Australasia, South America and Africa. All of these factors add to the enjoyment of an equestrian holiday. Most rides limit the group to 12 riders at the most, generally less. Exceptions are those trips which require a largish back-up team. They are particularly suited to single people, especially women, as they attract like-minded people and often avoid the dreaded single supplements, even though it may involve sharing a room with others of the same sex. It all depends on the destination. Equally there are places that cater for families, including youngsters, though the groups may understandably be larger. Riding clubs or simply a circle of riding friends can often get preferential rates by travelling together. Unless your foreign language skills are up to par, avoid single or heavily weighted nationality groups, as you could feel left out, especially when socializing in the evening. Americans, the British, Germans and, to some extent, the Swedes and French, make up the bulk of holiday riders. Special diets can be catered for. All equestrian holidays appear costly on paper, but remember, the prices listed should cover all accommodations, the use of a horse, tack and often saddle bags, around 6 hours of riding daily, a guide, transportation of personal belongings, camping equipment if needed, (although sleeping bags are not always included), all meals and, in some cases, drinks at dinner. This means that very little is needed in the way of spending money, other than for incidentals or shopping—if time and location permit. A rough guide to cost is given in the regional sections, but note that international flights are generally not included.

Agencies

Basically an agency, i.e. any company organizing riding holidays, takes the strain out of booking direct. The latter is always possible, especially in home territory and if travelling by car. Modern technology has made direct booking easy and it may even save you money in the long run. But if travelling further afield, especially abroad, agencies offer distinct advantages. First, they take away the bewildering choice of riding centers to choose from by promoting a limited number only. These, they claim, are ones that will appeal most to their clientele. This is based on their own research either as a specialist horse holiday company or by having an overall specialist knowledge of a particular region or country and good equestrian contacts. This means that some agencies will devote greater coverage to one destination than others, as in the case of Africa or France. A few agencies are household names, with riding just one of a number of holiday activities offered. Others are "boutique" operations without big budgets, but with a strong equestrian background. So shop around and see what each has to offer (some feature the same equestrian centers), comparing prices and conditions in much the same way as you would with traditional sun, sea and sand holidays. Secondly, agencies prime you with information on what you will need in the way of riding skills, vaccinations, visas and the like. They can also advise, and generally, arrange the most suitable international flights, along with transfers to and from the riding center. They also provide some financial security when you book. Agencies are also in the position to know when a center unexpectedly closes, or changes owners, sometimes to the detriment of the business, and can drop it from their programme. They can also monitor riders' comments, praiseworthy or otherwise.

Booking Individually

Having cited the advantages, it is also obvious that agency coverage is understandably restricted to those destinations they believe offer top-notch standards, equestrian and other-wise, and are located in popular riding regions. Those chosen may also be financially more powerful than others who are not big enough to warrant signing up with an agency. Yet their standards, size aside, compare favourably with a smaller business, perhaps with no more than 6 horses and a short season, holding as strong an appeal as a large yard with an indoor school, tuition, and all of the equestrian trimmings. It is like trying to compare a good B&B establishment with a top class hotel in London or New York. Both deliver the goodies, but in their own distinct ways. It should also be said that some centers, and this applies worldwide, have no desire to sign up with an agency. We have met some who are reluctant to even have their name mentioned, fearful they will have a flood of enquiries when they are content to cater for their fiercely loyal riders who make up small selective parties each year. These centers, by their very nature, are often expensive—which is where owners make their money.

Clothing

Clothing can often make or break a horse riding holiday. Basically it is a compromise between fashion and comfort—with considerable common sense thrown in. Fortunately, attitudes are changing rapidly, at least in the UK, and as long as you are smartly turned out there should be no raised eyebrows if jodhpurs sport a variety of colours and textures. Hacking jackets and military style macs are giving way to more casual, lighter materials favoured by walkers and are certainly easier to tie to a saddle or stuff in a saddlebag. It is local conditions, not dress code, that count.

If riding in Europe, especially in the British Isles and Ireland, you will be expected to wear an approved hard hat conforming to safety coding. In Britain this is the PAS 015 or EN1384. (In the U.S. it is ASTH-F11 67.) "Be seen to be safe," a British Horse Society slogan, is never more apposite then when riding in strange surroundings. Of course the temptation not to wear a hard hat is strong, especially when soaking up a hot sun or wanting to play the part. Yet a sudden stumble for whatever reason and your holiday could become a nightmare. Technology, however, is lending a helping hand. While once riders put talcum powder round the rim of a British hard hat to soak up the sweat to some extent, you can now wear a lightweight white Troxel hard hat with air vents and netting to keep out the insects. You can even buy a weather-proof cotton brim in the UK to go with it. (Hats of this kind can also be purchased in the U.S.) It may be bulky, but is at least cool, with the brim protecting both eyes and neck. These seem far less out of place in Africa or India than in conservative Europe, where the tendency is either to wear the traditional hard hat, or none at all. The French, Spanish and Italian riders are among the main offenders. This same, almost macho attitude, extends to America's Old West, where the cowboy culture calls the tune, and the familiar Stetson is revered. Sure it keeps the sun off your face, the rain off your neck, and the wind from your hair and can even be used as a water receptacle, but at a time when specially designed skull caps are being sold, over which you can place your Stetson, this is increasingly becoming an anachronism. Okay, so these have been criticized as being too bulbous and bulky, but surely in this high-tech age someone could come up with a traditional Western hat made of protective material. Beefy football players, hockey stars, and even English cricketers, now wear protective headgear. With litigation leading some American states to ban riders from even cantering (loping), the much loved cowboy hat has surely had its day.

Bring multi-stretch jodhpurs (with a spare pair in case it rains). Alternatively, you can wear light cotton breeches for hot climates, or even shorts, with short jodhpurs or dual purpose riding/leisure boots of which there are now an increasing number. Combine with short or full-length chaps to protect the legs from passing brambles, cactus and the like. Choose whatever permutation makes sense. In the case of Western riding, wear the tougher type of jodhpur jeans. Make sure they are well worn, as in not new, as they will almost certainly chaff. They should also be long enough not to ride up the leg when you mount. And, ladies, no casual jeans or slacks please! Chaps (from the Spanish word *chaperreras*) also make sound sense as protection against the weather. Wet jeans are extremely uncomfortable. Bandanas have multiple uses, from mopping your brow to keeping the sun from the back of the neck and the dust from your throat, and are handy wherever you are. Boots must have heels, suitable for gripping in the stirrups, whether factory made or custom crafted Western ones, or the leather or rubber ones worn elsewhere, especially in Europe. Any form of flat shoe will simply slip out of the stirrup irons as soon as your horse starts to trot. Rubber boots, preferably the familiar green Hunter or Wellington boots, are recommended for Iceland as leather ones will be ruined with river crossings and the like. This is worth remembering when in similar situations. Adapt accordingly. Bear in mind that whatever sort of boot you wear you will have to walk in them as well when leading horses up steep, and generally rocky, inclines. Women should wear suitable underwear that will not wrinkle or ruffle, producing horribly rubbed skin. Long silk and wool, or light wool long johns are far less likely to do so and are strongly recommended for long days in the saddle, especially if it is cold. A sports bra also makes sense. For warmer climates wear Aertex style pants and drip dry cotton shirts, preferably with long sleeves to protect arms from sunburn. Other essential items include a warm sweater, gloves (as hands can suffer from both heat and cold), bum bag or fanny pack (such as those worn by skiers), suitable riding socks, depending on the climate, waterproofs (in some instances these will be supplied), and "equipants" for the bonier members of either sex, which will help protect vital parts. This may all sound daunting, but several layers of clothing, which can be stripped off during the day, are more sensible than single, heavy items. Also advisable are sunglasses, with a lace or thong attached, a water bottle, sun screen, insect repellent (for use almost everywhere!), plasters, antihistamine cream for bites, and a small camera. Avoid light, plastic macs or capes which can easily tear or flap in the wind and frighten your horse. If you have a boney backside, use sticking plaster on your buttocks, first making sure you are in a sitting position as you would be on a horse. Do so standing up and it will simply come off. Sprinkle on some talcum powder too, or rub in surgical spirit to toughen the skin. You will also need casual clothes for the evening, and a nail brush is particularly useful after a day in the saddle. The main thing to remember is to dress for the occasion.

Insurance
Make sure you are covered for horseback riding while on holiday, as some policies only protect you for the occasional hour or so of pony trekking or basic trail riding in North America. This is an important distinction to draw at the outset, and confirmation should be obtained from your insurance company in writing, or clearly stated in the insurance certificate. Agencies can provide guidance here. Most policies cover leisure riding, but exclude hunting, competitive jumping, horse racing and/or professional riding of any kind.

AFRICA

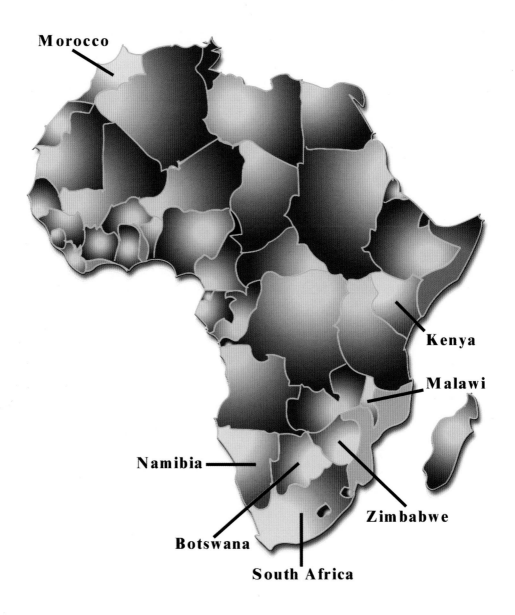

Morocco

Kenya

Malawi

Namibia

Zimbabwe

Botswana

South Africa

OUT OF AFRICA

by John Ruler

I
T WAS WHEN BARNEY CALMLY WARNED US, a group of seemingly vulnerable horsemen and women, to look out for marauding lions, that we really knew we were in Africa. Don't panic, was her message. The lions were likely to steer clear of humankind and, in any case, a shot fired in the air from the rifle slung alongside her husband's saddlebag would soon scare them off.

We never did see a lion, although one night their grunts were heard close to our base camp in Botswana's Okavango Delta, leading to an all-night vigil beneath the glare of headlamps from the safari jeep. We did see herds of wildebeest and zebra, watching them disappear from the approaching horses in clouds of dust. We also saw hippos wallowing and snorting in reeded lakes and cautiously skirted 'round pools where the piercing eyes of crocodiles peered sinisterly just above the water level. A few years later, while clambering amid the canyons of the Waterberg Plateau in the Northern Transvaal, our horses were brought to an abrupt halt when our South African guide calmly pointed-out a puff adder lying coiled in the long, dry grass. Two incidents which bring alive the thrills, and occasional anxieties, of horse safaris in Africa, where the human scent so feared by game is replaced by that of the far more acceptable horse. Giraffes dip their heads discreetly, warthogs, their spindly tails held erect, scurry by squeaking when they realise that the horses have riders, while great lumbering elephants stop and stare. This is Africa far removed even from the growing number of walking safaris. Provided that you are a competent rider, able to walk, trot, canter and, most important, control your horse, there is no real cause for concern. However, it is best to check first on the riding ability required and the best times to go, especially for game viewing. Both South and East Africa are well served by members of the African Horse Safari Association and by other competently run centers. The majority are featured in the brochures of many US and UK agencies which specialize in Africa, horse-riding holidays, or both.

Our hosts in Botswana were Barney and P.J. Bestelink, whose unique knowledge of the African bush bring out the best in their horse safaris based on tented accommodation deep in the Okavango Delta, the "Jewel of the Kalihari." The Delta is home to more than 500 species of birds and 18 varieties of antelope alone, in addition to lion, cheetah and elephant. Home for 5 days was one of the hundreds of small "islands" which dot the Delta, sleeping in fly tents, and listening to the sound of the bush, including a muttering hippo which pottered around in the undergrowth. It was late March. Later the region would flood, leaving much of the terrain we had ridden over underwater or swampland.

Memories of Okavango came flooding back months later in South Africa, riding back to base in the Waterberg Plateau (a 3 hour car drive from Johannesburg), when we crossed swampy grasslands, the horses' hooves slurping in the mud and the fast setting African sun creating rosy red strips across an inky black sky. What a contrast to the time Steve, a Virginian on his first riding trip outside the United States, sped off in pursuit of a herd of red hartebeest, his horse kicking up clouds of wispy yellow dust, or on a sunset ride when we chided a troop of baboons while sitting in their favorite cliff-top shelter. They replied in kind, jumping up and down in mock rage. Silly, but still part of the simple pleasures experienced on this 200 mile wilderness ride in the 42,000 acre Touchstone Game Reserve, sometimes almost barren, but never boring. During the 4 to 7 hours spent in the saddle, occasionally scrambling over rocks on foot to rest the horses, we spotted 2 rarely seen black and white crossed eagles drifting in the thermals. Then there were the rare white rhino (the word "white" not denoting colour, but actually a derivation of the German "writ" meaning wide, and applied to the mouth) and baleful eyed buffalo. Less dramatic, but supremely elegant are other veldt animals such as eland, impala, duiker and tsessebe.

Accommodation with Equus Horse Safaris, the tour organizers, has a delightful "Out of Africa" quality to it, especially when sitting amid the ice-cooled waterfalls at Palala River Lodge, the water bubbling Jacuzzi fashion around stiffening shoulders. Use the Lodge's wildlife checklist to mug up on what you have missed. We never saw giraffe or cheetah, but did learn about trees whose bark can be used as writing paper, or even bandages, and the healing properties of plants, including juicy strips of aloe used to soothe a horse's swollen leg.

Also operating in the Waterberg Mountains, and with a good reputation, is the Triple B Ranch. Home to the Baber family for over a century, it continues to operate as a working cattle and game ranch. Accommodation is based on a variety of lodgings of the thatched-colonial style. Guests can take an overnight game safari, try cattle mustering, or participate in the other sporting activities, such as swimming, tennis, volleyball, boating and fishing. Likewise Sarah-Jane Gullick, a gifted rider who previously worked with Equus Tours, now runs Horseback Safaris in a remote southwestern pocket of the Okavango Delta from mid-December to the end of February. The horses include Namibian, Hanoverian, Kalahari crossbreds, Boerperde, Freisian, and Moroccan Barb-Arabs. Accommodation is provided in luxury tented camps.

Although I cannot comment personally on riding in Kenya, Tristan Voorspuys' safaris come highly recommended, especially when based in the Masai Mara, a region teeming with game. This is riding *par excellence*, in a land beloved by Ernest Hemingway, a fast plains ride with long canters and gallops. Confident and comfortable at all paces are the criteria here. Ride with a herd of about 150 wildebeest and learn about the lives of the Masai, a warrior tribe with a proud past, renowned for their cattle husbandry. Horses used include Thoroughbreds (some from the race-track and converted to polo ponies), sure-footed and reliable. Another "close to nature" experience can be had on safaris in the Lewa Wildlife Conservancy which is situated in the northern foothills of Mount Kenya. Your guide is Pete Murray-Wilson, who was trained as a National Hunt Jockey in Great Britain by champion trainer, Ryan Price. The region is comprised of savannah, wetland, grassland, and indigenous forest. Great store is being placed on preserving wildlife, and Lewa is one of the leaders in black rhino conservation. It is also home to white rhino. Safaris are for a minimum of 2 riders and a maximum of 6. Duration is 2 to 6 nights, and trips can be tailored to accommodate those with only a few safari days available as well as those wanting to combine a conventional safari with a horseback experience in a genuine wilderness area. Arabs, Quarterhorse crosses, and Thoroughbreds, using English style tack, are found in the Mavuradonna wilderness, a region barely known outside Zimbabwe, yet only a 2 hour drive from the capital of Harare. The pace is slow, but only confident riders are suitable for the Explorer Safari, plunging deep into the heart of the wilderness.

In Malawi, Nyika National Park in the north offers a very different Africa. David Foot, of Heart of Africa Safaris, offers exploratory trips in the high plateau. Expect rolling grasslands populated with roan, antelope, zebra, and reedbuck. In summer, the grasslands are ablaze with wildflowers. Choose between staying at the main lodge and riding out each day, or join a 5 or 9 night trail ride. Terrain dictates that the pace is mainly walking, but with some faster stretches possible.

More recent African riding opportunities include Namibia, where a unique desert trail ride through undulating hills and mountain escarpments, starts near Winhoek, the capital. The Namib Desert/ Moon Valley Trail covers around 248 miles (400 kms.) across the desert to the coast at Swakopmund on the legendary Skeleton Coast. The ride begins in the hills, features a mountain range and a visit to an old gold mine, before reaching the desert with its unlimited space, solitude, and spectacular sunsets. The pace is moderate, with some long canters. Also new on the riding scene is Lesotho, the "Kingdom in the Sky," where the trails traverse mountain passes and some of the country's highest waterfalls. Guides are Basotho horsemen and village huts and farmhouses provide the overnight accommodation. The pace is understandably slowish, with faster riding where the terrain permits.

A F R I C A
by Bayard Fox

I WANT TO BEGIN BY TELLING YOU A LITTLE ABOUT MYSELF, so that you can put what I say into better perspective. For more than 25 years now my business and my passion have been running riding tours, and horses have been a big part of my life since I can remember. We keep 170 or so horses on our ranch here in Wyoming and organize riding tours on 6 continents the rest of the year. I also like the people I ride with and enjoy interacting with them. Another great pleasure is working with the wonderful, colorful bunch of characters who run our riding tours in different parts of the world.

I can't remember taking a riding trip that I haven't enjoyed, but, of course, some have been vastly better than others. One riding tour stands out above all. This is just my opinion, but it is shared by many of my friends who are among the thousand or so people we have sent on this trip in the last 20 years. My wife (who was raised in East Africa) and I used to lead it ourselves and have done it more than 20 times. It is consistently enjoyable, interesting and wildly exciting. Many have said it is the experience of a lifetime. It has certainly enriched my life.

African safaris are riding holidays where the speed of your horse and your riding skill could be the things that will save you from becoming "lion food!" The riding is that tough, yet the longest day is not much more than 30 miles. Most of it is at a walk, but there are some really wonderful gallops of up to 6 or 8 minutes. The dangers are statistically small and one is probably at greater risk in our crime-ridden cities. What keeps many people away is the cultural leap demanded, which few are prepared to make. We rode more than 200 miles without crossing a fence and only one paved road. We camped in the bush with nothing but a canvas tent and a Masai guard between us and the lions and hyenas, howling and roaring around us at night. We had our own camps, far from tourist haunts, which were moved on most days leaving little trace of our passing. The whole journey takes place in the country of the proud Masai, who still herd their cattle and protect them from lions and leopards with their spears—much as they used to do a century ago before the white man ever came to Africa. The traditional mixture of blood and milk is still a big part of their diet and they live in houses made of wooden frames covered with cow dung and mud. The Masai are a tall, slim people of Hamitic-Nilotic origin, who moved down from the north a few centuries ago and carved out a huge section of East Africa for themselves and their cattle. They had an invincible military machine, which was the terror of the surrounding Bantu tribes. Their long spears, short swords, huge buffalo hide shields and military tactics are reminiscent of ancient Rome. The training of young warriors was like that of Sparta.

Obviously, this kind of experience is not for everyone, so that the people who go are an exceptionally adventuresome, courageous and open-minded fraternity who revel in exotic new experiences and challenges. They have the common bond of an interest in horses, wildlife and primitive people. The interaction among such a group heightens the intensity of the experience. It is usually a diverse group of adventurers from many walks of life. On this last trip we had lawyers, a computer specialist, a toy designer, and a very successful sculptress who teaches a popular course at Yale.

The trip was led by Tristan, a former British Cavalry officer and keen polo player, who came to Kenya 15 years ago. He has mastered Swahili, the lingua franca of East Africa, and has an exceptional knowledge of the flora and fauna. What I particularly admire is his uncanny ability to identify over a hundred birds from their calls. That takes dedication! It is a privilege to go with a guide who can tell you all about the fascinating habits of every thing from dik dik to crowned cranes. Tristan also has an excellent string of horses, many of which he uses for polo. It is not easy to keep horses in top condition in East Africa, but he manages it and it is evident that he really cares about his animals far beyond their commercial value. He and his wife raise and train many of them themselves, which always means a great deal to me when I choose an outfitter because we do the same thing ourselves here in Wyoming.

The safari began at Tristan's lovely home, Deloraine, which was built at the height of the colonial era by Lord Francis Scott and is one of the great show places of Kenya. Its wide veranda and magnificent gardens have a spectacular view of the Aberdare Mountains which rise to over 13,000 feet. The attractive architecture of this solid stone house, with its large sitting room and dining room and its splendid bedrooms, has made it famous. Staying there brings more understanding to such marvelous books as *Out of Africa* or *West With the Night*. The drive from Deloraine to the start of the ride took most of the day and passed through some varied country, including enormous tea estates covered with bright green leaves as far as the eye could see. The last part of the route wound up through the Loita Hills at a snail's pace into remote country near the Tanzanian border. There are wide-open plains and smaller clearings interspersed by thick forests. Arrival in camp at Morijo was like a homecoming for me. The staff of 15 or so was there to greet us. Our sleeping tents are for 2 people and big enough to stand up in. The beds have sheets and blankets and are made up each day. Behind each sleeping tent was a toilet tent, and several shower tents were also set up. Hot water was ready, as it is every evening, so that we could all take showers. Cold beer was in the ice chest and the tea and coffee were hot. The horses were grazing around camp, some of them free and others tethered. We have had problems at times with them running off from camp because they were spooked by elephants, hyenas, etc., and one has to keep a careful eye on them. At night they are tied to a long rope stretched tight by a landrover at one end, with a tree to anchor it on the other. Masai guards tend the fires and keep a watch for marauding lions, which have been known to jump horses on the line at night. Some old friends were there, like Faraway, who is a fine polo pony and a beautiful ride. I remembered that Arnie Garvey, editor of *Horse & Hound*, had ridden him and loved him 3 years before. All 20 of the horses were in good condition and could gallop along for 2 or 3 miles without showing much strain.

Nights are quite cool at 7000 or 8000 feet, even on the Equator, and as the sun plunged down behind the hills we immediately felt a chill in the air. The staff had a bonfire going and we were all glad to bring our drinks and draw up our chairs around it. There is something cheerfully reassuring about a blazing fire at night in the African bush. Dinner was served with wine and the food was excellent. Fresh bread is baked each day and nearly every fruit and vegetable in the world is grown in Kenya's wonderful climate. There is a wide variety of meat, poultry and fish. As the nights progressed, we would often hear the captivating noises of wild Africa. The lilting cry of the hyena is very distinctive, as is the roar of the lion or the bark of the zebra. They are nostalgic sounds for me, like the cry of the coyote on a moonlit Wyoming night, a goose flying far overhead at the first light of dawn, or the electrifying bugle of a bull elk in the rut. They summon up images of the wild, untamed world which existed long before mankind, and which I fervently hope we will never exterminate through our heedless greed and arrogance.

The next morning, after a copious breakfast, we were off to test our horses and see something of the country. We climbed and climbed, up from the valley to the crests of the hills from where we could see forests, clearings and plains in every direction. Here and there on the hillsides were herds of Masai cows being tended and watched by warriors to ward off lions and see that they grazed in the right places. Each night at dusk, the cows, sheep and goats are driven back to the villages, which are protected by thick thorn fences to keep out lions and leopards. In this hilly, forested country there is not as much game to be seen as there is on the Mara plains, but we did see several bushbuck and reedbuck, as well as some colobus monkeys leaping through the trees with their spectacular black and white costumes. A few test gallops going along the crest of a hill at a slight upgrade where the footing was good went very well. All of us were in control of our horses and able to handle them without trouble, despite the size of our group of 17. We had ridden with them all before at our ranch or in India, so we knew what to expect of each other. We had made a lunch for our saddlebags and shortly after noon, we stopped on the crest of a hill for a picnic and a bit of a rest. We could see the wooded hills of Tanzania a few miles away, and with my binoculars I made out a herd of cape buffalo on a distant hillside. A brilliantly colored turaco flitted through the trees nearby and a bateleur eagle soared overhead with its distinctive wing markings and short tail. We munched our sandwiches and talked quietly for more than an hour. I slept soundly for 20 minutes, using my saddle as a pillow. Then it was time to saddle up again, and loop back to our camp. On the way, we passed several Masai *manyattas* (villages) with their thorn walls and cow dung huts. Women with their babies came to wave and stare. Most of the grown men were out with the cattle.

On arrival in camp, we turned our horses over to the grooms and headed for the showers and cold drinks. Those who felt like it, walked with a Masai guide to one of the *manyattas* a half a mile away to have a closer look at their way of life. The cows were just coming back and the women were milking them into gourds with swift, deft fingers before turning the calves in with their mothers for the night. Blood is take periodically from the cattle in small amounts to enrich the milk. The Masai thrive on this diet, although today, other less exotic food like corn meal is creeping in. The Masai seldom slaughter their cattle for meat. They feel that cows are their wealth, as sacred to them as money is to most of us.

The next day was a moving day, and we were off early through forests and then onto the plains, where huge herds of zebra and wildebeest turned to stare at us. The grass was grazed close to the ground like a golf green. We trotted out for a few hundred yards and eased into a canter, gradually increasing the speed until we were flying across the plain. The zebra and wildebeest entered into the spirit of things and would cut in front of us in an unmistakable challenge to a race. The horses' blood was up and they loved the excitement. By the time we reined in 6 or 7 minutes later, we must have covered more than 2 miles. The horses were breathing fast, but not too hard, and they quickly recovered. We walked on for several more miles to the base of the main spine of the Loita Hills, which go up to nearly 9000 feet. When it became steep, we got off and led the animals for 15 or 20 minutes until we reached the crest. There, we stopped for a rest and looked at a tremendous view stretching across to the Great Rift Valley to the east, and the escarpment above the Mara River to the west. The African haze of dust and wood smoke obscured the view after 50 miles or so. We had another picnic near the highest point and continued along the grassy crest of the hills at a walk until Tristan signaled a canter. The horses knew the place and were eager to be off. Before long, we were galloping again along the undulating crest. This time the grass was a bit longer and we had to watch for holes, but the horses know their business and carried us safely through for several more miles until we came to the end of the ridge. There, we turned east and headed down off the hills toward the plain at Entesekera, dropping 2000 feet or so very quickly. One could feel it get warmer as we descended. It had been a long day and the showers and cold drinks at our new camp under yellow-barked acacias were more welcome than ever. Somehow, as we pulled our chairs up around the fire that night with our drinks in our hands, we felt bonded together. We had had a glorious day; arduous, exciting, beautiful, and somehow very special. The staff had moved camp by truck while we rode and set it up again as if by magic. Our beds were made and towels hung up just as it had been the day before. It is not hard to understand why Isak Dinesen, Beryl Markham, Ernest Hemmingway and so many other artistic and talented people have fallen in love with this country. To me it was wonderful to be on this benign safari without either hunting or being hunted. Thirty-five years earlier I had had my times of horror and fear on this continent, which, like the ocean, can be cruel or benevolent, horrible or delightful.

Day after day we rode on and the camp we had left was moved again, only magically to reappear at the end of the day, when we rode in hot and tired to find everything ready under a new set of those lovely, spreading acacias with their feathery leaves. Bush babies and hyrax played in them over our heads at night. Each day held new adventures and new sights. We saw dozens of soft-eyed giraffes towering high into the air, often above the trees. The horses would stand with their ears pricked, staring at these incredible animals with their long necks and huge strides, which make them seem to be in slow motion at a gallop, although they are really moving fast. One day, we came to a wide plain which was obviously a place for a splendid gallop. In the far distance, we saw ostrich as well as eland, zebra, wildebeest and gazelle. I was up with the front runners, concentrating on the ground in front of me to avoid any possible holes or rocks when, suddenly, the horses veered almost 90 degrees to the left. I saw an ostrich coming straight for us with wings held far out and looking very large and impressive. It raced with us for some distance, running at a terrific rate and creating quite a stir among the horses who hadn't seen such antics before. We never knew what got into it. Perhaps it had nest nearby which it thought we were threatening.

The days blended with one another and in many ways we felt as though we had lived the lives of nomads for a very long time. The routines of camp, the horses and the staff all became familiar. For those of us who were born partly under a wandering star, this idyllic way of life struck a very responsive chord. There was talk of going back to the real world, but to me, this world is as real as any other and I have spent most of my life in something like it. At the Olare Orok Camp, the routine broke. We spent 3 nights there, and after a 35 mile ride the day before, we took a rest from the horses, and they from us. Instead of riding, we climbed into the landrovers and headed down the Mara River into the heart of the game reserve where domestic animals are prohibited. We saw several prides of lions, some on a kill, and 4 cheetah mothers with their cubs. Along the Mara River, we watched enormous hippos almost totally immersed in the water. They surfaced form time to time, blasting air from their noses like a diver clearing his snorkel. At night, they would leave the water to graze far from the river. Below, their great enemies, the crocodiles, were sunning themselves on a sandy beach, hardly moving. A few had their great jaws wide open as though waiting for an unwary animal to walk in. Some of them looked to be about 16 feet long and were as round as barrels. It is here, during the great wildebeest migrations, that crocodiles gorge themselves on the animals that lose their footing in the floods or fall back from the banks.

We continued down along the river and stopped for a barbecue lunch in a grove of trees. After lunch and a rest, we headed back toward camp by another route and spotted several herds of elephant, which we watched for a long time. There were some tiny calves, no more than a few months old, sticking very close to their mothers. Many of the elephants were tearing at the trees, often devastating them as they ate branches and tore away the bark. It reminded me a bit of what the beavers do to aspen groves near their ponds. The following day, we were off at dawn on our horses after a quick cup of tea and a biscuit so that we could be out on the plains at the first cool light of dawn. Patches of mist still clung to parts of the valleys and the sides of the hills and the huge herds of antelope, zebra and gazelle were busy cropping the grass. After a day's rest, and with the coolness of the morning, the horses were eager for a few gallops and we were glad to oblige. The wild game entered into the spirit of things adding to the excitement of it all. By 10:00 we were back in camp, ravenously hungry for a huge breakfast, which was not long in coming. Our laundry was already drying on nearby bushes.

Next, we crossed the Mara River at a shallow ford and headed up toward the escarpment, which towers more than 1,000 feet above the Mara Plain. In that part of the Mara, there were quite a few tourist buses which struck a bit of a false note for us after having had the wild bush to ourselves and the Masai for the last week. We stopped for lunch and a swim at one of the lodges on the Mara River. It was pleasant enough, but we only could shake our heads at the notion that people could experience Africa by staying in such a place and watching game from a minibus. It is a step up from watching game on a television program, but a very far cry from the intensity of our experience. The camp on the escarpment is one of the world's glorious places which brings exultation to my soul in a way no cathedral ever could. When they made the film, *Out of Africa*, they knew what they were doing in filming the picnic scene and the burial scene here, even though it is not the true place. It has a magnificent soaring view of the Mara Plain just below the Loita Hills and the Great River Valley in the far distance. To the south, one can see far down into the bordering Serengeti of Tanzania. It is cooler high above the plain and there is almost always a breeze. Much of my life has been spent camping, and I have stayed in some exquisite places on 6 continents, but if I had to pick one place, this is the one that jumps to mind before all others. It is a great treasure for mankind and would be an irreparable loss if we did not preserve its unspoiled beauty as well as the wildlife which thrives here.

The next morning, we were off again to our last camp up higher on the Mara River. We headed down off the escarpment and followed the river. It was a wonderful ride through forest and clearing. Tristan led some splendid trots and canters where the terrain allowed. We came close to several herds of elephant which made the horses tense in every muscle. Troops of baboons foraged on the ground or in the trees and sometimes skipped from rock to rock as they crossed the river, wary of lurking crocs. Once, Tristan swerved quickly in a thick place to avoid a solitary old bull buffalo. They have nasty tempers and often charge, although a good horse can outrun them quite easily. We got a good view of a group klipspringer, perched on the side of a cliff above the river. They have incredible agility, jumping from foothold to foothold on the nearly sheer rock face. A little after 5:00, we rode into camp near a bend in the river, where everything was ready, as always. There must have been more than 100 hippo in the pool at the bend, where my wife had once seen a mother hippo give birth. We spent the next 2 days riding out of that camp in the morning and evening or taking game drives in the landrovers to get close to the big cats and the elephants. Plenty of lions and cheetahs were about, and we saw them frequently. We watched the cheetah with our binoculars from a distance so as not to disturb them. They are daytime hunters, depending on their tremendous speed for short bursts to catch their game. Cheetah are the world's fastest animal and have been clocked at around 70 miles per hour. Unlike lions, they are usually solitary hunters. I could watch these graceful, beautiful animals for hours.

On the last evening, after the sun had set and darkness was fast approaching, we had one more glorious gallop across the plain. Over to the side, a group of giraffes watched us with interest and a herd of zebras kicked up its heels and dashed across in front of us. I turned Faraway over to a groom with much regret and thought of a snowy Wyoming winter into which a jet plane would soon plunge me. That night at dinner, there was the glow of a wonderful adventure shared mixed with the sadness of parting and leaving it all behind us. I wondered when the next time would be and whether Tristan and our staff would prosper in the meantime. Would the great herds of zebra, wildebeest and all the other game still thrive and would the Masai still be there in their red cloaks with their spears and herds of cattle? How about Tristan's beautiful string of horses? I know of nothing better to do than to send as many people as I can to experience this magic place. It is only if enough people care and support it with their dollars and their efforts that it can survive. So, I hope you will go, both to enrich your own lives and to preserve one of the great treasures on thisplanet.

About Bayard Fox and Equitour

Bayard Fox is the owner of Equitour in the USA. His agency offers hundreds of riding opportunities around the world. During the summer months, Bayard and Mel Fox operate Bitterroot Ranch in Wyoming.

AFRICAN HORSEBACK SAFARIS

www.inthesaddle.com

BASICS: Agent: **In the Saddle**, Laurel Cottage, Ramsdell, Tadley, Hampshire RG26 5SH, UK
Tel: 01256-851665   Fax: 01256-851667 (from UK)
Tel: (44) 1256-851665   Fax: (44) 1256-851667 (from US)
Email: rides@inthesaddle.com
In Botswana contact: Sarah-Jane Gullick, African Horseback Safaris, c/o P O Box 20538, Maun, Botswana
Tel: (267) 663154 (for urgent inquiries only)
Fax: (267) 660912
Email: sjhorses@info.bw

WHEN: Open all year except part of January and the month of February.

AIRPORTS: Johannesburg, Harare or Victoria Falls Airports in Zimbabwe or Windhoek Airport in Namibia. From these locations you should arrange to fly into Maun, Botswana. From Maun, you will be transported by light airplane to the airstrip at the horse camp in the Okavango Delta where the ride begins.

LOCATION: The Okavango Delta, Botswana.

PRICE: From £160 ($256) per night, per person, double occupancy. Prices vary according to the season and include all riding, game drives, night drives, walks when available, seasonal Mokoro trips, accommodation, all meals, all drinks (except liqueurs and special wines), and daily laundry service in main camp. Single supplement add 50% if unwilling to share. Roundtrip airfare between Maun and the camp, from £95 ($150) per person.

Sarah-Jane is an experienced, relaxed ride leader, who has worked in Africa for many years. The Okavango Delta, "Jewel of the Kalahari," is an incredible place with palm islands, flood plains, mopane forest and crystal clear waters, home to elephant, buffalo, giraffe, zebra, leopard, lion, wildebeest, and hundreds of other species! The Delta changes over the course of the year from open green grasslands to water-covered flood plains dotted with islands. While this safari is exciting, it is not strenuous and there is plenty of opportunity to relax. Riders need to be able to control the horse at all paces and feel comfortable and safe in the saddle. You are recommended to stay a minimum of 7 nights.

CHILDREN'S PROGRAM: No children under 12.

ACCOMMODATIONS: For the first 3 or 4 days of each trip you will stay in a base camp with large, luxurious tents, each with 2 comfortable beds and a traditional shower and toilet. Later you will move to either a tree house camp or tented fly camp, depending on flood conditions.

SPECIAL ACTIVITIES: Alternative activities include bird watching, game drives, walking trails, and canoeing, subject to seasonal changes.

MEALS: You will enjoy a light breakfast before your ride, an open-air brunch, teas, and a 3 course candlelit dinner. The meals are of excellent quality and the service is superb. Special diets can be catered for with prior notice.

RIDING STUFF: The horses are part and full Thoroughbreds, Anglo-Arabs, Kalahari crossbreds, Namibian Hanoverians, and South African Boerperds. They are responsive, well-schooled horses chosen for even temperament. After a light breakfast, you will enjoy a 3 to 4 hour ride before lunch. The pace varies from a walk to exciting gallops across the floodplains. After a shower, a siesta, and afternoon tea (with cakes!) there is another ride in the late afternoon. It is fascinating to watch the abundant herds peacefully grazing on the plains, and see colors change as the sun goes down. The Delta traditionally floods from May to September, allowing you many opportunities to enjoy exhilarating canters through the wetlands.

AUTHOR'S COMMENT: *Sarah-Jane is a well-known outfitter with over 10 years experience in Africa. She runs a relaxed, quality program, suitable for competent riders, eager to enjoy the prolific wildlife that still remains in Africa.*

HIGHLIGHTS
Abundant wildlife viewing • African wilderness • Extremely comfortable safari camps • The magic of Okavango Delta • English and Western tack • 4 to 6 hours in the saddle per day • Competent riders

HORSEBACK SAFARIS ON LEWA DOWNS

BASICS: For bookings and enquiries: Attention: Mr. Chris Flatt, Bush Homes of East Africa, Ltd., P O Box 56923, Nairobi, Kenya
Tel: 254-2-571647
Fax: 254-2-571665
Tel: (11) 254-571647
Fax: (11) 254-571665 (from US)
Email: bushhome@africaonline.co.ke
WHEN: All year round except for April, May and November.

AIRPORTS: Nairobi, Jomo Kenyatta Airport.
LOCATION: Lewa Wildlife Conservancy, situated in the northern foothills of Mount Kenya, 65 kilometers northeast of Nanyuki.
PRICE: Two Person Group: £300 ($480) per night, per person. Three Person Group: £269 ($430) per night, per person. Groups of 4,5 or 6: £256 ($410) per night, per person.

Lewa Downs Conservancy, located among the foothills of Mount Kenya, was founded in 1993. It is a non-profit organization, officially registered with the government of Kenya. As human populations and poverty are growing over most of Africa, intense pressure is being placed on the environment. This is the case in Kenya, where half of its indigenous wildlife has disappeared in the last 20 years. The solution, as Lewa Downs sees it, lies not in the enforcement of the old protectionist rules, which often failed to deal adequately with the needs of local communities for safety, economic freedom, and food. The Conservancy solution, modeled after similar operations in South Africa, is to fence the land, thereby protecting both the local communities and the wildlife. Additionally, by funding various aspects of local community needs, and in its capacity as an employer, Lewa Downs hopes to create and sustain a healthy and viable relationship between people and animals. The rides in the Conservancy are led by Pete-Murray Wilson, an experienced horseman, trained as National Hunt Jockey in Great Britain, by champion trainer, Captain Ryan Price. The riding is fast paced and requires experienced riders.

CHILDREN'S PROGRAM: Children must be over the age of 12 and competent riders.

ACCOMMODATIONS: Riders will stay at any, or a combination of, the permanent accommodations at Lewa Downs Wilderness Trails, Lerai Camp or Ngare Niti House.

MEALS: Home-cooked meals are freshly prepared on the ranch, using produce grown on the farm. Vegetarians will be catered for.

SPECIAL ACTIVITIES: Tennis, swimming, walks with experienced guides, and game drives for non-riders are all available alternate activities.

RIDING STUFF: The horses are Thoroughbreds or Thoroughbred crosses, well-schooled, and of good temperament. The land comprises savannah, wetland, grassland and indigenous forest. and also functions as a commercial cattle ranch. The Conservancy is home to both white and black rhino, Grevy and Burchell zebras, waterbug, warthog, situatunga, ostrich, oryx, kudu, impala, hartebeest, Grant's gazelle, giraffe, gerenuk, eland, and buffalo as well as a host of other species. As the program proceeds, farming has been reduced, the ultimate goal being to demonstrate that farming and wildlife are not mutually exclusive, and that is it possible to integrate wildlife conservation with ranching and tourism.

AUTHOR'S COMMENT: *Pete-Murray Wilson has added a new dimension to this attractive ride with his utilization of horses best suited for competent riders. Lewa Downs Conservancy has adopted an admirable program for wilderness preservation that should be welcome to riders.*

HIGHLIGHTS
Riding in the Lewa Downs Conservancy • Rides guided by Pete Murray-Wilson • Small group size of 2 to 6 • Superb wildlife viewing • For competent riders only • Safaris of 2 to 5 days

OFFBEAT SAFARIS LIMITED

www.ridingtours.com/africa/

BASICS: Equitor, PO Box 807, Dubois, WY 82513, USA
   Tel: (307) 455-3363 Tel: (800) 545-0019
   Fax: (307) 455-2354
   Email: equitour@wyoming.com
WHEN: Scheduled riding dates all year round except April, May and November.
AIRPORTS: Kenyatta International, Nairobi.
LOCATION: Southwestern Kenya
PRICE: Prices range from $320 (£200) to $350 (£218) per day, per person, double occupancy.

Offbeat Safaris' ride through Masai country has been the experience of a lifetime for many of the hundreds of intrepid riders who have done it over the last 20 years. The abundance and variety of wildlife is without comparison elsewhere and the Masai people are colorful and fascinating. This trip affords an exceptional opportunity to get "up close and personal" with big game animals and interact with the Masai at close quarters. Tristan and his guides know and love this country and its inhabitants and freely share their knowledge and experience with their guests. Camps are located far from civilization, deep in the African bush, where one often hears the roar of lions and the laugh of the hyena. Although Kenya is located close to the equator, the heat is usually not oppressive because most of the route lies at 6000 to 9000 feet above sea level. Nights are cool and you may feel the need to don a sweater and pull a chair up to the fire. In addition to customized safaris, there are regularly scheduled trips throughout most of the year.

CHILDREN'S PROGRAM: Children must be accompanied by an adult and must be experienced riders.

ACCOMMODATIONS: Sheets and blankets are provided for the beds in large, 2 person tents. Hot showers and toilet tents are conveniently situated nearby. Masai guards watch at night to keep lions from the horses. Some of the trips begin or end at the Deloraine House, a British colonial house built in the 1920s and still magnificent.

MEALS: Food and service are of the highest quality, a gourmet experience brought to the bush. This style of camping was made famous by Hemingway and Hollywood.

RIDING STUFF: Tristan is a keen polo player and has a fine string of horses (Thoroughbreds and Somali/Thoroughbred crosses), which are equally at home on the polo field or in a gallop alongside a zebra. The pace of the ride is fast at times, opening out to a 7 or 8 minute gallop when the terrain is favorable. The landscape varies greatly from high forested hills at 9000 feet to vast open plains where the grass is often cropped to golf course height by teeming herds of game. On camp moving days, riders carry lunch and a canteen in their saddlebags and there is a long pause at midday under a shady tree so that riders and horses can rest during the warmest part of the day. When the camp is not being moved, you will usually ride out early in the morning or evening. You might wish to a take morning or evening run by landrover to allow for better photo opportunities and closer proximity to lions and elephants. The longest day covers 35 miles and usually involves about 7 hours in the saddle. Riders always have the option of spending the day in the landrover.

AUTHOR'S COMMENT: *Tristan's ride always receives accolades for the wildlife experience and the campsite ambiance, where you'll receive the service and treatment you always knew you deserved. The opportunity to interact with the Masai culture make this an incredible and unique experience.*

HIGHLIGHTS
Outstanding wildlife viewing • English tack • 35 Somali and Thoroughbred horses • Experienced riders • Weight limit 185 lbs. (84 kg.) (13 stone) • Camel safaris • Customized safaris arranged • Landrover/riding combination safaris • Luxury 11 and 14 day safaris

SAFARIS UNLIMITED AFRICA LTD.

www.kenya-direct.com/safarisunlimited

BASICS: PO Box 24181, Nairobi, Kenya
   Tel: (254) (2) 891168 or 890435
   Fax: (254) (2) 891113
   Email: safunlim@africaonline.co.ke.
WHEN: All year round, except April and May
AIRPORTS: Jomo Kenyatta International, Nairobi

LOCATION: Great Rift Valley, Masailand in northern Kenya, 65 miles from Nairobi.
PRICE: Prices vary depending on itinerary and group size, starting around $300 (£188) per day, per person.

Safaris Unlimited was founded in 1971 by Tony Church, who pioneered Kenya riding safaris. Tony spent his childhood roaming the highlands of Kenya on foot with gun and fishing rod, and later by horseback. These early experiences provided the impetus for what was to become one of the most unique riding experiences in the world. Imagine riding the open plains, hunting for the pot, nights under velvet starlit skies, mingling with the warrior Masai, and enjoying gourmet meals cooked over an open fire. Safaris Unlimited, now operated by Tony and his son, Gordon, offers an exotic bush adventure which includes abundant natural beauty, a never-ending spectacle of wildlife, and high adrenaline gallops. Stationary holidays are offered year round from Longonot Ranch House, an 80,000 acre ranch located in the heart of the Great Rift Valley. The ranch is situated at 7000 feet and provides spectacular views. You may enjoy escorted walking trips or daily riding and gaze at some of the 475 species of birds that make their home on Lake Naivasha, not to mention zebras, giraffes, elands, impalas, gazelles, kongonis, warthogs, hyenas, jackals, and the occasional cheetah, leopard or Cape buffalo.

CHILDREN'S PROGRAM: Children must be accompanied by an adult. Longonot Ranch House is suitable for children under 12.

ACCOMMODATIONS: Fully staffed, luxury mobile-tented camps.

MEALS: Food and service are of the highest quality.

RIDING STUFF: You will be driven out to the base camp and set off on horseback over some of the most dramatic wildlife and scenic country in Africa. You ride each day for 6 or 7 hours across open country uninterrupted by fences, paved roads or even telegraph poles. You will be spellbound by the sense of space and freedom. Your sure-footed mounts are tacked up with comfortable, specially designed trekking saddles—saddlebags attached. The camp is moved by truck along bush roads while riders follow game trails across Masailand. Each afternoon you will arrive at a new campsite set up beside a spring or waterhole beneath spreading acacia trees—just in time for tea and hot showers before evening sundowners around the camp fire. The *syces* (grooms) attend to your horses on the picket line and provide special protection against predators. These safaris are only for experienced riders. Some of the safaris combine a landrover photographic holiday with time on horseback. On most safaris, you can expect to see the "Big Five" and at least 30 other mammal species.

AUTHOR'S COMMENT: *Tony Church, now joined by son Gordon, runs one of the most respected rides in the world. A number of very well known outfitters virtually demanded that I include this ride, which is kind of like being forced to eat a great meal!*

HIGHLIGHTS

Outstanding wildlife viewing • Handmade pigskin French trekking saddles • 25 Anglo-Somali and Anglo-Arab Kenya-bred horses • Intermediate riding skills: competent and confident at all paces • Weight limit 210 lbs. (95 kg.) (15 stone) • Camel rides and personalized safaris arranged • 5 to 16 day safaris all year except April and May (rainy season) • Longonot Ranch House is open all year round for day rides, stationary vacations and safari embarkation • Member: Kenya Association of Tour Operators and Kenya Professional Safari Guides Association

SOUTHERN OASIS & HIGH ATLAS VALLEY

www.perso.wanadoo.fr/cheval.daventure

BASICS: Cheval Adventure/Adventures on Horseback, Mas du Pommier, 07590 Cellier-du-Luc, France
Tel: (33) 4-6646-6273   Fax: (33) 4-6646-6209
Email: cheval.daventure@wanadoo.fr

WHEN: Southern Oasis, April; High Atlas, July/August.

AIRPORTS: Oasis Ride: Fez or Ouarzazate (via Casablanca); Atlas Ride: Marrakesh.

LOCATION: Oasis Ride is a beautiful 5 hour drive from the airport at either Fez or Ouarzazate; Atlas Ride is a 2 hour drive from the airport at Marrakesh.

PRICE: *Oasis Ride:* $1125 (£703) (1077 Euro) 10 days (7 riding), per person, double occupancy. *High Atlas Ride:* $1370 (£856) (1307 Euro) 10 days (7 riding), per person, double occupancy.

SOUTHERN OASIS RIDE: The first day is spent exploring Fez, former capital of the Moroccan Kingdom, an incredible city with miles of narrow, winding streets, closed to cars, where delicious aromas whafting from exotic food and spice stalls accompany visitors browsing among colorful shops selling traditional crafts. Once on horseback, you will ride from oasis to oasis in the luxuriant Ziz valley, where towering date palms and rich gardens feed small Saharan villages guarded by brick fortresses (*ksour*). Beyond the Ziz, riders sweep into the sands of the Sahara and the rose-tinted dunes of the Erg Chebbi. The vast expanse of space and light characteristic of the true desert will thrill you as the horses move out in fast gallops and you enter a realm where time seems to stand as still as the desert air. During the last day of your trip, you will drive to Ouarzazate to sample the varied attractions of the city and enjoy the delights of a comfortable hotel.

HIDDEN VALLEY OF THE HIGH ATLAS RIDE: This is a summer ride that takes you into the heart of the High Atlas mountain range, filled with the smell of pines, juniper and thuyas and home to the Berbers who ingeniously cultivate green oases in the shadows of its high, arid peaks. The Berbers are a friendly people, whose unchanging way of life and gracious hospitality (including delicious food and traditional mint tea) will make your trip an unforgettable experience. Due to the mountainous rocky terrain, the riding pace is usually kept to a walk and you may sometimes be required to dismount and lead your horse over rocky downhill areas. Neverthless, there will be opportunities to canter. Riders meet and depart from Marakesh, where they will spend a half-day and evening before starting out the following morning.

CHILDREN'S PROGRAM: Children under 16 must be accompanied by an adult.

ACCOMMODATIONS: Riders sleep in 2 person igloo-shaped tents.

SPECIAL ACTIVITIES: While riding is the main activity, immersion in an ancient, fascinating and colorful culture will stimulate all of your senses.

MEALS: Moroccans are renowned for their delicious, sumptuous meals and mint tea. You will not be disappointed! Wine is included with the evening meal. A full breakfast and picnic lunch is provided.

RIDING STUFF: Riders must be at ease at all paces, capable of riding confidently over varying terrain for several hours at a stretch. Riding in the Atlas Mountains is relatively easy, the pace often dictated by the rough terrain. In contrast, the Arab-Barb horses will move to the gallop on the desert ride. Riders must be able to handle very manageable but strong and willing horses.

AUTHOR'S COMMENT: *Morocco is an enchanting and charming world full of beautiful sights, tantalizing mysteries and intriguing customs of an ancient people, where hospitality is more than a tradition. Horses have always played a strong role in Moroccan history. These rides offer a comfortable opportunity to explore this exotic region and experience a culture that has remained relatively unchanged for hundreds of years.*

HIGHLIGHTS
Arab-Barb horses • English tack (calvary saddles) • Immersion in traditional old Morocco • Pre-Saharan villages and Bedouin or Berber (non-Arabian) villages and nomadic camps offering great warmth and hospitality. • Group capacity 15 • Oasis Ride is for experienced riders only • Atlas Ride requires intermediate level riding skills • 5 to 7 hours per day in the saddle

Southern Oasis:
Last villages
before the desert

High Atlas Valley:
Berber fortified villages in the valley.

NYIKA HORSE SAFARIS

BASICS: Nyika Horse Safaris, PO Box 2338
   Lilongwe, Malawi
   Tel: (265) 740-579   Fax: (265) 740-848
   Email: nyika-safaries@malawi.net
UK Agent: **In the Saddle**, Laurel Cottage,
   Ramsdell, Tadley, Hampshire RG26 5SH, UK
   Tel: 01256-851-665   Fax: 01256-851-667
   Email: rides@inthesaddle.com
   Website: www.inthesaddle.com
US Agent: **Equitour**, PO Box 807, Dubois, WY
   82513, USA
   Tel: (800) 545-0019   Tel: (307) 455-3363
   Fax: (307) 455-2354
Email: equitour@wyoming.com
Website: www.ridingtours.com

WHEN: Open April through the end of December.
AIRPORTS: Lilongwe. Flights from Lilongwe to
   Chelinda (via Mzuzu) are available through
   Air Malawi 2 times per week (Thursdays and
   Sundays) and cost $160 (£100).
LOCATION: Chelinda is approximately 180 kms.
   from Mzuzu - a 4 hour drive.
PRICE: *Base Camp Safari at Chelinda Trail Camp:*
   $170 (£106) per night, per person, double occu-
   pancy. *Luxury Tented Safaris* (2 to 10 nights):
   $200 (£125) per night, per person, double occu-
   pancy. Add 50% for single supplement. Prices
   include all meals, accommodations and riding.
   Drinks and local gratuities are extra. Park fees
   may be extra.

The meeting place for this safari is Chelinda Camp in Nyika's National Park, a true wilderness covering more than 3000 square kms. The rolling montane grasslands of the Park are unique in Africa. Wildlife includes eland, roan antelope, zebra, reedbuck, warthog, hyena, leopard, and many other species, with the possibility of sighting elephants and buffaloes as well. There is excellent bird watching and wonderful wildflowers including more than 200 species of orchids.

CHILDREN'S PROGRAM: Suitable for children.

ACCOMMODATIONS: Chelinda Camp sleeps 28 in rooms with twin beds and *en suite* baths. There is a separate bar/dining area. The luxury-tented camps used on safari include large walk-in safari tents, made-up twin beds, and hanging shelves. Towels, hot water bottles, water jugs, glasses and washbasins are provided as well as traditional bucket showers and long drop toilets.

SPECIAL ACTIVITIES: Bird watching, night drives, and trout fishing (bring your own rod).

MEALS: You will enjoy hearty cooked breakfasts, light packed lunches, and 3 course dinners, all prepared by the camp staff and served in the dining tent. Special dietary needs will

be accommodated upon prior notice.

RIDING STUFF: All rides are led by professional guides. The horses are Thoroughbreds and Boerparde crossbreds. Comfortable cavalry saddles are used. You will typically ride about 5 hours daily and get very close to the wildlife. David Foot can arrange to have suitable horses for all skill levels, and weight up to 200 lbs. Groups are very small, from 2 to a maximum of 6 people. The pace is generally a walk, but there is some faster riding. On the 10 day safari trip, you will change camps at least 3 times, moving from grasslands to higher rocky plateau, and finally towards the mountain peaks of Vitinthiza and Mwanda, before spending the final night back at Chelinda. In addition to the rolling montane grasslands, you will travel through evergreen forest patches, and over rocky outcrops, streams and bogs. Riding may involve many ascents and descents.

AUTHOR'S COMMENT: *This is a wonderful ride in a beautiful and remote part of Africa, an area abundantly populated with grazing herds. The terrain is unique and experienced riders, as well as novices, will have plenty to write home about. Your horse will be well suited to your skill level and you will enjoy a safe, but stimulating ride.*

HIGHLIGHTS
Beginning to advanced riding skills • Weight limit 200 lbs. (91 kg.) (14.2 stone) • Comfortable Western-like McLellan saddles • 5 hours in the saddle daily • 18 scheduled safari trips (5 to 10 days) • Traditional, vehicle supported luxury safari camps • Great wildlife viewing • Professional guides • Flexible schedule • Customized safaris

NAMIB DESERT TRAILS

www.ridingtours.com

BASICS: Reit Safari, PO Box 20706, Windhoek, Namibia

Tel: (265) 740-579   Fax: (265) 740-848

US Agent: **Equitour**, PO Box 807, Dubois, WY 82513, USA

Tel: (800) 545-0019   Tel: (307) 455-3363

Fax: (307) 455-2354

Email: equitour@wyoming.com

WHEN: High Season: Mid-February through mid-October. Low Season: July 12 to 24.

AIRPORTS: Windhoek, Namibia

LOCATION: The farm is located 65 miles southwest of Windhoek.

PRICE: High Season: $2280 (£1425) 13 days/12 nights, per person, double occupancy. Low Season: $2030 (£1269) 13 days/12 nights, per person, double occupancy. Riders over the weight limit must pay a 30% supplement for an additional horse. Bus fare from Swakopmund to Windhoek is $25 (£16). Dinner and lunch in Swakopmund are not included in the prices listed.

Namibia is home to the world's oldest desert, where the indigenous flora and fauna have won the battle against extinction, sometimes by ingenious methods. Your hosts, Albert and Waltraut Frizsche, were born and raised in Namibia, where Albert's grandfather arrived as a German soldier. They are extremely knowledgeable about the region, and confidently lead groups on this rugged and challenging ride. The trail covers over 35 kms. a day for 9 days, before emerging at the beach near the old town of Swakopmund on the Atlantic Ocean, where you will enjoy some spirited riding. With the possibility of spending 8 or more hours in the saddle each day, the physical challenge of this ride is equaled only by the rugged terrain. You will see mountain zebras, oryx, and other game animals, as well as old gold mines, leopard caves and an always startlingly beautiful landscape.

CHILDREN'S PROGRAM: Due to the strength and stamina required for this ride, it is not appropriate for children.

ACCOMMODATIONS: During the first 2 days riders stay at the base farm, which is about 65 kms. southwest of Windhoek. On the last 2 nights guests sleep at a cottage in the coastal town of Swakopmund. Camping accommodations consist of 2 person dome tents. Swags with sheepskin padding are provided for placement under your sleeping bag. Most nights can be spent sleeping without a tent, under the stars. Hot showers are available.

SPECIAL ACTIVITIES: Riding over the impressive dunes along the Atlantic coast.

MEALS: Meals are prepared over an open fire and often feature local game meat, as well as fresh produce and South African wines.

RIDING STUFF: The horses include Arabians, Haflingers, Trakehners, local crossbreds, and the famous wild horses of the Namib. English and Western saddles are used. You will ride through the central highlands at 2000 meters (6561 feet), following a 20 km. trail along red sand dunes, which takes you into the 50,000 acre Namib-Nauklluft Park and eventually through the Namib Desert. You will finish the ride by spending your last 2 nights at the Namibian coastal town of Swakopmund, located on the Atlantic Ocean

AUTHOR'S COMMENT: *This ride was launched when Albert decided to find out whether he too could survive the trip his grandfather had made across the desert on horseback more than 75 years ago. The answer is self-evident and the ride has been operating since 1992.*

HIGHLIGHTS

For fit and experienced riders • Weight limit 185 lbs. (84 kg.) (13 stone) • Western and English saddles • 6 to 10 hours in the saddle per day • Covers 35 kms. daily • Ride through the Namibian desert • Wildlife viewing

EQUUS HORSE SAFARIS

www.equus.co.za

BASICS: African Wildlife Safari on Horseback,
36 12th Avenue, Parktown North 2193,
Johannesburg, South Africa
Tel: (27) 11-788-3923 Fax: (27) 11-880-8401
UK AGENT: **In the Saddle**, Laurel Cottage, Ramsdell,
Tadley, Hampshire RG26 5SH, UK
Website: www.inthesaddle.com
Tel: 01256-851-665 Fax: 01256-851-667 (from UK)
Email: rides@inthesaddle.com
US AGENT: **Equitour**, Box 807, Dubois, WY 82513, USA
Website: www.ridingtours.com
Tel: (800) 545-0019   Tel: (307) 455-3363
Fax: (307) 455-2354 (from US)

Email: equitour@wyoming.com
WHEN: Open year round, except November.
AIRPORTS: Johannesburg International. Transfers
arranged at additional cost.
LOCATION: Waterburg Plateau, about a 3½ hour drive
from Johannesburg.
PRICES: *Bush Camp Safaris:* £110 ($180) per
night, per person, double occupancy.
Wilderness Safaris: £144 ($230) per night, per
person, double occupancy, all inclusive (1998
Rates) **Please Note: Slight variations in price
depending on the total package offered.**

Wendy Adams and her staff have been treating guests to extensive wildlife viewing and comfortable accommodations for years. Local fauna includes wildebeest, warthog, red hartebeest, klipspringer, bushpig, monkey, baboon, kudu, zebra, impala, hyena, aardvark, giraffe, cheetah, hippopotamus, crocodile, and many more. Experienced riders are permitted to ride in areas where black and white rhinoceros and buffalo can be found. All riding is on the Waterberg Plateau in the Lapalala Wilderness, a private reserve, world-renowned for black rhino conservation and environmental education, encompassing nearly 77,000 acres (35,000 hectares)of pristine wilderness, bisected by the great Palala River with its majestic gorge. The terrain is wild and rocky with lots of sheer cliffs, clear streams, grass-covered plains, shady valleys, and wonderful high mountain views.

CHILDREN'S PROGRAM: Not suitable for small children under the age of 8. Teenagers, if competent riders, are welcome.

ACCOMMODATIONS: The base camp safaris have 4 twin bedded luxury tents, spaced well apart for privacy, thatched central dining and lounge area. Each tent has a private veranda and *en suite* bathroom with hot shower and flush *loo*. On safari, riders will make use of other tent camps, log cabins, rock lodges and river huts.

SPECIAL ACTIVITIES: There is a small but cooling rock pool at the bush camp. Game and bird watching are also available.

MEALS: Fresh local produce and home baked bread are served whenever possible. Substantial brunches, and an afternoon tea follow a light breakfast. Dinner provides a good opportunity to relax and socialize during 3 course meals. The well stocked bar operates on the honor system. Special diets will be catered for upon request.

RIDING STUFF: Riders generally spend 5 to 7 hours a day in the saddle riding a variety of well-trained, locally bred horses, including Boerperd Arabs, Friesians and crossbred Saddlers of 14 to 16 hands. The horses are well cared for, responsive, alert, forward-going and well-tempered. Novices will enjoy riding through the wilderness area where the safer game resides, while experienced riders, as judged by the guides, will get plenty of chance to observe larger and potentially more menacing larger game. Vehicles support the Wilderness Safaris. Riders are evaluated on the first day by local guides, who will determine in what areas each guest may safely ride. Although there is good riding all year round, the winter months of June through September provide an ideal climate for riding—warm days with clear blue skies and cooler evenings. Where the going is good there will be opportunity for long trots and canters.

AUTHOR'S COMMENT: *Wendy and her staff offer a delightful way to experience the excitement of Africa's exotic flora and fauna, under conditions that insure a high level of creature comforts, good horses and exhilarating riding. Formed in 1989, this is the longest-established specialist horse safari company in South Africa.*

HIGHLIGHTS
Good wildlife viewing • Riding for novice to advanced (no beginners) at luxury base camp • Safaris require riders with at least intermediate skill • Comfortable trail saddles and English saddles available • Bush camp stays of 3 to 10 days • Safaris from 5 to 9 nights • Guest limit 8 • Professional field guides • Member: AHSA

HORIZON HORSE ADVENTURES AT TRIPLE B

www.inthesaddle.com

BASICS: Agent: **In the Saddle**, Laurel Cottage, Ramsdell, Tadley, Hampshire RG26 5SH, UK
Tel: 01256-851665   Fax: 01256-851667 (from UK)
Tel: (44)1256-851665   Fax: (44)1256-851667 (from US)
Email: rides@inthesaddle.com
In South Africa contact: Triple B Ranch, P O Box 301, Vaalwater 0530, South Africa
Tel: (27) 14755-3737 Fax: (27) 14755-3705
Email: tessa@smartnet.co.za

WHEN: Open all year.
AIRPORTS: Johannesburg. Transfers to the farm may be arranged at extra cost.
LOCATION: The ranch is situated in the Northern Province, a 2½ hour drive north of the airport.
PRICE: £95 ($152) per night, per person, d/o. Prices include all riding activities and pack trips, lodging, meals and alcoholic and non-alcholic drinks. Single room supplement adds 50% extra if you are unwilling to share.

Triple B Ranch, situated among the stunning Waterberg mountains, has been home to the Baber family for 3 generations. The ranch is a mixed cattle, crops and game ranch and is surrounded by private game reserves, making it the ideal base for Horizon Horseback Adventures. The Waterberg is a 6000 square km. wilderness area of outstanding beauty. It features wonderful vistas, rolling bushveld hills, gorges, clear streams and open plains and is rich in flora and fauna, including the white and endangered black rhino and over 300 species of birds.

CHILDREN'S PROGRAM: Children 10 and older may ride provided they have experience and wear an approved riding hat.

ACCOMMODATIONS: Guests stay at the Horizon homestead; a lovely colonial style house with 3 double rooms and a thatched rondavel, both with *en suite* facilities. There is a plunge pool, and a tennis court only a short drive away. While out on safari, guests will be accommodated in large, 3 person tents, with camp beds, pillows, and bush shower. The *loo* is a shovel and a view. You may wish to combine your stay at Horizon with a couple of nights at the Ant's Nest, the Babers' private game reserve and luxury lodge, where guided walks, game drives and upscale riding safaris are on offer.

SPECIAL ACTIVITIES: You may enjoy game drives to private reserves, guided bush walks, or simply roam the premises of this large, diversified farm.

MEALS: The food is of a very high standard and includes an early light breakfast, mid-morning brunch, afternoon tea, and a 3 or 4 course dinner. Dinner is served either in the house or the *boma*, while brunch may be on the veranda, in the house, *boma*, or even a bush breakfast. A hearty English breakfast is served after the morning ride.

RIDING STUFF: Triple B enables you to ride through a variety of terrain, traverse koppies, travel through thick bush, gallop across open lands, canter along miles of sandy tracks, or jump the cross-country course. Horizon prides itself on its quality horses; they are honest, forward-going and highly responsive and are always well-matched to the rider. The herd is over 50 strong, most are Anglo-Arab/Boerperd crosses, but there are also Arabs, Thoroughbreds, and Boerperds. Horizon offers a broad range of riding opportunities. On riding safaris, guests venture off into the neighboring Palala Conservancy to enjoy riding alongside a wide variety of game and camping out at night around a fire. The ranch experience allows you to enjoy rides which range from gentle explorations to long and fast. Cattle work and polo-crosse are excellent fun and provide unique riding experiences, while cross-country jumping brings its own challenges.

AUTHOR'S COMMENT: *Horizon offers an exciting riding experience where one is not only able to view game from horseback, but can also try some of the other challenging riding opportunities. Coupled with the excellent quality of their horses, the relaxed and friendly atmosphere provides good reason to visit Africa and enjoy a taste of the great wilderness in gracious and comfortable surroundings.*

HIGHLIGHTS

Game viewing on horseback during 2 night riding safaris in the Palala Conservancy • Morning and afternoon rides on the ranch • Cattle work • Polo-crosse • Cross-country course • Can accommodate all riding abilities • English or Stock saddles • Comfortable accommodations at the homestead • Recommended 7 to 14 days

CAREW SAFARIS-MAVURADONNA WILDERNESS

BASICS: UK Agent: **In the Saddle**, Laurel Cottage, Ramsdell, Tadley, Hampshire, RG26 5SH, UK Tel: 01256-851-665   Fax: 01256-851-667 Email: rides@inthesaddle.com Website: www.inthesaddle.com US Agent: **Equitour,** PO Box 807, Dubois, WY 82513, USA Tel: (800) 545-0019   Tel: (307) 455-3363 Fax: (307) 455-2354 Email: equitor@wyoming.com Website: www.ridingtours.com In Zimbabwe contact: Carew Safaris, Mavuradonna Wilderness, P. Bag 295A Harare, Zimbabwe Tel: (263) 4 -758194 or (263) 4-758196

Fax: (263) 4-773971
Email: carew@harare.iafrica.com
Website: www.zimbabwe.net/tourism/carew
WHEN: Open year round.
AIRPORTS: Harare Airport
LOCATION: The ride begins 180 kms. north of Harare.
PRICE: $220 (£137) per night, per person, d/o. Price includes all meals, local wine, beer, soft drinks and spirits in reasonable quantities, accommodations and riding. Single supplement add 50%, unless willing to share. There is an additional charge of $130 (£81) per person roundtrip for transfers from Harare.

The Mavuradonna Wilderness covers hundreds of thousands of acres of uninhabited wilderness and rugged terrain. The mountains are cleft by deep valleys and laced by perpetually running waters. Thundering rivers crash over mighty waterfalls during the rainy season, crystal clear streams and limpid pools beckon in the dry season. The Wilderness has been totally unpopulated since bushmen hunted these valleys and painted delicate portraits of the game. A mere 180 kms. from Harare, this is a land of startling beauty. The Great Dyke towers over the Zambesi Escarpment before cascading over 1000 feet into the valley. The area is inaccessible except on foot or horseback. From July to December you are likely to see a variety of animals and birds.

CHILDREN'S PROGRAM: Children are welcome if they ride well and can do the distances.

ACCOMMODATIONS: Safaris begin and end at Kopje Tops Lodge which can accommodate up to 12 guests in 6 rock and thatch-roofed chalets, with *en suite* shower and toilet facilities. Bat Caves Camp, where you will spend at least 1 night, is a comfortable bush camp with 4 thatched-roof cabins. Safari beds and mattresses are provided. Remote wilderness camps are set up under the stars with portable tents, or in the ancient bushman caves.

SPECIAL ACTIVITIES: You may wish to extend your stay at Kopje Tops Lodge, a most unusual set-up, with comfortable surroundings, good food, and some good riding territory. Visit traditional African villages or the famous Tengenenge Sculpture to the south of the Wilderness.

MEALS: Breakfast and 3 course dinners are served at Kopje Tops and the Bat Caves. Lunches are packed. House wine, beer and soda are included.

RIDING STUFF: Arabians, polo ponies, Thorough-breds, and Quarterhorse crosses, 14 to 16 hands, are used. The tack is English. The rides are generally slow paced. Riding time is 4 to 6 hours a day. Some or all of the riding can be arranged at the eccentrically beautiful Kopje Tops Lodge, or in combination with a visit to the Bat Caves Camp, where you may witness the evening flight of Egyptian fruit bats. You may also opt for the Mavuradonna Wilderness Trails which take you deep into the bush, following animal paths, tracking the elephants and other game. The rides are led by Jane Hunt, a professional guide, who grew up in Zimbabwe.

AUTHOR'S COMMENT: *This is a wonderful opportunity to visit one of the last remaining wilderness areas left in the world.*

HIGHLIGHTS
Ride through the uninhabited Mavuradonna Wilderness, Zimbabwe's last true wilderness • Customized trips • Group capacity 2 to 8 • Intermediate skill level • Pace slow, due to mountainous terrain

ASIA

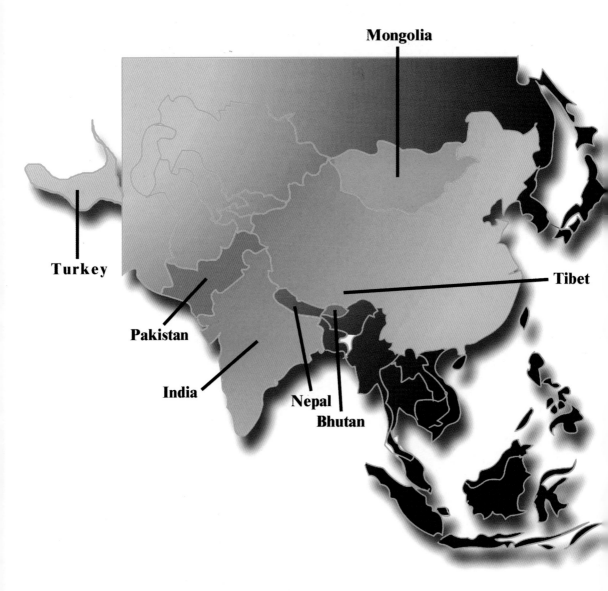

Mongolia

Turkey

Pakistan

India

Nepal

Bhutan

Tibet

INDIA

by John Ruler

ANYONE FROM THE WESTERN COUNTRIES contemplating a trip to India are automatically in for a culture shock. To do so on horseback is to jump in at the deep end—and it's worth every minute of it! Rarely in nearly 30 years of holiday riding have I been subject to such a bewildering kaleidoscope of colour and sound. The images are of riding through a heaving mass of humanity, of honking cars and gaudily decorated lorries making their way among strolling grey humped-back sacred cows nonchalantly eating from market stalls, and swaying camels. In contrast, the rural scene is one of perfect peace. Tilled fields where sari-clad women (and occasional men) flit like so many butterflies in vivid hues of blue, red and orange amid the dusty yellows and grey-greens of Rajasthan. Add the excited greetings of village children as you ride into town—the boys full of waves, the girls more bashful—the sight of people gathering water from the well or sheltering beneath the communal People Tree, and you quickly fall under India's enchanting spell.

Working much of the magic are the marvelous Marwari—the Merlins of equine world—whose distinctive inwardly curving ears, when seen from the saddle appear, as one wit remarked, as though looking through the sights of a rifle. Ranging in size from 15.2 to 16.2 hands high and with longish backs, they have a tendency to stride out at the trot. These delightful creatures have the stamina needed for around 6 hours of riding daily. Our group of 11 (including 3 Americans, 4 Brits, and 3 French) was organized by Raghuvendra Singh, simply known as "Bonnie," who proved to be a genial host with an infectious giggle, while still maintaining strict discipline over us. We needed it, as an element of sheer escapism ran strongly through the ride. The effect heightened by 2 grooms, resplendent in orange robes and bearing lances, who took up the rear.

The sights and sounds of India blur into one giant impressionist painting, the colour sharpened each evening when girls in bright red saris stole the limelight during cabaret style entertainment. After leaving the parkland setting of the Roop Niwas Palace Hotel at Nawalgargh, a gala night was staged at the Samode Place Hotel, made famous as a location shot in "The Jewel in the Crown" and "The Far Pavillions." Equally evocative was the night spent at Lohar Gal, a religious shrine set amidst the cool, calm palms of the surrounding Aravalli Hills. The pilgrims' rest house consisted of small, stone cells, a single candle, and camp beds which proved to be some of the most comfy sleeping arrangements we came across. Canvas latrines were provided in the back—the spartan side of riding in India. And no, we did not suffer from the infamous Delhi Belly. Freshly cooked food, supervised by Sunayana, our lady mentor and lynchpin of the back-up team, saw to that.

INDIA

by Billa Edwards

WHY GO TO INDIA TO RIDE? Because of its rich cultural heritage as well as its wide open spaces and breathtaking landscapes that all combine to create a heady mix. The entire land is ablaze with exotic traditions and people—India is about people, the different castes and how they relate to each other. India is a land of ancient cultures. Two of the world's greatest religions were born here. India is a land of paradoxes, where old and new thrive alongside each other and travelling is always an adventure. All your senses are heightened by the brilliant array of colours, the spicy aromas, the deep sense of spiritualism. Riding is for those who want to not only marvel at the world's greatest monument to love, the Taj Mahal, but also those who wish to experience the magic of India's quiet places, far beyond the tourist trail.

India mesmerizes you—its great monuments, its mad way of utilizing transport (you wonder how anybody ever gets anywhere or survives), its complex marriage system. Just when you think you are beginning to understand these complexities it becomes all too clear that there is so much more to see and learn. You begin to dream of your next visit and the one after that, you are caught by this extraordinarily beautiful, outrageous, awe-inspiring and, often, witty land.

The horses are a dimension in themselves. They are Marwari horses, a very old breed indigenous to India. There is a very ancient and rich Indian horse culture nowhere more evident than in Rajasthan, where legends and stories of heroic deeds of warriors and their steeds are still related with pride today. The following couplet illustrates a very endearing characteristic of the Marwari's place in the heart and psyche of the Rajput warrior.

Dhav to sooto mahal mein,
Neelo bandhyo thaan.
Sapne seem na sancchare
ari dhooje anthaan.

The lady of the house is in her palace, conversing with a friend about the peaceful ambience, she observes how peacefully her husband sleeps when his reliable steed is stabled nearby. Even she is confident that in such circumstances no enemy may even dream of violating the boundaries. The beauty of this couplet is found in the lady's belief that the presence of the horse permits the master his fearless slumber, the awe, admiration, envy and confidence the horse arouses in the wife, the fear the horse arouses in enemies. It is the horse that is credited with inspiring such confidence and peace.

On most safaris you will get a chance to ride a Marwari horse, characterized by their lyre-shaped ears that meet at the tips and are very special in lots of ways. Their loyalty, generosity of spirit, stamina, and hardiness, all make them ideal to ride for long distances. They can withstand a great range of temperatures and require relatively little food, all the while remaining unbelievably willing. Their spirit and enthusiasm leave no doubt that they too are enjoying the ride. The Marwari breed dates back to the 6th century if not before. They were the war horses of the Rajput warriors of what today are known as Rajasthan and Gujarat. Historical records describe huge numbers of cavalry, as many as 300,000 horses were kept ready in some places. It is interesting to note that even today in these same places, Marwari horses are still being bred. With the partition of India in 1947, and the advent of 4 wheel drive vehicles, the breed almost became extinct, but thankfully they are now making a comeback, due in part to their use on riding holidays, giving them exposure to the West.

So now you have a backdrop upon which to weave your dreams of what will be an adventure as much as a holiday. What can a riding safari offer that most other trips to India cannot? If you want to get way off the beaten tourist track away from coach trips and throngs of camera clickers, to get close to the heart of the country itself, then a safari on horseback is an excellent choice. Once you have left the international airport and the incredible noise and bustle of Delhi or Bombay far behind, the countryside, whether desert, plain, hill or mountain, will reveal a different India. Teamed with a group of like-minded people and a willing horse, you can discover a pastoral lifestyle that has not changed for centuries You will experience first hand the ways of a proud and honourable people, where the simplest of pleasures brings the shyest and warmest of smiles. You will wander through villages where children stare in wonder or run joyfully after you. The young men and elders give a cheerful greeting, "Namaste," with clasped hands and a bow of the head. Beautiful women in brilliant orange or fuschia robes look up from tending their goats or sifting corn, perhaps to wonder for a moment why a group of oddly clad strangers on horseback would wish to be there. "Are they lost? Wouldn't they prefer to go to the city?"

Biblical scenes are to be found at every turn. Saffron turbaned men with home-whittled wooden ploughs walk quietly behind compliant and well-matched cattle, clicking and grunting, "aah, aah" to guide them through fields preparing for the sowing. Or round and round on a turnstile to draw water from ancient wells and send it through channels hollowed out of the soil directing it to needy crops. In the desert, camels are used on the long daily round-trip to collect household water or fodder for livestock. Sometimes you may be invited by a householder to share their hot sweet tea. Offering refreshments to weary travelers is polite, and it must be as interesting for the hosts as it is for their guests. It provides a chance for riders to ease themselves from their saddles and stretch their legs whilst experiencing the natural warmth and hospitality of these simple farming people. In the presence of strange men many of the women will cover their faces in shyness or modesty, but occasionally female guests may be invited inside the house or compound to have a look around. This provides a sense of tremendous privilege, and you will notice that everything is spotless—floors swept, pots and buckets gleaming.

As the day draws to a close, the horses sense that they are nearing the camp and food. Your campsite has miraculously been erected, ready and waiting for your arrival. Grinning grooms come to help you dismount, taking your horse off to untack and settle her down for the night. You go in search of hot water to sponge down your weary body in anticipation of a good meal, good conversation and a good sleep under canvas. You speculate happily about what the next day will bring, when your horse, fresh as a daisy and ready to go, is brought for you to mount. Can adventure really be this luxurious?

About Billa Edwards and Indian Encounters

In 1984, after 6 years traveling through India, Billa Edwards started Indian Encounters. Her aim is to share with like-minded travelers her knowledge of and love for India. Because of this, she is in a unique position to guide and advise you on your travels—whether you are a single individual or part of a large group. Billa has spent all of her life with horses and her experiences cover every aspect of horsemanship, breeding, training, and riding in many different countries. This makes an ideal background for organizing riding holidays. The idea of horseback riding safaris in India was first conceived in 1987 and Indian Encounters has come a long way since then. The latest development for Indian Encounters is Jharokha, an Indian company created by Th. Saryendra Sing Chawra, which is locally based in Udaipur, and is best situated to coordinate all of the riding activities. Both operations are small and always try to ensure that a friendly and relaxed atmosphere prevails. The itineraries are carefully structured and organized, but there is plenty of scope for flexibility in order to take advantage of the surprise encounters that India so often magically produces.

RIDING IN INDIA
by Inder Jit Singh

NOT MANY PEOPLE ASSOCIATE THE INDIAN SUBCONTINENT with horses, and it is true that India does not boast of the large private stables that one can find in North America, Europe, Australia or South America. But whatever may be missing in terms of size, variety of breeds, and modern facilities, is made up for many times over in terms of lore, living history, and quality of experience—all of which result in an equine adventure like no other!

Did you know, that it was in ancient India that the riding stirrup was first invented? That on one of our rides you can actually visit a temple deifying the horse? That polo was, and still is, being played in its original form in the Indian Himalaya and the mountains of Central Asia, a form going back hundreds of years? Did you know that you can travel to witness the ancient equestrian skill of tent pegging in India, as performed by the Nihang Sikhs in the Punjab, or the Rajputs of Rajasthan, in the same style used by the Arabs and Moors who first introduced the skill when they crossed the Arabian Ocean to India in the 12th century? In fact, during the Tricentennial Celebrations (April 1999) of the birth of the Khalsa (the "Pure"), the name for the modern Sikh religion, you can join us to see the Nihangs displaying ancient martial skills on horseback, attired in dress and accoutrements unchanged since the 1700s, when they went to war. Some of these skills are described by Colonel Alesander Cunningham, the 18th century explorer, writing about cavalry-training in the Sikh court of Ranjit Singh in his classic book, *The History of the Sikhs.*

It is also in India that you can watch the polo players of Ladakh and Baltistan in the high Himalaya, playing at 12,000 feet above sea level in a high altitude desert, where there are few rules and no limit on the number of players. The game itself is unrestrained, players often carving a wedge into the crowd as spectators rush back to make way for the melee of horses. The game lasts for an hour and more, non-stop. In the desert state of Rajasthan, you can visit the cattle fairs, where people from hundreds of kilometres away converge annually at a holy pool or site. Due to the cost of travel, these pilgrimages have become a cattle exchange as well, to pay for the journey. The sights seen at these fairs at Pushkar, Naugaur, and Baneshwar, have remained unchanged since well before the time of Colonel James Todd, who made his horseback journeys here to complete his epic 19th century journal, "The Annals of Antiquities of Rajputana." One American visitor could not forget how a small and very modest optometrist's shop refused to charge because she was a foreign visitor. While riding in the desert, one simple and poor villager offered to bring water for us to drink, the most expensive and rare beverage he could offer. For pure fun, pageantry and ceremony, India's military is among the most colourful and historically rich in horse regiments, like the 61st Calvary, which won renown for defeating the Turks when fighting under Field Marshal Viscount Lord Allenby in Palestine during World War I. The "61st" still celebrates "Haifa Day" every September 23rd when it commemorates what is considered one of the last great victorious cavalry charges witnessed in recent history. You can see these mounted columns every 26th of January on India's Republic Day Parade.

This then is a glimpse of the places and experiences that are within your grasp while traveling on horseback in India—where it is affordable and realistic to ride into a mountain fortress or palace for the night, and to places where the James Bond film *Octopussy*, or "The Jewel in the Crown" and "The Far Pavillions" were actually shot. You can also spend the night at a jungle or desert camp with sloth bear or leopard and desert cat sighted from your Imperial Raj Tent. Facets of this experience were immortalized by Kipling and Corbett.

I look forward to the opportunity to lead you on an epic horseback journey, A ride into history, which promises to touch you like no other.

About Inder Jit Singh

Born in Shillong, Meghalya, Inder Jit Singh showed an early fascination with history, culture and biodiversity that was cultivated by an expedition he joined while still in high school. Along the way, Inder Jit graduated from the University of Jabalpur, has been awarded a prestigious Australasia-wide grant from Bio Diversity Conservation Network in the eastern Himalaya, and has personally led many expeditions. Since 1982, Inder Jit has been operating Tiger Paw Adventures, of which International Riding and Polo Holidays is a subsidiary. His interest in Indian history and the relationship with the horse is married to his own positive reaction to horses. Inder Jit played low-goal polo at the President's Estate Polo Club in New Delhi, and has learned the ancient art of tent pegging. He now pursues his interests in horses, eco-tourism, history, and adventure travel from bases in both British Columbia and India. For more detailed information, you can visit his website at: www.tigerpaw-adv.com.

MONGOLIA

by Arthur Sacks and Anne Mariage

TO MOST WESTERNERS, THE WORD "Mongolia" conjures up images of a vast, stark landscape, a place where dinosaurs once roamed, peopled by savage, nomadic tribes whose hordes of warriors on horseback, led by Ghengis Khan, swept across Asia, Russia and Eastern Europe on a quest to conquer the world. This view of the Mongolian landscape and people is far removed from present day reality. Nevertheless, Mongolia still offers a romantically exotic destination for the adventurous traveler.

There are numerous agencies that organize trips to various parts of Mongolia and they all describe beautiful and varying landscapes and a warm, hospitable people who have maintained an intimate relationship with other living creatures. Among other occupations, Mongolians breed reindeer, hunt wolves and fox with golden eagles perched on their wrists, and regularly milk their mares to make the potent drink, *airak*. The horse population of Mongolia is equal to the human population. Mongolian horses are short, sturdy, working breeds. The tack includes a variety of Tibetian, Chinese and Russian cavalry saddles.

A form of Buddhism venerating the Dali Lama is the prevalent religion, numerous altars testifying to the level of devotion. The Kazakhs, who live in the Altai Mountains, follow a liberal form of Islam. Accommodations are modest, although an effort is made to provide a modicum of creature comforts. Riders sleep (and eat) on some trips in traditional yurts—large, round, felt-covered tents. Luggage is transported by vehicle or pack animals. The Mongolian landscape varies from the dry, steppe-like Gobi Desert in the south, to thick forests in the northern regions, and to the high peaks of the Altai Mountains in the west. Many of the agencies that service Mongolia, offer side trips at either the beginning or end of the journey, including Ulambataar, the Mongolian capital, Hong Kong and China.

MONGOLIA: LAND OF THE HORSE

by Cynthia Davidson

TREKKING IN MONGOLIA, WITH ITS FAMOUS, semi-wild horses, is more than an amazing equine experience. For the rider, it means total immersion in an ancient culture and testing of physical capabilities. The ruthless Chinggis Khaan* started it all. In the 12th century, control of his vast empire was made possible by his mounted army's ability to cover great distances. The Khaan established an efficient communications system, with riders galloping 100 kms. a day across the vast, undulating grasslands. Today, Mongolians are still proud of their horsemanship. Out in the country, on our 10 day trek, we saw small children galloping amidst spumes of dust for maybe 60 kms. in preparation for the Nadaam Races. Our Mongolian guides expected us to trot and gallop for long periods in order to reach the next camp in good time. They would sweep past us shouting, "choo! choo, gallop, gallop" their long *dels* billowing around them, with their pinnacle hats firmly placed on their heads.

The gait of these game little horses was quick at all paces. The ride was uncomfortable even as they tripped along at the walk, like ladies in high heel shoes. A sitting trot was unimaginable and a rising trot hardly possible. It was best to emulate the wranglers, who stood poised in the stirrups, like ballet dancers, as their horses oscillated beneath them. Cantering and galloping were effected in a similar way. However, looking at our group of 12 from the rear, a position in which I often found myself, seats were meeting saddles, unlike those of our expert Mongolian horsemen. Nevertheless, galloping over those expansive plains in whatever style we found possible, proved to be an exhilarating experience. We sometimes raced for 15 minutes at a time, wielding our whips, while carefully watching out for marmot holes.

The leather saddles were brand new, but more roughly hewn than we were accustomed to. Underneath, there was wood, tubular metal, and a lot of felt. Nearly all of the saddles had to be customized with more felt after the first day's riding, to accommodate Western rears. Twin girths were constantly monitored by the wranglers, who stopped to tighten or slacken them according to the riding conditions. For the first few days of the trek we roamed the treeless steppe, homeland of our wranglers. The sun was unrelenting in a bright, ultramarine dome. It beat down on the parched, stony outcrops where we stopped for rests. The hobbled horses huddled together, resting their golden heads on each other's necks, as we drank our smoky, boiled water. It was hard to imagine that these seemingly loveable creatures would buck and kick at any unusual happening. It meant that they had to be approached with caution and only from the left side. They were nervous of cameras and flapping waterproofs. Although greatly respected by their owners, these horses are not treated as pets and have no names.

*More commonly known as Ghengis Khan.

Occasionally we would stop at a lonely *ger*, a nomadic, round tent with a wooden trellis frame, covered in felt and canvas. The dark, cool interior would engulf us all in welcome shade. We accepted bowls of *airak*, fermented mares' milk, still produced in the traditional, thousand year old way. Through our interpreter, Enkhtur, we talked of the traditions associated with entering a *ger* and receiving refreshment. We learnt something of the lives of our hosts and exchanged stories and pleasantries. The black-haired children came out to meet us with brown smiling faces and bemused expressions, as we attempted to speak to them in a foreign tongue. They would leap up on nearby horses to show off their riding skills, hoping to be photographed. There would always be a selection of horses around the *ger*, either grazing free or tethered to a high "washing line." Sometimes we were given a plate of clotted cream and delicious bread to share, as we watched a scene unusual to Western eyes. Two people are needed to milk a mare. The herdsman collected a sleepy foal, which was tethered with the other new arrivals. The young animal was held, often protesting, alongside its mother to stimulate the milk flow. The herdsman's wife, dressed in *del* and boots, dropped on one knee to squirt the milk into a bucket. Upon completion of the operation the foal was returned to his friends. He would probably get the real thing in the evening.

A few days into our journey, as we traveled north, we encountered magnificent green valleys and larch clad mountains. We rode through the Khan Khentii protected area and the Gorkhi Terelj National Park, east of Ulaanbaatar. By this time we were getting the measure of our horses. Chinggis (mine had a name by now) I found, was not averse to a little pat on his smooth, sand coloured neck, nor did he respond unfavourably to a stroke of his bristle brush mane, as we were riding along. Now more difficult manoeuvres, such as reaching down to a saddlebag to retrieve the water bottle, could be carried out without too much upset. However, I was never quite brave enough to try removing clothing or taking a photograph whilst mounted. All the time we were riding, our luggage was taken on a shorter route by horse carts managed by Mr. Dagva, his family and friends. Once we reached the difficult mountain terrain, the mode of transport was changed to yaks. At night, the horse cart people left us to return to the steppes and we had a farewell party. Both sides made reciprocal, complimentary speeches as we shared a meal together. We were given special pastries, made by Mrs. Dagva. She also introduced us to her home-distilled vodka, which smelt of horses and tasted strong, while her husband treated us all to a pinch of snuff. That sad night, beneath an amber sunset, we listened to traditional folk songs sung by our Mongolian hosts. Later, in our small tents, we were lulled to sleep by the sound of the stone-cold Tuul River rushing by. Once in the mountains, the air was cooler and the land was green and lush. We crossed numerous meadows, sparkling with wild flowers and we stopped for rests by huge, shady rocks and ancient larches. In the valleys, we pranced across rocky streams and galloped past massive, bulbous, rock formations looming in the distance.

To the Mongolian horsemen, the camp was always "just over there." They found their way by the sun and geographical landmarks. Born and raised in this vast landscape, distance meant nothing to them. Indeed, the white speck of our *ger*, nestling in a green haze, often looked to be "just over there," as we led our horses down a mountain side, or trotted across a wide valley floor. Two hours later, the camp still seemed at the back of beyond. Even by late afternoon the horses would do whatever was asked of them, after a day of no food or water. For those of us unused to the high altitude, a rest stop meant the unwelcome exertion of dismounting, and we would often carry on with our eyes fixed on that illusive camp. Reaching camp meant a shower or a cool river in which to bathe, followed by a 4 course meal, with soup, steamed bread and tasty stir-fry. Here, the toilet had a screen.

Hopefully, someone would have already erected our tent. With our saddles at our feet and the gentle sounds of grazing horses in our ears, sleep came easy.

To see something of this landlocked country, with its bloodthirsty and, more recent secret history of oppression, leaves a lasting impression. To discover it on horseback, galloping alongside Mongolian horsemen, transports you back, for a short while at least, to the awe inspiring times of Chinggis Khaan.

© Cynthia Davidson 1998

About Cynthia Davidson and In the Saddle

Cynthia Davidson, a travel writer, was kind enough to share her recent riding experiences during In the Saddle's 12 night July expedition to Mongolia. In the Saddle, owned and operated by Olwen Law and James Sales, is a member of ABTOT and specializes in riding holidays throughout the world. Olwen and James often participate on trips and, like other agency owners, are avid riders. Various riding trips organized by In the Saddle appear throughout this book and they are also listed in the section on travel agencies. All rides with Inn the Saddle are fully bonded.

HORSE RIDING IN BHUTAN/CHITWAN NATIONAL PARK IN NEPAL

BASICS: **Equitour: Peregrine Holidays Ltd.**, 41 South Parade, Summertown, Oxford, OX2 7JP, UK
Tel: 01865-511642
Fax: 01865-512583 (from UK)
Tel: (44) 1865-511642
Fax: (44) 1865-512583 (from US)
Email: 106357.1754@compuserve.com
WHEN: April 7. Exact date may change slightly.
AIRPORTS: New Delhi. Transfers to hotels included.
LOCATION: Bhutan and (optional) Nepal

(Katmandu and Chitwan National Park).
PRICE: Full Package: £1780 ($2848) 12 days/11 nights, per person, double occupancy, includes 5 days of riding. Single supplement add £300 ($480). Bhutan Ride (ends in Bhutan): £1200 ($1920) 8 days/7 nights, per person, double occupancy, includes 5 days of riding. Nepal Extension (Nepal only): £580 ($928) per person, double occupancy, includes internal airfare. Single supplement add £200 ($320).

This trip will be the first-ever riding holiday to Bhutan, a country still dominated by Tibetan Buddhism, high in the Himalayas. Riders/travelers should be willing to accept the unexpected, since Bhutan is not a country that caters to large numbers of tourists, unlike other areas of the Himalayas. Bhutan, nestled among the highest mountains, has kept its natural beauty intact and its valleys and mountainsides are covered with dense evergreen forests that have never been exploited. The small, pony-sized horses are indigenous to the area. Those choosing either the Full Package or the Nepal Extension will have the opportunity to enjoy game viewing on elephant-back in Chitwan National Park, a reserve where tiger, leopard, sambhar, barking and hog deer, wild boar, one-horned rhinoceros, sloth bear, crocodile, wild dog, and monkey roam freely. The later part of the trip in Nepal does not involve horseback riding. Guests will have the chance to go canoeing, and join 4 wheel drive trips to observe the wildlife.

CHILDREN'S PROGRAM: This program is not suitable for children under the age of 16.

ACCOMMODATIONS: A combination of hotel stays and tent camps.

SPECIAL ACTIVITIES: Bhutan, which limits tourists to 3000 a year, offers views of the Dzongs and monasteries that cling to a vertical granite cliff, 6000 meters (18,600 feet) above the valley floor. The site is unbelievable, testimony to mankind's ingenuity when inspired by faith.

MEALS: Meals are mixture of Bhutanese, Chinese, Indian and continental foods.

RIDING STUFF: The horses are a combination of local ponies and Haflingers, healthy and strong due to an abundance of fodder available throughout Bhutan. The first day of riding on local horses provides some spectacular views. During the second, third, and fourth days you will cover approximately 20 kilometers in 4 to 5 hours daily, eating lunch *en route*, riding through Bhutan. The next day's riding covers 28 kilometers and includes a visit to the Punakha Dzong. With a bit of luck, you will catch some fantastic views of the holiest peaks in the Himalayas, including Chomolhari. There is a 5 to 6 hour ride, covering 26 kilometers, on the sixth day of the trip. Day 7 you bid a fond farewell to the horses and spend the day sightseeing by car on your way to Paro. On the eighth day, you will either take a morning flight back to New Delhi or continue on to Nepal, Katmandu, and Chitwan National Park.

AUTHORS COMMENT: *If you want to experience something different, a place where few tourists have been, then Bhutan is for you. The culture of Bhutan is unique, protected by its self-imposed isolation until recently. Chitwan National Park in southern Nepal is one of the world's great wilderness reserves, an area of lush green forests, tropical climate, loaded with wildlife of every variety from elephants to tigers. This riding opportunity is part of a new eco-tourism trend, where riding is merely one part of a great adventure into this unique part of the world.*

HIGHLIGHTS
Visit the ancient kingdom of Bhutan • Views of spectacular Himalayan peaks • Riding between 2000 to 3500 meters (6000 to 10,000 feet) • On Full Package and Nepal Extension visit Chitwan National Park in Nepal

CORBETT'S TRAILS AND TIMES

BASICS: Agent: **Indian Encounters**, Creech Barrow, East Creech, Wareham, Dorset, BH20 5AP, UK
Tel: 01929-481421
Fax: 01929-480998 (from UK)
Tel: (441) 929-481421
Fax: (441) 929-480998 (from US)
Email: BillaEdwards@btinternet.com
WHEN: There are 2 rides per year: April 16 to April 30 and April 27 to May 11.

AIRPORTS: New Delhi. Transfers included.
LOCATION: Kumaon Region in the foothills of the Himalayan Mountains.
PRICE: £1225 ($1960) 15 days/14 nights, per person, double occupancy. Single supplement add £50 ($80). Price includes all accommodations, full board while on safari, B&B during non-riding portion.

Billa Edward's Indian Encounters offers exciting, well-planned adventures. In this case, the ride is organized around the life of Colonel James Edward Corbett, a courageous and famous hunter of the man-eating tigers that plagued Indian villages in the late 19th century, a visionary conservationist, and author. The first 2 nights are spent in New Delhi, and include a short sightseeing trip. From there, you travel by train to Agra and visit the Taj Mahal on the third day. You then journey (again by train) to Corbett Park and spend a few days riding elephants and searching for wildlife, including tigers. The riding safari begins on the sixth day, with easy riding through teak forests and many river crossings. There are plenty of opportunities to stop and take photographs. Each night will be spent camping on the grounds of forest lodges, a legacy of the British Raj, always chosen for the beauty of the surroundings. As each hour passes, the terrain continues to unfold offering breathtaking views across green valleys and gorges.

CHILDREN'S PROGRAM: There is no special program for children, but appropriate arrangements can be made.

ACCOMMODATIONS: On this ride 8 days are spent in hotels or lodges, 2 nights are spent traveling overnight by train, 4 nights are spent in comfortable tent camps. Each tent has proper twin beds, with sheets, quilts, and pillows. Toilet facilities are located in an adjacent forest rest house. Fresh towels and soap are available on a daily basis.

SPECIAL ACTIVITIES: Special trip to the Taj Mahal.

MEALS: Meals are a combination of Indian and Continental foods, with plenty of freshly cooked local produce.

RIDING STUFF: The typical riding day is 4 to 5 hours long. The first 2 days offer opportunities for trots and canters, thereafter, the pace remains at a walk. On the sixth day, you will get the opportunity to meet your sure-footed, Marwari horses and enjoy an introductory ride. Then you will ride, over the course of 2 days, through the heart of the reserve forest in an area where Jim Corbett spent a lot of time. The camp sites were selected for their spectacular locations. Following the second full day of riding, you will begin to climb up through the hills, camping along the way. The next day you pass over Sunbill Pass at 2300 meters (7360 feet) where, weather permitting, you may catch a gorgeous view of the high Himalayas. On the final day of riding there is a wonderful descent to Ratighat. From there you travel by car to Raniket and onwards the next day to New Delhi by train.

AUTHOR'S COMMENT: *Billa Edward's Indian Encounters is an agency born from a love affair with India. Her enthusiasm is contagious, her planning is excellent, and the trip promises you a wonderful opportunity to enjoy the Himalayas. Indian Encounters is the only agency specializing exclusively in horseback riding in India. While the riding portion of the trip is not especially strenuous, you will require a good head for heights and should be fit enough to walk over short rough patches.*

HIGHLIGHTS
Riding in the Himalayan foothills • 15 days/14 nights • 6 days of riding • Sightseeing and game viewing • Trip led by tour guide • Weight limit 15 stone (220 lbs.) (100 kg.) • English tack • Marwari horses • Elephant riding in Corbett Park

THE ARAVALLI HILLS

BASICS: Agent: **Indian Encounters**, Creech Barrow, East Creech, Wareham, Dorset, BH20 5AP, UK
Tel: 01929-481421
Fax: 01929-480998 (from UK)
Tel: (441) 929-481421
Fax: (441) 929-480998 (from US)
Email: BillaEdwards@btinternet.com

WHEN: October to March.
AIRPORTS: New Delhi. Transfers to hotel included.
LOCATION: Southern Rajasthan
PRICE: £1550 ($2480) 16 days/15 nights, per person, double occupancy, includes 7 days of riding and 7 days sightseeing.

The first full morning is spent sightseeing in New Delhi. You then take an afternoon flight to Udaipur, one of India's most romantic cities with lakes and palaces, busy alleys and streets of the old bazaar. Late afternoon on the third day takes you to the camping site at Kaladwas. That evening you will enjoy a performance of traditional "horse dancing" and an evening meal with cocktails. Thereafter you will stay at a different camp site each night over the course of 7 days, riding through wild and beautiful scenery, a land of river beds, valleys, and towering hills frequented only by local shepherds. The pace tends to get faster as the terrain flattens out, permitting long canters through open countryside. The ride is followed by a few days of rest and relaxation at Bijapur Castle while visiting Chittogarh, then on to Bundi and, finally, to Agra, home of the Taj Mahal.

CHILDREN'S PROGRAM: There is no special program for children.

ACCOMMODATIONS: The 8 camping nights are spent in comfortable tents. Each 10' x 10' domed tent has proper twin beds with sheets, quilts and pillows. There is a trailer nearby with W.C. and shower facilities. Fresh towels and soap are available on a daily basis. The camp sites are very beautiful, mostly close to lakes populated by a marvelous variety of birds, including Sarus cranes, geese, pelicans, kingfishers, and different species of duck. On the other 8 nights, accommodations are provided in hotels, palaces, and forts.

SPECIAL ACTIVITIES: A special dinner with cocktails and a performance of traditional "horse dancing." Visit to the Taj Mahal.

MEALS: Traditional Indian food consisting of freshly cooked local produce. Continental food may be served upon request.

RIDING STUFF: A typical riding day on Marwari horses involves 4 to 5 hours in the saddle, but there are 2 longer days averaging up to 6 hours of riding. While in the mountains, the pace is mostly walking as the terrain dictates. As you reach the plains, the pace increases with lots of opportunities to trot and canter. The ride passes through remote countryside dotted with little villages; where there are plenty of chances to stop for tea and catch a first hand glimpse of the native way of life. The people are very friendly and their excitement at your arrival on horseback is infectious and you will no doubt be a topic of conversation for several months to come. You will need at least moderate riding ability and a decent level of fitness. You should be able to dismount and lead your horse over the rougher sections and competent to control the horse at different paces in open countryside.

AUTHOR'S COMMENT: *Another exciting holiday from Indian Encounters offers good riding combined with comfortable accommodations, sightseeing, interaction with local folks, beautiful scenery, tasty food, and a well-planned journey through this exotic and colorful country.*

HIGHLIGHTS
Visit the Taj Mahal and the romantic city of Udaipur • Varied bird life • Riding through mountains and plains • Trip led by tour guide • Group size 8 • Weight limit 15 stone (220 lbs.) (100 kg.) • English tack • Marwari horses

HADOTI RIDE

www.horsebackholidays.com

BASICS: International Horseback & Polo Holidays
In India contact: D383, Defence Colony, New
 Delhi 110024, India
 Tel: (91) 11-4624879   Fax: (91) 11-4616137
 Email: inder.tigers@aworld.net
In Canada contact: 8034-112 B Street, Delta,
 British Columbia V4C 5A7, Canada
 Tel: (604) 501-1652   Fax: (604) 501-9213
 Email: info@horsebackholidays.com

WHEN: October to March.
AIRPORTS: New Delhi. Transfers from airport
 included.
LOCATION: Southern Rajasthan's Aravalli
 Mountains.
PRICE: $3100 (£1937) 13 days/12 nights, per
 person, double occupancy. Price includes all
 accommodations, meals, taxes, gratuities, and
 other land costs.

Operating since 1983, this magical adventure begins when you are picked-up at the New Delhi Airport and transported to a hotel (the former country home of the Nawab of Pataudi) on the way to Jaipur. On the following day, you will have a chance to enjoy browsing among the bazaars and sightseeing in magnificent Jaipur. The third day involves an 8 hour drive, as you leave the desert on your way south to Bundi. The actual ride commences on the fourth day and you are "on safari" until the tenth day, after which you will visit the Ramthambhor Tiger Sanctuary before returning to New Delhi.

CHILDREN'S PROGRAM: Children must be 14 or older.

ACCOMMODATIONS: Accommodations are in ancient fortresses, Imperial Raj tents, hunting lodges and similar establishments.

SPECIAL ACTIVITIES: You will spend 1 evening and a day exploring the Ranthambhor Tiger Sanctuary by vehicle, led by Inder Jit Singh, a keen naturalist, who is very familiar with India's flora and fauna.

MEALS: Meals are a mix of both Western and traditional Rajasthani foods, including exotic marinated and lightly spiced meats with pilaf, lentils, and oven-baked breads. Cereal and fruits are served for breakfast. All meals are served

hot. Cold and hot drinks are also available and beer may be purchased with the evening meal.

RIDING STUFF: The excellent horses include a mix of Thoroughbreds, halfbreds, and the native Marwari and Kathiawari breeds. The riding area is among the most scenic and lush in Rajasthan, bordering on the densely forested state of Madhya Pradesh. This ride traverses the landscape of India's southern Rajasthan in the ancient kingdom of Bundi. You will gaze with awe at the Bundi fortress, its medieval gates closed to outsiders at nightfall until recently. At the ride's end you will visit the Ranthambhor Tiger Reserve with its 12th century fort, jungle palaces and *jheels* (lakes) where you can see Sambhar stags wallowing in the marsh and mugger crocodiles sliding in and out of deep pools. There are also Macaque and Langur monkeys, peacocks, spotted deer and, of course, *sher* (the Hindi word for tigers). Riders will spend between 5 to 7 hours in the saddle daily. All rides are vehicle supported. The pace of riding varies but you may expect some short gallops, walks, trots and canters.

AUTHOR'S COMMENT: *Hadoti Ride takes you through Rajasthan's greenest areas. You will experience a heightened sense of adventure as you ride through alleys below ancient fortress walls and along jungle paths. You would not be the first traveler to be enchanted by India.*

HIGHLIGHTS
Experienced open country riders • 13 days/12 nights • 7 days of riding • Rides led by Inder Jit Singh and Bonnie Raghuvendra Singh • Capacity 6 to 12 riders (4 person minimum) • Weight 15 stone (220 lbs.) (100 kg.) • English tack • Well-trained, excellent horses • Special sleeping accommodations at ancient fortresses, Imperial Raj tents • Visit the Ranthambhor Tiger Sanctuary

© Phal S. Girota

RIDING WITH THE NIHANGS AND INTO THE HIMALAYA

www.horsebackholidays.com

BASICS: International Horseback & Polo Holidays
In India contact: D383, Defence Colony, New
Delhi 110024, India
Tel: (91) 11-4624879   Fax: (91) 11-4616137
Email: inder.tigers@aworld.net
In Canada contact: 8034-112 B Street, Delta,
British Columbia V4C 5A7, Canada
Tel: (604) 501-1652   Fax: (604) 501-9213
Email: info@horsebackholidays.com
WHEN: Approximately March 10 coinciding with
the Holla Mohalla Festival. Also, Nihang Ride,
October to March, and Binsar Ride, April to
early October.
AIRPORTS: New Delhi. Transfers included.
LOCATION: Punjab's Shivalik Hills and Kumaon
Himalaya District in Uttar Pradesh.
PRICE: Approximately £1560 ($2500) 14 days/13
nights, per person, double occupancy, includes
all land costs.

Inder Jit Singh offers up a fantastic new ride beginning with the Holla Mohalla, the Nihang Sikh's version of the Indian Holi, the festival of colors. The present day Nihangs are descended from an elite fighting group and they still take exceptional pride in their observation of martial traditions and the tenets of their faith. Nowadays, the Nihangs live in desert camps in the Punjab, land of 5 rivers. Each year during the Holla Mohalla, Sikhs dressed in traditional warrior uniforms ride for 5 to 7 days towards the foothills of the Himalaya near Anandapur, with war drummers and flag bearers, while reading their Sikh Holy Book. They do not use any leather in their tack, consistent with the Hindu belief that cows are sacred. You will follow the festival procession in a group of up to 6 riders, camping out for 5 nights. The second portion of the trip will include 3 nights of camping in the high Himalaya near the Binsar Forest, and 2 nights staying at the Binsar Valley Resort, owned by Mukul and Kalpana Joshie. On the return part of your trip you will stop at Agra to visit the Taj Mahal.

CHILDREN'S PROGRAM: Must be experienced riders, age 14 and older.

ACCOMMODATIONS: There will be nights of comfortable hotel stays in New Delhi, Agra and the Binsar Valley Resort, with the other nights spent at luxury camps, where you will be treated to exceptional service designed to ensure your comfort.

SPECIAL ACTIVITIES: You will spend an overnight at Agra and visit the Taj Mahal. There is also an optional visit to the Golden Temple

MEALS: Breakfasts and lunches are Western-style, with cereal, bread, nuts, butter and jam. Lunch includes salads, cold meats, potatoes, tea and juice. Dinner in the Punjab tends to be tandoori-style. In the Binsar area, the fare includes both Western food and tasty, traditional Indian dishes with curry and other spices.

RIDING STUFF: The horses in the Punjab are similar to the Kathiawari and Marwari breeds of the Rajasthan and Gurjat. Thoroughbreds are also used. Riding time will vary from 3 to 5 hours in the Punjab. The pace is mainly walks and trots with an occasional canter. The Himalayan portion of this adventure begins at 5000 feet (1666 meters) and moves to 8000 feet (2666 meters). You will spend 2 days at the Binsar Valley Resort and 3 days camping in high Himalaya. Binsar is in the Kumaon Himalaya, which was annexed from Nepal in 1815 by the English East India Company. Mounted on Tibetian Mountain Ponies, Haflingers, and crossbreds, the terrain will dictate a very modest pace as you gaze at 22,000 foot (7000 meter) peaks, while riding through the Binsar Forest. This area was once part of the ancient Hindostan to Tibet work route, and borders Nepal.

AUTHOR'S COMMENT: *From the vibrant colors and frenzy of the Festival, to the sublime peace of the high Himalaya Mountains—Wow!*

HIGHLIGHTS
English tack • 3 to 5 hours per day in the saddle • Intermediate riding skills •
Festival of Holla Mohalla • 5 day ride in the Himalaya

© Inder Jit Singh

All photos © Inder Jit Singh

PUSHKAR FAIR RIDE

BASICS: Equitour: Peregrine Holidays Ltd., 41 South Parade, Summertown, Oxford, OX2 7JP, UK
Tel: 01865-511642
Fax: 01865-512583 (from UK)
Tel: (44) 1865-511642
Fax: (44) 1865-512583 (from US)
Email: 106357.1754@compuserve.com
WHEN: October 25 to November 12. Exact dates may change slightly
AIRPORTS: New Delhi. Transfers to hotels included.
LOCATION: Rajasthan

PRICE: Full Ride: £2690 ($4304) 19 days/18 nights, per person, includes 11 days of riding. First Half Ride (ends at Pushkar Fair): £1380 ($2208) 11 days/10 nights, per person, includes 5 days of riding. Second Half Ride: £1665 ($2665) 9 days/8 nights, per person, includes 6 days of riding. Single supplement for all rides add £300 ($480). Dinners in New Delhi, Jaipur and Udaipur not included. Return flight to New Delhi for those leaving after the first half not included, cost is £65 ($104).

This fantastic ride through India's Rajasthan Province is part ride, part sightseeing tour of many ancient sites, cities with fascinating architecture, small Indian villages, and the Pushkar Fair, which is similar to a county agricultural fair in the West, but with exotic sights and sounds. It is generally attended by some 200,000 people and 50,000 animals, including camels, horses, and cattle that are bought and sold. The first part of the ride ends at the Fair. The second part of the trip takes you through scenes from an older India.

CHILDREN'S PROGRAM: Children must be at least 12 to 14 years of age depending on riding ability.

ACCOMMODATIONS: Guests sleep in a variety of accommodations, from modern hotels in cities to converted mansions, palaces, and deluxe tents. The tents are large enough to stand-up in and are furnished with cots, tables and chairs. There are toilet tents and hot water is available.

SPECIAL ACTIVITIES: Visits to the Pushkar Fair, Samode, Jaipur, Sardar Samand, and Kumbalgarh Fortress.

MEALS: The food is a mixture of Indian, Chinese and Continental cuisines. Full board is included on the ride.

RIDING STUFF: The tack is English and the horses are the indigenous Marwari breed, many of them former polo ponies. The average size about 15 to 16 hands high. You will ride 4 to 6 hours a day. You will change horses after the Pushkar Fair, meeting your new horses in Rohet, a 5 hour drive. On the first part of the ride, you will be transported from New Delhi to Dundlod Castle and ride in the semi-arid region called Shekhawati, where you will see some of the finest frescoes in the world. Over the course of 5 days the ride will take you through Mandawa, Nawal Garh, Lohal Gal, a religious shrine at the base of the Aravelli Hills, followed by a drive to Samode, then Jaipur and, finally, Pushkar. The second half of the trip encompasses a ride through ancient India including Rohet, Sardar Samand, several villages, Ranakpur, located on edge of the Aravalli Hills, and a ride to Kumbalgarh Fortress, which boasts a heavily forested sanctuary for sloth bear, leopard, wild boar, sambhar deer, and 4 horned antelope.

AUTHOR'S COMMENT: *This is a fantastic opportunity to enjoy one of India's most celebrated religious cattle fairs and enjoy a riding holiday that will take you through a wide variety of Indian landscapes, magnificent historical sites, and wilderness reserves. This is an ideal ride for experienced riders able to handle their horses at all paces in open countryside.*

HIGHLIGHTS
Incredible Pushkar Fair • Moderate pace • Intermediate riding skills • Weight limit 220 lbs. (100 kg.) (15.7 stone) • Accommodations in luxurious hotels, palaces and tents • Visit Rohet, Samode, Jaipur, Pushkar, Sardar Samand, Kumbalgarh Fortress

SHALIVAN STABLES

www.horsebackholidays.com

BASICS: International Horseback & Polo Holidays
In India contact: D383, Defence Colony, New
   Delhi 110024, India
   Tel: (91) 11-4624879   Fax: (91) 11-4616137
   Email: inder.tigers@aworld.net.in
In Canada contact: 8034-112 B Street, Delta,
   British Columbia V4C 5A7, Canada
   Tel: (604) 501-1652   Fax: (604) 501-9213
   Email: info@horsebackholidays.com
WHEN: October to March.
AIRPORTS: New Delhi (international flights);
Jodhpur (domestic flights) - 12 kms. from the
starting point; or Udaipur (domestic flights) -
80 kms. from the starting point.
LOCATION: Rajasthan
PRICE: *Jodhpur to Kumbalgarh Ride:*
£1812 ($2900) 12 days/11 nights, includes
8 days of riding. *Jodphur to Jodphur Ride:*
£1937 ($3100) 11 days/10 nights, includes 8 days of
riding. All prices are per person, double occupancy,
and include all internal air fares, accommodations,
meals, gratuities, taxes, and riding.

Rajasthan is an exotic land of ancient regal splendor, home of tent pegging and polo, with a long and varied history of horsemanship. This region of India is a land of royal forts and palaces now functioning as luxurious hotels in settings that evoke a great feeling of grandeur. The rides, led by Inder Jit Singh and Hargreev Bhatti, utilize quality spirited horses and offer great riding that moves you over varied terrain, through wilderness reserves, and to historical sites. The service is outstanding and, combined with excellent planning, allows you to enjoy this magical place to the fullest. All trips may be customized as your group desires.

CHILDREN'S PROGRAM: Experienced riders, ages 13 and older.

ACCOMMODATIONS: Accommodations are usually in old fortresses and large Imperial Raj tents. As you journey through the ancient kingdoms of India the accommodations provide not only a sense of India's rich history, but also comfortable, well-serviced places to rest, recuperate, and enjoy your meals.

SPECIAL ACTIVITIES: You will be staying at, or otherwise enjoying, many historial sites.

MEALS: Meals are a mix of both Western and traditional Rajasthani foods, including exotic marinated, lightly spiced meats in sauce with pilaf, lentils, oven-baked breads and a variety of local vegetable dishes. All meals are served hot. Lemon and orange juice squashes are also available.

RIDING STUFF: The rides take you through different regions of northern Rajasthan and require experienced riders, capable of controlling a horse at all paces. Riding time varies between 5 and 7 hours a day. Both rides are organized around the most prominent sites in each area and are sure to leave you dazzled. Kumbalgarh is a great fort with hundreds of temples sheltered inside its massive walls. The surrounding area in the Aravalli Mountains includes a wilderness reserve, where marsh mugger crocodiles, sloth bears, leopards and desert cats dwell. You will ride through jungles along the way. On the last day of the ride, you will dismount in order to trek with your horses to the fortress. The Jodhpur to Jodphur Ride, by contrast, allows for a faster pace since most of the riding covers desert flats and dunes. You will visit the famous Sadar Samand Palace, a lake resort and former hunting lodge of the Jodhpur Maharajas, as well as the mountain-top Rohetgarh Fort Palace. At the end of the trip, you will enjoy visits to Kumbalgarh and Jodphur. There is often nightly entertainment and lots of interaction with the local people.

AUTHOR'S COMMENT: *Your senses will have to respond to the stimuli of this ancient and exotic land. Add to that some fine horses and engaging hosts and you have the experience of a lifetime. This ride comes highly recommended by an English riding club.*

HIGHLIGHTS
Experienced riders • Rides led by Inder Jit Singh and Hargreev Bhatti • Minimum of 4 riders • Weight limit 15 stone (210 lbs.) (100 kg.)

© Phal S. Girota

© Inder Jit Singh

ALTAI and ARKHANGAI TRIPS

www.perso.wanadoo.fr/cheval.daventure

BASICS: Cheval Adventure/Adventures on Horseback, Mas du Pommier, 07590 Cellier-du-Luc, France
Tel: (33) 4-6646-6273   Fax: (33) 4-6646-6209
Email: cheval.daventure@wanadoo.fr
WHEN: June, July, August (every other February).
AIRPORTS: Ulaanbaatar

LOCATION: Mongolia
PRICE: *Altai Trip:* 13 days, $2250 (£1406) (2148 Euro) or 16 days, $2750 (£1718) (2623 Euro), per person, double occupancy. *Arkhangai Trip:* $2200 (£1375) (2100 Euro) 16 days, per person, double occupancy.

The Steppes of Central Asia are a paradise for huge herds of horses. Mongolia is 6 times the size of Great Britain, with a population of 2.5 million inhabitants and a like number of horses! The Steppe is not just a flat, monotonous plain, but encompasses sweeping hills and majestic mountains, carpeted with sweet-smelling flowers as well as great lakes and rushing rivers, giving way to larch and birch forests, tumbled granite rocks and lava flows. Everywhere there are clusters of white yurts with men coming and going on horseback, capturing horses with their *urga* or moving herds of yaks, sheep or Bactrian camels. The scene is reminiscent of Biblical times. The people are always friendly and hospitable, and you will be invited into native yurts or *ghers* to drink *airak* (fermented mare's milk) or gather round the campfire to chat and sing.

The initial meeting and departure place is Ulaanbaatar. The Altai Ride begins 1200 kms. west of the city and domestic flights take you to and from the riding area. You will be driven to the staging area for the Arkhangai Ride, 400 kms. northwest of the city, stopping along the way to visit the famous and impressive Buddhist monastery of Erdeni Zu, built with stones from Karakarum, the capital city of Genghis Khan's Empire. Domestic airlines carry you back to Ulaanbaatar at the end of the ride.

CHILDREN'S PROGRAM: Children under 16 must be accompanied by an adult.

ACCOMMODATIONS: Guests sleep in 2 person igloo-shaped tents during the ride and at hotels when in Ulanbaatar.

SPECIAL ACTIVITIES: Riding is the main activity, but you will have ample opportunity to explore the ancient and fascinating local lifestyle. There is good fishing at several of the stopping places. In Ulaanbaatar, museums display a magnificent collection of Gobi Desert dinosaur bones as well as artifacts of the Mongolian Empire of the 13th and 14th centuries. The famous Naadam national festival on July 11th features colorful archery competitions and wrestling bouts with participants in traditional costume. This festival is also the occasion for the famous horse races, ridden by up to 600 children galloping over courses as long as 74 kms.

MEALS: Three hearty meals a day are prepared for hungry riders, cooked on *estufas* that are transported by truck. Food includes soups with noodles or potatoes, mutton, tomatoes, and cabbage. Breakfast offerings include bread, jam, cheese, eggs, yogurt and pancakes.

RIDING STUFF: Riders must be at ease at all paces, capable of riding confidently over varying terrain for several hours at a stretch. You will ride for 5 to 7 hours daily. The native horses are comfortable, easy to handle and will offer you unforgettable canters in a wide diversity of unspoiled landscapes.

AUTHOR'S COMMENT: *This rugged version of a Mongolian riding trek is for experienced riders and travelers who thrive on long riding days and can deal with the unexpected. Few cultures have elevated the horse to the central role they play in this ancient culture, which has more than 120 ways to say "horse"!*

HIGHLIGHTS

10 to 12 day wilderness ride (depending on domestic flights)—transfers to riding area (2 to 3 days) • Naadam festival and sightseeing in Ulaanbaatar (3 days) • 2 native horses per rider • Russian cavalry saddles • For fit and intermediate riders • Group capacity 15 • Weight limit 178 lbs. (80 kg.)

THE VALLEY OF THE MUSTANG RIDE

www.horsebackholidays.com

BASICS: International Horseback & Polo Holidays
In India contact: D383, Defence Colony, New Delhi 110024, India
Tel: (091) 11-4624879   Fax: (091) 11-4616137
Email: inder.tigers@aworld.net
In Canada contact: 8034-112 B Street, Delta, British Columbia V4C 5A7, Canada
Tel: (604) 501-1652   Fax: (604) 501-9213
Email: info@horsebackholidays.com
WHEN: From May to September. Please note: This ride travels through a restricted area and is dependent on approval of the Government of Nepal by permission of His Majesty.
AIRPORTS: Katmandu for international flights. From Katmandu you must fly to Pokhara, where the trips begin, and then take a flight to Jomsom.
LOCATION: Mustang Valley in Nepal.
PRICE: £2812 ($4500) 19 days/18 nights, per person, double occupancy, includes all meals, accommodations, and riding (13 days of trekking, 6 days of travel or rest). Additional cost of airfare for 2 internal flights is approximately £100 ($160).

This first time trip, meticulously planned and led by Inder Jit Singh, is a fantastic, walking/riding trek along ancient trade routes on steep and narrow pathways, over high Himalayan suspension bridges, and through an area that the Nepalese government has just opened up to visitors. You will be among the first to explore this fantastic region. You must be able to adjust to unforeseen developments such as altered routes, changes in overnight destinations, and the like. Inder Jit is an experienced Himalayan outfitter, having taken his first such trip when only 15. This is a true adventure for the few, the brave, and the fit.

CHILDREN'S PROGRAM: The trip is not suitable for children.

ACCOMMODATIONS: Accommodations at the beginning and end of the trip will be in comfortable hotels with bathrooms *en suite.* During the trek, you will sleep in double fly dome or frame nylon mountain tents. Foam pads and sleeping bags are provided.

SPECIAL ACTIVITIES: You will be able to explore exotic Katmandu, and it's historic and interesting sites, including Freak Street.

MEALS: The food includes both Western and native Nepalese fare of rice, wheat bread, lentils, and meat (lamb) curries. Western meals consist of spaghetti, rissoles, tuna salads, etc. Experienced high altitude cooks will serve rice pudding and cakes among other desserts.

RIDING STUFF: You will ride rugged Tibetan mountain ponies fitted with equally rugged tack, accompanied by guides who will lead you through this high mountain horseback and walking adventure. The trek will take you over rivers, across wooden suspension bridges, and through ancient villages. The trip begins in Jomsom at 8900 feet (2730 meters)—the last place with phones and other modern conveniences—and heads straight into Mustang Valley, which is surrounded by Tibet on 2 sides. It can be a bit confusing because the Nepalese name for Mustang Valley means "Tibet." You will move through the entire valley over the course of 14 days. You will stop at ancient monasteries and visit rural villages which seem to belong to another age. The trails are very steep and narrow and some riders may choose to walk leading their mounts, although the horses are familiar with the route. One of the unique experiences you may encounter is watching the feeding of young colts as liquid butter is poured into their mouths while a "pony man" massages their necks to coax the fluid down their throats. This is done in order to prepare the young horses for the extreme cold they will experience.

AUTHOR'S COMMENT: *If you are very fit, are not afraid of heights and narrow trails, and can tolerate the schedule changes that may occur in very remote regions, you are in for an experience that will be difficult to match anywhere else. Oh, those bragging rights!*

HIGHLIGHTS
19 day trip • Ride through Mustang Valley—closed until 1992 • Combined horse and foot trek on narrow and steep Himalayan trails • Weight limit 176 lbs. (80 kg.) (12.5 stone) • Tibetan mountain ponies • Inaugural trip

Photos © Lila Bishop

THE PAKISTANI JOURNEYS

BASICS: Agent: **Ride Worldwide**, 58 Fentiman Road, London, SW8 1LF, UK
Tel: 0171-735-1144   Fax: 0171-735-3179 (from UK)
Tel: (44) 171-735-1144   Fax: (44) 171-735-3179 (from US)
Email: RideWW@aol.com
WHEN: April to November, 9 starting dates.
AIRPORTS: Islamabad. Transfers included.

LOCATION: Northern Pakistan. Riding areas include Chitral, the Shandur Pass, Kalash valleys, and rides to Hunza.
PRICE: From £1200 ($1920) to £1500 ($2400) per trip, per person, double/shared occupancy, includes all meals, accommodations and riding. Price varies for each trip. There is a small single supplement of £60 ($96).

Pakistan has few facilities for tourists and the areas you will be traveling through have even less, so creature comforts may suffer, but oh the trade off. Here you get to experience a way of life and scenery that makes it all worth while. You will ride through wide valleys flanked by ridges, sheer cliffs and some of the world's highest and most spectacular mountain peaks. You will follow narrow trails and sandy tracks, pass ancient villages, journey over grassy plains and high altitude prairies ideal for galloping. The rides are generally vehicle supported.

CHILDREN'S PROGRAM: The trip is not suitable for children

ACCOMMODATIONS: Pakistan offers modest hotels in the larger towns, many with private *loo*/shower and sometimes even air-conditioning. Other accommodations include government-owned rest houses, private homes (usually only available for those willing to share a room among 4 persons), or tented camps, which do not offer private rooms. When camping you will sleep in 2 person dome tents with camp beds.

SPECIAL ACTIVITIES: Rest breaks in the middle or at the end of your trip will offer opportunities to explore the local villages, shops, and special sites.

MEALS: Meals offer a mixture of native and European food. Breakfast includes eggs, *chappattis,* biscuits and jam. Lunch typically consists of tuna, cheese, *chappatis* and soup. Dinner is usually rice or pasta with vegetables. Tea, coffee and hot chocolate are available. The local food can be quite spicy.

RIDING STUFF: The horses are stallions from Badakshan in Afghanistan, between 14 to 15.2 hands. They are strong and willing and are trained to neck rein like polo ponies. Tack is English style made locally. Riding time averages 6 hours a day. All rides use Romance language or English- speaking, fully licensed, Pakistani guides. The **Nanga Parbat to Hunza Ride** is 16 days/ 15 nights with 9 days of riding and is offered at the beginning and end of the season, when the high passes are closed. This ride will take you through valleys surrounded by magnificent peaks to the ancient town of Hunza. The **Land of Kho and Dardistan Rides** are 16 to 18 day trips through the northwest provinces, where you will be surrounded by very high mountains. You can watch a game of *buskashi*, the national sport of Afghanistan, played with a sheep carcass— always an incredibly exciting display of horsemanship. You will travel over the Shandur Pass and, in July, enjoy the festival and polo tournament to end all polo tournaments. Finally, there is **A Short Ride in the Hindu Kush**, an 18 day trip that is as much a mountain expedition as it is a ride into un-mapped regions near the Afghanistan border only recently opened to outsiders. You will pass over rickety bridges, change routes to accommodate weather conditions, and even walk or ride a yak across the Darkot Pass, a snow-covered glacier. Be warned: This trip is only for fit, experienced riders with the spirit to experience the unknown.

AUTHOR'S COMMENT: *The trend in riding vacations is to find more exotic locations of great beauty and cultural variety. The rides in this area of Pakistan certainly qualify and you can rest assured that you won't be disappointed.*

HIGHLIGHTS
16 to 18 day trips • Group size limited to 6 • Weight limit 90 kg. (198 lbs.) (13.5 stone) • Spectacular mountain views • A true adventure

CAPPADOCIA TOUR

http://business.wec.net.comtr/Avanos/galip

BASICS: CEC Galip's Tour, Galip's Tour Travel Agency, Firin Sokak No.24, Avanos, Cappadocia, Turkey
Tel: (90) 384-511-4240 Fax: (90) 384-511-4543
WHEN: Extended treks from April to November.
NEAREST AIRPORTS: Ankara is 300 kms. from Avanos; Kayser is 80 kms. from Avanos
LOCATION: Cappadocia. Kayseri is a 1 hour drive and Ankara is a 3 hour drive to the southeast.
PRICE: $350 (£219) to $490 (£306) 8 days/7 nights, per person, double occupancy, includes all riding, accommodations, and most meals. All Day Ride: $35 (£22) per person, includes a picnic lunch. Local accommodations range from $10 (£6) per night, per person at a guest house to $30 (£19) per night, per person for a hotel.

Cappadocia means "Land of Beautiful Horses' and it is a region with a long history. Originally an independent kingdom, it later became a Roman province. During the 7th century, invading Arabs drove the Christian population of that time into the hills, where they carved churches and dwellings out of the soft rock and even created underground villages that you will visit. Avanos, where the ride begins, is Turkey's pottery center. Lillian Vanderzee, a charming and friendly English-speaking Dutch woman coordinates the rides. The area is filled with incredible rock formations, friendly people and is largely devoid of tourists. The landscape will often feel surrealistic, as you pass through a fantastic landscape created by ancient volcanic eruptions, now eroded by time. Riders also visit the remains of troglodite villages and travel through valleys and mountains with steep ascents, and descents, sometimes requiring riders to walk their horses.

CHILDREN'S PROGRAM: Children are welcome to ride with their parents. A horse cart may be arranged for the treks (1 adult and 3 children per cart).

ACCOMMODATIONS: Guests can choose from among 3 star hotels with private baths, pensions with shared baths, and camping. On point to point trips, vehicles will be used to transport you to your sleeping destination.

SPECIAL ACTIVITIES: Numerous historical sites including large, ancient, underground cities. Organized walking tours, exploring the rich historical heritage of this ancient region may be arranged.

MEALS: Turkish food is wonderful and includes fresh salads, pasta dishes, and Turkish pizza with meat or cheese.

RIDING STUFF: The basic riding holiday is 8 days/7 nights with 1 guide leader for every 4 riders. The horses are Arab and Arab crossbreds about 13 hands high. The tack is French and Turkish. Guests are divided into small groups in order to accommodate different skill levels. The terrain, at a height of about 1000 meters (3000 feet), varies. Guests ride on soft paths among the fields and gardens of the local people, through the valleys of Cappadocia and along river beds. There is usually an opportunity to enjoy some spirited canters on these rides. You might also wish to inquire about the special Full Moon Ride.

AUTHOR'S COMMENTS: *This riding opportunity was brought to my attention by an English riding club, The Order of Packriders, and their founder, Elizabeth Barrett, who says she will remember this ride as one "...of great kindness, good horses and an excellent guide." The recommendation, rest assured, was well deserved.*

HIGHLIGHTS
8 day/7 night riding tour • Guest capacity 8 • All skill levels • Weight limit 190 lbs. (86 kg.) (13.5 stone) • Guests choose between 3 star hotels, pensions or camping • Customized tours • Fascinating geological formations • Ride through an area rich in ancient history • Vehicle supported • Arab-Anatolian horses

AUSTRALIA

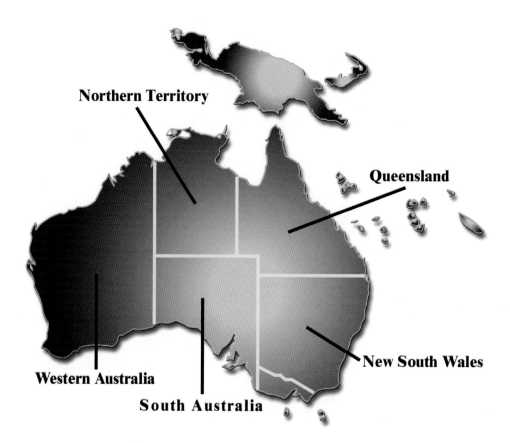

Northern Territory

Queensland

Western Australia

South Australia

New South Wales

A U S T R A L I A

by Nelly Gelich

"*Terra Australis Incognita*" read the world maps when King George III ruled England, when Louis XIV married Marie Antoinette, and when child prodigy Mozart delighted the courts of Europe with his music. With Captain Cook's arrival at Botany Bay in 1770, *Terra Australis* the '*incognita*' became '*cognita*'. It was about the time of the Boston Tea Party. So are we a young country? Yes, the written history we know is less than 250 years old. Are we an old country? Yes, because our other history, that of the Native Australians, going back 40,000 years is recorded in stone and tales. One could go on in that vein. Let's just say that Australia is a fascinating country full of contrasts in all aspects. We are an island, we are a continent, we are in the tropics, we are in the "Roaring Forties". You can ski our great mountains in the morning and enjoy dinner under a tropical moon in the evening. We all speak English—yet our original inhabitants speak many different languages only they understand. Our largest inland lake is mostly a salt pan extending over 9500 square kms., but can cover an area one-sixth the size of the entire continent after extreme rains. We have more dry riverbeds than wet ones. Vast deserts stretch towards dense rainforests. Not so long ago, the only indigenous predators were man, crocodiles and sharks and there were no domesticated animals. Dingos, the wild dogs, came from somewhere a few thousand years ago, but they never really flourished. However, marsupials of many shapes and sizes had a pretty good time. Kangaroo are found throughout Australia. There are various species including wallaby, wallaroo, and euro. They are all adapted to their environment from snow-tolerant alpine big greys to inland big reds, rock wallabies and rainforest tree kangaroos. Captain Cook and those who came after him, brought horses, dogs, cattle, sheep, camels, the cursed rabbits, cats, chickens, geese, ducks, goats, donkeys, foxes and many other critters.

For a long time Australia was used as a penal colony for the wayward sons and daughters of Mother England. So the nucleus of modern Australia was made up of prisoners and their wardens, some administrative personnel, explorers and fortune seekers from everywhere. We have had gold rushes as big as any. Other precious metals and minerals were, and some still are, plentiful — diamonds and opals probably the best known. Even now, many families go 'fossicking' for their annual holiday and delight to find gemstones, especially good quality sapphires and specs of gold. Over the last 200 years, Australia has been the 'Lucky Country" for many, many people. For others, such as those who died on the long journey out here or suffered the horrors of the penal institutions of the last century, it was anything but lucky. It is a country of contrasts indeed. People from many nations have joined us over the years. The results are great achievements on the intellectual, artistic and culinary fronts. Do we have good food!

Horses have played an important part in Australia's history. The only way to explore this vast country in the early days was on horseback. A handful of "unattractive" horses arrived from the Cape Colony (Africa) in 1788. They were said to be of English and Spanish stock. Once landed, they thrived. More horses joined them from Chile and Peru, purebred Arabians from India and England, and Timor and Welsh Mountain ponies. Only the tougher ones survived the early sea journeys, which could take up to 12 months. The settlers and explorers soon recognized their dependence on horses for the job in hand. Careful breeding and culling of the weak led to the emergence of the Walers—later to become known as the Australian Stock Horse. In 1848, J.C. Byrne wrote, "...the race of horse at present in use in Australia is not to be surpassed in the world for symmetry and endurance. It is hard to say exactly how they are bred. . . . Much pains have been bestowed on the breeding of these animals and the results have rightly rewarded the exertion . . ."

Australia was opened up by mounted settlers droving their livestock from the coastal plains across mountain barriers and through dense forests to find rich pastures and devastating deserts alike. Lawmen had to have good horses, and the outlaws ("bushrangers") generally had better. Tales of their feats are endless. These were horses whose average working day meant covering 60 to 80 miles, carrying riders, packs and gear. Many 100 mile rides per day had to made in emergencies. We commemorate these feats of endurance with the annual 'Tom Quilty' 100 mile ride. Walers supplied the British armies on the Indian subcontinent and Africa. In the Middle East campaign during the Great War, 12,324 horses went overseas. Most of them carried 20 stone with rider and equipment and often covered 70 to 80 miles on a daily basis for 2½ years.

At the Sydney Royal Show in 1938, Ben Holt jumped a world record of 9'6". In 1946 in Cairns, Golden Meade jumped 8'6" (unofficial). The official Australian record was established by Golden Meade and Flyaway in 1946. Oh yes, they can do dressage too. Horses like Debonnair represented Australia quite credibly in Grand Prix Dressage. We hope to prove our equestrian worth again at the 2000 Olympics in Sydney! Why not watch and complete your trip with a hands-on experience? We are a nation of horse people. In 1918, when the human census was just over 5 million, we had more than 2.5 million horses. The proportions have changed of course, but not our love for horses. The reverence we have for the 'Man from the Snowy River' is an example. Today, our population numbers 18 million, 80% of which live in the southeastern part of the country. Our horse population is down to 1.5 million, including the feral Brumbies. And talk about size—the largest cattle station, located in southern Australia, is the size of Belgium!

So my dear holiday maker, when you come to Australia to ride, and you read in the specifications that you will be riding Australian Stock Horses, look forward to your adventure, because you'll be riding the best. Even if not always registered breeding stock, Australian horses are still good, reliable, surefooted and level-headed companions for your ride. There may even be a "pure Brumby" or two—wild now, but actually domesticated horses that gained their freedom from servitude to man in some way or the other. For instance, there is Stella, a Brumby caught as a foal and trained, and Wizard, son of a wicked Witch who invited a Brumby stallion to share her mountain paddock for a bit, both well loved trail horses of John and Jackie Williams of Khancoban Trail Rides in the Snowy Mountains. Let's be romantic and imagine that Wizard's sire descended from a wild black stallion, still talked about with respect and awe a hundred years later by the mountain folk.

You may ask, "where can we ride in Australia?" Your question will usually be countered by, "when do you want to come?" Don't forget all you Northern Hemisphere folks, our seasons are the opposite of yours, your summer is our winter. Our fabulous Kimberley country in the northwest is only suitable from May to September, when Kimberley Pursuits, Equitrek's choice, offers rides from 2 to 7 days. These truly vast spaces under the bluest of skies are at their best at exactly the time when you can't ride in the Snowy Mountains. From November to February the beautiful coast area around Cairns, whilst great for diving, is just too darned hot and humid for riding. Peter Brown at Mount Molloy will take you through rainforest, beach and tableland for anything up to 10 days. He'll teach you to play the didgeridoo as well! These times are great for the "Centre" too, as for instance with Ossie at Alice Springs. Most inland areas are extremely hot and dry from November to February, when even some of the rides near Sydney can turn out to be very hot—this is the time to take to the mountains and experience the "Snowys" in all their grandeur. These rides can be accessed either from Sydney or Melbourne, depending on which side of the Alps you want to ride. The Snowy Mountain season extends from October to April.

Khancoban Trails and Talbingo Trails specialise in camping rides from 2 to 10 days. Because their groups are small, each guest gets great personalized attention. If you want to ride in the "Snowys" but don't care to sleep in a tent—great! Annemarie and Jack of Snowy Mountain Horseback Adventures will take good care of you. If you want lots of interaction and the fun of larger groups, John Rudd will ensure an equally good time for both experienced and less accomplished riders. Another great ride, where you'll encounter lots of Brumbies, is at Wangarra, and small groups are again the norm. Debbie and Malcolm, on the Victorian side, have a nice trick—a Black Tie Dinner, complete with silver candelabra. It's great fun after a hard day's ride to a mountain shelter hut. You will sleep in a tent, but dine in style! Don't forget your gladrags, they are a must. You can also do a "mountains to the sea" experience and finish with a brisk gallop along the beach. Cattle drives into and from the high county are wonderful experiences, the riding and scenery are unmatched.

There are also good rides right along the east coast of the continent, which run all year. For instance, on the New South Wales coast, between Sydney and Brisbane, Peter Kelly and his wonderful Arabs journey at a brisk pace from B B to B&B in very beautiful country, with hills and forests as far as the eye can see. A little further north, we enjoy a super "Heritage" trail from 3 to 5 days and, just north of Brisbane, Bob Sample and his splendid horses will satisfy the most expert riders. Six times a year, Lyn Tainsh will even take you from the mainland to Fraser Island—the world's largest sand island. Quite often too she will "pub crawl" with you in the Sunshine Coast Hinterland. Great horses! There are other pub crawl opportunities too in New South Wales and in western Australia. Cattle drives are always seasonal in their areas, but can be arranged most times of the year.

We offer a wide variety of rides including 10 day packhorse trips or treks, week long escapades in the bush with supplies brought along by vehicle, rides from B&B to B&B or shelter to shelter, and stationary rides from a base going out to different places daily. The latter can be farm and country stays like Millamolong Station, Belltrees, and many, many others throughout the country. You can tag along on the daily tasks of moving cattle or sheep, ride the range, enjoy day rides to picnic spots, or laze around the pool, take walks and watch the wildlife. Brush Gully, close to Sydney, provides charming, boutique accommodations and an excellent riding venue. Some of our farms—or stations—as we like to call them, have excellent facilities for many activities including sailing and other water sports. Some are well-established breeders of polo ponies (mainly Australian Stock Horses) and they don't mind teaching you how to hit the ball and let you play a chukka or two depending on your talents.

You can opt for day rides if time is short or make special arrangements for personalised treks. Many of our operations are of the smaller type, without set departure dates, so you can negotiate a time to suit you. It can be a little awkward to make arrangements long distance, especially if a minimum of 4 is required in order to make the trek happen, and you should enlist the aid of Equitrek Australia to coordinate that. You can choose from among slow rides to fast rides, comfortable to challenging, basic to luxury. If you would like a mix of fun and polishing your skills, many of our leading equestrians are happy to make themselves available if they can fit it in between their commitments. Holidays and vacations like these are very popular. It is always a great surprise to visitors to discover just how accessible our 'greats' can be.

Australia offers riding to match the best in the world. We have a broad variety of terrain and climate. Our horses are more than up to the job of providing a great holiday. Our people are friendly, genuine and very highly individualistic. Because our rides are generally small, you can always be sure that you will be treated as an individual. We don't have internal borders, passports or wars, and if English is the only language you speak, then the Aussie expression of "no worries mate" will be as reassuring under any circumstances as a hug from your best friend!

About Equitrek Australia

As the name suggests, we invite people from around the globe to come and "equitrek" Australia, and have done so since 1991. We offer unequalled horse riding adventures to all who love horses and nature. Three to 12 day treks allow full appreciation of the beauty of rugged mountains, great plains, endless forests, and even an island or two. "Equitreks" are about fun, relaxation, achievement, and rich memories. Your enjoyment and safety are our prime considerations. Designer treks are a specialty. Whenever possible, we match your wishes, time frame and expertise, even the wishes of non-riding family and friends are accommodated.

BRUSH GULLY GUESTHOUSE

BASICS: 5 Little Valley Road, Mandalong, New South Wales 2264, Australia
Tel: (61) 2-497-72864   Fax: (61) 2-497-73448
Email: bghosp@aljan.com.au

WHEN: Open year round. The mild climate is best enjoyed during Australia's spring and fall seasons, which are opposite to those in the UK and the US.

AIRPORTS: Sydney - a 90 minute drive. Transfers can be arranged.

LOCATION: Brush Gully is located 60 miles north of Sydney on the east coast, at the foot of the Watagan Mountains and 100,000 acres of forest.

PRICES $122 (£76) per day, per person. Children between 3 to 15 are charged at half the adult rate.

Situated on a 50 acre Arabian horse farm, only 90 minutes from Sydney, Brush Gully combines the home life of a genuine Australian family with professional hospitality. Owners Jennie and Greg Ireland present excellent food, very good horses, an intriguing house, and a spellbinding natural setting. Tall trees, pasture, and Australian native gardens ascend to spectacular, rugged mountains behind the house. Bird life is abundant. Kangaroos, wallabies, possums, and echidnas wander about . . . naturally.

CHILDREN'S PROGRAM: Children are welcome to enjoy biking, games, swimming pool, TV and countless videos. Parents are expected to supervise their children. However, with prior notice, supervision may be arranged at additional cost.

ACCOMMODATIONS: Guests stay in one of 3 large rooms with either *en suite* bathroom or private bathroom facilities. There are queen-sized beds, electric blankets, fluffy bathrobes, hair dryers, and other conveniences. The house is contemporary in style, with a pool, open fire, guest lounge, and dining area.

SPECIAL ACTIVITIES: In addition to riding, there is tractor driving, fishing in the dam, bushwalking, mountain adventure hiking, photography walks, beachside picnics, cruising by chartered yacht on Lake Macquarie, horse-drawn carriage rides, deluxe aromatherapy massage, hypnotherapy, cooking classes, tours of local wineries, shopping trips to Sydney, scenic helicopter flights, hot air ballooning, tandem skydiving, and more. Facials and pedicures are also available.

MEALS: Jennie Ireland is a professionally-trained chef, who has previously worked at some of Sydney's finest dining establishments. There is a full breakfast. Lunch is normally a buffet that includes soup, pasta, quiches, pies and pastries. Dinner fare varies from traditional Australian roasts to Asian/Thai cooking. Desserts are Jenny's speciality. There are special delights offered for vegetarians. Fine wines are served with dinner.

RIDING STUFF: Jennie is also a horseperson, having ridden since she was 9 years old. Brush Gully is set amidst rolling hills, lush valleys and rugged mountains, so riding adventures can be designed to satisfy everyone from the least experienced to the most competent rider. Most of the herd are sure-footed Arabians, trained for endurance. Saddles vary from American Cavalry and Australian Stock saddles to English Dressage saddles, with sheepskin coverings used to provide a comfortable seat. Riding times vary from 2 to 5 hours a day, covering 15 to 50 kms. The trained staff of ride leaders have a sound knowledge of the area, terrain and weather, as well as professional people skills and first-aid training. They even have their own medical practitioner available should the need arise. Riding speeds are adjusted to suit conditions in terms of people, horses, and climate.

AUTHOR'S COMMENT: *Brush Gully provides world class meals, a relaxed atmosphere. and excellent horses. There are plenty of challenging and beautiful areas to ride in and the Irelands' concern for their guests guarantee that this will be an exceptional experience.*

HIGHLIGHTS
Gourmet food • Comfortable, quality accommodations • Ride through eucalyptus forests • 20 minutes from the beach • 10 minutes from Lake Macquarie • Fly fishing • Spectacular mountain scenery • 10 guest maximum

KELLY'S BUSHRANGING ADVENTURES

www.equitrek.com.au

BASICS: Agent: **Equitrek Australia**, Club Equitrek, 5 King Road, Ingleside New South Wales 2101, Australia
Tel: (61) 2-9913-9408   Mobile: (61) 2-018-444-117
Fax: (61) 2-9970-6303 {International}
Tel: (02) 9913-9408 (from Australia)
Email: nelly@equitrek.com.au
WHEN: All year round.

AIRPORTS: Sydney Airport (International); Port Macquarie is a 1 hour flight from Sydney.
LOCATION: New South Wales "Holiday Coast" hinterland - a 4 hour drive from Sydney, or 5 hours by train.
PRICES: $116 (£72) per day, per person, double occupancy.

This is Equitrek's "favorite ride." Australia's "Holiday Coast" is not quite halfway between Sydney and Brisbane. Ideal climate, miles of sparkling beaches, huge forests, rainforests, and superb scenery justify its name. The 50,000 acres of forest offer superb riding trails, enjoyed by both riders and their horses. With so much riding country available, the best way to fully savor the experience is to ride from place to place. Although the pace is brisk, there is time to enjoy delicious creekside picnics, stop to gaze at scenic vantage points, and observe the local wildlife going about their business. Hills and valleys make for varied going. Stunning, panoramic views across mountains and valleys to the distant sea, 40 km. away. Get that camera out of the saddlebag!

CHILDREN'S PROGRAM. Programs during school holidays are available for capable young riders over 12.

ACCOMMODATIONS: The secluded lodgings along the way might best be described as B&B style, offering warm hospitality, excellent meals, and all of the creature comforts you might desire at the end of a great day's ride. *En suite* bathrooms and hot tubs are available at most places.

SPECIAL ACTIVITIES: Alternative activities include all water sports, whale and dolphin watching during season, diving, snorkeling, sailing, white-water rafting, tennis, golf, wonderful bush walks and guided eco-tours, even rock climbing, abseiling, and hang gliding. There are good art and craft galleries and tranquil gardens for the less active.

MEALS: All dietary requirements can be met - advance notice please! The meals along the ride are in the very good to extraordinarily good category. High quality local foodstuffs range from seafood to fruit. Lunch picnics are enjoyed at beautiful locations.

RIDING STUFF: You will ride specially picked Arabs. The horses all come from successful endurance strains. They are well cared for and fit, eager to tackle long rides day after day. Certainly not your average trekking horse. Intelligent, alert and safe, they are pure joy for capable riders. Owner, Peter Kelly, takes great care with their training and fitness level. He also takes care to monitor the riders' comfort along the way. With so many trails there is usually both a short and long way to any destination, and a fit group of riders will enjoy the longer route at a faster pace, delighting in long canters and exhilarating gallops. If, however, a group member feels "achy," s/he will not be ignored—appropriate measures are in place. No need to suffer! Please come prepared with appropriate comfortable riding gear. Luggage is transported for you and safety helmets are available.

AUTHOR'S COMMENT: *This well recommended ride comes with all of the ingredients for a good time for experienced riders—good horses, good food, and good accommodations. No wonder Equitrek feels comfortable promoting this ride as one of the very best Australia has to offer. It is always a rider-pleaser.*

HIGHLIGHTS
For experienced riders • Australian Stock saddles • Well-bred Arabians • 5 to 7 hours of riding a day • Medium to fast paced riding • Quality food

KHANCOBAN TRAIL RIDES

BASICS: PO Box 91, Khancoban, New South Wales
2642, Australia
Tel/Fax: (61) 260-769-455
Email: ktrtrail@khancoban.albury.net.au
WHEN: September through May.
AIRPORTS: Sydney. Albury Airport is the closest
local airport served by Kendall Airlines or
Hazelton Airlines. Roundtrip transfers to riding
center are $76 (£48) per person, with lower
rates available for groups.
LOCATION: Khancoban is 28 kms. southeast of
Corryong on the Alpine Way and 80 kms. north
of Thredbo, on the western slopes of the
Snowy Mountains.
PRICES: $274 (£172) 3 days/2 nights, per person;
$549 (£343) 7 days/6 nights, per person; $671
(£419) 10 days/9 nights, per person. Also, 2
and 5 day rides are available.

Khancoban Trail Rides operates 2 to 10 day horseback and fly fishing safaris into the Snowy Mountains. They offer a personalized service, keeping the group size down to 10 riders. The safaris run through Alpine National Park with spectacular alpine scenery, and the Snowy Mountains, which always provide panoramic views. Back-up is by 4 wheel drive vehicle, with pack horses used for the more remote locations and on the longer safaris. There is nothing quite like the Australian Alps, with tall blue gums, majestic alpine ash, gnarled and stunted snow gums, flowering shrubbery, and delicate orchids producing a kaleidoscope of color and beauty.

CHILDREN'S PROGRAM: Suitable for children 12 years and older. Children under 12 must demonstrate good riding skills.

ACCOMMODATIONS: Riders may stay at Lyrebird Lodge at the beginning and the end of a trip. It is located in a beautiful setting. On the rides guests camp-out. All equipment will be supplied including tents, self-inflating mattresses, hard hats, and extra warm clothing if needed.

SPECIAL ACTIVITIES: Fly fishing opportunities are excellent and you are likely to catch a glimpse of Australia's wild horses.

MEALS: Breakfast consists of fresh fruit, cereal, delicious porridge, lashings of bacon and eggs, toast, coffee and juices. Lunch is prepared before riding to be carried in saddle bags and served with Billy tea and Jackie's special fruit cakes. Dinner is prepared around the campfire and consists of cocktail hour with *hors d'oeuvres,* followed by a full dinner of chicken, beef or mutton accompanied by vegetables, fresh fruit, dessert, port or chocolate.

RIDING STUFF: Hearty crossbreds will carry you over rugged mountains and deep valleys. This ride is not for beginners. You will pass fern-filled gullies, steep wooded ridges, cool alpine streams, meadows, rushing rivers and travel through the ever-changing foliage of the forests and woodlands. You will see Brumbies (semi-wild Australian horses), hear the dingos cry, and catch glimpses of Australia's unique fauna including kangaroo, wallaby, emu, wombat, and other species. The terrain is generally steep and rough, with many creek and river crossings. The riding pace is mostly at a walk with opportunities to let your horse stretch out across the open plains if desired. Riding time is usually 5 to 6 hours per day.

AUTHOR'S COMMENT: *Khancoban's owners, John and Jackie Williams, provide good horses, good food, guides with extensive knowledge of the Snowy Mountains, and a desire to please. This is one of the finest riding opportunities in Australia's Snowy Mountains.*

HIGHLIGHTS
2 to 10 day trips • Australian stock horses, crossbreds • Australian Stock saddle or English all-purpose saddle • 6 hours of riding per day • Intermediate to experienced riders • Brumby wild horse viewing • Fly fishing • Spectacular Snowy Mountain scenery • All adventure week including riding, white-water rafting, fishing, and abseiling

MILLAMOLONG STATION

www.millamolong.com

BASICS: PO Box 25, Mandurama, New South Wales 2792, Australia
Tel: (61) 2-636-75241   Fax: (61) 2-636-75120
Email: millamol@lisp.com.au
WHEN: Open year round.
AIRPORTS: Orange or Cowra in New South Wales. Transfers can be arranged.
LOCATION: A 4 hour drive from Sydney and a 2½ hour drive from Canberra.
PRICES: *Singles:* $98 (£61) per day, per person. *Twins:* $85 (£53) per day, per person. Suites from $104 (£65) per day, per person, 2 or more guests. Prices include accommodation at the Homestead and 3 meals per day. Reduced rates for children. *Farmhouse:* About $24 (£15) per day, per person, room only. *Optional Extras:* Up to 4 hours of riding a day $30 (£19) per person. *Polo School:* $61 (£38) per day, per person. *Pony Pack Ride* (for children ages 8 to 14): $256 (£160) to $320 (£200) 5 days/4 nights, per child, includes meals, accommodations, horsemanship lessons, riding lessons, competitions, and more.

Polo and kangaroos? Trail riding with emus, working cattle, swimming, tennis courts, qualified instructors, polo tuition by arrangement…is it heaven or Australian horse fun? There are abundant opportunities to engage in almost any type of horseback riding activity imaginable for the entire family. With over 250 stock and polo horses, Millamolong is the genuine item. Good terrain and natural beauty, abundant wildlife, a diverse riding program along with comfortable accommodations, including a fine restaurant and lounge area, all combine to make Millamolong a great horseback riding holiday destination.

CHILDREN'S PROGRAM: Children are welcome on the Pony Pack Ride, but they must be over 8 years old for trail riding.

ACCOMMODATIONS: Guests stay in elegant, well-appointed Homestead rooms with luxury beds, private bathrooms, log fires. Alternatively, you can stay in the historic Farmhouse with a kitchen and dining room for self-catering and a games room.

SPECIAL ACTIVITIES: There is river and pool swimming in season, fishing for trout or carp, tennis courts, bush walks, mountain bikes, visits to local vineyards, limestone caves and historic local towns.

MEALS: Healthy country cooking with fresh ingredients, including farm produce.

RIDING STUFF: Someone must have failed to tell owner-managers Prue and Murray McMillan and James Ashton that the future lies in specialization. Quite simply, Millamolong offers an unusual combination of horseback riding activities, with cattle mustering (round-ups of cattle or sheep), jumping lessons, polo instruction, trail riding, Pony Pack Rides (a week-long children's instructional program), and trail riding. They maintain a herd of 250 horses, breeding for both cattle work and polo, that should keep you plenty busy. The area offers enjoyable riding terrain with rolling hills, rivers, some dirt roads, a polo field, camp-outs on demand, and a jumping arena. With a guest capacity of 55, Millamolong Station offers very comfortable accommodations for the budget-minded as well as those looking for a more upscale setting. The Farmhouse was built during the 19th century and the newer Homestead dates back to the 1930s.

AUTHOR'S COMMENT: *Millamolong Station was recommended to me by one of Australia's top riding holiday experts. It offers a uniquely Australian combination, kind of a cross between an upscale Argentine estancia, a U.S. dude ranch, and a cattle farm. Hosted by able and willing people, it is an ideal place to have fun, Aussie style.*

HIGHLIGHTS
Charming country hospitality • Diversified riding program • Instruction in polo, trail riding, and mustering cattle • Lessons for beginners • Novice to experienced • Comfortable accommodations with *en suite* or private bathrooms • Abundant wildlife

THE 2000 OLYMPIC RIDES

www.equitrek.com.au

BASICS: Agent: **Equitrek Australia**, Club Equitrek, 5 King Road, Ingleside, New South Wales 2101, Australia
Tel: (61) 2-9913-9408   Mobile: (61) 018-444-117
Fax: (61) 2-9970-6303 {International}
Tel: (02) 9913-9408 (from Australia)
Email: nelly@equitrek.com.au
WHEN: Before and after the Year 2000 Olympics in Sydney.
AIRPORTS: Sydney Airport (International).

LOCATION : New South Wales
PRICES: *Pre-Olympic Ride:* $1648 (£1030) 7 days/7 nights (5 days of riding), per person, double occupancy, all inclusive. *Post-Olympic Rides:* Option 1 $1504 (£940) 7 days/6 nights (5 days of riding) per person, double occupancy, all inclusive; or Option 2 (Snowy Mountain Ride) $1537 (£960) 7 days/6 nights (5 days of riding), per person, double occupancy. Prices subject to change.

Nelly Gelich, owner and operator of Equitrek Australia, has graciously agreed to promote these rides offering 3 different options. Although everything about these rides is subject to change, prices and availability included, riders would do well to book early and, if possible, as a group. The rides were designed for sophisticated experienced riders who, it is anticipated, will be attending the Olympic equestrian events and would like to catch a glimpse of Australia on horseback as well. The Pre-Olympic Ride is a fast paced, inn to inn type ride on well-trained Arabs, suitable for endurance riding. The Post-Oylmpic Rides offer 2 options. The Snowy River Ride (Option 2 above) depends entirely on weather conditions in the Snowy Mountains. The Olympics are scheduled to take place during Australia's spring season, and snow conditions might prevent a high mountain ride. The other Post-Olympic riding opportunity (Option 1 above) is at a very upscale, cattle and horse breeding property, founded in the early 1800s and is still run by the same family—now going on the 6th generation. This ride offers inn based trail riding, polo, and a cross-country course, in addition to beautiful countryside, fine accommodations and meals. All 3 riding options will provide you with a glimpse of the best of Australian horsemanship. Any one of them would be a perfect addendum— the highlight of your Olympic experience. One of the riding destinations on the Option 1 Post-Olympic Ride, will have served as home to the U.S. 3 Day Eventing Olympic team prior to the ride.

Pre-Olympic Ride:
This is a fast paced inn to inn ride featuring Arabian horses, trained for endurance, offering B&B accommodations, mostly with *en suite* facilities, very good food and some long hours in the saddle.

Post-Olympic Rides:
Option 1
The object here is to enjoy a superior Australian equestrian facility that offers experienced riders good cross-country riding, polo, and trail riding amidst beautiful surroundings and rather luxurious accommodations.

Option 2 (Snowy Mountain Ride)
This is a great ride through the famous Snowy Mountains. Unfortunately, the timing will make it quite dependent on weather conditions, i.e., whether the higher mountain passes are still covered with deep, impassable snow.

A complete description of these options will be made available at the following website: www.ridingholidays.com

These particular riding opportunities were developed at the request of The Compleat Traveller for our readers. It is a once in a lifetime opportunity to enjoy the best of equestrian activities at the Olympic level, while getting a chance to strut your own stuff, riding in the land of kangaroos, funny expressions, and a very friendly people. We urge you to get your dialing or email fingers to work and call early. Due to the confusion that will inevitably surround the Olympics, including the difficulty of obtaining flights and accommodations in the Sydney area, etc., Equitrek will attempt to assist you with all aspects of your Australian trip if required. So, be more than a mere spectator, "take five," enjoy the action, become a part of it, and learn to talk Australian, but if you are less than musically gifted, please leave those didgeridoos alone.

Nelly Gelich at work in her office.

HIGHLIGHTS
Riding in Australia before and after the 2000 Sydney Olympics • Polo • Upscale comforts • Cross-country riding • Endurance-like inn to inn • 3 different riding options

PUB CRAWLS ON HORSEBACK

www.bec.com.au/glen/horseback/

BASICS: Bullock Mountain Homestead, Bullock Mountain Road, Glen Innes, New South Wales 2370, Australia
Tel: (61) 2-67-321-599   Fax: (61) 2-67-323-538
Email: pubcrawl@northnet.com.au
WHEN: Open year round. More than 17 starting dates annually.
AIRPORTS: Sydney to Glen Innes by Tamair. (Special rate for Pub Crawl riders.)
Free transfers from Glen Innes Airport
LOCATION: A 7 hour drive from Sydney; 4½ hours from Brisbane. Located near the New England Highway running between Brisbane and Sydney
PRICES *Basic Pub Crawl:* $548 (£342) to $619 (£387) 6 days/6 nights, per person, includes 4½ days of riding. *Ride the Divide:* From $1085 (£678) 10 days/9 nights, per person.

The renowned Pub Crawls on Horseback has been rated as one of Australia's top 10 adventure holidays. Now under the ownership of Steve and Allison Wood (a couple sneaking-up on their 30th wedding anniversary), the ride has been invigorated by a new energy. The tour departs from Bullock Mountain Homestead, near Glen Innes, and captures the spirit of the old Australian way of life, traveling over old stock routes and often following trails used by Cobb & Co. (Australia's early stage coaches). Even those with little riding experience can have the time of their lives, taking in the historical villages of Emmaville, Torrington and Deepwater, staying in old bush pubs at the end of a great day on horseback. In addition to the Pub Crawls, there are mini-Pub Crawls, the Great Divide Ride for experienced riders, a Murder Mystery Ride, and more.

CHILDREN'S PROGRAM: The Pub Crawl is not recommended for children under 12 unless parents can verify their riding ability, but there are family weekend riding and accommodation packages.

ACCOMMODATIONS: Bullock Mountain Homestead has single bunkhouses for 16 persons and 3 rooms with double beds. All rooms have the shared use of 3 bathrooms. The hotels provide similar style accommodations with shared bathroom facilities. All beds have electric blankets and some form of heating during winter months.

SPECIAL ACIVITIES: During the rest day in Torrington, bush-walking tours are organized to take in the sights, including Thunderbolt's (bushranger/outlaw) cave and lookout. After a BBQ lunch, you can visit Old Mystery Face, a unique natural granite rock formation, or visit the remains of an old arsenic mine.

MEALS: Breakfasts include a variety of cereals, toast, bacon, eggs, sausages, rissoles and tomato, with orange juice, tea and coffee. Lunch is carried in your saddlebag for eating along the trail, except on the rest day when a beautiful BBQ is provided. Dinners are all candlelit 3 course affairs with wine served on the nights at Homestead. Vegetarian and special dietary needs are catered for upon advance notice.

RIDING STUFF: The typical riding day begins at 7:00 a.m. to allow time to feed and saddle the horses and give them a chance to digest their breakfasts. Riders eat at 8:00 a.m. and the ride begins at 9:00 a.m. You will cover 20 to 25 miles (about 5 to 6 hours in the saddle) traversing open plains, gorges, country lanes and river crossings. Lunch is usually eaten by a river or in a bush setting. There are plenty of areas where you can trot and canter and more experienced riders will have opportunities to gallop. Most of the ride is cross-country through private properties with very few paved roads in sight. There are plenty of photo stops along the way. Riders normally arrive at the pubs by 3:30 p.m., in time to have a drink and a hot shower before dinner at 7:00 p.m.

AUTHOR'S COMMENT: *This long established ride has been infused with the energy and enthusiasm of its new owners and you may expect some positive changes as the Woods stamp their own brand of expertise on one of Australia's most popular rides. Steve Wood is a former automotive engineer and active businessman in the community. Allison Wood, a lifelong horsewoman, is ably assisted by Joe Williams, an experienced rider and 8 time Pub Crawler before he joined the crew.*

HIGHLIGHTS:
Australian tack • 5 to 6 hours a day in the saddle • Australian stock horses • 1 to 10 day packages • Novice to experienced • Comfortable accommodations • Abundant wildlife

CLIP CLOP HORSE TREKS

http://Internet-connect.com.au./clipclop

BASICS: Eumarella, 249 Eumarella Road, Lake Weyla, Via Noosa, QLD 4562, Australia
Tel/Fax: (61) 7-5449-1254
Email: morr@m140.aone.net.au
WHEN: March to November.
AIRPORTS: Brisbane. Transfers to Noosa about 1½ hours. The nearest local airport is at Maroochydore, Queensland.
LOCATION:.North of Brisbane, on the coast.

PRICES: *Two Day Camp-Out Ride:* from $214 (£134) 2 days/1 night, per person. *Five Day Hinterland Pub Ride* (in Noosa hinterland): $597 (£374) 5 days/4 nights, per person, includes 4 days of riding and accommodation in historic pubs. *Fraser Island Trek:* $1189 (£743) 7 days/6 nights, per person, includes 6 days of riding.

This riding opportunity comes highly recommended. Clip Clop Treks is located on the Sunshine coast of Noosa- known for the beauty of its beaches and national parks, which are under strict environmental and planning protection, and for the quality of its restaurants. A broad range of holiday activities are available including water sports, such as sailing, kayaking, river cruises, and surfing. Travelers would be wise to spend a few extra days exploring this delightful area.

CHILDREN'S PROGRAM: The rides cater primarily to adult guests, although competent young riders, if accompanied by parents, will always be welcome.

ACCOMMODATIONS: On the Fraser Island Trek there is "5 Star" camping which includes large tents with camp beds and mattresses and a central marquee for dining. Hot showers are available daily. On the Hinterland Pub Ride you will stay in historic Australian pubs, 2 to a room with shared facilities.

SPECIAL ACTIVITIES: The area is rich in water sports of all types, golf, international standard resorts, where accommodations may be arranged, and lots of shopping opportunities.

MEALS: The chefs pride themselves on serving meals of exceptional quality. Australian wine is served with many of the meals. Special dietary requirements can be catered for, if notified in advance.

RIDING STUFF: Clip Clop maintain 25 horses of mixed breeds, including Australian Stock horses. Their tack is Australian Stock and English. The horses are very fit, friendly and well-mannered. They are trained to move on a loose rein. They also have dressage-trained horses available for educated riders. Lessons are available for guests who are willing to allow extra days and there is a 3 day minimum program for beginners. The ride on Fraser Island is divided into experienced and beginners groups, suitable to their skill levels. The terrain includes undulating hills with sand tracks covered in leaf litter, isolated inland lakes, and ocean beaches. You will pass through rain forest and open sedge land with lots of plant life. There will be plenty of trotting and cantering. The scenery is just beautiful. The Hinterland Pub Ride takes guests through hill country with sweeping ocean views, over rugged mountain ranges, and cross-country through rain forest and farmland. Again, there's lots of trotting and cantering with a few steep climbs and descents to add to the excitement. On the Two Day Camp-Out Ride you pass over Tinbeerwah Mountain to the Noosa River and there is 1 steep climb.

AUTHOR'S COMMENT: *Well maintained horses, excellent food, great riding terrain, and well planned trips make this an exciting addition to our ride offerings from Australia. Clip Clop is a very well run operation and riders and travelers to this area will certainly feel rewarded.*

HIGHLIGHTS
Eco-tourism adventures • Fraser Island, the world's largest sand island, designated World Heritage Site • For competent riders and beginners • Group size limited to 12 • Complimentary masseuse on Fraser Island Trek • Fully stocked bar on all overnight trek • Located on beautiful Sunshine Coast, Queensland, Australia

HORSE TREK AUSTRALIA
(Owned and operated by Piabun Aboriginal Corporation)

BASICS: PO Box 473, Albion 4010, Queensland, Australia
Tel: (61) 7-3256-1300   Fax: (61) 7-3256-1220
Email: piabun@ozemail.com.au
WHEN: Open year round.
NEAREST AIRPORT: Brisbane International - a 2 hour drive, transfers included.
LOCATION: Conondale Range Wilderness area in southern Queensland.
PRICES: $900 (£563) 8 days/7 nights (Saturday to Saturday), per person, double occupancy, includes 7 days of riding.

Horse Trek Australia has been in operation since 1985, providing exceptional quality riding for international guests. The horses are bred, reared, and trained by the world-renowned Sharahd Endurance Stud - a division of Piabun Aboriginal Corporation. Piabun is an Aboriginal owned and operated corporation. The name, "Piabun," is derived from the local Aboriginal Gubi Gubi word meaning "a place of spiritual healing and dreaming." The horses have undergone extensive training and endurance competitions, which keeps them fit and athletic and guarantees a terrific riding experience. The riding trails are through government-owned forestry land in an area composed of subtropical rainforests, with staghorns, tree ferns and palm trees mixed with eucaplyptus forest, hoop pine plantations and open grassland. Bird life is a special feature of the area. Rides are led by qualified guides, including Bob Sample, an Australian champion endurance rider, along with indigenous Aboriginal guides well informed about the local history, flora and fauna.

CHILDREN'S PROGRAM: Children ages 7 through 12 years are welcome, but must be competent riders and accompanied by an adult.

ACCOMMODATIONS: Private rooms with *en suite* bath facilities, shared with adjacent room.

SPECIAL ACTIVITIES: On Wednesdays there is a guided tour to Noosa Heads Beach Resort, shopping, swimming and sightseeing, followed by a 3 hour evening ride.

MEALS: All basic food requirements are satisfied by a good selection of meals, drinks and snacks (including a glass of wine or beer at dinner). Vegetarian and special dietary requirements will be catered for.

RIDING STUFF: Queensland has a subtropical climate, which allows for good riding conditions throughout the year. Winter nights can be frosty, but are usually followed by warm days, while hot summer days are usually followed by balmy cool nights. Although all of the horses are well trained and responsive, some are spirited while others are very quiet. Horses are selected to suit each rider's ability, experience, and confidence. Riders must be able to post at the trot for extended periods. Experienced riders will have ample opportunity for fast-paced riding. The horses are Arabian and Anglo-Arabian crossbreds. Riding time is approximately 4 to 6 hours daily. There is a much talked about evening ride through the forest, where you must place complete trust in your horse's ability to move you through countryside that you can feel, but not necessarily see. The experience is memorable and builds a new and trusting relationship with your mount.

AUTHOR'S COMMENT: *Horse Trek Australia remains one of the top holiday riding outfitters in the world, catering to guests with a variety of riding abilities. Bob Sample remains as one of the best and most well-known endurance trainers worldwide.*

HIGHLIGHTS
Outstanding Arabians and Arabian crossbreds • Australian Stock endurance saddles • Spectacular wildlife viewing • Intermediate riding skills required • Member: Endurance Riders Association and Outdoor Tour Operators Association

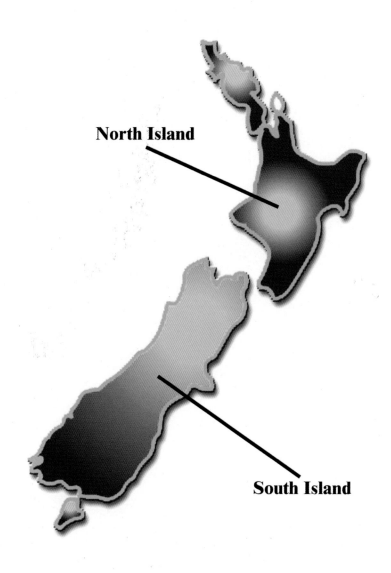

North Island

South Island

NEW ZEALAND
by Rob Stanley

NEW ZEALAND, "Aoetearoa," is a unique and special part of the South Pacific, known for its all-Black rugby team, kiwi fruit and its success in The Americas Cup. It is also a country synonymous with great horses and horsemen. From that awesome race horse, Pharlap, to Charisma and Mark Todd of Olympic fame, the horse has a special place in the hearts of most New Zealanders.

Since 1868, when Samuel Marsden brought the first horses to New Zealand, a strong horse culture has developed and participation is extensive. There are regular pony club, dressage, show jumping and eventing competitions held around the country and, of course, several Hunts such as the Brackenfield Hunt on South Island and the Pakuranga Hunt in the north. They hunt twice a week during the winter months and enjoy strong support. The breeding and racing of good race horses is also close the hearts of many "Kiwis." New Zealand bred horses have distinguished themselves overseas both on the track and in other equestrian disciplines, particularly 3 day eventing. Many of the world's top owners and trainers are represented at the yearling sales held each year at the Karaka complex near Auckland, where New Zealand's top yearlings are sold at auction. There are also many Thoroughbred studs in the region. It is not surprising then that there should be a good selection of riding holidays available throughout New Zealand.

The People
Because of its geographic location, New Zealand is often confused with Australia. While we enjoy a special and competitive relationship with our "colonial cousins," New Zealanders are fiercely independent and the culture is quite unique— a blend of Polynesian and European cultures with a rich inheritance of warm, genuine hospitality which often develops into lifetime friendships with visitors.

The Horses
You will find most of the more popular breeds of horse and pony in riding establishments throughout New Zealand. Thoroughbreds, Arabs, Appaloosas,Clydesdales, Quarterhorses and Connemara Ponies are probably the most common. The progeny of the New Zealand Thoroughbred horse crossed with these other breeds have proven their worth in the varied terrain and climate of New Zealand. Some outfitters breed their own stock so that they are well accustomed to the climate and conditions in which they work.

The Terrain
The story of New Zealand's natural history, enshrined in the myths and legends of the Maori, is also visible in its terrain. The bush-covered and forested hill country with still active volcanoes, Ngarahoe and Ruapehu, of the central North Island tell the story of New Zealand's birth.By contrast, the more open country of South Island and the Southern Alps with its glacial valleys, snow-fed rivers, lakes, and fertile alluvial plains display yet another part of that history.

The Riding

New Zealand consists of 3 main islands, North Island, South Island and Stewart Island. While there is no riding centres on Stewart Island there is plenty to choose from on North and South Islands. Recreational riding opportunities abound in New Zealand and the diversity of terrain is as refreshing as its renowned clean, green environment. You can enjoy a refreshing canter along a sandy beach in the morning and watch the sunset from horseback in the mountains later that same day. New Zealand is becoming increasingly popular as a multi-day riding destination. It is seen as a relatively safe country to ride in, there are no snakes, bears, lions or other man-eating species to be concerned about and you can actually drink the water from the streams on most of the rides (always check with your guide first). Better yet, New Zealand has a favourable exchange rate with most countries.

There are many riding centres offering trail rides of up to a full day near the main population centers as well as professional operators running longer pack trips of up to 10 days, based mainly in the more rural areas. It is not difficult for the enthusiast to build an itinerary. Short rides and wagon rides based around orchards and wineries are also available in some regions. North Island offers plenty of riding opportunities ranging from a few hours to a few days. Within an hour or so of Auckland, New Zealand's largest city, one can be riding amidst the solitude of beautiful white sand beaches and bush of the semi-tropical Northland, or you can choose to enjoy a quality farmstay, riding out daily and returning at day's end. Further down the island, near the thermal resort of Rotorua, it is possible to join the *tangata whenua*, the Tuhoe tribe (dubbed the "Children of the Mist" by 19th century ethnographer, Elsdon Best) and ride through the mystical bush country and rivers of Urewera National Park.

The South Island has many multi-day riding options and with companies such as Hurunui Horse Treks, just north of Christchurch, one can ride the high country sheep and cattle stations and through the beech forest of Lake Sumner Forest Park in the Southern Alps, from Hamner Springs, the Alpine thermal resort, to the sea at Kaikoura, famous for its whales, dolphins and rock lobster. Further south at Cadrona Valley, riders can join rides of varying lengths through the high country of central Otago and its Lakes District on Appaloosa horses—only a stone's throw away from the home of 'bungy jumping," adventure capital of the world, Queenstown. You will also be within a day's drive from the majestic splendour of Milford Sound and remote Fiordland. Central Otago is also well-known for its annual Cavalcade, where hundreds of horses and riders, along with wagons, spend several days in the saddle following different historic trails to converge on a specific site to celebrate the horse and times gone by. Wagon Treks are also run regularly between Hamner Springs and Nelson, travelling through the high country and stations of the Clarence, Wairau and Motueka River Valleys.

Accommodations

There are many accommodation options for the rider in New Zealand. On multi-day rides and pack trips, one may choose from tents and rustic shepherd's huts in the mountains, or take a more exclusive holiday, riding from 1 sheep and cattle station to another, staying at quality farmstays along the way. There are also those that offer day rides from their farmstay and residential riding schools.

Safety

The New Zealand Tourism Board, along with the Adventure Tourism Council and the adventure industry itself, are very strong on setting and maintaining high standards of safety and quality assurance. The International League for the Protection of Horses also runs an approval scheme for riding schools and trekking centers. When you come to ride in New Zealand you should first check to see if your intended riding destination is run by an approved operator who adheres to the industry code of practice and is a "Kiwihost" trained company. Any company displaying "The New Zealand Way" brand has had to meet rigid criteria and have proven performance and commitment to quality and the environment. At present, there are only 2 riding companies who have achieved this level of accreditation.

Other Activities
New Zealand is an outdoorsman's paradise, with several species of deer, chamois, thar and wild boar as well as ducks and Canada geese to hunt. Brown and rainbow trout are found in most lakes and rivers throughout the country and salmon also are caught in the South Island rivers, such as the Rakaia, Rangitata and Hurunui. Saltwater fishermen are also well catered for in New Zealand, from big game fishing in Zane Grey's "El Dorado" and Northland's Bay of Islands, to fishing for the likes of cod and grouper in the south. There are many professional guides available and some companies offer hunting and fishing options in conjunction with their rides. New Zealand provides travelers with the opportunity to take part in a full range of adrenaline-pumping adventure activities, including sea kayaking, swimming with dolphins, white water rafting, mountain biking and jet boating, as well as more passive ecological and cultural tours. There is something for everyone.

Climate
Average Temperatures:
Summer: 20º to 25º Centigrade (70s Fahrenheit)
Winter: 12º to 15º Centigrade (50s Fahrenheit)

How to Get There
New Zealand is well serviced by Air New Zealand and the other international airlines that fly regularly into it's international airports at Auckland and Christchurch from North America, United Kingdom and Europe.

Transport Within New Zealand
Moving around in New Zealand is easy with good regular road and rail options. There is a ferry service between the North and South Islands, 2 major airlines and some smaller ones offering flights to all the major cities, and some of the smaller ones.

About Bob Stanley

Bob Stanley along with Mandy Platt own and operate one of New Zealand's outstanding rides, Hurunui Horse Trails on New Zealand's South Island. He has consistently been a leader in bringing the entire package of New Zealand rides to the public.

NORTH RIVER TREKS

BASICS: Helmsdale Road, RD2, Waipu, North Island,
New Zealand
Tel: (64) 9432-0565
Tel: 0800-RIDE-GGS (New Zealand only)
Fax: (64) 9-432-0562
Email: northvr@igrin.co.n3
WHEN: Open year round.
NEAREST AIRPORTS: Whangarei, North Island -
a 40 minute drive; Auckland International -
a 2 hour drive.

LOCATION: A 2 hour drive north of Auckland.
PRICE: *River Explorer* (1 hour ride): $25 (£15) per
person. *Off the Beaten Path* (3 hour ride): $60
(£37) per person. *The Caves* (full day ride): $95
(£59) per person, incl.lunch and caving; *The
Woolshed* (overnight ride): $150 (£94) per per-
son, d/o, incl. all lodgings, meals and 3 hours of
riding per day. *The White Sands* (2 full days):
$250 (£156) incl. lodgings, meals and 5 hours
of riding per day.

North River Treks was established by Ian and
Anna Benson in 1991 with a view towards
diversifying their cattle farming business.
Since then, the popularity of trekking has seen
the demise of the cattle farm, while the horse
trekking operation has expanded from 10 to
30 horses. The Bensons also breed horses and
keep about 20 young stock on their farm. With
access to over 40 kms. of trails on 5000 acres
of bush, river, beach and farm land, the variety
of scenery and terrain will amaze you. On the
overnight rides you will visit the glow worm
grottos of the Waipu Caves.

CHILDREN'S PROGRAM: Children under 12 with
little or no riding experience may take rides of
up to 1½ hours. Those over 12 with some experience may participate in all of the day rides.

ACCOMMODATIONS: All overnight trekkers
will sleep in a sheep shearing shed. This is
basic accommodation (mattresses on the
floor) with a hot shower, toilet and kitchen.
For those of you engaged in day riding there
are a variety of accommodations available in
the area ranging from budget to luxury.

SPECIAL ACTIVITIES: Extended caving and
abseiling trips can be arranged in the extensive network of limestone caves in the area.
Dolphin watching and fishing trips can also
be arranged locally.

MEALS: The all day rides includes a BBQ lunch
(home grown beef and salads). On all overnight
trips you will have a cooked breakfast (bacon
and eggs with fruit and cereal) and a BBQ dinner. Vegetarians are catered for upon request.

RIDING STUFF: The vast variety of the terrain
will fascinate you. From fertile river flats to
green sheep farms, with panoramic views of
the coast and outer islands; from a stony bot-
tom river valley surrounded on both sides by
steep bush-clad hills colored in every shade of
green imaginable to 14 kms. of white, unspoiled
sandy beach. The temperate climate allows the
rides to operate year round, the most popular
time being December to March. There are rides
to suit all riding levels. One to 2 hour rides are
offered daily as are half day rides. On all day
and longer rides you will visit the glow worm
caves. On the 2 day trek, riders will travel
along an east coast beach. Experienced and
trained KiwiHost guides make it their business
to ensure that every ride is conducted safely
and with concern for the environment. There
is 1 guide for every 5 or 6 riders, and groups
are split (when necessary and possible) into
different skill levels, allowing more experienced riders to enjoy the challenge of steep
hills, river crossings and a faster pace.

AUTHOR'S COMMENT: *The Bensons will graciously welcome you to New Zealand's rural
area. As professional farmers, they are knowledgeable about the land and the people who
inhabit a region that is, for many of us, a
remote and exotic place. Glow worm caves,
convenient for when the power goes out, and
some great beach riding await you.*

HIGHLIGHTS
Small groups • Glow worm caves • Varied scenery • Australian stock saddles •
Day rides and overnights • 7 customized tours • All skill levels • KiwiHost Council
Business (trained guides) • ILPH approved riding facility • Member: NZ Adventure
Tourism Council and NZ Adventure Horse Riding the Best of New Zealand

PAKIRI BEACH HORSE RIDES

BASICS: Rahuikiri Road, Pakiri Beach, 2 RD, Wellsford, New Zealand
Tel: (64) 9-422-6275
Fax: (64) 9-422-6277
WHEN: Open daily year round
AIRPORTS: Auckland International
LOCATION: The farm is a 1½ hour drive from Auckland; a 2 hour drive from Paihia Bay of Islands; and 20 minutes from Wellsford.

PRICE: Full Day Rides: $90 (£56); Half Day Rides: $57 (£35); 2 Hour Rides: $40 (£25). Farmhouse accommodations with 3 meals: $74 (£46) per night, per person, double occupancy. Ngapeka House: $154 (£96) per night, per person, double occupancy, add $41 (£26) for 3 meals per day. Beach Cabins: $66 (£41) per night, per cabin, add $41 (£26) for 3 meals per day.

Pakiri Beach Horse Rides is a family owned cattle and sheep operation covering 2000 acres. The farm occupies land on which the great Maori Chief Te Kin and his daughter Rahui once lived. Riders can opt for overnight safaris in the summer or stay at the farmhouse. There are great beach rides, with wild dolphins often visible along with the occasional Orca whale. Sharley Haddon, one of the owners, runs the riding operation. She is a delight to spend time with, knowledgeable about the region, and eager to promote a good time.

CHILDREN'S PROGRAM: Children under 5 are welcome, but only for only for short rides on a lead line. Children under 12 cannot participate in overnight safaris, but may join all day rides.

ACCOMMODATIONS: There are 3 options: Ngapeka House, with 4 bedrooms, TV, dishwasher, and magnificent views of the ocean; beach cabins, situated among the sand dunes, are small but very private, with a double bed, bathroom and kitchen unit; or you may choose to stay at the central farmhouse in a double bedroom with *en suite* bathroom. On summer safaris you will sleep overnight in cabins or tents.

SPECIAL ACTIVITIES: You can enjoy a genuine Maori *hangi* meal—delicious food cooked underground. Minimum of 6 persons.

MEALS: Breakfast and evening meals are served family style in the farmhouse kitchen or outdoors in summer for a BBQ or *hangi*. Lunch is casual, often a picnic on the trail. Special diets can be catered to and there are excellent restaurants in the area.

RIDING STUFF: In addition to some 57 assorted riding horses, suitable for all skill levels, the family maintains 25 pure-bred Arabian stud horses. Located on the ocean, Pakiri is ideally situated for beach riding along miles of pristine white sand, unpopulated, but alive with bird life, dolphins, bright sun, and the sound of hoofbeats. Additionally, riders may choose a 2 to 6 hour ride through farmland and New Zealand rain forest on trails that offer some spectacular scenery. The tack is mainly English, with some Western and some Stock. In addition to the overnight safaris, overnight guests who possess an appropriate level of skill, are welcome to help with the daily chores of the farm on horseback. Riders will be grouped and ride according their abilities and more experienced riders will have plenty of opportunities for faster riding.

AUTHOR'S COMMENT: *Pakiri Beach Rides offers some the most spectacular beach riding this side of Atlantis. The farm provides a warm family atmosphere and members of the host family will happily regale you with stories and share their knowledge of local history. One of your hosts, Laly, played rugby for New Zealand and will be pleased to tell you about his experiences and his Maori heritage.*

HIGHLIGHTS
Isolated Pacific Ocean beach ride • 2000 acre coastal cattle and sheep farm • Cattle and sheep work on horseback • Dolphin watching • Rides through New Zealand rain forest • Farmhouse accommodations • Member: New Zealand Adventure Tourism Council

TE UREWARA ADVENTURES OF NEW ZEALAND

BASICS: Ruatahuna, Privat Bag, 3001, Roturua, NZ
   Tel: (64) 7-366-3969   Fax: (64) 7-366-3333
   Email: biddlemarg@clear.net.nz
WHEN: October to June
NEAREST AIRPORTS: Rotorua
LOCATION: A 2 hour drive west of Rotorua.

PRICE: $60 (£38) per day, per person; $184 (£115)
   2 days/1 night, per person, d/o; $298 (£187)
   3 days/2 nights, per person, d/o; $347 (£217)
   4 days/3 nights, per person, d/o; $397 (£248)
   5 days/4 nights, per person, d/o. Prices include
   all meals, accommodations and riding.

Nestled away in the hills, far beyond civilization, is a wondrous place, which legend has it, is home to the *Children of the Mist*—the Tuhoe tribe. To get there, you must travel beyond the tarseal, past gravel roads and the last remaining power pole, to a place where no 4 wheel drive can go. You will taste life in an area where the only way in or out is by foot or on horseback. It is the doorstep to Te Urewera National Park and home to Whare and Margaret Biddle of Ruatahuna. Their backyard is the largest stand of virgin native forest on North Island. The Biddles love their simple way of life and enjoy sharing it with others. The rides are unique and exhilarating, they transport you back to a place where time stands still. There are few luxuries, but the living is uncomplicated; cooking over open fires and bathing in mountain streams. The Biddles love to share their culture and customs and their knowledge of local Maori history, hospitality, Maori medicinal plants, traditional fishing and cooking techniques.

CHILDREN'S PROGRAM: Children are welcome, but must have riding experience.

ACCOMMODATIONS:. Accommodations are in 2 person, igloo-shaped tents, with insect screens, floor complete with *lilos* or blow-up mattresses, sleeping bags and sheets. You may also get a chance to stay at a traditional Maori Meeting House that can sleep 20 people comfortably. New Zealand Department of Conservation huts are also available complete with bunks and mattresses.

SPECIAL ACTIVITIES: Fly fishing the wilderness of the Whakatane River offers a grand experience for the keen fisherman. Brown or rainbow trout abound and you can learn the traditional fishing habits of the Maori, setting the eel basket, torching, and bobbing. Te Urewara National Park is home to red and rusa deer. There are also wonderful opportunities for photography, meditation, and relaxation.

MEALS: Breakfasts include a variety of cereals and cooked foods. Wholesome lunches with salad are often eaten *en route*. Dinners consist of hearty meals prepared by a hand well-versed in cooking over an open fire.

RIDING STUFF: The horses are Clydesdale crosses, Arabians, and Pacers. The average time in the saddle is 3 to 5 hours a day. The saddles are Western or Stock. You will ride through the Te Urewara National Park as well as privately owned land and there will be frequent river crossings. The area is home to the Tuhoe tribe and your ride hosts Whare and Margaret Biddle are themselves *Children of the Mist* as the Tuhoe are called. There are no power poles and the region is uninhabited and inaccessible except on horseback. The Tuhoe culture predominates and you will be informed of the proper protocols.

AUTHOR'S COMMENT: *The Biddles are a delight to know, willing and able to introduce you to the unique culture of the Children of the Mist who inhabit North Island. Te Urewara Adventures is truly a complete holiday, stimulating, educational, and relaxing. It will broaden your horizons and the riding is fun too!!*

HIGHLIGHTS
For intermediate riders • Weight limit 185 lbs. (84 kg.) (14 stone) • Stock saddles • 3 to 5 hours in the saddle per day • Good fishing—from the back of a horse! • 15 horses • Member: New Zealand Adventure Tourism Council

HURUNUI HORSE TRAILS

www.horseback.co.nz

BASICS: Hewetts Road, "The Peaks", Rural Delivery, Hawarden, North Canterbury, New Zealand   Tel/Fax: (64) 3-314-4204 Tel: 0800 HURUNUI (487-8684) (from New Zealand only) Email: StanleyR@xtra.co.nz

WHEN: Open year round. Principal trekking dates from November to April.

AIRPORTS: Christchurch International - a 1¼ hour drive. Transfers from airport included for some rides.

LOCATION: Hurunui horse center is located 100 kms. north of Christchurch.

PRICES: *Mountains to the Sea Ride:* $793 (£495) 8 days/9 nights, per person, double occupancy. *The Real Thing:* $702 (£438) 8 days/9 nights, per person, double occupancy. *Station to Station:* $910 (£569) 5 days/6 nights, per person, double occupancy, includes superior accommodations with hot showers at farmhouses. *Seaward River:* $286 (£179) 4 days/3 nights, per person, double occupancy. *Overnighter:* $130 (£81) per person, double occupancy. *Covered Wagon Treks:* $832 (£520) 5 days/4 nights, per wagon (4 adults maximum).

Hurunui Horse Treks began operating with a handful of horses in 1987. Today, they are recognized as New Zealand's leading high country outfitter with over 50 horses, offering a range of multi-day pack trips and trail rides through the spectacular high country of New Zealand's Southern Alps. Proprietors, Rob Stanley and Mandy Platt, have many years of experience and are supported by a team of dedicated, professional guides. Their programs give riders the opportunity to interact with families who own the sheep and cattle stations along the way. Most rides are suitable for riders of all skill levels, but certain rides, like the *Mountains to the Sea Ride*, are only for experienced riders who can handle a challenge and long days in the saddle. Hurunui also operates multi-day *Covered Wagon Treks* between the alpine thermal resort of Hanmer Springs and Nelson via the rugged Rainbow Track. These treks are great for anybody to enjoy with plenty of fishing and swimming opportunities.

CHILDREN'S PROGRAM: Children must be at least 12 years old for 4 and 8 day pack trips. There are no age restrictions for the Wagon Treks.

ACCOMMODATIONS: Varies from sleeping under the stars to tents and rustic backcountry huts; from historic cob houses to modern bunkhouse quarters with showers and flush toilets at some of the stations. The *Station to Station Ride*, however, provides for quality farmhouse accommodation on most nights.

SPECIAL ACTIVITIES: Fishing (brown trout and salmon) and hunting (red deer, wild pig, and chamois) options are available by prior arrangement.

MEALS: Good wholesome Kiwi meals, including cooked breakfasts are supplied by the station owners along the way. Where possible, riders cook over an open fire. Vegetarians and folks with other dietary concerns will be catered for.

RIDING STUFF: The horses are hunter types, including Thoroughbred/Clydesdale crosses between 15 to 17 hands, bred on the stations and hills. There are also purebred and crossbred Connemara ponies. Most of the rides involve between 4½ to 6 hours of riding a day, except for the *Mountains to the Sea Ride,* which includes days of 6 to 8 hours riding. The riding is varied and differs each day, ranging from riding along tracks and river flats to following cattle and game tracks over mountain ranges, crossing both quiet streams and big rivers. Wherever possible, guests ride separately from the pack horses and the pace can include trotting and cantering for those able.

AUTHOR'S COMMENT: *Rob and Mandy Roberts provide excellent rides and are leaders in promoting New Zealand riding holidays. Their website is particularly useful. They offer a wide variety of rides, and the currently favorable exchange rates for Brits and Americans make this a very attractive holiday in a beautiful and friendly country.*

HIGHLIGHTS

Professional guides • Australian stock saddles • From 8 day/9 night rides to ½ day treks • Covered wagon treks • Riding to suit all skill levels • Fishing • Hunting • Explore the culture and natural history of the High Country • Member: Adventure Tourism Council • Accredited: New Zealand Way • ILPH approved facility

NEW ZEALAND BACKCOUNTRY SADDLE EXPEDITIONS

http//kiwiadv.co.nz/Otago/BackCountrySaddles.htm

BASICS: Cardrona, RD1, Wanaka, New Zealand
  Tel: (64) 03-443-8151
  Fax: (64) 03-443-1712
WHEN: Open all year for 2 hour option. Pack trips are available from November to April.
NEAREST AIRPORTS: Queenstown.
LOCATION: Backcountry Saddle is located 27 kms. from Wanaka and 35 kms. from Queenstown over the Crown Range on an unpaved road. Please Note: Not all car rental companies will allow you to travel over unpaved routes.

Alternatively, you can take Highway 6 – a 135 km. drive. There is a free courtesy coach supplied from Wanaka to the stables.
PRICE: *Two Hour Rides:* $16 (£10) per person for children under 15; $24 (£15) per person for adults. *Full Day Ride:* $60 (£37) per person, includes lunch and 5 to 6 hours of riding. *Pack Trips:* $68 (£42) overnight, per person; $195 (£121) 3 days/2 nights, per person; $234 (£146) 4days/3 nights, per person, includes all accommodations, meals, and riding.

New Zealand Backcountry Saddle Expeditions has been in operation for 14 years under its current owners, Debbie and Darrin Thomas, benefiting from both the breeding and tack selections made by its founders. The combination of the Appaloosa horses and the Western saddles means that trekkers can journey safely and comfortably in these parts. The terrain can be challenging, but it is always worth the effort. There are breathtaking views of snow-capped mountains, covered in tussock grass that you never quite get used to.

CHILDREN'S PROGRAM: Children 4 and over can participate in 2 hour treks led by guides. The longer treks are unsuitable for young ones.

ACCOMMODATIONS: On extended rides, the camp site includes a modest hut, which was used by drovers up until about 1960. The hut contains a basic toilet and running water by way of a crystal clear mountain stream. Campfires are lit, the cards come out and the story-telling begins.

SPECIAL ACTIVITIES: Visit the Cardrona Hotel established in 1865, or try your hand at gold panning.

MEALS: Breakfast includes cereal, fruit, and home-made bread. Lunch consists of sandwiches, fresh fruit, and baked goods. Dinners include smoked chicken, steak or lasagna with vegetables, and salads.

RIDING STUFF: Working with a herd of 20 well-trained Appaloosa horses, the Thompsons like to customize their trips to the needs of each group they work with. The stables are situated at 2100 feet (656 metres) and the riding goes up from there. Both the trails chosen and the pace of the ride depend on the level of riding experience within the group. The extended pack trips for larger groups are all supported by pack animals. The pack trips are organized around sites of historical and natural interest, including Lake Wanaka and Arrow River. You will also cross the Crown Mountains, where a view of Mount Cook is sometimes possible, spending 6 to 8 hours in the saddle daily. Picnic lunches are served along the way.

AUTHOR'S COMMENT: *Debbie and Darrin believe that if you bring the right set of attitudes to one of their extended pack trips, you will walk (or ride) away with a smile on your face and a sense of having captured a little bit of what makes New Zealand so special. New Zealand has a very friendly culture and tremendously varied terrain and the "2 Ds" offer up a healthy dose of the best of its backcounty. The basic style of this riding holiday is similar to that of wilderness outfits in the U.S., but the terrain and culture are strictly New Zealand.*

HIGHLIGHTS
Western tack and saddles • 20 Appaloosa horses • 2 hour to 4 day trips • Views of snow-capped mountains • Novice to experienced riders • Challenging terrain • Safety equipment supplied • 3 and 4 day pack trips to Motapu Valley (5 to 7 hours riding per day) • Member: Best of New Zealand

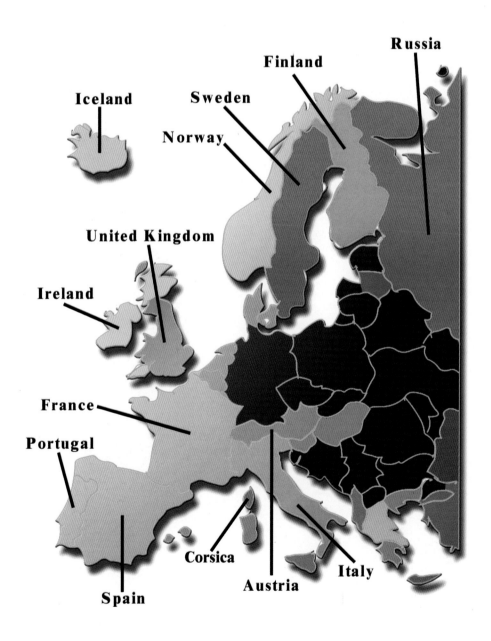

Russia

Finland

Iceland

Sweden

Norway

United Kingdom

Ireland

France

Portugal

Corsica

Italy

Austria

Spain

AUSTRIA

by John Ruler

LTHOUGH GENERALLY NOT RATED HIGHLY in terms of tourist attractions, horseback riding is available in Austria, much of it at the local level. A scenic landscape of mountains, lakes, and flower-covered meadows cannot be ignored. In the case of Austria, the Haflinger, a sturdy Tyrolean breed, basically a mixture of palomino and chestnut in colour, provides the perfect equestrian vehicle for exploring the mountainous terrain, if only for an hour or two. In winter, these delightful Disney-like characters, around 14 hands high, with shaggy manes, are used to draw the sleighs. There are organized rides along the Watch River in Lower Austria and the border area between the Danube River and the Czech Republic, which offer a blend of meadows and forests conducive to long gallops or canters (lopes). This is a land of knights and nobles, best experienced in the spring when the Alps are still covered in snow. Another ride featured in this book, crosses the border into Southern Bohemia.

To many, the Tyrol means Austria, with high mountains, splendid slopes, glaciers and lush meadows. Ebbs has a huge Haflinger stud as well as a riding school. At Gerlos, the Kroller guest ranch offers Western riding in winter as well as summer. Other riding centers, often with a good-sized indoor school, can be found at St. Ulrich am Pillersee, Steeg, Steinberg, Walchsee, Weer and Wildschonau. A variety of rides through the National Park in the Hohe Tauern mountain range are possible, offering from 1 day excursions to 2 day rides with 7 nights accommodation in the Park. A week long ride, available in July and August, staying in mountain huts overnight is also possible. Any mention of Steiermark would be incomplete without emphasizing the famous Lipizzaner at Piber stud near Graz, 200 years old in 1998. This stud was first used for breeding military horses and they have been breeding Lipizzaners, which are used by the world-famous Spanish Riding School of Vienna, since the 1920s. Book well in advance for the School's regular performances as tickets are hard to come by. There are Lipizzaners too at Amplwang im Hausruckwald in Upper Austria, along with nearly 200 Icelandic horses and 15 Warmbloods. They also offer carriage driving courses, another branch of equestrianism for which Austria is renowned. Hungarian and Polish Warmbloods join their Austrian counterparts at Neusiedl am See in Burgenland, bringing a touch of the Hungarian Plain to this little known border region.

FRANCE

by John Ruler

ITH FRANCE MORE THAN TWICE the size of the British Isles, a large proportion of it rural in nature, it is hardly surprising that equestrian attractions are equally as extensive. Differences in climate and terrain are also enormous, making some regions far more suited to simple trekking or hacking, while others may be well be suited to the faster pace sometimes demanded by long distance rides covering around 25 miles a day. These are known as *randonnees* in France, and feature overnight stops, full back-up service for luggage, and a guide. You are also expected to look after your horse, although help is always at hand. Thanks to American and UK agencies, inclusive riding holidays are now far more available, though the bulk of riders remain the French themselves, encouraged by the professional approach to equestrian tourism generally. This means that many centers, some small and well patronized, may not even appear in the holiday brochures, only to be discovered by those travelling independently. Note too that the language problem can be acute, especially in more remote regions, so brush up on your French.

France also benefits from a vast network of bridleways, well mapped out and provided in handy book form, with information on routes, overnight stops, hiring horses, vets and farriers available from local authorities. All this is put to good use by the horse holiday companies, who between them cover a wide spectrum of options, not simply in terms of scenery, but also in the type of riding holiday they offer. Just over the English Channel, Nord and Pas-de-Calais, a traditionally rural area of lush pastures and an abundance of old towns, is ideal for short breaks. Typical of these is a 3 day, 36 mile trek, with riding in the rolling hills and along the beach in the region between Cap Gris-Nez and Cap Blanc-Nez (easily accessible from London via Dover and P&O Stena Line ferry to Calais or by Eurostar from London in less than an hour). Accommodation is a *gite* (basically country style self-catering) or a *chambre d'hotel*.

Similarly, short break opportunities offered by British-based companies in Normandy, the gorgeous region known for its fiery calvados (an apple brandy), cider, spotted cows, and Mont St. Michel, with its amazing alleyways, nooks and crannies. One British company offers a 5 day, 120 mile *radonnee* which ends with a gallop across the vast bay in which Mont St. Michel stands. Another 5 day trip by the same British company includes a ride on the huge Utah Beach, which played a key role for the Allies in the D-Day landings during World War II. Another ride takes you to Barfleur, a delightful village with a dramatic lighthouse, and then on to Manoir d'Herclat in Neville for a traditional Normandy lunch. Historically, the valleys of the Loire in central France with their huge forests have been considered prime riding holiday country. There are the castles to start with, plus the charm of French provincial life, and cuisine to match. In what is loosely termed the Dordogne, the castles of Perigord provide a dramatic and romantic backdrop to river and valley rides through a region rich in delicacies such as sweet chestnuts, truffles, and goose live pate.

Bordeaux likewise is famed for its wines, and you can ride through the vineyards, meadows, woods, and orchards near the resort of La Rochelle (further north on the Atlantic coast), which hosts a 5 day ride geared to ability and riders' choice in terms of pace.

But it is even further south that you find the main holiday riding locations. It was in the Corbieres Hills that I dozed off while on horseback in the warm September sun and when I awoke, it was difficult to comprehend what century I was in! Such is the Camelot quality in this land of the Cathars (a religious sect crushed by Rome as heretics), whose hilltops castles remain as shrines to their simple faith. You will quickly develop the habit of tucking into the local delicacies and top class wines. This is classic horseback riding country, with wide coverage given by a number of companies. One company offers independent farm to farm rides, map reading your way along marked bridlepaths and tracks. Another programme, based on self catering in a converted grange, take you to the Aude Valley, near the walled town of Carcassonne, where its preserved medieval quarter rightly draws the crowds. There are more sites of historical interest in the Cevennes hills and mountains of southern France, using horses based on Barb, Hispano, and American breeds, where the Knights Templar fought religious wars. Although the rides can be challenging, with the need to lead your horses when the going gets too stony, the reward is discovering a region of stone-walled villages, forest tracks, boundless plateaux, and hillsides. The food is pretty good as well and, in one case, is prepared by a top French chef. You can choose between country hotels or bivouacs if you want to explore the more remote regions.

Albi, with its famous cathedral in the mid-Pyrenees, is a sightseeing stop during a 7 day farmhouse *randonnee* in the Tarn Valley, riding for 2 to 4 hours daily in small groups. You can also play golf, tennis, or walk. Non-riders are welcome. The Pyrenees attract considerable interest, with a number of exciting equestrian explorations along the Franco-Spanish border, going up as high as the snowline. Locally bred Merens horses are used in the High Cerdagne. A fastish pace, using Andalucian horses, is set for one of the Provence rides, featured in this book, where olive trees, lavender, and the sound of cicadas provide a true Mediterranean flavour on the week long journey. The Camargue (a word said to be derived from the Greek words for reed and field) is a strange, compelling area. The swampy delta land of the river Rhone is home to the "white horses of the sea" which thrive on a diet of tough grass and salt water. Their origins have never really been defined and they blend as easily into the marshes and lagoons as do the pink flamingos. Black bulls, reared on ranches, are rounded up by the *gardians* (cowboys) for branding and for use in bull games, as opposed to bull-fighting. Riding here is very much exploration, with the chance to join in a fall *randonnee* to the Roman-walled city of Aigues Mortes and experience the traditions of the Camargue at the Salt Festival.

Other examples of organized rides, through international agencies, can be found among the Auvergne, volcanic mountains well off the beaten track, and in Vercors-Trieves, a fairytale national park in the French Alps. Fast riding is promised on Moravan, an island in the heart of Burgandy, with long gallops during the 5 to 7 hours ridden daily. Expect rolling hills, large forests, rivers, lakes and villages full of character. Even then you have barely scratched the surface.The annual directory of *Tourisme et Loisirs Equestres en France* boasts 1001 riding ideas and addresses. This is an invaluable tool for the more independent rider, although it is often by personal recommendation that you come across tours such as those run for groups of 8 to 10 by Jean-Paul Bonetat visiting the Loire chateaux. All this is in addition to simply staying in France, possibly as a family, touring by car, or camping, with riding just one of the available options. Whatever your choice, you can be sure that your equestrian wishes will be granted.

GERMANY AND THE BENELUX COUNTRIES

by John Ruler

BETWEEN THEM, GERMANY AND THE Benelux countries of Belgium, Holland and Luxembourg, have a huge concentration of riding centers—the majority of them, however, serve their own nationals and are pretty well booked year round. This means that there is less in the way of organised long distance rides than are found in France, the UK, or Ireland, though this in no way precludes the enthusiast from joining half or sometimes full day hacks, often in some delightfully rural settings.

With the Germans providing the largest number of holiday riders outside their own country, and with a keen desire to learn new skills, it is scarcely surprising that many German centers, especially in towns and cities, concentrate more on instruction than on actual hacking, and are much more likely to be located in and around the main tourist regions. Bavaria is one example where, like Austria and Switzerland, riding is often found in smaller towns and villages, and can involve a long and involved journey. Riding is certainly available in the Allgau Lower Alps, while the more pastoral scenery of meadows, woods and rivers can be found in central and northern Swabia. Interestingly, one British based company which offers instructional holidays above the town of Bernkastel-Kues in the Moselle region, has now added a 5 day riding tour based at the Halflingerhof at Rosshaupten in southern Bavaria. This was due to overseas pressure for exploratory rides and involves 5 hours daily in the saddle using Haflingers. In Baden-Wurtemberg, the Black Forest lends itself to at least one long distance ride, staying overnight in country inns, while the Rhineland-Palatinate—famous for its castle hotels - has a number of riding centers close to Koblenz, at the confluence of the Rhine and Moselle Rivers. To the north, there is riding round the delightful old Hanseatic town of Lubeck, and in Lower Saxony the Luneberg Heath. The area north of Hanover is obvious riding country with its many miles of sandy tracks, moorland and, in late summer, masses of heather.

Saxony, in what was once Communist East Germany, offers a surprisingly beautiful landscape of forests, lakes and mountains, ancient cities, and a fair sprinkling of riding centers as I discovered during a visit in 1994. Expect to speak German when making inquiries. Locating local riding centers in this region requires patience, as East Germany is still relatively unknown to tourists—even among tourist offices, used to selling the West. This is where specialist firms prove so useful. Utterly different, but very much an equine holiday, is a horse-drawn coaching holiday in Bavaria, a fairytale trip, as your smart yellow and black coach—once a private French omnibus—trundles along the route taken by the famous King Ludwig, ending up at Neuschwanstein Castle, a turreted knight's castle of Disneyland proportions. I took this two-in-hand carriage trip in 1993 and found it to be far better than anything fiction could conjure up.

I also recall a unique cycling *cum* horse riding holiday in Holland, based at Dwingeloo in Drenthe which, together with Groningen and Friesland, make up the so-called Top of Holland. Forget canals and windmills, this is a sylvan setting dotted with pristine villages where shaggy coated sheep, peculiar to the region, are rounded-up by shepherds on one of the largest wet heathlands in the whole of Europe. With 700 miles of cycleways, along with an envious amount of equally scenic bridle paths, this ride illustrates how good horseback riding can crop up in the most unexpected places. The fact that you can easily switch to a cycle—something many of you may not have done for years - only adds to the interest. The region is also home to some superb gardens, created by artists from Amsterdam. Nor does this preclude riding in more obvious locations. There are beach rides between The Hague and the Hook of Holland, and in Gelderland (scene of allied landings during World War II). The De Hoe Veluwe National Park, with its vast acreage of woodland, heath, sand dunes and fens, is considered as being among the best riding country in Europe.

With some of Europe's sandiest beaches as well as the Ardennes offering some of the best in bucolic and culinary delights, there is certainly scope for riding in Belgium—often taken up by the Belgians or their continental neighbours. But it is to the Ardennes that you must turn for the greatest concentration of equine opportunities. Made up of parts of the provinces of Liege, Luxembourg and Namur, the Ardennes is a wild country of forest and heath, steep valleys and marshy plateaux. Better still, there are clearly defined trails in the Luxembourg province which offers made to measure guided tours as well as long trails. Considerable efforts have been made to create tracks which allow horseback riders, hikers, and cyclists to enjoy a richly rural area, with superb restaurants, hotels and guest houses, some with their own riding stables. One person who sampled the riding at Haras du Poteau equestrian center at Odeigne, half way between Vielsalm and La Roche-en-Ardenne, tells of hearty family cooking and 5 hour forest rides. Delve a bit deeper and you will be surprised at what you find. This certainly applies to Belgium's next door neighbour, Luxembourg, where longer rides include the Tour de Luxembourg, the Upper Sure Lakes Tour, the Seven Castles Tour, and the Luxembourg Little Switzerland Tour. There is also a ride through the Eifel and Ardennes. It was once said that for its size, little Luxembourg has more horses *per capita* than anywhere else in Europe. Suffice it to say there are around 20 centers, including those around Luxembourg city and other popular tourist spots.

HUNGARY

by John Ruler

ORSEBACK RIDING IN HUNGARY FLOURISHED under Communism, with a specialist section of Ibusz, the state travel organization, producing a comprehensive programme on which a number of holiday agencies happily relied. This network has largely collapsed since the advent of the free market, with promotion being centered more on the money-generating attractions of Budapest and other such crowd-pullers. There is hope, however, of renewed interest being shown, especially in the American market. Such attention is welcome in a country whose historic links with horses go back many years. Hungary is not a country for beginners, as riders are expected to cope with anything from a walk to a gallop through vast tracts of land with no fences or even hedges. Mile long gallops or canters (lopes) are frequent, often along the edge of huge maize fields or across farm land belonging to giant estates. There is riding also in forests, hills, by lakes—and in them—as well as on the Great Hungarian Plain, although the scenery here can become somewhat tedious. Hungarian half-breds are often used. Hungarians are an old Eastern European breed, whose ancestors were bred first with Spanish and Arabian horses and now with the powerful Hanoverian and Holstein lines from German and English Thoroughbreds. The result is a type of horse that is not too large, but sturdy—ideal for cross-country work.

Of the various organized rides available in Hungary, the Tokaj-Hortobagy Ride features 6 days of riding and includes the Puszta of Hortobagy National Park with herds of horses, grey cattle and geese. You might also get a chance to meet the *csikos*, herdsmen with daredevil riding skills. The steppes provide perfect galloping country, so you need to be experienced. The Tokaj, in turn, takes in vineyards famous for their wine. The Matra Danube Ride is the more scenic. This ride first takes you to the former royal hunting grounds, before crossing the Danube by ferry (with the horses) at Visegrad. You then ride in the Matra mountains, alongside lakes, and across meadows speckled with huge sunflowers. The Rakoczy Mountains are situated in a little-known region of dense forests and rugged mountains in the Tokaj wine country. Accommodation is provided in hunting lodges or small hotels, which serve spicy Magyar-style food.

Stick to these and you have a good sampling of Hungarian riding opportunities, travelling in groups of 5 to10, spending 4 to 6 hours in the saddle daily. Other options are available, some based on the various studs dotted round the country. Carriage driving, a great Hungarian tradition, is also possible, with courses available at centers such as Szilvasvarad, with its Lippizzaner stud. It should be stressed that German is the second language in Hungary, and it is wise to inquire whether tuition is available in English before booking.

ICELAND
A PERSONAL VIEW

by John Ruler

P AUL, OUR GROUP LEADER, called it his "piece of paradise." I didn't argue when, aftera tough 3 hour haul through a black Icelandic lava desert, we'd arrived in a valley so vividly green we rubbed out eyes, reddened and rimmed with volcanic ash, in sheer disbelief. Everything in this land of geysers, glaciers, waterfalls and muttering mud pots has an almost extraterrestrial quality to it. Whether you take a 5 to 6 hour ride close to the capital city of Reykjavik, or the longer 8 to 9 hour ride, which includes a coach trip to Gullfoss (Golden Falls), or tackle the 8 to 18 day highland ride, you will meet the "mean machine" that makes it all possible: the incredible Icelandic horse. This gutsy little creature, dating back to Viking times, reaches little more than 13 hands high, yet can easily carry a man of up to 20 stones (280 lbs.). Not content with that, it has 5 gaits: the familiar walk, trot, canter (lope), pace and the tolt. The tolt is basically a running walk which, once mastered, provides a perfect ride, even if your classical English seat goes to pot as you sit back much more than usual with your legs deliberately sticking forward. The footfalls are back left, front left, back right, front right. It is said that you can drink a glass of champagne at the tolt without spilling any. There is also a pace in which the horse moves 2 feet simultaneously. This gait is used for short stretches at high speed in racing. Forget the latter and just gawk politely when the experts do it. Concentrate instead on the tolt, winning congratulations all around when it is accomplished, but suspecting your equine companion has provided a helping hand, or rather, hoof. Thanks to Elli, in particular, for showing how comfortable it is to cover a daily distance of between 30 t0 40 kms. (18 to 25 miles) during the 9 day/8 night Myvatn ride, which traces a triangular route in the remote north, roughly bounded by the fishing port of Husavikand Lake Myvatn.

We were 20 riders in all, with a herd of 40 Icelandic horses (NOT ponies please, despite their small stature) so that our mounts could be rotated every few hours. The summer rides help prepare the horses for the sheep round-up in the fall—tough work in harsh weather, but an activity in which a growing number of foreign tourists now take part. Ours, in comparison, was a tamer ride, although we did cover about 200 miles. We were usually blessed with fine weather. The heavy-duty orange waterproofs carried in our saddlebags remained dry and folded. We swapped and tacked up fresh horses every few hours, releasing what felt like an old friend back into the herd before taking on a new companion, each with a character of its own. Tvistur, who calmly bore me across the fast-flowing Laxa River and through pine forest, with the sun glinting off the bark of the silver birches, became a strutting whirlwind on the grit road. My tolt quickly became a tilt, and I was provided with more of a plodder for the long ride across a lunar landscape in which each lump of lava seemed to be harbouring a lurking troll. Changing horses is part of the fun, with 15 basic colours and colour combinations from which to choose. Tivistur was neither bay nor chest-nut, but then neither was he dun. Some are similar to the creamy dun of a Norwegian fjord, others truly black and white. You quickly get to know their names, as you do the names of fellow guests. You are, after all, alone in a landscape that swiftly changes from being gen-tly alpine to decidedly desert. Small pink and while flowers punctuate the black, atmos-pheric land surrounding Hverfjall, a blackened volcanic crater left by an eruption 2500 years ago, which provides a jaw-dropping diversion.

At Asbyrgi, an ancient hoof-shaped bite in the earth that has left a canyon 200 feet high. According to Viking legend, the hoof of a warrior's horse made it. I would believe anything of an island that can spew out so many geological goodies. The Myvatn Ride illus-trates many of them; others add new dimensions. One 12 day/11 night tour (for experi-enced riders only) follows the ancient trail Sprengisandur, travelling some 350 kms. (220 miles) north to south. Another entitled Northern Exposure, includes riding along North Atlantic beaches before turning inland towards a region of lakes. In the east, riders meet herds of reindeer, while the Golden Circle tour (8 days/7 nights) is geared towards the less experienced rider and includes a number of popular sights, such as Gullfoss and Geysir. This tour is also more suited to families, as is a newly introduced farm-based holiday, which is less than a 2 hour drive from Reykjavik. Two farms are used, each with hot pools heated by geothermal waters. Take Note: Accommodations on the Highland rides range from schoolhouses to converted farms and mountain huts. Sleeping bags and mattresses are supplied, but expect to sleep on the floor. Hot dishes served in the evening, are fresh-ly prepared by a back-up team and are wholesome and plentiful, usually including fish or meat. Ask first if you have dietary requirements. Riders personally prepare lunchtime sandwiches from the buffet breakfast. Bring your own duty-free beer and spirits, since none are available for purchase *en route.* Wear rubber boots, preferably of the green Hunter or Wellington type, because of the river crossings, and take plenty of warm clothes and casu-al gear for the evening. Don't forget to carry film, as Icelandic prices are high. For reasons of hygiene, all boots, saddlebags, etc., must be disinfected before being brought into Iceland. A veterinarian will do this and issue a certificate, which you may be asked to pre-sent on arrival. Rides are held from late June through early September, depending on loca-tion. Allow for a mixture of weather, though it will never be that hot.

ITALY
by John Ruler

While riding is undoubtedly available elsewhere in Italy, equestrian eyes focus largely on Tuscany and Umbria, regions rich in Italian tradition. Steep mountain ranges give way to soft hills lined with vineyards and dotted with olive groves and open fields glowing with sunflowers and bright red poppies. Go in the late spring, and you will find Tuscany ablaze with ginestra (genista to the horticulturally-minded), whose petals gently part as you press your way on horseback through avenues of yellow blossom. Less familiar are miniature gladioli and cyclamen. All this, plus pine-covered hills and slopes shaped like giant scallop shells, help to make it ideal riding country. There are always chances for some fast canters (lopes) along dusty tracks or through flower-strewn meadows. It has been some years since I stayed at the Rifugio Prategiano in Montieri, southwest of Sienna in the Alta Maremma region, but I still retain fond memories of the locally bred Maremma horses—fit, agile and ideal for covering up to 40 kms. (25 miles) daily. Watch out for the strange grey cattle which are rounded up by Clint Eastwood-style cowboys, the *butteri*. This Michelin Guide listed, stone-built hotel, rustic in style, with a restaurant serving Tuscan specialities, provides a comfortable base for a series of options, including 2 exploratory rides, in which you return to the Rifugio daily by minibus while the horses stay put. One ride stays inland, with a visit to the ruins of the San Galgano monastery in the higher part of the Maremma hills. Another takes riders to the coast for long gallops along the sand and the chance to swim with the horses in the sea. A center-based programme offers 4 to 7 hours riding daily, with lengthy picnic lunches in the sun.

Similarly, there is a farm-based ride near the ancient town of Tuscania, less than a 2 hour drive north of Rome, steeped in Etruscan history. Again, fine Tuscan fare is on the evening menu, which features dishes often prepared with olive oil from the farm. Other options in the region, include a ride based at the Antico Casale di Scansano, a 100 year old estate farmhouse, completely restored as a 4 star property. Non-riders are always welcome, but a self-drive car in which to explore the surrounding countryside is recommended. The Chianti Ride, covering the famous wine growing region between Florence and Sienna, with overnight stops at farms, inns and small hotels, is offered by English-born, Jenny Bawtree, who has had many years of equestrian experience. A couple of nights are spent at her home in Rendola. One British company also features spring and grape harvest rides from a base only 15 minutes from Sienna which, in August, plays host to the famous Palio horse race in its main square. May and September are ideal months for Tuscany. There is also Western-style riding on offer from Vallebona, with riding groups restricted to around 6, sometimes even smaller. Umbria, wedged between Latium, Abruzzi and Tuscany, features the hilltop city of Perugia and Assisi, the birthplace of Saint Francis. The Malvarinna Trail Ride in Umbria offers comfortable accommodations, good riding, and superior food.

Riding is by no means confined to Tuscany and Umbria. Look out for centers recognized by ANTE (*Associazione Nazionale per il Turismo Equestre*). Many are essentially riding clubs, since horseback riding is, to a large extent, the province of wealthier Italian professional men and women and is not really promoted as a tourist attraction in the same way, for instance, as skiing. This applies to some extent in other Mediterranean countries as well, and it is often left to overseas companies to realize the potential. This is not a criticism, but a fact, and few tourist offices can be expected to provide detailed equestrian information, other than perhaps at a local level. This leaves holiday riders to fend for themselves, often discovering some excellent riding along the way. If your Italian is good, so much the better. Most clubs welcome experienced riders, and often arrange weekend rides or even longer treks that you could join. You can also look for more general weekend equestrian packages or hacking in the Veneto and Venice region, also the Campania and Naples regions, with Calabria providing an almost Alpine flavour. Other places to ride include Piemonte (Aosta Valley), Lombardy (Lakes Garda, Como and Maggiore), Abruzzo, and Rome (with longer summer treks in the national park). The Italian islands of Sicily and Sardinia also a have a scattering of riding, with a 5 day ride possible on the delightful island of Elba.

POLAND

by John Ruler

OLISH TOURISM, TO A LARGE EXTENT, has placed the emphasis strongly on historic centers such as Cracow, though with a nod towards outdoor activities of which horse riding is just one. While the sport enjoyed brief recognition following the collapse of Communism, under which the stud farms had flourished, it is now generally available only if you ask and is not usually mentioned in the main vacation brochures. A pity because, as I found back in 1991, the potential is certainly there. With a heritage of horse breeding stretching back to the famous 17th century Polish cavalry, it is hardly surprising that equestrian standards at the studs were high. Of those I saw, the stud at Sierakow, some 45 miles (72 kms.) from Poznan, provided basic, but comfortable, accommodation. Overnight trails, generally using Wielkopolska (Great Poland) horses, take you through a gentle landscape of woods, lakes and fields. There is little or no road work, and the ubiquitous horse-drawn carriages transport the luggage (as well as any non-riders), following an intricate network of rural tracks.

I also visited the Racot Stud, some 30 miles (48 kms.) south of Poznan, former residence of a Polish prince, interesting for its neo-classical façade, but lacking in scenic interest. The highest praise is reserved for the privately-run Hotel Osiniec, the name of a hamlet close to the pleasant old town of Gniezno, which is itself about 30 miles from Poznan. With guests restricted to 14, a lively bar, BBQs, and traditional Polish fare, there is a family feel to the place which is what riders want when traveling in an out of the ordinary place such as Poland. Other centers include Lack, around 7 miles (12 kms.) east of Plock, 62 miles (100 kms.) northwest of Warsaw, Iwno, close to Poznan, with an excellent stud of full blooded horses, and at Kadyny, a hotel complex and the former residence of Prince Wilhelm II, located on the shore of Vistula Bay, 36 miles (75 kms.) from Gdansk in the northeast, a region with a rich horse breeding tradition.

You will also find riding elsewhere in Poland through one specialist company which features the Mazurian Lake District as the perfect riding center. Suffice it to say that the combination of studs (there are said to be 1000 nationwide), with a surfeit of unspoilt scenery, make sound equestrian sense for anyone prepared to make their own arrangements. After all, Poland has about 900,000 horses (the sixth or seventh largest equine population worldwide) from which you can choose!

PORTUGAL

by John Ruler

I T WAS ONCE KNOWN AS LUSITANIA, so it is hardly surprising that Portugal is best known in equestrian circles for its royal breed of warrior horses, the Lusitano. Not unlike the Spanish Andalucian in appearance, this flamboyant descendent of the Iberian warhorse, from 15.2 to 16 hands high, is master of the dressage ring, although not so much in the classical German style, but more a fiery version, born of the battlefield and the bull-ring. The fact that the breed performs well in the cork forests, olive trees, and coastal pastures makes the sparsely populated Alentejo region ("beyond the Tagus"), some 170 miles south of Lisbon, an obvious equestrian playground for holiday riders.

The riding options are enormous. A typical example is the colourful Blue Coast Ride during which you ride 6 to 7 hours a day in groups of up to 12. Expect brisk, long canters (lopes) along miles of sandy tracks, with the need to walk the horses on particularly steep downhill and uphill stretches. Exploring the villages and sampling local varieties of goat and sheep cheese are among the highlights which include the flowers and herbs, especially in springtime, an ideal season in any case. Overnight stops are either in the villages, or back at the base.

Other rides are equally romantic. The 8 day Dolphin Coast Ride, where riders can watch dolphins playing at the mouth of the River Sado, for instance, is somewhat similar to the Blue Coast Ride. There is also the Silver Coast Ride, which offers 8 days of riding through the wildlife refuge of Mafre, with overnights in hotels or guest houses; and an 8 day ride close to the rugged mountains of Extramedura which separate Portugal from central Spain. With its rolling hills, lakes and flower- covered meadows, this is perfect riding country. Indeed, as is the entire region. Overnights are spent in small hotels, some rooms furnished with antiques. Alternatively, you can ride for 3 hours daily either with a group or take an individual lesson for part of the time. Impeccably trained Lusitanos will help the less experienced rider come to grips with the piaffe and passage, shoulders-in, and extensions of dressage. This still allows time to try other activities, such as walking, canoeing, carriage driving, or visiting the Portuguese Royal Stud.

If you wish to totally immerse yourself in dressage, riding courses are available, among others, at the Quinta da Fonte Santa Equestrian Centre, located in Canecas, some 10 kms. (4 miles) north of Lisbon. The Director is Francisco Bessa de Carvalho, a senior rider with the Portuguese School of Equestrian Art. Courses are geared to riders looking to maximize learning in a limited period of time. Two lessons are given daily over a period of 4 to 5 days. A 7 day program includes 12 private riding lessons and 7 nights accommodation at the riding center. "The soft, round backs of the Lusitanos and their docile temperament are ideally suited to this work... and to all riders—from novice to advanced," wrote one pupil. Certainly the holiday rider can expect to find the principles of classical equitation, epitomized by the proud style of the legendary "Master"—the late Nuno Oliveira, to be preserved and patiently practiced in the Portuguese countryside. Look out, too, for the Alter-Real horses, bred from Andalucians and originating at Vila de Portel Sud in the Alentejo province, which imported around 300 mares from the Jerez district of Spain during the mid-18th century. They remained much in demand as *haute école* horses until the Napoleonic invasion of 1821, but in subsequent years they were crossed with a motley collection of breeds. Nevertheless, the Alter Real survived, and now this compact breed has become a good saddle horse which, like the Lusitano, lends itself to pleasure riding.

You may well find some riding centers along the southern Algarve coast, an off-season hideaway for many Brits, where Bermuda buttercups bloom in the winter fields and, in spring, crocuses, grape hyacinths, iris, and narcissi can be seen. Wild herbs and rock plants add spice to the cliff tops. Pinetrees Riding Centre, run by British Horse Society instructor Beverley Gibbons, is the first center approved in Portugal by the Association of British Riding Schools and features both lessons and hacking mainly on pure or part-bred Lusitanos. The Centre is located at the Cas dos Pinheiros, half way between the exclusive resorts of Quinta do Lago and Vale do Lobo. The nearest town is Almancil, less than 2 miles away, and Faro airport is just 20 minutes by car. This is ideal for those seeking a sunshine holiday with perhaps golf or other sports, but with the chance to enjoy some decent riding as a bonus. Two hour hacks for the fit and competent—with picnic rides of 3 to 4 hours in the cooler weather—are available, with 1 hour rides for those able to manage a rising trot. Beverley is able to offer accommodation in her villa, which sleeps 9, adjacent to the Centre. Riding clubs, riding schools, and Riding for the Disabled groups (which Beverley and other foreign nationals strongly support at a local level) are especially welcome. The Centre also appeals to single travelers on their own who would like to meet others. The riding is through pine woods, alongside the area's famous golf courses, and lakes. Look out for sheep in the Ludo Valley, with its orange and avocado orchards, also the Sao Lourenco Church. Sand tracks lead to a long sandy beach. Most routes are within the Ria Formosa Nature Reserve, which is rich in birdlife, butterflies, and wild flowers. Another center well worth considering is the Quinta do Paraiso Alto, Bensafrim, Lago, run by Jinny Harman and the second riding center in Portugal to achieve ABRS status. The stables are set among wide-open scenery for riding into the hills and towards the west coast.

THE RUSSIAN HORSE TRADITION

by Anne Mariage

THE COSSACK IS THE MOST POPULAR horse-related figure in the Russian imagination. The Cossacks tended to live in remote areas, away from the control of authority, and were often regarded as outlaws. Cossack society was led by Ataman, an elected chief on whom all members of the community relied throughout their lives. Today, the Cossacks inhabit the vast, southern Eurasian territory of the former Soviet Union. Their ethnic origins are not only Russian but also Ukrainian, Kirghize, and Kazakh, from whence the term, "Kossack" originates. Historically, their communities were comprised mostly of peasants who were trained for war in order to protect themselves from bandits and rival communities. They were also very experienced horsemen.

The Cossacks developed what has proved to be the most efficient tactical use of horses: guerrilla warfare. This tactic was used to defeat Napoleon's troops when they invaded Russia in the early 19th century. The Cossacks' use of horses, however, was more the result of psychological orientation than military need. By dint of repeated harassment by light, mobile cavalry troops, the French troops were demoralized, unable to use their heavy cavalry and cuirassiers to keep the Cossacks at bay.

The tactics of Genghis Khan and the Hungarian Hussars were influenced by the Cossacks' mastery of horses in battle. All 3 cultures were characterized by their devotion to horses as the key to survival. A display of impressive horsemanship used to intimidate and demoralize their enemies, led to the development of the Djiguitovka, a warlike exhibition where the Cossacks demonstrate their skill at trick riding. Unlike the use of the circular arenas in the West, the Cossacks rode in straight lines and projected a masculine, military image in their native dress and long mustaches.

Under Tsarist rule, the Cossacks eventually were integrated into the Russian Imperial Army. The Tsars used them for special missions and to patrol the Russian Empire's vast borders. Their integration into the Russian military created a demand for more horses and new breeds were developed. One of these breeds was the Donski horse, bred at Rostov on the river Don, which were used widely in Russia and the Ukraine. Another breed was the Orlov, named for Count Orlov, one of Catherine the Great's many lovers. The Orlov was known for its speed as a trotter, with long strides to pull the *troika*. Crossbreds also developed, such as the Orlov-Rostopchine, a light harness and riding horse, depicted in many 19th century paintings. Their elegance appealed to the Russian aristocracy. Another crossbred, the Terski, combined Russian and full-bred Arab bloodlines and originated in the Northern Caucasus. Among the heavier breeds of Russian horses were the Vladmir, Gashkir, Kabardin, and Tcherkess. The Akhal Teke, bred in Turkmenistan, were legendary for their speed, brilliance, vigor and stamina.

In Russia, the *troika* has been used to impress and dazzle people since the 17th century, much in the same way as the Cossacks used horses in the Djiguitovka. With a *troika*, 3 horses are harnessed abreast. The horse in the middle maintains a fast trot, while the horse on the left canters on its right front foot with the neck and withers turned left, and the horse on the right canters on the left front foot with the neck and withers turned to the right. Small bells are attached to the harness to enhance the effect.

Today, Russia faces serious economic problems. Shortages in fuel and spare parts have led to the reappearance of horses as work animals on Russian farms, where they graze on large tracts of undeveloped land. The Russians' dependence on and esteem for horses continues today. Near St. Petersburg stands the world's only cemetery for horses, and every year Russians celebrate the "Day of the Horse."

About Anne Mariage and Cheval d'Aventure

Anne Mariage is the owner and operator of Cheval d'Aventure. Anne's overwhelming love affair with horses, and her equally well developed desire for adventure, has led to the creation of a small, friendly group of riders who repeatedly return for still another adventure. With 27 years of experience under her belt, Anne is a font of hard-earned knowledge. She is fluent in French and speaks and writes English quite well. Anne is a delightful person and it has been a pleasure to work with her. Four of the rides sponsored by Cheval d'Aventure are featured in this book.

SCANDINAVIA
DENMARK, SWEDEN, NORWAY AND FINLAND
by John Ruler

Space, solitude, and scenery, these 3 attributes, to a large extent, sum up what to expect from all 4 sparsely populated Scandinavian countries, whose attraction lies in providing a reliable range of outdoor activities, of which walking, white-water river rafting and cycling tend to take priority. Horseback riding, however, still plays a prominent role, with the native breeds providing some of the finest horseback riding I have encountered. Tack is generally of a high standard with comfortable saddles for long distances. Okay, so the sun shines less strongly than in the south, but the long days of June, July and August can be comfortably warm (although, in some regions, you will want to watch out for the inevitable mosquitoes). You won't be involved in much road work, but will basically be exploring a surprisingly varied landscape with any overnight stops generally at local inns or guest houses, or in well equipped log cabins. The food is easy on sensitive stomachs, with daily picnic lunches prepared by guests themselves from a comprehensive buffet-style breakfast table. Expect the going to be rugged, be ready for rain, and keep warm. The reward, especially during the long summer days, are well worth while. It is easy to see Scandinavia as a land of forests, lakes or fjords and, to some extent, this is true. But each country offers something distinctive for the rider. Inclusive riding holidays, however, are few and far between, in line with the more individual, tailor-made approach to Nordic tourism generally. While a high standard of living results in high out-of-pocket costs, prices are far lower than they were a decade ago.

DENMARK

You will need to do a bit of delving, but the Danes, a gracious and friendly people who speak English well (with German close behind), will happily help you to discover riding stables at a local level. Many centers are more like clubs, with decently sized indoor schools and a clubhouse, complete with cozy bar and restaurant. The terrain is far from flat and featureless, but a pleasing blend of fields, woods, lakes, streams and rivers. Farmhouse vacations make sense for the family, and the use of a horse or pony is often possible. Much of the vacation riding lies in western Jutland on the North Sea coast, with an abundance of beaches, often using Icelandic horses (not ponies please, despite their size) and also the Jutland horse which, in the Middle Ages, bore armored knights into battle. Many centers are geared towards families, and horse riding camps are popular throughout Denmark. Look out for driving offers—the Danes are naturals when it comes to carriage work.

SWEDEN

Largest in land size of the 4 Nordic countries, Sweden has begun to expand the scope of its equestrian holidays to include mountain riding and forest safaris, pony treks, and wagon and sledge tours in Swedish Lapland. You can even join a cattle drive! Typical of those outfitters trying to make their mark is the Blekinge Riding Trail in the southeast, bordering on the Baltic Sea, where you hire a horse and ride individually, following a trail some 200 kms. (124 miles), with meals and overnight accommodation arranged at farms along the way. A map and route description are provided, each stage being between 20 to 30 kms. (12 to 18 miles). You can book a minimum of 2, and up to a maximum of 8 days, leaving time for a day of rest or other activities. Many riders, however, are rightly wary of riding alone, so it is wise to enlist a companion for what seems a tempting offer. Alternatively, Smaland, also in the southeast, has a 5 day forest safari in which a small group of riders spend 5 hours daily exploring a region of old villages with red cottages, farms, and small lakes. Evenings are spent Western style around a fire, with overnights spent in Lappish tents. Guided treks on Icelandic horses for 1 or more days are based in conservation areas around Varberg on the west coast.

NORWAY

Faced with a landscape of fjords, forests, and mountains, riders are somewhat restricted by the terrain in Norway—at least with respect to speed—but possibilities do exist, if only on a small scale and local level. Between Oslo and Bergen, not only do you find some of the finest scenery, but 8 day riding tours are featured around Alvdal, home to moose and brown bear. You ride the delightful Norwegian mountain horses through dense forests, over moss-covered plains, and through rocky highlands. Enter the Rondane National Park and you are in reindeer country, where eagles and falcons fly. Meals are taken in the open accommodation is of the basic mountain hut variety or in teepee style tents, where you sleep on reindeer skins.

Among other riding centers, are those at Sandelfjord on Oslo fjord. Latvik in the same locality offers rides across Hardangervidda based on Rjuka in the Telemark region. You can also enjoy some cantering at Geilo, Ardalstangen, Vradal and Morgedal. There is even said to be riding in the far north close to the Russian border.

FINLAND

It was less than a decade ago that the Equestrian Federation of Finland told me that, "despite the beautiful scenery and the scarce population which would make the country ideal for riding holidays, we don't have much to offer visitors..." Fortunately, I knew better. Although some riding centers sometimes have difficulty in finding a horse for the casual caller, most major resorts can come up with the equestrian goodies, if only for an hour's hack in this land of forests and some 60,000 shimmering lakes. Riding lessons, hack, and treks are also available from centers in and around the capital city of Helsinki.

In the tourist regions of Finnish Lapland, riding is more on a level with other outdoor sports. One British company (In the Saddle) features the Oulanka Trail in southern Lapland. Located just south of the Arctic Circle, near Kusamo, next to the Russian border, the ride follows the famous Bear's Ring Trail, a route well-known to walkers. The horses are Finnish, a medium size breed, nimble-footed, and with great staying power. This is a remote region where small groups of no more than 6 riders willing to forego luxury can experience some of Europe's last wilderness. Meals are provided at the end of the daily 25 to 30 kms. (15 to 18 miles) ride, with accommodation in heated tents, mountain cabins, or traditional Finnish lavu (sort of a lean-to). Meals are prepared on site, and there will be the occasional opportunity to ease aching limbs in a sauna.

There are a series of summer and winter treks using the sure-footed Icelandic horses, with their unique tolt, a 4 beat pace with equal intervals between the foot falls (see Iceland for more detail). One of them, the Wilderness Trek in Ruunaa, runs from May to September and takes place in the ancient forests in Finnish Kareilia. Another, in Rautalampi, central Finland, some 80 kms. (49 miles) from Jyvaskyla, takes in the lakeland, with wilderness paths, farms, and the opportunity to try rowing or sample a genuine smoke sauna along the way. This trek is run by a company specializing in social interaction and teamwork training, and offers other outdoor pursuits as well as riding. The final choice is a winter trek in Lapland. This ride is based in Kittila, in the far north, where temperatures can drop to −20° Centigrade (that's "cold" in Fahrenheit). Nights are spent in a cozy wilderness cabin. You might glimpse an Arctic eagle, or a herd of Santa's reindeer... These rides are all utterly different, so select with care. Go during the summer solstice and you could ride all night long.

SLOVENIA
by John Ruler

S LOVENIA HAS A CHEQUERED HISTORY in which the stud has come under military attack. During World War II, it was liberated by General Patton and, more recently, was in danger from the Yugoslav Upheavals. Nevertheless, the famous Lipica stud is still flourishing in Slovenia, a peaceful country which has more in common with alpine Austria and Italy than with the old Yugoslavia of which it was once a part. There are now around 200 horses at Lipica. These include some 25 breeding stallions helping to secure the lineage of the Lipizzaner horses, dating way back to the 18th century. In fact, the original stud was founded even earlier by Austrian Archduke Charles in 1580. Even better, instruction, hacking and carriage lessons are available, using these legendary white (and we do mean white, not grey) horses, booking individually and staying at the Hotel Klub. Another attractive alternative is a stay at the nearby self-catering Diomed farm, which has a license to breed Lipizzaners. At yet another farm house, Medljan Primorska, a mile or so from the coast, there is a riding school which uses Lipizzaners. There have also been satisfactory reports of the equestrian center at Struga, located in the renovated stables of a medieval castle, where race horses, saddle horses, and Thoroughbreds are used. The Ranch Kaja and Grom, closer to the capital of Ljubljana, is geared towards youngsters, demonstrating that the scope of riding activities available on "the sunny side of the Alps" is considerable.

S P A I N

by John Ruler

I N THE EARLY SEVENTIES, it was virtually left to one English couple to pioneer riding holidays in Spain's Sierra Nevada. Using maps borrowed from the military, which was obliged by law to ride the routes to keep them open, they enlisted the help of local *posadas* (country inns) in remote mountain villages to provide overnight stops for horses and riders alike. By the mid 1970s, Aventura were running 15 day rides which took you from their base at Orgiva, across the snowline at Trevelez, and back via towns such as La Calohorra, which boasts a splendid renaissance castle.

Other companies have now taken their place. The *posadas* have running water and showers, where once you used a pitcher and basin. The straw mattresses and the huge iron bedsteads are probably long since gone as well. What has not altered is the ability of Spain to attract holiday riders, not so much on the coast where stables tend to cater for the tourist trade, but further inland where the scenery is matched by a pace of life that has changed little and where the sound of clattering hooves is music to the Spanish ear. Ride into a village, tether up the horses and join the locals in a bar for a drink and *tapas.* It is a scene which is repeated throughout Andalucia—the main holiday riding region. The popularity of this area is due in no small measure to the use of Andalucian horses, a medium sized breed whose ability to pick their way piaffe fashion through the most demanding terrain is amazing. They may display a certain degree of arrogance, yet are willing to please. All of which is very much in keeping with the spirit of this most southerly slice of Spain, where horses, bulls and sherry barons bring a storybook ambiance to your stay.

Ride an Andalucian horse as I did in 1998, neck reining and using the Vaquero saddle (similar to and just as comfortable for sitting long hours as its Western counterpart), and the image is complete. A wonderfully thick sheepskin seat and large metal stirrups which envelope your feet, are bonuses. So too, is the carpet the olive and sweet chestnut groves of the Finca el Moro in a paintbox of blue, yellow, orange and white. You will also find bright splashes of colour in the surrounding villages—the blue tiled spire of the church at Los Marines, the terra cotta rooftops at Valdelarco, and the fiery flautists and drummers practicing for the fiesta in the Moorish town of Almonaster La Real, where even the sound of firecrackers failed to startle the horses. Catering for a maximum of 6 competent riders, Finca el Moro is a 70 acre working farm in the Aracena National Park, in northern Andalucia, run by an English couple, Nick and Hermione Tudor, that epitomizes the considerable efforts being made to attract overseas riders. The fact that gourmet style dinners reflect local dishes is an added attraction. Accommodations are provided in tastefully restored 2 bedroom farm cottages with *en suite* facilities, shared lounge and kitchen and a sun terrace. Finca el Moro also organizes walking holidays, which are ideal for non-riding companions.

Beach rides on a curving swathe of firm, fresh sand provide a 3 mile gallop along the little known Costa de la Luz, and form part of the mixed bag of programmes at the Finca Los Romeros, near Barbate, overlooking Cape Trafalgar. Still in Andalucia, although far to the south on the Atlantic Coast, a 1½ hour car drive from Gibraltar. April proved to be an ideal time for a week of flexible local riding based around the Finca, with daily sorties of 4 to 5 hours allowing for some challenging rides, largely free of road work. We rode along the sandy tracks of the surrounding pine forests, enjoyed a cliff top ride towards Vejer de la Frontera, a fabled hilltop town of Moorish origins, and got the adrenaline flowing on a beach ride. It is a happy blend, with the chance to rest weary legs at the Finca's tiny bar or flop out in your white washed villa accommodation. There is also the culinary skill of Enrique, the chef, to look forward to. Alternatively, there is a 125 km. (77 mile) circular route, with the horses staying overnight at local farms and riders returning to the Finca daily by mini-bus. The longest section is a 7 hour ride over the plains and the spectacular Sierra de la Plata. The average riding on other days is around 4 hours. Both holidays include a visit to the sherry center of Jerez de la Fontera for a stunning performance at The Royal Andalucian School of Equestrian Art. This show lavishly illustrates the artistic skills of the Andalucian breed whose nobility and grace stems from sturdy Arab stock.

The Trafalgar Trail Ride, based at Bolonia (a 2 hour drive from Malaga airport), covers similar ground, with overnight stops in Vejer and the coastal village of Zahara de los Atunes. This is complemented by an Atlantic Ride, with a chance to swim, by yourself and with the horses. Another ride provides the opportunity to join the pilgrims on the route to El Rocio across the unique Cota Donana, with a host of Spanish riders, the girls wearing bright flamenco dresses, and covered wagons festooned with banners and flowers, on their way to pay homage to the Virgin of Rocio, also known as the Blanca Paloma (White Dove). There is music, singing and dancing along the way. Non-riding friends can join on foot or by wagon. Similar celebrations happen at the annual horse fair in Jerez de la Frontera, where you can combine a visit with riding. Yet another combination is a stay at the Cortijo el Morrito, just 30 kms. (18 miles) from Seville, a family estate set in rolling countryside, which offers riding lessons with tuition in English, or hacking among olive and cork trees. Ideal, too, for non-riding partners.

If the Sierra Nevada (Snowy Mountains) appeals (I have fond memories of forests of mountain oak and wild alpine flowers), Dallas Love has been operating in the Alpujarras region for over 10 years above the village of Bubion, as has Rafael Belmonte of Cabalgar Rutas Alternativas, who has been delivering quality rides for 17 years. Although I have not ridden with Dallas, the rides come recommended by the likes of *Horse & Hound* magazine. The route follows ancient bridle paths and drovers routes dating back to the Moorish occupation. The pace may often be slow, but there are opportunities for canters (lopes). You get spectacular views in a region where mules outnumber cars, freshly cooked local fare is served in village restaurants, the sweet smell of herbs fills the air, and you get the chance to pick pomegranates. Naturally, the horses are Andalucian, using military style saddles. In the Spring of 1998, Dallas organized rides in the Sierra Morena, which extends through the provinces of Seville, Cordoba and Jaen, and is home to private estates breeding bulls and horses.

A 9 day/8 night ride to Ronda starts with an overnight stop at the Hurricane Hotel in Tarifa, where riders (around 6 to 10 in number) are matched to horses before departing for calls at a string of remote villages. Overnights are spent at such delightful old towns as Jimena de la Frontera, Gaucin (staying at a country house run by an English lady), Cortes de la Frontera, and, finally, Ronda, which is dramatically situated above the narrow gorge of Gaudalevin and reeks with regional atmosphere. The pace varies from walking along mountainous tracks (once used by bandits) to long canters (lopes) along forest tracks. Spring and fall are the best times to visit Andalucia, i.e. from March to May and September to October. The days are warm to hot and generally dry.

Equestrian holidays can be found elsewhere in Spain as well. In Catalonia, 50 kms. (31 miles) south of Tarragona, lies the Finca Jacaranda in the Burga Valley. The horses have mostly been brought over from Scotland, although there are some Andalucians too. English tack is used and English spoken. After the initial selection of horses, a programme is arranged with the guests. Accommodation is at a local guest house serving traditional Catalonian cuisine. Elsewhere in Catalonia, the 9 day Gran Penedes ride is literally only 3 miles from the popular Costa Brava. This ride follows old Roman roads with overnights in cozy estates, sometimes dating back to the 15th century, guest houses and castles. Close to the French border, in the Catalan Pyrenees, Spanish Arab and Barb crossbreds are used at the 15th century farmhouse of Can Jou. Your hosts for the ride, which includes 7 nights and 6 days of riding to the Mediterranean coast at Roses, are Englishman Michael Peters and his family. Just west of the main Pyrennean chain, the Sierra de Guara features riding across some pretty wild country, staying in simple farmhouses and country hotels. The days are quite long, demanding good riding skills and fitness from groups of around 8.

In Extremadura, the transhumance, i.e. the movement of livestock to mountain pastures, dates back to Roman times. Nowadays, you can join the *vaqueros* for part of the cattle drive. Other 8 day rides are based in the Gredos National Park and the Monfrague National Park, located in the northern part of Extremadura, which between them occupy most of south central Spain. There are 2 other unusual rides. First, is the Road to Santiago de Compostela, following in the footsteps of the pilgrims who have made this journey one of the most famous pilgrimages in the western world. This ride crosses the region of Galicia in northwestern Spain, which is utterly different from the south, with woods of oaks, yews, beeches and hazel. Stops include a night in the cells of an old Benedictine abbey. Similarly, in Majorca you leave the tourist resorts of this most popular of the Balearic islands, for a unique 8 day ride, staying overnight in some of the island's monasteries. The ride is based at the Finca Son Menut in the southeast, only 20 minutes from Cala Mondrago. You can also stay there for a holiday of lessons and hacks. Many years ago, while staying at the monasteries, I reflected on how much better it would be if you could visit on horseback rather than by car. It is a measure of the degree to which the island, and mainland Spain generally, have taken up the challenge that my dream has come true.

SWITZERLAND

by John Ruler

I F NOTHING ELSE, WINTER POLO ON THE FROZEN lake at St. Moritz, introduced in 1985, has drawn attention to equestrian activities in Switzerland. Polo aside, it is left to the visiting rider to make his or her own arrangements, relying largely on regional tourist offices. As with neighbouring Austria, the terrain varies considerably, particularly south of the Alps, where the weather in the Italian-speaking Ticino region becomes almost Mediterranean. Fortunately, this compact country is well geared to the independent traveler, with tourist passes giving hefty discounts on rail, boat and postal coaches. The best advice to would-be riders is to select your canton (the name for Swiss regional divisions going back to the 13th century) and then look for decent stables. In the Grisons, for instance, there is certainly riding at St. Moritz and Davos, while at Engadin, a valley of the Inn River in eastern Switzerland, there are 8 day trail rides using Freiburg horses with Western tack. Other popular spots include the hub around Lake Lucerne, near Zurich, in the Bernese Oberland, the Fribourg, Jura, and the Bernese Jura, mostly French-speaking with horse-drawn carriage tours a popular attraction. Similar carriage offers can be found in the Grisons and central Switzerland.

THE UNITED KINGDOM AND IRELAND

by John Ruler

BLESSED BY A LONG HISTORY OF HORSE BREEDING, Great Britain and Ireland have an equestrian know-how which is reflected both in their approach to riding standards and the diversity of equestrian experiences available. Better still, they have the scenery to match. Unfortunately, riding centers are often located in the major tourist areas which can attract novices and the inevitable nose-to-tail rides. Avoid these, and you have some of the finest riding country in the world. One way is to choose the less crowded "shoulder months" when the horses are more fit and eager to go. Scotland, in particular, enjoys some of the best weather in late April, May and June, also in September and even into October, which allows visitors to dodge the mid-summer mosquitoes. The same can roughly be said of Wales and the West Country counties of Devon, Cornwall, and Somerset, though both have their fair share of rain, hence the greenness. Ireland, likewise has numerous "soft" days (i.e. rainy) which is the price you pay for some superb settings. Ireland also adopts a more aggressive selling policy when it comes to equestrian tourism with appropriate literature aimed at the holiday rider. Sadly this cannot always be said for mainland Britain, although both the Welsh and Scottish trekking and riding associations do help to address the problem. So too do some individual centers, some of which appear in both UK and overseas tour companies' brochures. Otherwise it can be a bit of a hit and miss proposition.

Many centers now recognize the need to match high equestrian standards with a similar approach to accommodation—thanks, in no small measure, to a generation of grown-up riders who demand far more than the bunk beds and baked beans tolerated when they were still pony mad kids. This is reflected elsewhere in a country where riding standards have always been high, but where comfort was far too often an afterthought. Fortunately, things ain't what they used to be, and adults seeking a room with private bath and central heating will find riding centers offering a range of quality accommodation from self-catering cottages to guest houses, B&Bs, pubs, or 4 star country hotels in the locality. Some even form part of a recognized Camping and Caravan Club site. Saddling-up for a weekend away has rarely been simpler, thanks to the popularity of mini-breaks where hotels offer special off-season rates. Some even offer actual riding packages. Alternatively, you can make use of the hotel deal and arrange for riding nearby. Book early, however, as weekends are quickly booked by local riders.

All this may sound daunting, but with careful planning you can discover a real stunner of a vacation. Transfers are a consideration, especially if you are arriving from overseas. Check first with the center, as they can often arrange to collect you at the airport or railway station. If travelling with the family, look out for centers which offer alternative outdoor activities such as golf, sailing and fishing for the non-riding members of your group. This is not unlike the North American guest ranches, where riding is only one of several options, and the amount of riding is geared to the size, character and commercial interests of the property concerned. You can also take instructional holidays, blending lessons in a variety of disciplines, from dressage to show jumping, with hacking in the area. Carriage driving, even polo, and sidesaddle are also in the frame.

If riding is all that counts, select with care. Pony trekking in British Isles and Ireland is largely for novices and often frustrating for those with riding skills. But, if the idea is to explore the countryside in a leisurely and safe manner—in that it succeeds. Because your route will basically follow mountain tracks, moorland, and old drovers' roads, it is frequently impossible to do more than walk. The knack is to find a center where groups are split according to riders' abilities, with group size restricted to no more than 12, and preferably less. You will not only move a little faster, but may even get in some short, sharp lopes or canters, which are not practical for beginners. The alternative is trail riding (different in concept from the North America interpretation of "casual," rather than "indoor" riding). In Britain, this involves long distance riding for the experienced equestrian, covering around 20 to 25 miles daily at a fastish speed and at all paces. This can be daunting if you are unused to an English saddle, although comfortable cavalry style saddles are common practice. Strictly speaking, the aim is to stay somewhere different each night, but some rides involve returning to base on a daily basis. You will also have to face the vagaries of weather—which is why hot water and a hearty meal are generally part of the package, often with a choice of hotel or B&B accommodation. Many of them have licensed bars, or you can bring your own drink. You will also be expected to look after your own horse, from grooming to catching it in the overnight field—a chore most happily accept, as the horse quickly becomes a close companion. Expect to spend about 6 hours daily in the saddle, with a lunch break after the first 3 hours.

Much of what is outlined above concerns your choice of location, which is why I've left this to the last. While the rest of Europe offers some spectacular scenery, better weather, exotic wines and food, few regions can offer the same range of equestrian options and in such diverse locations. Centers vary in size and serve different needs. It is whether the riding is good and suits you that ultimately matters.

SCOTLAND

There is much more to Scotland than the Braveheart image of mountains, lochs and glens. They are there all right—in abundance, but it is more a matter of matching location to what you want from your riding holiday. To the south lie the Borders, true horse country, where once marauding bands of Scots and English clashed amidst a landscape of sweeping hills, desolate in parts, but providing fine, fast riding. Come during the summer and you will catch the pageantry of the Common Ridings and Festivals, with towns such as Peeble, Hawick and Selkirk playing host to hundreds of horsemen to mark those historic clashes. To the northeast, in the Highlands, lies the Grampian region, where the famous Highland pony—the largest and strongest of Britain's mountain and moorland breeds—is very much in evidence. This is also the location for one of Scotland's most exciting equestrian expeditions—the Ten Day Trail, which includes 8 days and 1 day of rest, from Aberdeenshire in the eastern Highlands to the Atlantic Coast close to Kyle of Lochalsh and the island of Skye, a distance of 200 miles. For textbook scenery, pure and simple, the true Highlands are north of Inverness—the region of Great Glen and Loch Ness of Nessie fame. Instruction on Highland ponies is offered at Grantown on Spey and, at Spaen Bridge, there are trail riding holidays on Icelandic horses. To the southwest, Argyllshire plays host to some real barn storming rides from the Castle Riding Center based at Brenfield, overlooking Loch Fyne.

The biggest is the Wild Boar Trail, 7 days of riding which includes long gallops across sandy beaches, discovering ancient coastal castles, and crossing the brooding moors, with their sky-blue lochs and only the cry of the curlew or lone red grouse flapping furiously, to disturb the peace. Equally, riders can sample a mini- trail ride, join a riding clinic, or enjoy a family holiday with sailing, golf, and mountain biking available close by.

WALES

The fact that one of Britain's best loved breeds, the Welsh Mountain pony, is still found living wild or semi-wild, in Wales' medley of mountains, valleys, and rivers, speaks volumes. Wales is horse country, and while there is a strong emphasis on trekking, especially in season, there is also ample scope for more serious riding. Don't knock trekking either, as already stated, it is often the best way to explore some pretty rugged country. If you want something more elaborate, then the Trans-Wales Trails based at Talgarth, Powys (in mid-Wales) offers a 6 day/7 night trail ride covering 110 miles. Other rides, less strenuous but still geared to experienced riders, feature castles and the chance to sample local ales in country inns. Close by at Llangorse, Myfanwy Mitchell springs an equestrian surprise with a small selection of Welsh Cobs or cross-bred toughies, seemingly designed to tackle the Black Mountains. Myfanwy's program includes a 50 mile circular ride for small groups of 6, staying overnight at Llanthony Abbey, a bizarre 12th century bastion of Christian history. Beach rides add to the attractions of western Wales coastal resorts, with considerable scope for instructional and family holidays. North Wales' Rhiwiau Riding Centre is located in an area, as famous for its seaside resorts as it is for Snowdon (which, at 3560 feet, is the highest mountain in England and Wales), provides stunning views, especially in the Snowdonia National Park. Valleys, lakes, even derelict gold mines, blend to provide the backdrop for mostly road free riding. Welsh farmhouse food and accommodation honed to meet the high tourist board standards, complement the wide range of equestrian options available throughout the principality.

ENGLAND

Slip over the Bristol Channel from Wales, and the West Country offers a horseman's haven, with traditional tourist attractions a bonus (although best avoided during the summer season). While there are adult-only rides, the target is often family or teenage trade, so select wisely. Scenically, Cornwall's Bodmin Moor covers long stretches of spring turf bringing new challenges to those who can cope, in an often windswept and inhospitable landscape. Devon, famed for Dartmoor and home to one Britain's toughest native ponies, offers a less dramatic, gentler, wooded face with considerable emphasis on farmhouse style accommodation. Exmoor, its burnished hills the inspiration for the hymn "All Things Bright and Beautiful," slides into Somerset, less commercially frenetic, rich in wildlife and sporting an abundance of flowers in May and June. No long trail rides, but plenty of choice, including instruction at the highly regarded Porlock Vale, Porlock Weir. Mendip Hills, neighboring Avon, attracts visitors to the Lynecombe Lodge Riding Centre, a multi-activity center with riding as the main draw. Further south, Hampshire's New Forest, 200 square miles of woodland and heath, once the hunting grounds of kings, draws those on weekend hotel bargain breaks. Riding is available close by or, in some cases, on the hotel grounds. New Park Manor, which lays claim to once being Charles II's hunting lodge, is one such example. Time your visit for September and watch the annual drifts when the New Forest ponies are rounded-up for the sales.

Northern England, which is generally less urban, also has pockets of riding. The Cumbrian Lake District in the northwest has high profile scenery of lakes, fells and peaks that are particularly attractive when seen from the saddle. For a less commercial setting, ride with Barbara Burton at D & P Equestrian, which is based in Cautley, Sedburgh, where the Westmoreland Fells meet the Yorkshire Dales, the grey-green Fells contrasting sharply with the paint box richness of the Dales' pastureland and woods. Geared to small groups of competent adult riders, using tough half or pure bred Welsh Cobs, this is equine exploration at its best, with inspiring scenery and the chance to enjoy choice rural accommodations in the evening. The same can be said for elsewhere in Yorkshire. Harrogate, home to the Yorkshire Riding Centre run by dressage gurus, Christopher Bartle and Jane Bartle-Wilson.There is also the Peak District of Derbyshire with carriage driving courses at the Red House Stable, Darley Dale, Matlock.

Ten years ago, Tina Sutton of Albion Rides set out to evoke the history and romance of the Norfolk region of East Anglia which, along with Suffolk, is strewn with green lanes linking rustic villages. Now, her small groups, limited to around 6 riders, enjoy a unique glimpse into the local flora and fauna with some speedy rides along Marriott's Way, a long deserted railway track. You ride in the grounds of Blickling Hall, reconstructed in Jacobean style during the 17th century. Albion, incidentally, is the ancient word for Britain. England can spring some equestrian surprises in areas not even mentioned. You can ride along London's Rotten Row, around a mile long, or sample local rides in the southeastern counties of Kent, Sussex, and Surrey. These are often just as rewarding.

IRELAND

Whether breeding, betting or simply sitting on the back of them, horses are a part of Ireland's heritage throughout. No wonder that Irish horse holidays are riding high and are fiercely promoted on both sides of the Atlantic by an all-Ireland alliance through an Equestrian Holidays brochure. Every center in the Republic is Irish Tourist Board and AIRE (Association of Irish Riding Establishments) approved and, in some instances, by the British Horse Society as well. Remember, however, that Eire uses the Irish pound or "punt," while Ulster uses the pound sterling, and that the exchange rates are not the same. The difficult task is deciding whether, as in England, Wales and Scotland, you want a full-blown trail ride, with overnight stopovers staying at a variety of pre-booked accommodations. An increasingly popular alternative is to base yourself at one of Ireland's highly rated country hotels or farms that have their own stables and ride out each day. The range is huge and so is the terrain. To the west, lie the lakes, mountains, and forests of Sligo, made famous by the writings of W.B. Yeats, with a variety of rides where you can go exploring on your own through Horse Holidays at Grange. A creamy blue sea washes the seemingly endless yellow strands backed by fields and white-washed cottages—Ireland as we imagine it. The Sligo Trail offers 3 days by the sea and 3 through the mountains and forests. The Donegal Trail in the northwest offers a 2 week blend of coast, rugged mountains, and forests. Maps are provided and pre-booked accommodations arranged. Long time trail rider, Willie Leahy, is your guide for the Connemara Trail amid the latticework of rugged stonewalled fields and enough folklore to have leprechauns leaping in sheer delight. The Killarney Reeks Trail explores the highlands of Kerry which include the majestic MacGillcuddy's Reeks, Ireland's highest mountain range. All of these rides join forces under the Horse Riding Ireland banner. In sharp contrast, the 6 day, 120 mile long,

Wicklow Trail Ride lies only a mere 12 miles from cosmopolitan Dublin, and covers around 25 miles daily in County Wicklow, the so-called "Garden of Ireland." There is a little bit of everything, from forests to mountains and lakes. Take your pick of overnight stops in luxury manor house hotels or a combination of hotels and guest houses.

In northern Ireland's County Down, the British Horse Society approved Drumgooland House and Equestrian Center, set in 60 acres with its own trout-stocked lake, likewise offers a series of guided trail rides. These take place in the vast sandy beach at Newcastle, the ancient ruins of Dindrum Castle, and Crows Lane where, in the words of the song, " the Mountains of Mourne sweep down to the sea." But you needn't join a trail ride. Some centers offer shorter breaks or the use of their facilities. Others, like the Bel-Air Hotel and Riding School, Ashford, County Wicklow, said to be the oldest established riding school in Ireland, offers residential holidays with a choice of hacking or improving your skills. They are not alone. Many centers, some on large estates, pander to the riders' creature comforts as well as equestrian needs. You will not go hungry in Ireland. The giant breakfasts will see to that, along with a jar or two of the black stuff (i.e., Guinness) in the evening.

If you want to improve—or even regain—your jumping skills, then Frenchman Eric Pele, a graduate of the world-famous Cadre Noir and trainer with the French national Stud, can coax the best from you, whatever your strengths and weaknesses. Even dressage, which some find boring, comes over as an exciting partnership between rider and horse. Eric's week long summer courses, formerly based at Flowerhill House, near Ballinsloe, County Galway, a region well known for breeding quality jumping horses, will soon be relocated in County Down in Northern Ireland. The cross-country course at Flowerhill has nearly 100 fences, and there is a huge all-weather school. Likewise, Greystones Equestrian Center, Castle Leslie, Laslough, County Monaghan offers 5 to 7 day cross-country or improve-your-riding programs as well as combined riding and instruction, with hacking in the surrounding countryside of forests and lakes. Again, there is an all-weather school. Full board is provided at The Hunting Lodge, a large Victorian house on the estate, with restaurants serving local cuisine. The Center also features hunting, currently a contentious subject in the British Isles with a ban on fox-hunting still threatened. Special weekends are set aside in season for first timers as well as more advanced riders.

CASTLES RIDE

www.horsevacations.com

BASICS: Eastern Trekking Associates/Susan Eakins, 2574 Nicky Lane, Alexandria, VA 22311-1312, USA
Tel: (703) 845-9366   Tel: (423) 933-0219
Fax: (703) 379-4059
Email: susaneak@erols.com
WHEN: Late June through October.
AIRPORTS: Vienna or Munich
LOCATION: Upper Austria. The ride originates at the Reiterhof inn which is situated exactly midway between Munich and Vienna, north of Linz in Oberosterreich. Trains stop at Linz. Riders can take a bus to Unterweissenbach, where they can arrange to be picked up or rent a car }(explicit, detailed driving directions will be provided upon request).
PRICE: S1180 (£737) 8 days/7 nights, per person, double occupancy, includes 6 days of riding, breakfast and evening meals, and accommodations.

This is a delightful ride mostly at a moderate pace that works best if you possess at least intermediate skill and a certain degree of fitness. There will be sufficient time before leaving the Hof to match horses with riders and make any necessary changes. You will be riding through a province of 64 castles and monastery ruins, some dating back to the Holy Roman Empire. The ride is very well organized and attracts riders from all over Europe. The Ride Master speaks English, as will many of the guests. Riding together in Austria always produces a warm camaraderie.

CHILDREN'S PROGRAM There is no children's program.

ACCOMMODATIONS: Guests sleep at the comfortable Reiterhof inn and spend 3 nights at other pensions. All rooms have private baths.

SPECIAL ACTIVITIES: Sightseeing in Munich and Vienna.

MEALS: Breakfasts consist of hearty Austrian dishes. Lunch is not part of the package, but on all day rides you will stop at restaurants/pubs. Remember to carry some cash, as plastic is not always accepted. Dinner consists of home-cooked food, Austrian style, occasionally accompanied by live music. At one of the stops you will be treated to homemade potato poppyseed noodles.

RIDING STUFF: The horses include Argentine Criollos, Lippizaners, several Quarterhorses, a few Paints, at least 1 Appaloosa, and other breeds. You will be introduced to your horse and learn how to groom and tack him in accordance with "house rules." The first 2 days of riding will take you through deep woods, alongside blooming meadows, bubbling brooks and the village of Hackstock. On the second day the pace picks up and this is the time to decide if you are well matched with your horse. The third day involves a change of accommodations following a day of riding through a wild ravine, peaceful green meadows and several tiny hamlets. The fourth day takes you to Rapottenstein Castle, a 12th century jewel, and along an abandoned railroad line in the great Weinsberger Forest, which is still among the holdings of the imperial Hapsburg family today. During the next 3 days you will ride out from the Hof through forests, meadows filled with wildflowers, green pastures, cultivated fields and along isolated trails, visiting the ruins of Ruttenstein and Prandegg Castles and passing many more along the way. Weather conditions may affect the ride and you are urged to bring warm clothing and rain gear.

AUTHOR'S COMMENT: *This ride will allow you to exercise your horseback riding skills on ideal terrain. Interesting historical sites, Gothic and Romanesque castles and the natural beauty of the surrounding landscape add to the pleasure of riding among like-minded horse enthusiasts.*

HIGHLIGHTS
Western or English tack • Intermediate skills • Weight limit 225 lbs. • Riding in the foothills of the Austrian Alps • 4 to 6 hours on horseback per day • Covers 220 kms. • Well-trained, powerful horses • 6 days of riding

EXPLORERS' RIDE

www.horsevacations.com

BASICS: Eastern Trekking Associates/Susan Eakins, 2574 Nicky Lane, Alexandria, VA 22311-1312, USA
Tel: (703) 845-9366 Tel: (423) 933-0219
Fax: (703) 379-4059
Email: susaneak@erols.com
WHEN: June through October.
AIRPORTS: Vienna or Munich.
LOCATION: Upper Austria. The inn is located in the Muehlviertel, exactly midway between Munich and Vienna, north of Linz in Oberosterreich. Trains stop at Linz. Riders can take a bus to within a few kilometers of the inn (Unterweissenbach), where they will be collected by a staff member, or can rent a car (detailed driving directions available upon request).
PRICE: $1000 (£625) 8 days/7 nights, per person, double occupancy. Price includes breakfast and dinner, all accommodations, and riding.

Come to the land of strudel and the Alps! In Austria, the trails wend upwards and upwards through the forest to reach high meadows where goats, sheep and cattle graze. You'll experience a beautiful, rural economy tended by friendly, animal-loving people. This ride provides a delightful introduction to Austria for riders with at least 2 years riding experience.

CHILDREN'S PROGRAM: Children must be skilled riders, over 10, and accompanied by an adult.

ACCOMMODATIONS: Guests return each evening to the comfortable country inn. All of the beds are graced with luxurious eiderdown comforters. Every room has a shower, toilet and phone. The sauna and solarium are available to all guests. The absence of televisions encourages lively interaction among the guests who gather in the central lounging area.

SPECIAL ACTIVITIES: You may wish to spend some time in Munich or Vienna, before and/or after the ride.

MEALS: Breakfast is plentiful and hearty. Lunch is not part of the package, but on all day rides you will stop at local restaurants or pubs. Be sure to carry some cash for lunch, since credit cards are not always accepted. Dinner is an enjoyable affair, consisting of Austrian style, home-cooked dishes prepared by Hermine, the Ride Master's wife.

RIDING STUFF: The horses, including 20 Argentine Criollos, a few Lippizaners, some Quarterhorses, a few Paints, an Appaloosa and other breeds, are powerful, agile, trustworthy and well-cared for. You will be introduced to your horse on the first day and given specific instruction to permit you to groom and tack your horse according to "house rules." On the following day there is a short introductory ride to ensure that you have been matched with a suitable horse. You will ride down old cart paths, through wooded countryside and pine forest moorland to Tannemoor Nature Preserve, where on warm days you will be invited to take a dip on horseback in Rubener Schwemm Brook. One day you will visit the ruins of an ancient castle and enjoy lunch at a nearby farmhouse, before riding back to the farm at day's end. The vacation includes a long ride through wild country, a friendly glass of schnapps distilled by the farmer who serves it, and a home-cooked lunch at a rustic inn. After a late afternoon ride to a local inn for dinner, there will be an evening ride back under the stars. On the last day you will enjoy your longest ride through a beautiful high plateau. You should be confident that you can comfortably spend some hours in the saddle before undertaking this moderately paced ride.

AUTHOR'S COMMENT: *Spend a week in Austria at an established inn on a family farm. This is a comfortable way to enjoy a stimulating international atmosphere combined with wonderful horseback riding.*

HIGHLIGHTS
Western (must request in advance) or English tack • Intermediate skills • Weight limit 225 lbs. • 4 to 6 hours on horseback per day • Ride covers 200 kms. • Well-trained, powerful horses • 6 days of riding • Group size 10 or smaller

SOUTH BOHEMIA RIDE

www.horsevacations.com

BASICS: Eastern Trekking Associates/Susan Eakins, 2574 Nicky Lane, Alexandria, VA 22311-1312, USA
Tel: (703) 845-9366   Tel: (423) 933-0219
Fax: (703) 379-4059
Email: susaneak@erols.com
WHEN: Late June through October.
AIRPORTS: Vienna or Munich.
LOCATION: Upper Austria, halfway between Munich and Vienna, north of Linz in Oberosterreich. Trains stop at Linz. Riders can take a bus to Unterweissenbach where pick-up can be arranged, or rent a car (detailed driving directions will be provided upon request).
PRICE: $1180 (£737) 8 days/7 nights, per person, double occupancy, includes breakfast and supper, horses, tack, and guides.

This is a moderately fast ride with a true international flavor. Your group of riders from various countries will spend the first few days in beautiful Upper Austria before crossing over the border into South Bohemia where you will change to Czech horses and meet your new guide. The journey will take you over varied terrain including high mountain meadows, wooded hills, and along waterways with stops at various points of interest. This is an unusual trip, somewhat off the beaten path, that is sure to provide some unforgettable memories.

CHILDREN'S PROGRAM: Children must be 12 or older, accompanied by a parent, moderately skilled riders, and able to spend long hours in the saddle.

ACCOMMODATIONS: Guests sleep in comfortable country inns along the way and a former manor house converted to a charming pension in the ancient Czech village of Tschechien.

SPECIAL ACTIVITIES: Sightseeing in Munich and Vienna. Zurich is only a 4 hour drive.

MEALS: Breakfasts and dinners are substantial and tasty. Lunch is not part of the package, but on all day rides you will stop at local inns. In Leopoldschlag, riders stop at a pizza shop to eat and will be treated to Bohemian noodles (*povididatschkerin*) at the site of an ancient cloister in Bohemia. Dinner is a lively affair, as guests enjoy hearty, home-cooked fare, to the accompaniment of live music on occasion.

RIDING STUFF: The horses include Argentine Criollos, Lippizaners, Quarterhorses, Paints, an Appaloosa, and other breeds. This ride requires a high intermediate skill level as you will be galloping on the straightaways and climbing up and over immense bluffs on narrow ledges. You must be comfortable at all paces and capable of spending long hours in the saddle as well as willing and able to tack and care for your horse daily. Luggage is transported for you. Pack light, but be sure to bring proper riding gear including boots, chaps or half chaps, rainwear, a warm sweater, and a hat. On the first day, riders are paired with suitable horses and taken on an introductory ride to ensure compatibility. Adjustments will be made as necessary. While in Austria for the first 4½ days, you will travel through high plains and meadows, over wooded hills, along sparkling streams and mountain brooks. Highlights of the Austrian part of the trek include visits to the medieval trading city of Freistadt, the Forellenhof (Trout Manor) at Mitterbach, the centuries old but still turning Leithen Mill and the pilgrimage site of St. Leonhard. Once over the border into the Czech Republic, you will be transported by van to the Pension Kalliste, where you will be refitted on Czech horses and introduced to your Czech guide. Bohemia offers a landscape of grassy hillocks, boxwood plantations, woodlands, meadows filled with wildflowers, and a visit to the beautiful historic city of Krumau, known as "Venice on the Moldau."

AUTHOR'S COMMENTS: *An outstanding riding terrain makes this ideal if you are looking for a spirited ride. The history of the area as well as its natural beauty add to your pleasure. The fine horses are cared for with skill and concern.*

HIGHLIGHTS
Western or English tack • Intermediate skills • Weight limit 225 lbs. • Riding in the foothills of the Austrian Alps and through Bohemia in the Czech Republic • 4 to 5 hours on horseback per day • Covers 220 kms. • Saturday to Saturday • Well-trained, powerful horses • 6 days of riding

FINNAIR RIDING TOURS

BASICS: FINNAIR USA or call your local travel agent.
Tel: (800) 950-4768   Fax: (212) 499-9036
Email: george.garber@finnair.com
Website: www.us.finnair.com
Official Tour Operator (US): NORVISTA, 228 E.
45th Street, New York, NY 10017
Tel: (800) 677-6454   Tel: (212) 818-1198
Fax: (212) 818-0585
Email: sales@norvista.net
Website: www.norvista.net
Official Tour Operator (UK): NORVISTA, 227
Regent Street, London W1R 8PD
Tel: 171-409-7334
Fax: 171-409-7733
Email: reservations@norvista.co.uk
Website: www.norvista.com

WHEN: May to September. See below for details.
AIRPORTS: Helsinki. Tour prices include transfers from Helsinki to your destination by air and, in the case of the Southwestern Finland Icelandic Horse Trekking Tour, by train and car.
LOCATION: Helsinki is the central meeting place. Riding locations are spread throughout Finland.
PRICE: See below for details. All tours include free transfers from Helsinki. The Southwestern Finland Icelandic Horse Trekking Tour includes transfer from the Helsinki Airport, while the other rides require Finnair flights to destinations in Finland. Prices (1999 rates) include all meals, accommodations, helmets, saddlebags and horse gear.

It is always exciting when a new riding program is established, and Finnair's tours, in a country that is ideally suited for riding, are worth getting excited over. The 4 tour alternatives each reflect the characteristics of that specific part of Finland where the riding occurs. The Ruunaa Icelandic Trekking Tour takes place among the ancient forests found in Finnish Karelia. The Rautalampi Icelandic Horse Tour gives you an idea of the lake land wilderness terrain typical of the heart of Finland. There are also 1 to 3 day treks in southwestern Finland along the ancient "King's Road," as well as other Short Ride options from which to choose. The involvement of Finnair ensures a quality, well-planned holiday. The sparse population, its considerable size, the beautiful terrain, and English-speaking guides, make Finland an appealing riding alternative. Rugged 5 to 8 hour a day riding tours will challenge your body, while you experience the beauty of a pristine environment. While most of the rides do not require advanced riders, experience in horseback riding as well as a degree of physical fitness are desirable. These tours provide an excellent opportunity to hone your practical horsemanship in Finland's peaceful wilderness terrain.

CHILDREN'S PROGRAM: Children should be at least 14 years old for all rides except the Rautalampi Icelandic Horse Trekking Tour, where 13 is an acceptable age.

ACCOMMODATIONS: The Southwestern Finland Icelandic Horse Trekking Tour does not involve an overnight stay. The Rautalampi Horse Trek involves 2 nights in shared accommodations in Sahala Manor at the Rautalampi Icelandic Horse Center and 6 nights in wilderness cottages. The Wilderness Trek in Ruunaa involves 6 nights in cottage rooms for 2 to 6 persons.

MEALS: Three meals a day are provided on all treks. The dishes served reflect traditional Finnish fare, which takes advantage of the bounty of each season. You will enjoy some of the delicacies of the region in which you will be riding. Fresh fish, game, and berries prepared in the traditional Finnish manner will be just one of many memorable highlights of your trek.

AUTHOR'S COMMENT: *Finnair's involvement promises a bright future for this new program that will surely became a staple of the riding holiday industry. It's nice to see a country that places such high value on preserving its natural environment.*

HIGHLIGHTS
Ride the Karelian forests near the Finno-Russian border • Ride through the picture perfect lake country • Varied riding through mountains and plains • Trisp led by English-speaking tour guides • Small group size • Weight limit 220 lbs. (100 kg.) (15.71 stone) • Icelandic horses on most tours

FINNAIR RIDING TOURS (continued)

THE WILDERNESS TREK IN RUUNAA

PRICE: Starting at $2019 (from New York)/£915 (from London) 7 days/6 nights, per person, includes airfare, accommodation in 2 to 6 person cabins, full board, insurance, and 5 days of riding.

WHEN: May, June, August, and September.

AIRPORT: Joensuu Airport. Transfers to Lomaprittis are included.

LOCATION: Finnish Karelia.

This tour takes 7 days/6 nights with 5 days of riding. This is a trek through the famed bear country of the vast Karelian forests, not far from the Finno-Russian border. Tranquil rivers, roaring rapids, quiet marshlands, majestic elks and other wild animals will capture your hearts and minds. The tour covers 130 kilometers, and involves 5 to 8 hours a day in the saddle travelling 30 to 40 kilometers through difficult forest terrain. Riding experience and physical fitness are desirable. Helmets and saddlebags will be supplied. There are 10 scheduled departure dates from May 17 to September 20.

Following your arrival at Joensuu Airport, you will be transferred to Lomapirtti Inn in the village of Jongunjoki, and introduced to the staff. The next morning off you go on a 35 kilometer trek, riding along the sandy riverbanks of the Haahnjoki River and finally moving over into marsh land, which must be crossed on causeways! The day ends at Ruunaa, a vast area famous for its abundant, freely-flowing rapids, where a relaxing sauna will greet you. On the second day, you will ride along the banks of wilderness rivers, marvel at the roaring rapids, and complete an exciting river crossing by way of a wooden hanging bridge. In the evening, you return to Ruunaa Hiking Center for another sauna and a delicious dinner of genuine Karelian dishes. You will shoot the rapids in original wooden boats and enjoy a cabin on the banks of the Neitikoski Rapids. On the fourth day you will ride as close to the Finno-Russian border as is permitted. The day will end at a loggers' cabin. From here, you turn northwards, riding down narrow sand roads near the border. On the last day of trekking you pass through ancient Karelian forests, where the bears dwell. This area is the site of the Finno-Russian Winter War, and many places still show signs of that conflict. You will also visit the Varnanen caves as well as the home of a legendary Finnish bear hunter, Mr. Väino Heikkinen, resting that night at the Lomapirtti Inn, where another hot sauna awaits you.

THE RAUTALAMPI ICELANDIC HORSE TREK

PRICE: Starting at $2035 (from New York)/£899 (from London) 7 days/6 nights, per person, double occupancy, includes airfare, full board, insurance, and 5 days of riding. A 2 day, weekend version of this trek is also available.

WHEN: May to September.

AIRPORT: Jyvaskyla Airport.

LOCATION: Jyvaskyla is located in the lake country of central Finland, called Savo.

You arrive at the ride location by taking a direct Finnair flight from Helsinki to Jyvaskyla, where you are transferred some 80 kilometers from the airport to the Rautalampi Icelandic Horse Center, which is housed in historic Sahala Manor, a large working farm engaged in modern agriculture and forestry. The stables are home to 65 Icelandic horses and 42 foals. The region is filled with picturesque lakes and the terrain varies from vast green forests, interrupted by occasional wilderness paths and logging roads, to softly rolling hills, tidy cultivated fields surrounding traditional farmhouses, and blue lakes. Ideal for riding, the area provides a reasonable challenge, with participants spending 5 to 8 hours in the saddle daily at a moderate pace. Physical fitness and some riding experience is desirable.

The days are long, leaving birds to their singing through what would be evening hours in less northerly locations. On the first and last nights accommodations are provided at the Sahala Manor. You will enjoy saunas at several stops. Accommodations along the trek include guest houses and you will also spend 4 nights in basic wilderness cottages and inns. This ride through the beautiful lake district is designed to cultivate a spirit of cooperation, achieved through working together to solve problems, build camps, groom the horses, and prepare meals. Group size is 8 to 14 persons.

FINNAIR RIDING TOURS (continued)

ALONG THE BEAR'S RING TRAIL

PRICE: Starting at $1900 (from New York)/£839 (from London) 7 days/6 nights, per person, double occupancy, includes airfare, full board, insurance, and 5 days of riding.
WHEN: First week in June to first week in September.
AIRPORT: Kuusamo Airport. Transfers to the horse farm in Oulanko are included.
LOCATION: Southern Lapland in Oulanko National Park.

Oulanko National Park and nature preserve is located just south of the Arctic Circle and is remarkable for its river valleys, gorges and canyons. The vegetation is a mix of coniferous, birch, and mountain ash as well as dense undergrowth. Home to 50 different species of birds (many of them rarely found elsewhere in Europe), the forest is also inhabited by elk, reindeer, brown bear, wolf and lynx—all wary enough of humans to keep out of your way. The daily rides are from 4 to 6 hours and cover 25 to 30 kilometers of forested terrain. The Finnish horses are rugged and versatile, accustomed to traveling through forest, across rivers, and along rocky trails. Guests should have a basic knowledge of riding, be fit enough to spend 6 hours in the saddle daily, and have a spirit of adventure.

After your arrival at Kuusamo Airport, you will be taken to the farm, where you will meet the horses and overnight in a cabin. The trek begins the following morning at Savijoki River and takes you past Rupakivi rock formations to Oulanko canyon. You spend the night in a cabin or heated tent. Tuesday's ride offers the wild beauty of the river, rapids, and virgin forest of Oulanko. A cabin with sauna and shower await you beside the Kiutakongas Rapids at day's end. On Wednesday, the group heads towards the Russian border, where a sandy river beach provides the chance for a fast gallop. In the evening, try swimming with the horses. The night will be spent in an Oulanko cabin with sauna or in a heated tent or lean-to. Thursday's route follows the river to Kahiamo fjord. On Friday the trek takes you past Finland's most powerful rapids, along Alakokoski canyon to the quiet village of Juuma, the re-entry point to civilization. A final sauna and celebration await. On Saturday, you transfer to the airport to begin the return trip home.

SHORT RIDES

Short Ride programs can be combined with other tours, rides, or business trips using Finnair as the carrier. You can obtain assistance with these arrangements through your travel agent or NORVISTA.

THE KING'S ROAD: SOUTHWESTERN FINLAND ICELANDIC HORSE TREKKING TOURS

PRICE: $189 (£109) 1 day, per person; $330 (£189) 2 days/1 night, per person; $449 (£259) 3 days/2 nights, per person.
WHEN: May to September.
AIRPORT: Helsinki Airport.
LOCATION: The King's Road, Lesola in southwestern Finland.

This is a 1 day ride which begins at Minna's Stables at the Lasola family farmhouse, about an hour's drive from Helsinki. Transfers, either from Helsinki, the Helsink-Vantaa Airport, or the Karjaa train station, are arranged. The riding is quite extensive, covering 50 to 60 kilometers, and basic riding skills are necessary. Your destinations on this 1 day trek in Uusimaa are the authentically restored villages of Mustio and Fiskars in southwestern Finland, sites of 400 year old iron works. The Lasola farmhouse is also 400 years old and has been owned by the same family since 1609. The riding terrain is hilly and follows the route of the old King's Road, dating back to the time when Finland was a part of Sweden. You will pass idyllic villages, rivers, lakes and ride through green forests. There are 2 possible destinations from which to choose. One, the Mustio Manor, was first mentioned in Finnish history books in the 14th century. You will visit this old royal manor, known for its wooden 'castle,' built in the 1780s and its Baroque style gardens, originally landscaped in 1787. The other option you may choose is Fiskars, a village which grew up around iron works founded in 1649, which lies on the shores of a beautiful river. The restored village is currently home to a unique community of artisans and artists with their exhibitions and workshops. At either destination you will be offered, time permitting, the opportunity to wash away the dust with a swim in a sparkling lake or relax in the soothing warmth and steam of a Finnish lakeside sauna.

LE MOULIN DU CHEMIN

www.inthesaddle.com

BASICS: Agent: **In the Saddle**, Laurel Cottage, Ramsdell, Tadley, Hampshire, RG26 5SH, UK
Tel: 01256-851-665
Fax: 01256-851-667 (from UK)
Tel: (44) 1256-851-665
Fax: (44) 1256-851-667 (from US)
Email: rides@inthesaddle.com

WHEN: Open year round

AIRPORTS: Paris. Le Moulin du Chemin may also be reached by ferry, train or coach. Transfers included from Poitiers (train from Paris or coach from UK).

LOCATION: Le Moulin du Chemin is located 240 miles southwest of Paris.

PRICE: Low Season (January to April and October to December): £540 ($864) for riders; £450 ($720) for non-riders. High season (May to September): £590 ($944) for riders; £490 ($784) for non-riders. All prices quoted on basis of 6 night stays, per person, double occupancy, and include wine and other drinks, use of mountain bikes, all meals, lodgings and riding. There is an additional charge for singles during high season.

Le Moulin du Chemin is an old converted mill run by an English couple. Its limited guest capacity ensures a peaceful and relaxed atmosphere and is appropriate for non-riders as well as riders. The area is bounded by ancient hedgerows, a wonderful patchwork of tracks that meander through woods, past apple orchards and ponds, alongside lush meadows and small fields where Parthenasie cattle graze. The streams are unpolluted, the countryside sparcely populated, but full of wild animals, birds, butterflies, and flowers. The local history dates from pre-Roman times and there are plenty of local attractions that reflect the early Roman presence in this region.

CHILDREN'S PROGRAM: There are 2 ponies, 14.2 hands high, that children from about age 8 can ride. Child-minders and babysitters need to be arranged in advance for younger children.

ACCOMMODATIONS: There are 3 comfortable guest rooms at Le Moulin du Chemin, accommodating a maximum of 8 guests. Each room is tastefully furnished and has its own bathroom and tea and coffee facilities.

SPECIAL ACTIVITIES: There is a swimming pool, mountain bikes, boules, artists' materials and a library. There are excellent local golf courses. There are nearby hiking trails, ancient churches and rural markets. It is an easy drive to Saumur, the equestrian capital of France.

MEALS: Leisurely, tasty meals are served in either the dining room, *al fresco* in the shade of the patio, or beside the pool for BBQs. Breakfast consists of hot crusty baguettes, croissants and fresh coffee, tea or chocolate. Lunch is either a picnic, a traditional spread in a friendly farmhouse, or back at Le Moulin du Chemin, where *aubergine* pasta bake, deep fried Camembert, or trout may be served. Dinner is a multi-course feast ranging from chicken in mustard sauce, to quail and spiced rice. Special dietary needs are catered for. Wine, beer and soft drinks are always available without charge.

RIDING STUFF: Since group size is generally 5 or less including your BHSI guide, the pace will be tailored to the group. The tack is English. The horses and ponies currently range from 14.2 to 16.2 hands high. You will be offered the opportunity to groom and tack up horses if you are so inclined or want to learn. All of the riding takes place on morning jaunts, usually involving 4 hours on horseback, so that you are free to relax in the afternoons. The pace is mostly at a walk, trot and canter. The tack is English style.

AUTHOR'S COMMENT: *Riders come to Le Moulin du Chemin for the pleasure of it, rather than for a purist's riding trip. Its laid-back atmosphere and charming countryside, with hundreds of miles of local tracks, makes this a very enjoyable riding holiday.*

HIGHLIGHTS

Charming rural French countryside • Swimming pool • Mountain bikes • 7 days/6 nights with 5 days of riding • Intermediate riding skill required • Sunday evenings to Saturday departures • Open year round

MUDININA HORSE TREKKING CENTRE

http://www.teaser.fr/corsenet/pub/m/madun/madun.html

BASICS: Centre Tourisme Equestre A Mudinina Domaine de Croccano, Route de Granace km3, (Sartene) Corsica F20100, France
Tel: (33) 495-771-137 Fax: (33) 495-734-289
Tel (mobile): (33) 608-435-634
Email: christian.perrier@wanadoo.fr
WHEN: Open year round for stationary riding holidays; March to October for treks.

AIRPORTS: Figari Sud Corse (40 kms.); Ajaccio (80 kms.). Air France or Air Liberte from Paris and Nice.
LOCATION: Island of Corsica (Sartene).
PRICE: Deluxe 6 to 7 day trips: $815 (£526) per person, double occupancy. Camping trips, 6 to 7 days: $498 (£321) per person, double occupancy.

On this picture perfect island, host Christian Perrier has created an exciting riding program. Corsica is large enough to provide some excellent 6 and 7 day treks, including mountain treks, coastal treks and combinations of the two. Guests enjoy comfortable accommodations and wonderful Mediterranean food. The 2 camping trips follow the wild coastline. Island trekking begins in April and ends in October, but visitors may enjoy riding year round at Christian and Claudine Perrier's comfortable home located in the rural hills. Christian also organizes annual rides in Tuscany and Sardinia.

CHILDREN'S PROGRAM: Children over 8 can enjoy riding with their parents on the stationary program. Children over 12 may participate in treks.

ACCOMMODATIONS: Accommodations vary. There are 2 camping rides; 4 rides where you sleep in comfortable country houses; and 4 rides where you enjoy hotel or inn accommodations along your trekking route. The stationary stay is at an old Corsican granite house, overlooking the sea, with 4 comfortable bedrooms and 3 bathrooms.

SPECIAL ACTIVITIES: On stationary holidays, you are within a short drive from tennis, all water sports, fishing, golfing and the mountains. In addition, Christian arranges walking treks.

MEALS: Quality Corsican and Mediterranean foods made from tasty local products.

RIDING STUFF: The mounts are small, surefooted Corsican horses and the tack is English. Christian maintains a free roaming herd of 33 horses, which he breeds and trains. Luggage is generally transported by vehicle. The 2 camping trips move along the wild Sartene coastline, while the 8 luxury trips alternate between an inland mountain trip, a mountain to sea trip, and a coastal trip. You will ride for approximately 6 hours a day over rugged terrain and experience is required. Corsica offers an incredible landscape, a combination of mountains and water, that makes this trip a riding delight. On many of the trips you will enjoy a swim with your horse. The pace of the ride varies as dictated by the terrain. In the mountainous areas, walking dominates, but galloping is possible on the grassy plateau or along the coastline by the sea. Due to the riding skill required in the rugged and changing terrain, riders must be fit and weigh less than 200 lbs. (90 kg.) (14 stone).

AUTHOR'S COMMENT: *Christian's much praised rides came to my attention several years ago and we are glad to welcome him into our book. Those who visit for a riding tour on the French island of Corsica will not be disappointed. Christian is multi-lingual, fluent in French and English. A small piece of riding paradise awaits those of you who take the time to visit this off-the-beaten-path island.*

HIGHLIGHTS

Competent riders required for all trekking trips • Stationary holidays suitable to all riding levels • 8 inn to inn treks on Corsica • 2 camping trips • All Corsica treks-6 or 7 days • Christian also leads treks in Tuscany and Sardinia • Weight limit 200 lbs. (90 kg.) (14 stone) • Ride through crystal clear water • Group limit 5 to 12 • Member: FFE and DNTE

PYRENEES MOUNTAIN RIDE

BASICS: Inntravel, Hovingham, York Y06 4JZ, UK
   Tel: 01653-628811
   Fax: 01653-628741 (from UK)
   Tel: (44) 1653-628811
   Fax (44) 1653-628741 (from US)
WHEN: March to October.

AIRPORTS: Toulouse - a 2 hour drive.
LOCATION: Inland from Perpignan near the border of France and Spain.
PRICE: Prices start at £779 ($1246) per week, per person, double occupancy and includes airfare from London.

These rides traverse some of the most scenic areas of southwestern France as you move over hills and through the valleys of the wonderful Corbieres region in the warm foothills of the Mediterranean Pyrenees, west of Perpignan. The area is home to many beautiful 13th century Cathar strongholds, which still dominate the valleys and villages producing a wonderful feeling of timelessness. Each riding day ends at either a farmhouse or country inn set in rural splendor. Experience and fitness are required to deal with the pace and long hours in the saddle. Despite the rugged and changing terrain, there will be many opportunities for exhilarating canters and gallops.

CHILDREN'S PROGRAM: Not suitable for children.

ACCOMMODATIONS: Riders stay in charming farmhouses and occasional small country inns with simply furnished private bedrooms. Showers and washing amenities are sometimes provided *en suite*. Single travelers may be accommodated in one large room.

MEALS: Continental breakfasts and picnic lunches with wine are provided *en route*. Dinner is a leisurely meal to be enjoyed with fellow riders and your host, consisting of tasty farmhouse fare, accompanied by robust Corbieres wines. Vegetarians are catered to with fresh locally grown produce.

SPECIAL ACTIVITIES: Discover the remarkable history of the medieval Cathar heretics and the myths and legends that still hold sway among the local people. There are still rumors of fabulous treasure reputedly hidden here by the Cathars—perhaps you'll find it!!

RIDING STUFF: The riding is exciting and demanding with long hours in the saddle. On some days you will ride up to 8 hours through unspoiled and enchanting scenery. Each morning you will groom and prepare your horse for the day's riding and, at the end of day, you will brush, feed, and turn the horse out. Groups vary in size from 4 to 9 riders. English-speaking guide leaders, Jean-Claude and Nicole, are both expert riders. While there are some variations in the route due to changes in weather conditions, you will generally ride past lush vineyards, ascend the foothills of the Pyrenees, cross rivers, and visit the castles and quaint villages of the region. The overall terrain is quite dramatic, including mountain tracks, vineyards, river gorges and ancient villages. Small groups of adventurous travelers can chose to ride independently from farmhouse to farmhouse without the benefit of a tour guide. This exciting option requires considerable riding experience and the ability to read a map, but may well prove to be the experience of a lifetime for those seeking a challenge. You will get a taste of what it was like to journey to distant places before the advent of modem transportation replaced the excitement of foreign travel with drudgery. Luggage is moved by car on all trips.

AUTHOR'S COMMENT: *A delightful and spirited ride through the lower Pyrenees for those looking for a bit of a thrill, while enjoying this romantic and charming area of France. Good horses, lovely surroundings, excellent food and wine—this ride has stood the test of time and pleased many riders.*

HIGHLIGHTS
Farmhouse to farmhouse • Experienced riders • Weight limit 13 stone (185 lbs.) (82 kg.) • Sunday to Sunday • Up to 7 hours of riding per day • Group size under 9 • Unguided tours may be arranged • For fit and experienced riders

THE HEART OF PROVENCE

BASICS: Inntravel, Hovingham, York Y06 4JZ, UK
   Tel: 01653-628811   Fax: 01653-628741 (from UK)
   Tel: (44) 1653-628811
   Fax: (44) 1653-628741 (from US)
WHEN: March to October
AIRPORTS: Marseilles. Transfers included.
LOCATION: Provence. The riding center is a few
   miles from Aix-en-Provence
PRICE: From £965 ($1544) including British Airways
flight from London to Marseilles; From £812
($1299) including Channel crossing from Dover to
Calais; From £772 ($1235) from Marseilles with
transfers to property. Prices are for 6 day/7 night
trips, per person, double occupancy, includes
accommodations, 6 days of riding, and meals.
Single supplement add £60 ($96), but shared
accommodations may be available upon request.

The Heart of Provence Ride comes highly recommended for the quality of the horses, accommodations, and food. This fast-paced ride is best suited for experienced riders. Additional rides may be available for 2 or more less confident riders. The region is well known for its magnificent scenery and sunny warm climate, ideal for riding from early spring to late October. There is a break during the hottest periods of July and August. Your guide leader, Jean Claude Chouard, is an enthusiastic and accomplished horseman. This is a "must do" holiday for proficient riders, and double that if you have never visited Provence.

CHILDREN'S PROGRAM: The minimum age is 14. Teenagers who are proficient and accompanied by an adult are welcome.

ACCOMMODATIONS: You will enjoy quality accommodations in hotels and farmhouses while your horses rest in specially adapted horse boxes. Four of the properties have swimming pools. Luggage will be transferred each day.

MEALS: This ride will afford the opportunity to enjoy the best of Provencal cooking and the company of your fellow adventurers. Mediterranean cuisine has been acclaimed the healthiest–and tastiest. Home made terrines, ripe Provencal peppers and vegetables, delicious fish dishes, and wine with dinner. Generous and imaginative picnic lunches. Vegetarians will be catered for.

SPECIAL ACTIVITIES: The ride offers the opportunity to experience some of the lesser-known corners of this beautiful area of France.

RIDING STUFF: Fit, forward-going Andalucian horses are used for the ride which maintains a brisk pace for an average of 6 hours per day. You will splash through the river Durance, near Jouques, and ride on to the regional park at Luberon on your first day. The second day takes you across the rugged Luberon hills to Reillanne on horseback. On the third day, which is the longest, you wander over hills and valleys and wind your way along shepherds' tracks and traces of an old Roman road. On the fourth day, your journey takes you past the extraordinary moon-like landscape of Provencal Colorado to the village of Viens and the nearby welcoming Hotel St. Paul. The following day, you ride past the village of Lurs to La Grange, a Ferme Equestre that breeds Quarterhorses. At the conclusion of the ride, you will enjoy a final dinner at Ferme St. Lazare, where you relax and reflect on a week of superb riding. Each morning you will groom and tack-up your horse, ready for the day's adventure. At the end of the day, your mounts are untacked and fed before dinner. By the end of the week, these loveable and gentle horses will have become your firm friends. All rides are led by Jean-Claude, who speaks English and will join you for dinner each evening, while the horses rest nearby in his specially-designed horse boxes.

AUTHOR'S COMMENT: *Good food and accommodation, wonderful horses, and a pace suitable for the truly proficient rider, make this highly-recommended ride a pleasing experience for those who enjoy the challenge of a good, hard ride that is vehicle supported and ends each night in comfortable hotel-like surroundings. This is an excellent ride for single travelers.*

HIGHLIGHTS
Exciting riding for proficient riders • Forward-going, fit Andalucian horses • Excellent English tack • 9 scheduled riding dates • Quality accommodations • Group size 2 to 6 riders • Weight limit 13 stone (185 lbs.) (82 kg.) • Rides led by English-speaking Jean Claude Chouard • Hot, sunny climate

ICELANDIC RIDING TOURS

www.ishestar.is

BASICS: Ishestar ehf, Baejarhraun 2, 220
Hafnarfjorour, Iceland
Tel: (354) 565-3044   Fax: (354) 565-2113
Email: info@ishestar.is

WHEN: Year round for 1 day trips; all other trips,
June through September.

AIRPORTS: Keflavik International Airport - a 40
minute drive from Reykjavik. Four and a half
hour flight time from New York City. Daily
flights from London and Glasgow. Transfers
included from airport for longer rides and from
Reykjavik to riding center for 1 day rides.

LOCATION: Rides all over Iceland.

PRICE: *One Day Rides:* $40 (£25) to $140 (£87)
per person. *Stationary "Holiday Farm" Rides:*
from $1045 (£653) 8 days/7 nights, per person,
double occupancy. *Riding Tours* (2 to 18 days):
from $161 (£100) per day, per person, double
occupancy. Prices include accommodations,
full board, all transfers, rainwear, sleeping bag,
saddlebag, safety helmet, and 3 to 4 horses
per person.

Ishestar is Iceland's, and the world's, largest outfitter with more than 1300 horses. It offers an extensive holiday riding program on Icelandic horses. There are 3 basic types of riding tours: the year round 1 day tours designed for overnight business visitors and tourists; the 2 to 5 day tours designed to give you a great opportunity to see Iceland on horseback; and the 8 to 18 day adventurous Highland tours. On every tour, other than the 1 day rides, you will experience the beauties of Iceland while logging some 5 to 7 hours per day in the saddle at a brisk pace. The pace is a function of the unusual and very smooth "tolting" gait of the Icelandic horses as well as the fact that, on any given day, you will change mounts 3 or 4 times. Your alternative mounts run as a free herd along with the mounted horses while the staff and guest riders help to drive them! The gait of the Icelandic horse drives you into the saddle, eliminating the need to post, while maintaining the rider in a comfortable seat. At Icelandic horse shows, horses moving at much faster gaits than the tolt are mounted by thirsty riders carrying filled champagne glasses to demonstrate the smoothness of this unique movement.

However, riding anything for 7 hours is bound to tire you out. The horses don't wear shock absorbers – ditto for the riders. Ouch! In other words, these trips are for people who are looking for a physical challenge of sorts, measured though it is. Sharing this type of experience in groups consisting of as many as 18 guests plus a herd of 60 horses, riding through a terrain that more often than not appears to be the stage setting for a film, is a tremendous experience. The large number of rides offered are an indication of their popularity, the number of returning riders who want new alternatives, and the quality of these rides.

The planning that goes into running a successful Iceland wilderness ride is astonishing. Just when you are tired, a hot stream or thermal pool will appear. Your days on horseback end at places that offer more than pup tent comforts for a weary group. The rhythm of the ride, the secret of every successful outfit, is exquisite. There is a good balance between heavy-duty physical exercise followed by moments of rapture as you gaze at the latest geological wonder the country offers. Add to that the ever present thermal pools, heated lagoons and streams, and you have a country that knows how to take some of the tired out of your body and leave you wanting to get up and do it again.

Guests are driven from the airport at the beginning of the ride in Ishestar buses and returned in Ishetar buses at the trip's end. All transfers are included in the package.

HIGHLIGHTS

Year round single day tours on horseback • Icelandic horses • Novice to experienced • 8 days/7 nights stationary farm stay • 31 starting dates for 8 to 18 day riding tours • 20 starting dates for 2 to 5 day tours • Group capacity between 16 and 18 guests • Each guest assigned 3 to 4 horses per tour • Driving herd of 50 to 60 horses

ICELANDIC RIDING TOURS (continued)

CHILDREN'S PROGRAM: Children receive a 25% discount, but they must be older than 10 and be able to ride for long hours.

ACCOMMODATIONS: Most of the longer rides involve a first and last night in comfortable guest houses in Reykjavik, where single or double rooms are available. On point to point riding tours, you will generally sleep in a variety of accommodations, varying from co-ed mountain huts to schools, farmhouses and guest houses. Hot springs, hot pools and swimming pools will often be available when showers are not. The mountain huts are warm and most offer indoor w.c. and running water. You will sleep in large rooms with 8 to 12 beds in sleeping bags. All of the tours are designed to provide the most comfortable arrangements possible without sacrificing the chance to enjoy Iceland's natural beauty.

SPECIAL ACTIVITIES: Riding is, of course, the special activity, although you always will be directed to the unusual and spectacular natural features of Iceland. A careful review of the company brochure will reveal some variation in the trips, including rides among the reindeer and whale watching.

MEALS: Good food is a concern and a source of pride in Iceland. Guests are served large breakfasts and prepare lunch packets from the breakfast buffet. At the mountain huts, dinner is prepared and brought to you in a kitchen van which also transports your luggage. You will be greeted with warm food after your day's ride.

RIDING STUFF: Riders may expect to spend 5 to 7 hours a day in the saddle, covering 25 to 40 kms. daily. Each rider rotates among 3 or 4 horses during the day, while the resting horses move freely along in a herd driven by staff and riders. There are very few places in the world where you can let horses run alongside the riders and this is a rare thrill, reminiscent of the kind of thing you may have only seen in "cowboy movies." The horses will generally move at a tolting gait which covers ground rapidly. The special gaits of the Icelandic horse make it unnecessary to post at the tolt which generally places you comfortably in the saddle and makes riding a pleasure. Horses are switched every few hours to keep them fresh. At faster paces, the Icelandics remain very comfortable horses to ride, requiring much less physical exertion than most other breeds. Intermediate level riding experience is definitely not necessary on most rides, but "intermediate fitness" is advisable. The horses' movement is very smooth, but it is not the same as sitting in a Rolls Royce and you will get tired. Like all horses, Icelandics vary in their degree of athleticism and the more experienced riders will be assigned to stronger, more athletic horses.

The various rides are distinguished by the amount of ground covered daily and the difficulty of the terrain. Rock formations, glaciers, geysers, thermal pools, reindeer, whale watching, active and dormant volcanoes, and seemingly endless lava fields are all things you may not experience anywhere else on this planet. You will ride through mountains, streams, valleys, highlands, along smooth beaches and over rocky terrain.

The weather is subject to change several times in the course of a day and rain gear is definitely advisable. Even though the sun shines nearly 24 hours a day during the summer riding season, if you wait 5 minutes in Iceland, the weather is sure to change. Temperature is generally above 60° Fahrenheit (15° Centigrade) in the summer and over 30° Fahrenheit (0° Centigrade) in the winter. The climate is actually a lot easier to tolerate than the country's name would suggest.

THE TOURS

Day Tours: All single day tours begin and end in the Reykjavik area, take 4 to 7 hours, and are organized around notable sites. The riding varies from a 1½ to 6 hour ride and includes transfers to the riding center as well as lunch. For weekend travelers to Iceland, or for those of you passing through, this is a wonderful opportunity to experience Icelandic horses while visiting some areas of interest.

ICELANDIC RIDING TOURS (continued)

KJOLUR RIDE (10days/9nights): Ishestar's most popular tour ride will introduce you to a wide variety of Iceland's natural wonders. You will visit lakes with floating icebergs, geothermal regions, lava fields and mountains. You will ride for 5 to 7 hours daily, covering 30 to 45 kms. Accommodations include guest houses, holiday farms and mountain huts.

THE GOLDEN CIRCLE (8 days/7 nights) and **GEYSIR-GULFOSS SPECIAL** (5 days/4 nights): Both of these tours accommodate advanced to less experienced riders and cover 30 to 40 kms. daily. Accommodations offer the luxury of either a holiday farm or guest house. You will see geysers, waterfalls, mountains, and rivers while enjoying comfortable sleeping arrangements.

SNAEFELLSNES (9 days/8 nights) and **SNAE-FELLSNES BEACH RIDES** (5 days/4 nights): A very pleasant ride along beaches and through mountain areas dotted with lakes. You will enjoy some beautiful riding on the west coast of Iceland along sandy beaches. Depending on tidal conditions, there may be some sunlit night beach riding. Riding consists of 5 to 7 hours per day (30 to 40 kms).

MYVATN (9 days/8 nights): One highlight of this ride is the opportunity to get in some good whale watching, weather permitting, plus a beach party under the midnight sun. You will ride 5 to 8 hours a day, visiting magnificent waterfalls, Lake Myvatn, hot pools, and geothermally heated swimming pools.

EGILSSTADIR (10 days/9 nights): This magical ride covers Iceland's eastern region, an undeveloped area that is home to large herds of reindeer. The largest glaciers in Europe, the old volcano Snaefell, valleys, mountains and canyons provide the background. Accommodations include summer hotels, holiday farms, and mountain huts. You will spend 5 to 7 hours per day on horseback.

SPRENGISANDUR (12 days/11 nights): For those who want to test skill and fitness, this is the ride for you! It covers 350 kms. in 9 days of riding and is recommended only for experienced riders able to spend long days in the saddle. The ride moves north through a stark landscape graced with glaciers, numerous rivers, waterfalls, and Mount Arnarfell. Accommodations are provided in hotels, huts, and at a holiday farm.

LANDMANNALAUGAR (10 days/9 nights): Another tour into paradise that covers the interior of Iceland, including the natural hot bath region from which the ride takes its name. You will ride through lava fields dating from 1480, past volcanoes, onto a big glacier, and through a continually changing environment.

HOLIDAY FARM SPECIAL (8 days/7 nights): This trip is designed for families who prefer more comfortable accommodations and less riding. The program includes 5 nights at a holiday farm where you will be able to do some riding, visits to the Gullfoss waterfall and a world-famous geyser, as well as ancient ruins.

There are several other rides of varying lengths and equal merit. It is the combination of incredible horses, a landscape that will leave you wondering when you boarded the rocket for the moon, and some excellent planning which allows you to enjoy the beauty and unusual geological features of this unique country.

AUTHOR'S COMMENT: *The temptation with Icelandic horses is to say, "Look how cute they are!" and that would be the truth, or at least half of it. Quite simply, they are more than cute. They are strong, smooth-moving horses ideal for trekking and riding with pace over varied terrain. Iceland is of the earth and yet it is not. It is certainly worth the time for riders, travelers and the simply curious. So let's meet in friendly Reykjavik, hoist a schnapps, and go off into the "land of the moon" to perform our own version of the "moonwalk" on a remarkable breed of horses amidst volcanoes, glaciers, geysers, hot springs, whales, reindeer, mountains, lakes, rivers, 24 hour sun, and free roaming horses.*

ALLIE CROSS EQUESTRIAN CENTRE

BASIC: US Agent: **Laura Pray**, Crazy Oaks Farm, Rt.2, Box 331B, Charleston, WV 25324, USA
Tel: (304) 744-8270   Tel: (800) 757-1667
Fax: (304) 744-2324   Email: laurapray@citynet.net
UK Contact: Willie Leahy, Allie Cross, Loughrea, County Galway, Ireland
Tel: (353) 91-841216   Fax: (353) 91-842363
Email: tct@tinet.net

WHEN: Hunting, mid-October to March 1; Cross-country, late September to March 1

AIRPORTS: Galway; Shannon; Dublin

LOCATION: Loughrea, central east coast of Ireland.

PRICE: Hotel: £815 ($1305) per week, per person, double occupancy, add £90 ($144) per week for single; B&B: £675 ($1080) per week, per person, double occupancy, add £50 ($80) per week for single occupancy; Self catering: £422 ($675) per week in area rental cottages. Capping fee (hunting) £75 ($120) per day. There are also many self-catering places in the area.

Jumping the famous stone walls of Ireland, hunting with the Galway Blazers 1 to 3 times during your week long stay, a cold brew, good accommodations, the charming Leahy family—what more could you want out of life? If stonewall jumping and hunting sound like too much for you, the Centre will be happy to accommodate with an individually designed program to improve your jumping skills, while allowing you to enjoy some great cross-country riding through the beautiful farms and forestland of County Galway. Non-riders will find plenty to do, especially if a vehicle is arranged, including drives to the ocean and shopping in nearby towns in between visits to your favorite fishing spot or golf course.

CHILDREN'S PROGRAM: Children should be age 12 or older to hunt and at least 7 years old for trail riding, jumping and cross-country.

ACCOMMODATIONS: Accommodations are in 3 or 4 star Irish country hotels and inns with private baths. The inns and hotels reflect the cultivated charm of a bygone era. The B&Bs tend to be newer, but private baths cannot be guaranteed. You may also choose a self-catering program.

SPECIAL ACTIVITIES: An ideal location for sightseeing as well as shopping. Connemara, the Aran Islands, the cliffs of Moher, and the famous monastery at Clonmacnois are all easy day trips.

MEALS: Breakfast is usually a communal meal served as you appear between 8 and 10 a.m. Lunch is a picnic, sometimes in a local pub or the Leahy kitchen, but often right in the field with the horses. Dinner is always a social affair. At the hotels, 4 course meals featuring local products are served, while the B&Bs serve hearty, country meals. Vegetarians will be accommodated, but please notify Laura before departure of any special dietary needs.

RIDING STUFF: The County Galway Hunt is one of the oldest and best known in the world. There are 2 theories on how this hunt got its nickname, "The Blazers." One is that the members burned down a pub in a post-Hunt celebration, and the other is that the name reflects the rapid pace at which they travel through the countryside. Whatever the case, the Blazers are well known for being very friendly to visitors and the "stone wall country" makes for some great hunting. The week's ride at Allie Cross will include at least one visit to Dartfield, where the Leahys have a fantastic cross-country course, created by a top European designer, featuring one of the best water complexes in Ireland. Jumps range from Novice through FEI Intermediate level—this means from "fairly small" to "really big," for those not familiar with eventing lingo. It is a great opportunity to learn from a horse who really knows his stuff.

AUTHOR'S COMMENT: *Catch the fever! Join the boys of Galway for a romp in the countryside…a bit of a nip, the call of the huntsman, and away we go. The County Galway Hunt is certainly a time-honored tradition. Alternatively, you may use the week to improve your cross-country skills in a land where field jumping still thrives.*

HIGHLIGHTS
Monday to Sunday accommodations • Hunt with the Galway Blazers • 1 to 3 hunting opportunities per visit • Customized cross-country jumping program • Approved by Irish Horse Board, Association of Riding Establishments

CONNEMARA and COAST TRAILS

BASICS: US Agent: **Laura Pray**, Crazy Oaks Farm, Rt.2, Box 331B, Charleston, WV 25324, USA
Tel: (304) 744-8270   Tel: (800) 757-1667
Fax: (304) 744-2324
Email: laurapray@citynet.net
UK Contact: Willie Leahy, Allie Cross, Loughrea, County Galway, Ireland
Tel: (353) 91-841216 Fax: (353) 91-842363
Email: tct@tinet.net

WHEN: April to September
AIRPORTS: Galway; Shannon; Dublin
LOCATION: West Ireland
PRICE: Hotel: £825 ($1320) per week, per person, double occupancy, add £90 ($144) per week for single occupancy; B&B: £650 ($1040) per week, per person, double occupancy, add £50 ($80) per week for single occupancy.

Well-known owner Willie Leahy and family will entertain you on this granddaddy of all horseback riding vacations. Attention is paid to each rider to ensure a quality ride for guests of varying skill and fitness levels. Just as pace is adjusted to fit individual needs, the accommodations cater to a variety of desires. In all cases, you will find your hosts incredibly charming, the horses willing and able, the country beautiful, and good humor seldom absent. Non-riders are offered an attractive package of alternatives that permit them to join the riding crowd nightly for drinks, food and fun. Non-riders should carefully plan their trips by reviewing all of the alternatives in advance with Laura Pray.

CHILDREN'S PROGRAM: Qualified riders over 7, but you must speak to Laura Pray to discuss details.

ACCOMMODATIONS: Accommodations are in 3 or 4 star Irish country hotels and inns, always charming, with private baths. The B&Bs tend to be newer houses, but private baths cannot be guaranteed.

SPECIAL ACTIVITIES: Cycling, golf, fishing, walking, sightseeing and shopping alternatives may be planned for non-riders.

MEALS: Breakfast is served as you appear between 8 and 10 a.m. Lunch is a picnic, usually right in the field with the horses, but sometimes outside a local pub. Dinner is always a group affair. At the hotels, 4 course meals featuring fresh seafood, beef, and lamb are on offer. The B&Bs serve good country meals. Vegetarians can be accommodated, but if you are staying at a B&B, please let Laura know in advance.

RIDING STUFF: Riders may bring their own saddles or enjoy the English or Western saddles provided. The horses vary from purebred Connemaras, Thoroughbreds and Irish Draughts to Irish Hunters (T'bred-Draught cross) and Connemara-Thoroughbred crosses. Riders generally should expect to spend 5 to 6 hours a day in the saddle, except on the relaxed ride, where riders spend 3 to 4 hours a day on horseback. On all trips the scenery will vary from mountains to seacoast, with opportunities for gallops, jumping, cantering and other activities. Attention is always paid to individual rider needs and riders may opt for all or none of the more vigorous riding activities. Ocean swims with horses are a regular part of all trips. Expect some gorgeous greenery throughout your trip to the land of Shamrocks.

AUTHOR'S COMMENT: *If there was ever a casting call for the perfect Irish rogue, Willie Leahy would have to be nominated! Willie has a wicked sense of humor, is a wonderful provider of entertaining trips, and possesses a knowledge of horses equal to the very best. Like most equestrian service providers, Laura Pray has a contagious enthusiasm for this ride and it can be catching.*

HIGHLIGHTS

Connemara Trail Ride/ Coast Trail – 6 days/6 nights • Relaxed Connemara Ride – 6 days/6 nights/5 days riding • English or Western saddles • Novice to experienced • From exciting beach riding to beautiful inland mountains • Vehicle supported • Approved by Irish Horse Board, Association of Riding Establishments

DRUMGOOLAND HOUSE and EQUESTRIAN CENTRE   www.travel-ireland.com/drumhrse

BASICS: 29 Dunnanew Road, Seaforde, Downpatrick, County Down, BT30 8PJ, Northern Ireland
Tel: 013968-11956
Fax: 013968-11265 (from UK)
Tel: (44) 1396811956
Fax: (44) 13968-11265 (from US)
Email: frank.me_leigh@virgin.net

WHEN: Open year round.

AIRPORTS: Belfast - a 45 minute drive; Dublin - a 2 hour drive. Transfers available by arrangement.

LOCATION: A 10 minute drive from Newcastle and Downpatrick; a 30 minute drive from Belfast.

PRICE: *Trail Rides:* £519 ($830) to £685 ($1096) 6 days/6 nights, per person, double occupancy, includes accommodations with full board; or £287 ($459) to £359 ($574) 3 days/3 nights, per person, double occupancy, includes B&B accommodations. *Horsemanship Holiday:* £575 ($920) to £725 ($1160) 7 days/7 nights, per person, double occupancy, includes breakfast, lunch (and dinner with some programs), accommodations and riding. *Weekend Riding Break:* £135 ($216) 2 days/2 nights, per person, double occupancy, includes 6 hours of riding and B&B accommodations.

Drumgooland House is a friendly, family-run operation. Horse people to the bone, owners Frank and Alice McLeigh offer quality accommodations, good horses, sensitivity to nervous or inexperienced riders, and a well-trained staff. Three members of the family have been on the Irish national teams. All guides are trained and carry mobile phones. On trail rides, guests are divided into separate groups to accommodate different skill levels. Rider safety hats will be supplied. This is a well respected riding center located on 60 acres with a trout stocked lake and adjoining equestrian center.

CHILDREN'S PROGRAM: The horsemanship program that combines lessons with trail riding can be especially designed for children. Children accompanied by an adult may participate in trail riding.

ACCOMMODATIONS: There are several alternative packages, including farm and country house stays at Drumgooland House and Slieve Cobb Inn or B&Bs. The former includes all meals. Accommodations are approved by the Northern Irish Tourist Board.

SPECIAL ACTIVITIES: There is a trout stocked lake at Drumgooland House, 6 golf courses within a 20 minute drive, coarse fishing, bike riding, and more.

MEALS: You will enjoy a full Irish breakfast wherever you stay and a picnic snack lunch daily, except Wednesdays, when guests visit a local pub for lunch. On trail rides, town and country house accommodations include meals at a different restaurant each night.

RIDING STUFF: Drumgooland House has 50 Irish bred horses for your riding pleasure. Trail riding is vehicle supported and well planned, with good opportunities for some brisk beach canters as well as extended trots while moving through beautiful areas which include lakes, the Mourne and Slieve Na Slatt Mountains, forests and the golden sandy beach at Newcastle. The *Horsemanship Holiday* offers ground instruction on horse care as well as 12 hours of lessons (including show jumping, basic dressage, and cross-country riding), 5 hours of trail riding, a half day beach ride, and 3 hours of trekking. *The Weekend Riding Break* package is ideal for less experienced riders and includes 1 hour of tuition and 6 hours of riding.

AUTHOR'S COMMENT: *Drumgooland House, a large country house which comes highly recommended, offers a classic example of Irish hospitality. It is located in County Down which is characterized by gentle undulating terrain. Be sure to watch for the seals near the estuary if you take the beach ride at Newcastle.*

HIGHLIGHTS
3 and 6 day trail rides (must be able to trot and canter) • Guest capacity 10 • 7 day horsemanship programs with trail riding • Weekend break packages • More than 50 horses • British Horse Society Approved

El RANCHO HORSE HOLIDAYS, LTD.

www.iol.ie/kerry-insight/elrancho/index.html

BASICS: Dingle Peninsula Trail Rides/El Rancho Farmhouse & Riding Stables, Ballyard, Tralee, County Kerry, Ireland
Tel/Fax: (353) 66-21840
Email: elrancho@iol.ie
WHEN: Open Easter to October 1.
AIRPORTS: Shannon - a 2 hour drive.
LOCATION: Dingle Peninsula in southwest Ireland. Kerry is only 12 miles from the property.
PRICE: *Dingle Peninsula Trail Ride:* £525 ($840) 7 days/7 nights, per person, d/o, includes all accommodations (5 nights at farmhouse with *en suite* bath and 2 similar options), all meals, 6 days of riding. *Mini Trail Rides:* £332 ($532) 8 days/7 nights, per person, d/o, includes 4 nights B&B accommodations at El Rancho farmhouse with full board, 2 hour treks to Slieve Mish mountains and Queen Scotia's Glen, join the Dingle Peninsula Ride for 3 days trekking with full board and accommodations. *Farmhouse Stay*: £218 ($350) per week per person, d/o, includes guest house B&B accommodations plus 4 treks to the Slieve Mish mountains and Queen Scotia's Glen (2 hours each). Prices listed are for high season. Other combinations possible.

Operating since 1967, proprietor William J. O'Connor has created a loyal following of happy trail riders. This ride takes you through beautiful country where the movie *Ryan's Daughter* was filmed, and offers opportunities for thrilling gallops along miles of golden sandy beaches alternating with treks through mountain gorges and along fuchsia-lined green trails. Vehicles transport luggage. You will spend your days riding the trails of Slieve Mish Mountains or racing along Kilcummin, Stradbally, Tralee Bay and Derrymore beaches and will certainly appreciate the awesome beauty of this land, the friendliness of its people, and the quality of the horses.

CHILDREN'S PROGRAM: Children can participate if they are experienced riders.

ACCOMMODATIONS: Accommodations are provided in Irish Tourist Board approved farmhouses and B&Bs with bathrooms *en suite.* Accommodations are selected with great care, with concern for your comfort a priority.

SPECIAL ACTIVITIES: On stationary holidays you can enjoy nearby tennis, fishing, golf and shooting. Shopping for high quality handicrafts in Dingle, touring Blenner's Mill, visiting an ancient beehive hut built by a monk over 1000 years ago, and the singing pubs of Tralee, are among the many delights of this scenic peninsula.

MEALS: All trips offer full Irish breakfasts, lunch packs, and 3 course dinners, topped off with desserts and complimentary Irish coffee drinks. The evening meals are a delightful and relaxing part of the total experience.

RIDING STUFF: English tack on Connemara ponies and Irish Hunters are standard. The 8 day trips begin on Sundays with a beach ride that moves inland, stopping at Peter Daily's Pub. Riders will average 4 to 5 hours in the saddle with opportunities for some exciting beach gallops. You will also enjoy riding through wild boglands, enchanting forests, past waterfalls, along winding streams and through valleys, where the sound of hooves competes only with the music of rippling river waters and the bleating of lambs. You are expected to help look after you assigned horse. Riders must be able to gallop a straight line and canter a figure 8 in open fields.

AUTHOR'S COMMENT: *Thirty years of trail riding experience has given this experienced outfitter a thorough knowledge of what his clients need. These trips offer good riding, a spectacular environment, and the typically friendly interaction with the local folks that experienced travelers have come to expect of their Irish vacations. Videos available on request quoting C-T.W.R.V.*

HIGHLIGHTS
Intermediate and fit riders for all trekking trips • Weekly trips • 3 day mini trips • Weight restriction 185 lbs. • Exciting riding along beaches and through rugged inland mountains • Group limit 10 • Approved by Irish Horse Board, Association of Riding Establishments

ERIC PELE: "The Art of Horsepersonship" AT BROOKVALE FARM

BASICS: Brookvale, 57 Lisbane Road, Saintfield, County Down, Northern Ireland
Tel/Fax: 01238-510390 (from UK)
Tel/Fax: (44) 1238-510390 (from US)
WHEN: Will operate year round beginning Spring 1999.
AIRPORTS: Belfast International – a 45 minute drive to the Farm; Belfast City Airport – a 30 minute drive; Dublin City Airport – a 2 hour drive.
LOCATION: Brookvale Farm is a 45 minute drive from Belfast.
PRICE: £650 ($1040) 7 days/6 nights, per person, double occupancy, includes all meals, accommodations, plus 24 hours of tuition.

Brookvale Farm, Olivia and Eric Pele's new home, will be opening for the 1999 spring season. The US has Monty Roberts, and its fictional "Horse Whisperers" to teach them the ways of the horse and new ways to interact with them, and Europe has Eric Pele. Eric combines the holistic principals of rider and horse interaction that Roberts suggests with the classical methods he learned as a graduate of the prestigious *Cadre Noir* of Saumur in France. The result is a training program that pays as much attention to the relationship between horse, rider and the environment, as it does to classical posture, aids, and control that tradition dictates. "The goal is to help produce *sympathetic, efficient* riders."

CHILDREN'S PROGRAM: Children must be 16 years of age or older.

ACCOMMODATIONS: Accommodations are provided at the Dufferin Arms Hotel, about a 20 minute drive from the Farm. The Dufferin Arms is a recently renovated hotel with its own Irish-style pub/restaurant. All of the rooms have *en suite* baths. The hotel is located on the shores of Stangford Lough, and is only a mere 100 meters from the magnificent, old but fully restored, Killyeagh Castle.

SPECIAL ACTIVITIES: Guests may take a boating trip on Stangford Lough. There is a golf course less than 1 kilometer from Brookvale Farm and many others nearby. There is hiking in the nearby Mourne Mountains, 30 kilometers from the Farm, or you can enjoy visiting St. Patrick's grave in Downpatrick. There is also an aquarium nearby.

MEALS: Riders are offered a hearty Irish breakfast, lunch, and a quality Irish pub-style dinner at the hotel.

RIDING STUFF: Riders must be experienced in at least 2 of the 3 disciplines of dressage, show jumping and cross-country in order to benefit from the level of training provided. You must have enough confidence to jump over 1.1 meters (3.6 feet) on a trained horse. Eric uses a variety of horses, up to 16 of them, including well-trained mounts able to jump more than 1.25 meters (over 4 feet) and do lateral work as well, plus some 5 to 6 year olds, and 5 school-master hunting types. Video analysis, lessons, lectures, and the use of multiple horses per student are all part of Eric's unique classical training program. There is also some trail riding in conjunction with the program in the Mourne Mountains. The weight limit is 95 kg. (210 lbs.) (15 stone). A personalized follow-up program can be arranged for return guests

AUTHOR'S COMMENT: *I like to think of Eric as offering the classicist's version of "horse whispering" to produce an increased awareness of the horse as part of the package of skills needed to become a more efficient rider. If you find yourself struggling through competitions, somehow always directing your horse an inch too close to that jump, and/or having them quit on you with an intermittent regularity, then you need this training program. If you are locked, as many of us are, into your riding mistakes, Eric will offer fresh insight on how to grow and improve as a rider, rather than moan and blame the horses.*

HIGHLIGHTS
English tack • Equitation training • Training in dressage, cross-country, and jumping • Requires riders with experience in all areas • Lectures, discussions, demonstrations • Riding on a variety of competition-trained horses • Group size limited to 6 riders • Saturday to Sunday stays

HORSE HOLIDAY FARM

http://homepage.tinet.ie/~horseridingireland

BASIC: Tilman and Colette Anhold, Grange, County Sligo, Ireland
Tel: 0035371-66152
Fax: 0035371-66400 (from UK)
Tel: (353) 7166152
Fax (353) 7166400 (from US)
Email: hhf@tinet.ie

WHEN: Year round

AIRPORTS: Dublin Airport for international flights. From Dublin you can fly into Sligo Airport or drive (about 50 minutes), take a train (about 3 hours), or a bus (about 4 hours).

LOCATION: Northwest Ireland, on the Atlantic Coast.

PRICES: *Riding by the Sea:* £650 ($1020) 6 days/7 nights, per person, d/o, includes 6 days of riding. *The Sligo Trail:* £468 ($750) to £500 ($800) 6 days/7 nights, per person, d/o, includes B&B. *The Donegal Trail:* £937 ($1500) to £1000 ($1600) 15 days/14 nights, per person, d/o, includes B&B, 12 days of riding. *Hunting and Cross Country Packages:* £450 ($700) to £770 ($1300) 8 days/7 nights, per person, d/o, includes B&B with 5 course dinners, 4 days cross-country riding, 2 days hunting (cap fees included). *Winter Weekend Specials:* from £350 ($550) 5 days/4 nights, per person, d/o, includes B&B with 5 course dinners, unlimited riding.

Horse Holiday Farm is a well known outfitter with 25 years of experience, specializing in self-guided point to point riding trips. Small groups of experienced riders, capable of spending some 6 to 7 hours a day on horseback following well-marked maps will enjoy an adventure not easily available elsewhere. You should have a good understanding of the fundamentals of horse care to insure the maximum satisfactory interaction with your horse.

CHILDREN'S PROGRAM: No children's program.

ACCOMMODATIONS: Accommodations at Horse Holiday Farm or neighboring guest houses offer comfortable quarters with *en suite* facilities. On trail riding holidays, designated accommodations are prebooked with a concern for maximizing your comfort.

SPECIAL ACTIVITIES: The riding will take through many areas where you can rest, visit a local pub, or stop to sightsee whenever it suits you.

MEALS: Hearty Irish breakfasts are always filling and delicious. Lunch can be packed for your ride or purchased at a pub along the way. Dinner is not included on all trips, but can always be purchased at the farm houses where you will stay.

RIDING STUFF: Tack is English. The horses, mainly Irish Hunters and some Connemara ponies, range in height from 14.2 to 17 hands. They are well-mannered, experienced and sure-footed. You must be able to walk, trot, canter and gallop with confidence. There are a number of riding programs. *Riding by the Sea:* Includes 6 days of riding along the beaches that surround the farm and over the nearly 400 acre cross-country course. A horse will be assigned to you and you are free to ride as much or as little as you like. *The Sligo Trail:* Includes 6 days of trail riding along a well-marked route. Maps are provided to guide you. This ride is designed to allow for 3 days of beach riding and 3 days traveling through the mountains and forests of Sligo. Saddlebags are supplied. Since you carry your own luggage— pack accordingly. *The Donegal Trail:* This offers a modified 7 day program as well as a 14 day program (12 days of riding). You will ride through forests, rugged mountains and along the pristine beaches of County Donegal. During the winter months, Horse Holiday Farms offers 4 day riding by the sea specials as well as fox hunting and cross- country riding.

AUTHOR'S COMMENT: *This well-known ride offers small groups a wonderful opportunity to enjoy self-guided trips—the experience of a lifetime.*

HIGHLIGHTS
Self-guided point to point riding • English saddles • Experienced riders • Thrilling beach riding through beautiful inland mountains • Weight limit 14 stone (196 lbs.) (89 kg.) • Group size under 10 • Approved by Irish Horse Board, Association of Riding Establishments

MALVARINA TRAIL RIDE

www.equestrianvacations.com

BASICS: Agent: **Cross Country International**, PO Box 1170, Milbrook, NY 12545, USA
Tel: (914) 677-6000
Tel: (800) 828-8768 (North and South America)
Fax (914) 677-6077
Email: xcintl@aol.com
WHEN: March through November.

AIRPORTS/TRAIN STATIONS: Rome. Foligno train station.
LOCATION: Assisi
PRICE: $1400 (£875) 7days/6 nights, per person, double occupancy, all-inclusive with 4 days of riding. Single supplement add $150 (£94).

Ride along the ancient roads from Roman times, through beautiful, countryside dotted with buildings that reflect Italy's history. You will ride to a 16th century church on your way to a tiny convent built in 1426 at an elevation of 2400 feet—the very spot where St. Francis and his followers used to retire to fast, pray and meditate. On other days, you will ride to a medieval castle at Coppepino, pass by Spello, a city with 100 churches, visit the Mount Subsasio National Park at 3800 feet, as well as other interesting sights along the way. Riding in Italy is a trip through the history and culture of earlier times, offering a glimpse of the slower paced lifestyle still found in the rural villages of this area. Each night you return to Malvarina, where some world class meals will serve as the perfect finish to the day's adventure.

CHILDREN'S PROGRAM: Children must be comfortable on horseback and be able to walk, trot and canter.

ACCOMMODATIONS: Comfortable accommodations include large beds and *en suite* bathrooms.

MEALS: The cuisine has been favorably reviewed in *Bon Appétit* as among the best in Umbria. In fact, chefs from all over Italy come to Malvarina to learn the secrets of Umbrian cooking. Breakfast descriptions alone should stimulate your culinary juices, consisting of fresh ricotta cheese and home-made *marmellate* (jams), freshly baked *biscotti* or cakes from Maria's kitchen, tasty breads, fresh fruit, Italian expresso and *caffé latte*.

SPECIAL ACTIVITIES: Non-riders are welcome and, if you rent a car, you will have plenty of alternative activities to keep you busy. This area reflects Italy's long and varied history. On Wednesday, your day off from riding, transportation to Perugia and Assisi is provided.

RIDING STUFF: This is a 6 day ride, ideal for those who want to enjoy all the pleasures of Italy plus riding. The comfortable accommodations feature large beds, *en suite* bathrooms and some of the best cuisine in Italy. Building an appetite will be easy on brisk rides through the surrounding countryside. You will spend 4 full days in the saddle with 1 day off to see Umbria via more modern transport. You will ride through miles of olive groves to Assisi, a charming town most famous as the home of St. Francis of Assisi, the great lover of animals. On another day, you will travel into the mountains, passing many Roman ruins and visit a lovingly-restored village and castle. You will also ride to one of the region's highest points, Mount Subasio. From here you can see the cities of Assisi and Perugia. One day you will head for the Hermitage, where St. Francis spent years in prayer. Riders dismount to walk up to this holy site, enjoying the beautiful views and peaceful silence.

AUTHOR'S COMMENT: *Malvarina is the epitome of a great European vacation, enjoyable horses, great food, and a region that is both attractive to ride through and rich in Italian culture and history.*

HIGHLIGHTS
Experienced riders • Group limit 12 • English and Western tack • Comfortable accommodations • Excellent cuisine • Sunday to Saturday

THE HEART OF TUSCANY RIDE

BASICS: Inntravel, Hovingham, York Y06 4JZ, UK
Tel: 01653-628811
Fax: 01653-628741 (from UK)
Tel: (44) 1653-628811
Fax (44) 1653-628741 (from US)
WHEN: March to October
AIRPORTS: Pisa - 2 hours by train or car. Transfers from Folloncia train station are included.

LOCATION: Central Tuscany, southwest of Florence and Sienna
PRICE: Prices start at £765 ($1224) per week, per person, double occupancy and include airfare from London. Alternatively, you can arrange to rent a car through Inntravel and drive to Tuscany.

April in Paris is nice, but try Tuscany on horseback and you will travel through history enjoying excellent food, a wonderful climate, and some very good riding. Tuscany is one of those special places blessed with an abundance of charm, beautiful sites, ancient ruins, pleasant weather, a very romantic atmosphere and it is rich in history. This is the stuff of which dreams are made! Non-riders, provided that they rent a car, will have plenty of things to do and places to go. Rifugio Prategegiano is a well-established inn that has been providing quality enjoyment for many years. This region of Italy has a long tradition of horse breeding and riding.

CHILDREN'S PROGRAM: Suitable for competent riders over 15.

ACCOMMODATIONS: Guests stay in comfortable bedrooms rustically decorated with lots of old wood and pristine white walls. All rooms have showers and WCs.

MEALS: The evening meal is a time for outrageous exaggerations of the day's events while enjoying excellent pasta dishes as well as steaks and other treats, accompanied by Chianti wines.

SPECIAL ACTIVITIES: Riders will be busy on horseback, but non-riders who rent a car will find an abundance of delightful activities, from driving along the Mediterranean coast to visiting ancient towns filled with Roman ruins that have survived all over Tuscany. The truly energetic will want to visit Florence, where there are almost too many things to do.

RIDING STUFF: Rifugio Prategegiano uses only Maremma horses, which are fit and agile and can easily handle up to 25 miles daily. The tack is English. On either the Maremma Trail Ride or The Trail to the Sea, you will cover 100 miles on horseback, but will be transported by minibus to and from your horses each day. The horses are left at local farms and riding centers while your tired bodies are driven back to the Rifugio. The Maremma Trail Ride includes treks through valleys, woodlands, and a Maremma cattle farm as well as visits to Renaissance estates, hot springs, and ancient ruins. On the Trail to the Sea, you will spend at least 1 day riding along the Ligurian Sea, where you can enjoy some exciting gallops and a swim with your horse. You may also choose a local riding program which begins and ends at Rufugio Prategegiano each day. This ride typically involves 4 to 7 hours in the saddle daily. The pace varies and there will be some good opportunities for fast riding. Riders will travel though forests as well as plenty of open countryside, suitable for a gentle but varied pace.

AUTHOR'S COMMENT: *Vacation destination to thousands of riders over the years, the landscape, the horses, and the property are sure to delight. Tuscany is very romantic, an ideal place to visit and ride.*

HIGHLIGHTS
Tuscan countryside • Experienced riders • Group limit 12 • Weight limit 13 stone (182 lbs.) (82 kg.) • Sunday to Sunday • English tack • Trail rides through Maremma or to the Ligurian Sea with nightly bus rides back to the property • Leisurely riding beginning and ending at property nightly • Hotel quality accommodations - listed in Michelin Guide

ALCAINCA DRESSAGE PROGRAM

www.ridingtours.com

BASICS: Agent: **Equitour**, PO Box 807, Dubois, WY 82513, USA
Tel: (800) 545-0019   Tel: (307) 455-3363
Fax: (307) 455-2354
Email: equitor@wyoming.com
WHEN: Year round.
AIRPORTS: Lisbon. Transfers are free for stays of 5 nights or longer.
LOCATION: Alcainca is located 30 kms. northwest of Lisbon, only 15 kms. from the Atlantic Ocean.
PRICE: $150 (£94) per night, per person, double occupancy. Single supplement add $20 (£13) per night. Price includes horses, instruction, accommodations, meals, beverages, and taxes.

Taking lessons apart from someone other than your regular instructor is often not very helpful. There are exceptions of course and Alcainca's program would certainly stand out as one of them. The chance to ride Lusitano stallions and receive classical instruction provides an opportunity to improve your riding techniques and knowledge that is difficult to turn down, especially if dressage is one of your interests as a rider. This is an established, well-tested program that has been providing high quality instruction for years.

CHILDREN'S PROGRAMS: There are no special children's programs.

ACCOMMODATIONS: Guests stay in a guest house on the premises of the training center. The guest house has 3 bedrooms with 2 shared bathrooms. The property has an outdoor swimming pool and a bar.

SPECIAL ACTIVITIES: The Atlantic Ocean is only 15 kms. away and the famous cloister at Mafra is a short drive (5 kms.). Lisbon is under 30 minutes by car. The nearby town of Sintra, has been found to be one of the most picturesque towns in Europe by many, including the poet Byron.

MEALS: All meals are served in the dining room located off the riding hall. The meals are plentiful and wholesome with an emphasis on fresh fruit, vegetables, and seafood. There are restaurants within walking distance if you prefer a change.

RIDING STUFF: The horses are either pure-bred or part-bred Lusitanos, mostly stallions. The breed is world-famous and frequently exported. Classical dressage saddles are used for lessons and Portuguese military-type saddles are used for the trail rides. The program offers instruction from beginning levels through Class M, Dona Vaquera Spanish riding style, and introduction into *haute école* dressage is possible. There are both indoor and outdoor riding rings. You will have the option of taking up to 4 hours of lessons per day, which may mean tired muscles and saddle sores, as you are expected to work hard. The riding master is Georges Malleroni who studied classical dressage under Nuno Oliveira, the great Portuguese master. For variety, you can take an occasional trail ride among the hills and woods surrounding the center.

AUTHOR'S COMMENT: *Alcainca offers an exceptional opportunity to study classical dressage at a reasonable price. The sturdy Lusitano stallions are not only beautiful, but extremely well schooled to a high level of performance in the art of dressage. The instruction in English is top flight. The immediate surrounding area is rich in history, which allows you to enjoy a cultural experience as well.*

HIGHLIGHTS
Lusitano stallions • Up to 4 hours of instruction per day • Additional trail riding options • Classic dressage instruction • Temperate climate • From beginners to advanced riders

BLUE COAST/ MIRA ATLANTIC / TRAIL TO THE END OF THE WORLD

BASICS: Agent: **Peregrine Holidays Ltd.**, 41 South Parade, Summertown, Oxford OX2 7JP, UK
Tel: 01865-511642
Fax: 01865-512583 (from UK)
Tel: (44) 1865-511642
Fax: (44) 1865-512583 (from US)
Email: 106357.1754@compuserve.com
WHEN: Open all year.
AIRPORTS: Lisbon or Faro. Free transfers from Faro.
LOCATION: Southwest Portugal, north of Algarve in Alentejo province.
PRICE: *Blue Coast Ride:* £492 ($787) 8 days/7 nights, per person, double occupancy, includes 6 days of riding, 5 to 6 hours daily. *Mira Atlantic Ride:* £396 ($635) 8 days/7 nights, per person, double occupancy, includes 6 days of riding, 3 to 4 hours daily. *Trail to the End of the World:* £895 ($1432) 15 days/14 nights, per person, double occupancy, includes 12 days of riding, 5 to 6 hours daily.

These popular rides have been a staple of the riding holiday industry for years. The rides are led by English-speaking hosts, Robert Lee and Sheila Greenwood. There are many combination rides offered, including a modified Mira Atlantic Ride combined with dressage training, as well as a 2 week ride that combines elements of the Blue Coast and Mira Atlantic Ride. The Algarve area is sparsely populated and offers great contrasts, including lush green valleys, rolling forested hills, and, in season, fields of wildflowers. In addition to the flora and fauna (there are over 200 species of birds) the area is rich in the remains of Roman and Moorish conquerors.

CHILDREN'S PROGRAM: Children must be accompanied by an adult and demonstrate riding competence.

ACCOMMODATIONS: Accommodations are in traditional local hotels, which are clean, comfortable, with lots of charm and private bathrooms. On the Blue Coast Ride you will sleep at 3 different hotels, while on the Mira Atlantic Ride you will stay either at a 3 star hotel in the town of Milfontes or choose an upgraded option.

SPECIAL ACTIVITIES: Organized around different activities for each trip.

MEALS: Breakfast and a large mid-day meal with wine are served on the trail, in the best Portuguese tradition. Dinner is included on the first and last nights only.

RIDING STUFF: The Blue Coast Ride with its 5 to 7 hour riding days, often at an exhilarating pace, provides experienced and fit riders with good opportunities to enjoy extended trots and canters. Riding through a combination of coastal sand dunes, inland forests and farms you will enjoy a varied environment and visit interesting Portuguese towns connected by ancient sand tracks used by oxen, donkeys, horses, and mule drawn carts. In contrast, the Mira Atlantic Ride offers fewer hours in the saddle at a more moderate pace than the Blue Coast Ride. The Trail to the End of the World covers similar ground, but extends the holiday to 14 nights and 12 days of riding. There is even a combination Mira Atlantic Ride which includes classical Portuguese dressage instruction.

AUTHOR'S COMMENT: *Reasonable prices, a moderate climate, beautiful scenery, and terrain suited to spirited riding, have made Portugal a popular riding destination. You will not be disappointed.*

HIGHLIGHTS
English tack • From intermediate to intermediate plus riding skills • Weight limit 12.5 stone (175 lbs.) • 7 to 14 night holidays • 4 to 7 hours riding per day • Rides through Portugal's Blue Coast • Point to point and hotel based vacations • Pure and cross-bred Lusitano horses

THE RUSSIAN ADVENTURE

www.perso.wanadoo.fr/cheval.daventure

BASICS: Agent: **Cheval Adventure/Adventures on Horseback**, Mas du Pommier, 07590 Cellier-du-Luc, France
Tel: (33) 4 66 46 6273   Fax: (33) 4 66 46 6209
Email: cheval.daventure@wanadoo.fr
WHEN: February, 9 days (6 riding).
AIRPORTS: Arrive Moscow, depart St. Petersburg. All land transfers included.

LOCATION: The ride is located 600 kms. north of Moscow; 600 kms. east of St. Petersburg. A night train with a comfortable sleeping compartments will transport you to the starting point for the ride.
PRICE: $1260 (£788) (1200 Euro) per person, double occupancy.

Have you ever dreamt of riding across fresh powder snow or gliding along to the tinkling of *troika* bells and the echoing chimes from winter-shrouded monasteries, then warming up beside a log fire in an *isba*? This ride is no dream! Soft gallops in fine powder snow, the squeak of the *troika* as horses trot along, precious icons in fortified monasteries are offered deep in the heart of "old Russia," with scenery unchanged since the times of Chekov and Dostoevski. You will travel through undulating countryside along small country roads and tracks blanketed in snow, cross pine and birch forests, pass over vast frozen lakes, and stop near Ferapontovo and Kirillov monasteries with their onion domes and rich collections of icons and frescoes dating back to the Middle Ages. You will receive a warm welcome from the hostess as you gather around a steaming samovar in private homes where guests eat and sleep in traditional *isbas*. The intense cold of the "Russian Winter" is made bearable by very dry air and the sun.

CHILDREN'S PROGRAM: Children under 16 must be accompanied by an adult.

ACCOMMODATIONS: Basic facilities in warm private homes, many with steam baths.

SPECIAL ACTIVITIES: Visit famous old monasteries and participate in traditional Russian winter activities.

MEALS: Enjoy a late breakfast of hot tea and biscuits on the ride. Upon arrival at 3 or 4 in the afternoon, tea and local specialties are on offer, followed by a family style meal in the evening.

RIDING STUFF: The Terski and Orlov breeds, traditionally used for racing, are willing, fit and docile. The tack is local. The traditional *troika* is a sleigh pulled by 3 horses harnessed abreast. The *duga*, pulled by a single horse, is still in common use in the country. You may choose between riding on horseback or in a sleigh, or alternate between the two. In either case, it is important to be fit. If you ride horseback, you must be at ease with all paces and capable of riding confidently over varying terrain for several hours at a stretch. An attentive guide attends to individual and group needs while negotiating your way through the intricacies of rural Russia.

AUTHOR'S COMMENT: *Please note that while this trip does not require experienced riders if you choose only the* duga *or* troika*, a high degree of general fitness is still necessary to endure the physical strain and rigors of the famous Russian Winter, which has sent several invading armies into retreat! Fortunately, warmth is just a country house and a pot of tea away, while you enjoy the great beauty and rich historical heritage of Mother Russia. This ride offers a unique and often astonishing riding experience. You might enjoy spending some additional time sightseeing in St. Petersburg at the end of the riding adventure.*

HIGHLIGHTS

Snow riding and sleighing in the countryside • Guest capacity 15 • Ride through forests, over frozen lakes, past old monasteries • Physical fitness and stamina required even for *troika* or *duga* • Experienced riders for horseback • Evening meals and accommodations in private homes • Local Orlov and Terski breeds

ANDALUZ ADVENTURE

BASICS: The Andaluz Adventure/ Finca Los Romeros, Canada del Alamo, Apartado 35, (WW) 11160 Barbate (Cadiz), Spain
Tel: (34) 956-437294   Fax: (34) 956-437271
In UK please contact for bookings: **Ms. Jennie Ward**, Horns Hill, Nether Compton, Sherborne, Dorset DT9 4QA, UK
Tel/Fax (call first): (0)1-935-817567
WHEN: Open all year

AIRPORTS: Gibraltar. Transfers included. Jerez is a 1¼ hour drive; Seville is a 2¼ hour drive; and Malaga is a 2½ hour drive.
LOCATION: Southern Spain, Costa de la Luz.
PRICE: Trail Riding Holidays (April through Oct): $1040 (£650) per person, d/o; Local Riding Holidays: from $672 (£420) low season to $1000 (£625) high season, per person, d/o. Discount of $80 (£50) for second week.

Experienced riders will have wonderful opportunities for spirited gallops on willing and able horses through Parque Natural, a state-owned nature reserve. The reserve was created to protect the unique flora and fauna of this area and includes one of Spain's largest natural pine forests. This ride has been featured on BBC television and in the UK press, including a January 1995 article in *Horse and Hound* by the ever-charming and dapper John Ruler and a November 1997 article in *Horse* magazine.

CHILDREN'S PROGRAM: There is no special children's program.

ACCOMMODATIONS: Guests stay at Finca Los Romeros. Rooms are comfortable with *en suite* bathroom, a front patio terrace facing gardens, and a swimming pool with views overlooking Cape Trafalgar and the Atlantic Ocean.

SPECIAL ACTIVITIES: Every Thursday, when the horses rest, there are escorted trips to the Royal Andalucian Equestrian School in Jerez' followed by sherry tasting and *tapas* at a local bar. Guests may opt instead for a relaxing day of sunbathing and swimming at the large pool on the property or enjoy a walk on the beach. A car will increase your options to enjoy local history, wildlife, and golf. There are also mountain bikes for hire.

MEALS: Hearty local Andalusian home cooking with lots of locally grown vegetables. Vegetarian dishes are available. Meals are served around a farmhouse table with menu choices available for the evening meal. The region is well known for its fresh fish. Free beer, wine, spirits and soft drinks are offered around the pool, during all meals and there is a "help yourself" bar available 'round the clock.

RIDING STUFF: There are 2 basic, 7 day holidays. Participants in Local Riding Holidays ride through Parque Natural, pine forests, rural countryside and along empty beaches with plenty of opportunity for long canters and beach gallops. Trail Riding Holidays cover 125 kms. in 5 days of riding. On the latter, horses are left overnight at local farms while the guests are brought back to Finca Los Romeros each afternoon. This ride offers plenty of beach gallops, long canters over bull breeding plains and a spectacular ride over the sierra with views of Africa.   Except for high summer rides you will spend for 3 to 5 hours a day on horseback. Rides are led by English-speaking guides familiar with the area. Horses are 15 to 16 hands, sure-footed and forward going. They are well tended, but if you wish to help groom and tack up your horse, you are welcome to do so.

AUTHOR'S COMMENT: *Expect some challenging rides, largely free of any road work, with canters through the switchback of soft, undulating sandy tracks in the shady pine forests. The horses enjoy themselves as much as the guests, and the swathe of golden sand at Barbate is a reminder that the Atlantic Ocean attractions of the Costa de la Luz have yet to lure the lotus eaters of the better known Costas.*

HIGHLIGHTS

All riding holidays 7 days/7 nights/5 days riding • Guest capacity 8 riders and up to 4 additional non-riders • Ride through sandy pine forest paths, farm tracks and beaches, past old monasteries • For experienced riders • English saddles • Weight limit 176 lbs. (80 kg.) (12.5 stone) • Guests stay in rooms with *en suite* baths

CABALGAR RUTAS ALTERNATIVAS

BASICS: 18412 – Bubion, Granada, Spain
  Tel/Fax: (34) 958-763-135 (from US)
  Tel/Fax: (0034) 958-763-135 (from UK)
WHEN: Open all year.
AIRPORTS: Malaga. Transfers may be arranged.
  Malaga is about a 3 hour drive from Bubion.
LOCATION: Midway between Granada and Malaga,
Bubion, located in Alpujarra, a UNESCO classified biosphere, is the starting point.
PRICE: $723 (£452) 7 days/6 nights, per person, double occupancy, includes 7 days of riding.
$1188 (£742) 9 days/10 nights, per person, double occupancy, includes 9 days of riding.

Rafael Belmonte has been trekking in this region for 17 years and offers everything from daily rides to vigorous 9 days treks. He wants riders to experience a less-traveled Spain, reminiscent of the country in the 18th and 19th centuries when life moved at a slower pace. Bubion is the starting point for all of the trips, an area of Spain that is a meeting ground between the Muslim and Christian worlds. Rafael also leads riding holidays in Cuba.

CHILDREN'S PROGRAM: There is no special program for children, but youngsters 8 and older are welcome if they have had at least 2 years of riding experience.

ACCOMMODATIONS: While some trips offer camping experiences, most trips will end each day with riders sleeping in clean and friendly pensions and/or charming Andaluz hotels—always the most comfortable accommodations available in the area.

SPECIAL ACTIVITIES: Riders can visit local vineyards for wine tastings and tours of the cellars. Rafael often brings a guitar for singing around the fire at night. Where possible, there are trips to local fiestas for dancing and occasional flamenco.

MEALS: The food is typically Andalucian. Breakfast includes *café con leché* with various breads and jams or more traditional food such as tomatoes, garlic, and olive oil on bread. Lunch consists of salads and choice of omelettes or local seafood, Alpujarra ham, and various country sausages and meats. At least one *paella* is usually served on each trek with lashings of delicious local wine.

RIDING STUFF: Rafael maintains a herd of about 15 rugged, well-behaved horses. They are strong and agile, but docile. The longest and most complete ride is Sierra Nevada Cabo de Gata, a 9 day trip with 4 to 6 hours of riding daily, that takes you through 2 nature reserves, including the Tabernas Desert (the most important desert-like zone on the continent, and the scene of numerous spaghetti-Westerns) and Sierra Alhamilla. The ride ends at the beautiful beaches of Cabo de Gata. Rafael also leads a long ride to Mulhacen Peak. This ride follows old bridlepaths that snake through numerous ravines where cold snow-melt waters run. The plants of the high Sierra are alpine and mediterranean, as are the upland meadows scented with lavender, thyme, and rosemary. In the valleys you ride along extremely small paths among rows of mulberry, peach, fig and plum trees, filching ripe fruit as you pass. The aromas of fennel, mint and anise rise from the long grasses. The rural villages you ride past are reminiscent of an earlier Spain, now preserved by the absence of tourism. Where possible, the pace includes canters and even gallops. These rides are recommended for riders with at least some experience in open country riding.

AUTHOR'S COMMENT: *Rafael Belmonte, the owner and operator of Rutas Alternativas, is an entertaining and charming man, fluent in numerous languages, including English. His riding program is among the very best and, with his Moorish dark looks, you may feel yourself part of a marauding band of gypsy bandidos!!*

HIGHLIGHTS
English or Western tack • Intermediate skill level on longer treks • 1 to 9 day treks • 4 to 6 hours of riding per day • Rides through Las Alpujarras in the Sierra Nevada to snow-capped Mulhacen Peak at more than 10,000 feet (3482 meters) • Rides toward sea and desert • Customized treks • Hispano-Arabic crossbreds

FINCA EL MORO

www.inthesaddle.com

BASICS: Agent: **In the Saddle**, Laurel Cottage,
  Ramsdell, Tadley, Hampshire RG26 5SH, UK
  Tel: 01256-851-665
  Fax: 01256-851-667 (from UK)
  Tel: (44) 1256-851-665
  Fax: (44) 1256-851-667 (from US)
  Email: rides@inthesaddle.com
In Spain contact: Finca el Moro, Aracena, Spain
  Tel/Fax: (34) 959-501-079
WHEN: Selected weeks throughout the year,
February to June and September to November.
AIRPORTS: Seville, Spain. Transfers included.
LOCATION: Finca el Moro is a 1½ hour drive from
  Seville, in northern Andalucia, near
  Extremadura and Portugal.
PRICES: £530 ($850) 7 days/7 nights, per person, sin-
  gle or double occupancy. Price includes 5 days of
  riding, all meals and accommodation. Gratuities,
  alcoholic drinks and air fare not included.

Finca El Moro is a 70 acre working farm located in the midst of Aracena National Park. It is owned and operated by Nick and Hermione Tudor, who came from England some 10 years ago. The area is completely rural, and you may see wild boar, deer, genet cat, mongoose, fox, and badger in addition to numerous bird species. Your hosts are knowledgeable and charming. This holiday offers good riding, beautiful terrain, and fine farm-fresh food. March through May is a particularly beautiful time of year, graced by a profusion of flowers and bird life, while October brings some beautiful autumn colors and abundant fungi (mushrooms).

CHILDREN'S PROGRAM: The program is not suitable for children, unless they are competent riders and part of a larger group.

ACCOMMODATIONS: There are 2 fully restored cottages on the property. One cottage has 3 bedrooms, the other has 2 bedrooms, all with *en suite* bath or shower and terrace. Each cottage has a shared lounge and kitchen area. Big log fires, heated towel rails in the bathrooms, electric radiators, fully equipped fridge, and cooker all add to your comfort.

SPECIAL ACTIVITIES: There is a spring-fed open-air swimming pool, good bird watching and walking trails with maps.

MEALS: You make your own breakfast in your cottage from ingredients supplied to you, eggs, fruit, muesli, fresh bread, homemade jams, coffee, etc. Lunch is a selection of delicious *tapas* in a local bar with coffee or a drink. One such *tapas* lunch consists of local sausage cooked in white wine and garlic, a salad, and fresh goat's cheese with local honey. Dinner is a 3 course affair eaten together at the main farmhouse, for example, a bowl of mushroom soup made from fresh picked chantrelles followed by a casserole of local venison with vegetables from the garden.

RIDING STUFF: The area offers delightful riding country that takes you through sweet chestnut woods, cork oak forest and along wide tracks. You will seldom touch paved road and then only to cross it. Group size is limited to 6 and you should be a fit and competent rider, although novices may be accommodated depending on the group. The horses are strong, fit Andalucian horses ranging from 14.2 to 16 hands high. Some of the horses are locally bred and trained by Hermoine. You ride in a Vaquero saddle, which is similar to a Western saddle, covered by a thick sheepskin seat. From Sunday to Tuesday you will spend up to 6 hours in the saddle daily, exploring different routes and returning to the farm each afternoon. Wednesday is a rest day, and on Thursday guests embark on an overnight ride into big open cattle country, crossing the Sierra along an old smuggling route to Portugal. Friday you return to the farm via an old drovers' trail that is still used to drive sheep and goats north toward summer grazing.

AUTHOR'S COMMENT: *The joy of riding these Andalucian horses, sporting Vaquero saddles and large metal stirrups, is matched only by the courtesy shown by hosts, Nick and Hermione Tudor. With groups limited to only 6, this is a house-party style holiday, in which friends discuss the day's riding experiences over specialty dinners, each neatly recorded in daily diary form for riders to keep. Just as well, since each day brings new sights, and, above all, the ability to briefly become part of a way of life in which the horse is revered and the sound of hooves can bring a village—especially the local bar—to life. A real touch of class...Viva L'Espana!!*

HIGHLIGHTS
Excellent trail riding • Beautiful Andalucian horses • Vaquero saddles with sheepskin seats • Small group size 6 maximum • Rides through Moorish villages • Visit a 10th century mosque • Excellent food

SIERRA NEVADA: THE CONTRAVIESA AND ALPUJARRA RIDES

www.inthesaddle.com

BASICS: Agent: **In the Saddle**, Laurel Cottage, Ramsdell, Tadley, Hampshire, RG26 5SH, UK
Tel: 01256-851-665
Fax: 01256-851-667 (from UK)
Tel: (44) 1256-851-665
Fax: (44) 1256-851-667 (from US)
Email: rides@inthesaddle.com

WHEN: March to November. *The Contraviesa Ride* is offered during the spring and fall, and *The Alpujarra Ride* is offered during the warmer summer months. There are 15 scheduled ride dates, Saturday to Saturday. Additional dates available for private groups with a minimum of 4 persons.

AIRPORTS: Malaga or Granada. Transfers are included from Granada.

LOCATION: Bubion, Andalucia is the starting point for the rides. Rides are in the Sierra Nevada, the highest mountain range in Spain.

PRICE: *The Contraviesa Ride:* £699 ($1118), or *The Alpujarra Ride:* £669 ($1070) 8 days/7 nights, per person, double occupancy, includes 6 days of riding, all accommodations and meals, except dinner on the sixth day. Single supplements: *Contraviesa Ride* £65 ($104); *Alpujarra Ride* £45 ($72)

The Sierra Nevada covers an area of a 1000 incredibly varied square miles, a rich tapestry of Roman, Moorish, and 19th century Spain laid before your eyes in areas of Andalucia that are still well off the more heavily traveled tourist routes. These often praised rides are conducted by Dallas Love, an Englishwoman, who moved to this area with her parents during the 1960s. In the spring and autumn rides take place in the Contraviesa mountain range, which is close to the coast, warm and arid. During the hot summer months, guests ride high in the Sierra Nevada, which benefits from the natural air-conditioning of higher altitudes.

CHILDREN'S PROGRAM: These rides are appropriate for teenagers who are experienced riders.

ACCOMMODATIONS: The accommodations are provided in small, family run village hostels and hotels, in twin bedded rooms, usually with *en suite* facilities. They are clean and pleasant. Luggage is transferred for you.

SPECIAL ACTIVITIES: If you have the time to stay on for an extra day or so, Granada and the stunningly beautiful Alhambra Palace are well worth a visit.

MEALS: Breakfast is Continental style, lunch is either a substantial picnic carried on horse-back, or eaten at a local restaurant or bar. There are a range of small restaurants or pensions offering a selection of food for your evening meal.

RIDING STUFF: The superb horses are Andalucian and Andalucian crossbreds, ranging in height from 15 to 16 hands. All of them have been broken in and schooled by their owner, your guide, Dallas Love. They are fit, happy, and strong, which makes riding them a real pleasure. Although these rides are best suited for experienced riders, Dallas maintains a limited number of horses for the less advanced. The terrain can slow the pace, but there will be plenty of opportunities for canters and gallops. The very steepest descents require dismounting and leading the horses, suggesting that these rides are not for people who suffer from vertigo. Andalucia is a region of great natural beauty, with a great variety of plant life that varies according to the altitude. Following ancient bridlepaths and drovers' routes, dating back to the Moorish occupation and earlier, you will journey through a beautiful land, dotted with the remnants of earlier times.

AUTHOR'S COMMENT: *We are happy to have this highly recommended riding opportunity in our book. Presented in the best tradition of Andalucian horsemanship, these rides will not disappoint.*

HIGHLIGHTS
Unhurried riding through spectacular mountain area • Ride for competent riders with some exceptions possible per group • 5 to 7 hours riding a day • Coastal mountain riding • Inland high mountain riding • Excellent horses

HAURIDA SKOGS HAST SAFARI

BASICS: Lena Dahl, Lindforsa, 57892 Aneby, Sweden
  Tel/Fax: (46) 390-31016
  Email: tonga@mail.bip.net
WHEN: May to September.
AIRPORT: Jönköping (reached via Stockholm
  International Airport). You can also travel
  direct by car from Stockholm or Gothenburg, or
  take a coach or train. Riders are met at
Jönköping by arrangement for the ¾ hour drive
  to Aneby, where the ride is located.
LOCATION: The Highlands of Smaland, a little-
  known rural province in southern Sweden.
PRICES: $570 (£355) 5 days/4 nights, per person,
  includes 4 days of riding. Transfers from
  Jönköping are included. A 2 day ride may be
  arranged as well as customized trips.

An attractive riding alternative offered by English-speaking owner/operator, Lena Dahl, is this 5 day forest safari in Smaland, an uncommercialized, richly rural region in southeastern Sweden. Northern Swedish Coldblood horses take groups of around 6 competent riders through a magical landscape of woods, lakes, and flower-strewn meadows, blissfully traffic-free as road work is virtually non-existent, where you will have a chance to put these gentle giants through their paces. What proved outstanding on a 2 day trek, says author John Ruler, was riding into Asens, a restored village where the land is still farmed using turn-of-the-century farming methods. Girls in traditional smocks provide a smiling welcome at the distinctive ruby red timber home of Tekla, a fiercely independent old lady who died at the age of 91 and whose life is depicted inside, while the horses graze outdoors.

CHILDREN'S PROGRAM: Program is suitable for children over 13.

ACCOMMODATIONS: Overnight stops are either in well-equipped wooden huts with bunkbeds and electricity, their roofs thatched with turf, or in specially made teepee type tents of the kind used by the Lappish people of northern Sweden. Guests can also opt to stay at guest houses.

SPECIAL ACTIVITIES: Fishing, canoeing, swimming and saunas round out some alternative activities offered for your enjoyment.

MEALS: Typical Swedish food from the region is cooked at the evening BBQ, including Smaland's famous sausage made from barley and minced pork, beef or elk and spiced with white pepper or ginger. Grilled perch is also popular and for dessert, cheesecake is a specialty.

RIDING STUFF: The horses are northern Swedish Coldbloods, once used in farming and forestry. A strong and willing breed, they are highly suitable for the forest and lake trails. A combination of Western style saddles and English bridles are used and the ride is designed for both inexperienced and experienced riders. Daily rides of about 5 to 6 hours feature a varied landscape that includes forests, hills, fields of wildflowers, and small lakes. The riding portion of the trip covers 4 days. Comfort and reliable horses are what makes this ride tick—also the chance to swim, Swedish fashion, in ice-cold lakes, see the occasional elk or deer, or simply enjoy covering some 25 miles (40 kms.) a day at a variety of paces.

AUTHOR'S COMMENT: *This is a wonderful way to discover the secret Sweden in the little-known highlands of Smaland, with forests, lakes and meadows, during a few days of riding that is mercifully free of road work, and most certainly peaceful. Don't be deceived by the northern Swedish horses, they may look a bit bulky, but they have a good turn of speed and are ideal companions for cross-country work. Asens, an overnight stop, is a restored village where turn-of-the-century farming methods are still being used. Fascinating...*

HIGHLIGHTS
Riding Swedish Coldbloods • Ride through forested, rural Sweden • 6 hours of riding per day • Western saddles, English bridles • Visits to the restored village of Asens

ALBION RIDES

BASICS: Duck Row, Cawston, Norwich, Norfolk
NR10 4EZ, UK
Tel/Fax: 01603-87-1724 (from UK)
Tel/Fax: (44) 1603-87-1724 (from US)
WHEN: Open all year.
NEAREST AIRPORTS: Norwich - a ½ hour drive
LOCATION: A 3 hour drive from London.
PRICE: *1½ Hour Rides:* £16 ($26) per person; *2½ to 3 Hour Rides:* £32 ($52) per person; *All Day Rides:* £60 ($96) (Summer Rates, March 26 to October 1) or £45 ($72) (Winter Rates, October 2 to March 25) per person, includes 4 hours of riding with pub or picnic lunch and 1 drink. *Special Summer Ride* (March to October): £246 ($393) 3 days/3 nights, per person, d/o at a luxury hotel with half board, or £171 ($273) per person, d/o at a B&B, both include 2 full days of riding and a 1½ hour ride on the last day. During the winter months (October to March) the same package is £30 ($48) less.

Tina Sutton's riding centre is viewed as one of the most novel and enjoyable places to ride in the UK. Only 3 hours from London by car, Albion offers a chance to engage in some spirited riding on fit horses. This is an ideal side trip for London visitors looking to experience a quality English riding establishment. All Day Rides start at 9:30 a.m. and finish between 3:30 and 5:00 p.m. This is a great opportunity to work off jet lag, relax after a round of business meetings, or simply escape the mad scramble of "see it all" touring. Brits already recognize Albion as providing a fascinating glimpse into one of England's most historic regions.

CHILDREN'S PROGRAM: No special programs.

ACCOMMODATIONS: The local hotel is situated in a Georgian Square in the nearby market town of Reepham, close to antique shops. The hotel provides *en suite* luxury facilities, including a swimming pool and an up-to-date health center. Another option is a comfortable B&B run by a friendly, knowledgeable family of riders who will make you feel very welcome. There are camp sites available nearby on the site of a ruined mansion.

SPECIAL ACTIVITIES: North Norfolk adjoins Norfolk Broads National Park. Both areas are within easy reach of excellent facilities for coarse, game, and sea fishing, bird watching, sailing and cruising. There are good golf courses, lovely beaches and historic houses. A vehicle is very useful.

MEALS: Pub lunch with drink or picnic with drink are part of the 3 night package. Hotel stay offers half board and there are many excellent restaurants and pubs in the area.

RIDING STUFF: Riders are generally expected to be competent and able to control their horses at all paces while riding in a group. The horses are good-natured, corn fed, and fit. Guests are expected to help groom and tack horses at the start and end of each day. There will be good opportunities for long, safe canters through varied countryside, villages, parkland and farmland. The terrain includes sandy, peaty tracks, stony paths, some flat undulating plains, open farmland and woods, but no steep or hilly areas—in general, very good land for riding. Groups of riders are always small and emphasis is placed on providing a flexible and friendly environment. We couldn't resist quoting Tina's latest report from Albion: "...This week we have seen a Roe Deer with its fawn and a group of Red Deer, including 3 stags with full antlers. We have seen wild Columbine, Ragged Robin, and wild Lily of the Valley. All these plants are rare. I count it as a privilege to see them growing!"

AUTHOR'S COMMENTS: *What makes Tina's ride so satisfying is her knowledge of the flora and fauna native to this region which is also rich in history. Blickling Hall, a particularly fine National Trust property reconstructed in Jacobean style in the 17th century, is but one of the many historical sites in the area. Albion is the ancient name for Britain and this region, with its grassy bridleways flanked by high hedges, heathlands and sparsely populated villages, is evocative of a gentler, more romantic era.*

HIGHLIGHTS
Irish Drafts, Cobs, crossbreds • English Tack • Experienced riders only • Weight limit 14 stone (200 lbs.) (90 kg.) • Day rides • 2 day/3 night riding trips • Group size 6

D & P EQUESTRIAN ENTERPRISES

BASICS: Low Haggart Farm, Cautley, Sedburgh, Cumbria, LA10 5NE, UK
Tel: 0153-962-0349 (from UK)
Tel: (44) 153-962-0349 (from US)
WHEN: Holidays Rides: April to October. Hacking: All year round
AIRPORTS/TRAIN STATIONS: Manchester – a 2 hour drive. Either Oxenholme Station on the Euston/Glasgow line or Kirby Stephans Station on the Carlisle/Settle line. Less than a 30 minute drive from either station.
LOCATION: Cumbrian Falls, Yorkshire Dales National Park, about a 30 minute drive from the English Lake District in central Yorkshire.
PRICE: £150 ($240) to £180 ($290) 2 days/1 night, per person, d/o, all inclusive. £575 ($920) 7 days/6 nights, per person, d/o. Prices vary depending on the type of accommodation chosen. Day Rides: £45 ($72) per person, includes a pack lunch and 4½ to 5 hours of riding.

Owners Barbara Burton and Linda ffrench Devitt offer a wonderful riding experience through the Yorkshire Dales National Park, a lovely area of rolling hills, enchanting green wilderness, and romantic mists. Barbara's late father, John Parson, pioneered trail riding in Ambleside more than 40 years ago, and Barbara herself is a knowledgeable expert on horse riding holidays. Familiar with the needs of holiday riders, the fine quality of her horses reflects favorably upon her experience. D&P has consistently earned high accolades from the UK equestrian press. North Americans will love the feel of this "up the fell, down the dale" riding experience.

CHILDREN'S PROGRAM: Children under 16 must be experienced and competent riders and accompanied by parents.

ACCOMMODATIONS: Guests may choose from a menu that includes basic farmhouse, B & Bs, traditional English inns with *en suite* bath, bar and restaurant, and hotels. You will be offered a choice wherever possible.

SPECIAL ACTIVITIES: Golf, fishing and mountain biking as well as visits to the Yorkshire Dales in the Lake District.

MEALS: Hearty English breakfasts will begin your day. Lunches and dinners offer the very best of home cooking and traditional English fare.

RIDING STUFF: This is a truly a magical area in which to ride. "From where we were, high on the fells, we [saw] the tufted grass soft and springy beneath the horses hooves, the view of classic proportions, the gray green of the fells contrasting with the paint-box richness of the meadows and sudden clumps of wood. The centerpiece was undoubtedly Smardale, the nature reserve set off by an old viaduct part of a now disused railway line," is John Ruler's description. And, in the words of Barbara Burton: "You can see so much in a short time. It varies from hills to meadowlands, with dales and barns in some of the fields. Within a half day you can cover four different types of scenery." The horses range from 14.2 to 16 hands. They are attractive animals, large-boned, easy to handle, and in wonderful condition. Riders need to be experienced as this is open country riding, with climbs and descents and a spirited pace that requires fitness as well as skill.

AUTHOR'S COMMENT: *Take a mixture of moorland and dales and combine it with the bubbly personality of Barbara Burton, blend well, and you have the recipe for a wonderful riding holiday. Add her reliable team of half and pure bred Welsh Cobs, and the picture is complete. This is adult riding for small groups, appreciative of local flora and fauna (and legends), who, after an exhilarating 6 hours in the saddle, like to unwind in hand-picked accommodations. Choose either a country hotel or a farmhouse; each serving the finest in local fare. For Brits, this is great chance to discover a bit more about the lesser-known Cumbrian/Yorkshire border. For overseas visitors, D & P Equestrian offers a dramatic slice of the British landscape.*

HIGHLIGHTS
Beautiful, wild riding country • 12 horses • Welsh Cobs, Thoroughbred crossbreds, Cob types • Deep-seated saddles • English tack • Experienced riders • Weight limit 15 stone (210 lbs.) (95 kg.) • 2, 4 and 7 day riding holidays • Up to 6 hours riding a day • Group size 6

ARGYLL TRAIL RIDING

www.equestrianvacations.com

BASICS: Brenfield Farm and Estate, Ardrishaig, Argyll, Scotland PA 30 8ER, UK
Tel: 01546-603-374   Fax: 01546-603-225
North and South American Agent: **Cross Country International**, PO Box 1170, Millbrook, NY 12545, USA
Tel: (800) 828-8768 (North and South America only) Tel: (914) 677-6000
Fax: (914) 677-6077
Email: xcintl@aol.com
Website: www.equestrianvacations.com

WHEN: Open year round.
AIRPORTS: Glasgow, Scotland.
LOCATION: The riding center is located in Argyll, on the west coast of Scotland, a 90 minute drive from the airport.
PRICE: *Gourmet Trail:* $2500 (£1562); *Wild Boar Trail:* $2100 (£1312); *Rob Roy:* $1750 (£1094). All rides are 8 days/7 nights, per person, double occupancy includes all accommodations, meals, and 6 days of riding. Single supplement for all rides is $180 (£113).

Robert the Bruce, Rob Roy, Mary Queen of Scots, Bonnie Prince Charlie, and Robert Burns are among the famous, or infamous, personages who have inhabited this land of rugged and tenacious people, where myths and legends have helped to create a romantic tradition. The Scottish Highland region is one of the most beautiful parts of the British Isles. Its purple heather, crisp blue skies, green hills, and somber gray rocks have inspired writers and painters for centuries. This is an area of great historic interest and spectacular natural beauty. Much of the area is inaccessible by car, but not by horse. Argyll Trail Riding is a family run equestrian center with a reputation of being one of the finest trail riding centers in the world. They offer a variety of riding options from daily hacks to trail rides that span 7 days and cover 25 to 40 miles a day through some of the most exciting horseback riding country in Europe. The 3 rides are fast paced rides in the beautiful Highlands. Special pub rides and beach gallops are regularly offered on weekends, and there are riding clinics year round.

CHILDREN'S PROGRAM: Argyll Trail Riding caters for all ages. Ponies are available on a daily basis for pony trekking on the Brenfield Estate.

ACCOMMODATIONS: Guests may stay at the farmhouse during stationary holidays. On the Argyll Trail Ride, you may choose a hotel or guest house, most with *en suite* bathrooms or even spend a couple of nights at a castle.

SPECIAL ACTIVITIES: Archery, clay pigeon shooting, and mountain biking are some of the alternative activities available.

MEALS: The meals at Brenfield Farm are warm, social affairs—a time to gather around and get to know your fellow riders. The area restaurants are excellent with a fine selection of places specializing in seafood, including fresh Scottish salmon, beef, or venison.

RIDING STUFF: The Argyll Trail Ride will take you through hills and glens, across streams, past ancient ruins, and along lochs. The pace will be fast where possible and slower as the terrain dictates. You may either jump over or go around stone walls and ditches encountered along the way. This exciting trail ride includes a brisk beach gallop as well. You may even take a swim with your horse. The horses, Scottish Hunters and Cobs, are fit and have stamina.

AUTHOR'S COMMENT: *Argyll Trail Riding offers the type of equine experience in which Scotland excels. The horses are eager and the landscape fulfills everyone's Highland fantasy of sun-streaked, deep, vivid blue lochs and miles of rolling moorland. Daydream to you heart's content, for this is the secret side of Scotland that can only be seen from the saddle. Expect an adrenaline-pumping pace while riding with Tove Gray-Stephens, especially during the 2 mile gallop along the sandy beach between Duntrune Castle and the Crinan Canal. Also, be sure to give my regards to Monty, the gentle giant who has all the reliability required of a holiday horse, but with a turn of speed to suit the occasion.*

HIGHLIGHTS
English and Western tack • Intermediate skill level for the Argyll Trail Ride • 7day/6 night Argyll Trail Ride–May to September • Training and trail riding programs year round • Member: BHS

HAYFIELD RIDING CENTRE

www.hayfield.com

BASICS: Hazelhead Park, Aberdeen, Scotland
AB15 8BB, UK
Tel: (44) 1224-315703
Fax: (44) 1224-313834 (from US)
Tel: 01224-315703   Fax: 01224-313834 (from UK)
Email: info@hayfield.com
WHEN: Open year round.

AIRPORTS: Aberdeen - a 20 minute drive; taxi fare $16 (£10).
LOCATION: On the outskirts of Aberdeen in the middle of Hazelhead Park. A 1 hour flight from London's Stansted Airport and cheaper than the train.
PRICE: £75 ($120) per day, per person, double occupancy. Group discounts available.

The Hayfield Riding Centre, owned and operated by Sue and John Crawford, is set in beautiful parkland surrounded by forests and golf courses. One of Scotland's leading BHS approved training centers, Hayfield offers well-equipped, specialized training in every riding discipline except racing. All riding programs are customized to take into account individual training needs. Alternatively (or in addition to instruction), you can enjoy some relaxed trail riding. Versatility makes Hayfield an ideal setting for families with different skill levels and interests. John Crawford is a BHS certified "trainer of trainers" and an excellent teacher with 30 years of experience.

CHILDREN'S PROGRAM: Children ages 6 to 18 are welcome if accompanied by an adult.

ACCOMMODATIONS: There are 8 individual rooms providing a choice of single, double or adjoining family accommodations. The rooms are cozy and quiet. Bathrooms are shared. There are also many good hotels in the area for those who prefer a taste of luxury.

SPECIAL ACTIVITIES: There are country walks, good golf, gliding, shooting, bowls, fishing, swimming, nightlife, theatre, excellent restaurants, and many other sights nearby. Inverness and Loch Ness are within a 100 mile drive and Edinburgh, at 130 miles, is also within driving distance.

MEALS: Meals are wholesome and simple and will satisfy most tastes. Breakfast is Continental style. A light snack lunch and full sit-down evening meal are provided. Haggis can be ordered and guests are free to help themselves to tea, coffee and snacks at any time.

RIDING STUFF: All of Hayfield's staff members compete in either eventing, show jumping, cross-country, or dressage and the boss and his son play polo, so you are among people who know and appreciate good horses. An individual riding program will be designed for each rider. Hayfield's 45 horses provide an ample range of choices from quiet, "bomb proof" mounts to those that are sure to give their riders a thrill. In addition to its training program, Hayfield encourages guests to take advantage of daily breaks for some delightful afternoon trail riding which is also geared to individual rider needs. You can, of course, arrange to absorb as many lessons as your stay permits, but the option to trail ride will always be available. Try your hand at imitating John Wayne and ride Western style or jump in a sidesaddle. If shows are being conducted in one of the arenas you may be permitted to participate.

AUTHOR'S COMMENT: *For Americans and Brits alike who are looking for relaxed riding, the Grampian region offers a lively cocktail of Scottish charm, with considerable wildlife and some stunning scenery of the heather-clad hills variety. There are castles and malt whisky distilleries about. Hayfield is ideally situated in Hazelhead Park, close to Aberdeen, and offers the best of both worlds. There are rides in parklands, forests or down by the riverside, even a gallop along the beach is possible. In contrast, Aberdeen, the "Granite City," is a regular winner of the Britain in Bloom competition and offers plenty of nightlife, be it theatre, pubs, clubs or restaurants. With a full range of instruction, Hayfield is just the right place to hone your riding skills. Owner John Crawford is quite a character and superb horseman.*

HIGHLIGHTS

Cross-country training, show jumping, dressage training • 2 indoor riding arenas • Qualified multi-disciplined staff • Sidesaddle, Western and English tack • Polo training (extra) • 45 horses • Golf course on doorstep • Trail riding • Approved: British Horse Society

ELLESMERE RIDING CENTRE

BASICS: Llangorse, Brecon, Powys, LD3 7UN, Wales, UK
  Tel: 01874 - 658429 (day/evening)
  Tel: 01874 658252 (daytime only) (from UK)
  Tel: (44) 1874-658429 (day/evening)
  Tel: (44) 1874-658252 (daytime only) (from US)
WHEN: Open all year for full and half day rides;
  April to October for longer rides.
AIRPORTS: Cardiff or Bristol - a 1½ hour drive from either airport. Also, Abergavenny Railway Station - a 14 mile drive, pick-ups arranged.
LOCATION: Black Mountains in the Brecon Beacons National Park, Powys.
PRICE: £189 ($300) 2 days/1 night, per person, d/o; £320 ($510) 3 days/2 nights, per person, d/o; £399 ($638) 4 days/2 nights, per person, double occupancy. Half and full day rides priced on request. Extra night with breakfast and dinner add £30 ($48) per day. Trips may be extended.

Myfanwy Mitchell, owner and operator, offers an exciting riding program through some of the prettiest country in Wales. You are guaranteed a small group, lots of attention when necessary and a varied, often stunning riding area in the Black Mountains on strong, spirited Welsh Cobs and Cob crosses. Wales always offers a pleasant diversion from more harried lifestyle, and riders will especially enjoy the beautiful countryside.

CHILDREN'S PROGRAM: Must be over 12 and competent riders.

ACCOMMODATIONS: Comfortable B&Bs, farmhouses and small country inns along the way. Some *en suite* bathrooms are available. Provided that rooms are available, you may stay at the interesting and unusual 12th century Llanthony Priory which has been converted to a small inn.

SPECIAL ACTIVITIES: There are water sports, including sailing, canoeing, and windsailing on nearby Llangorse Lake as well as bird watching, fishing, mountain biking, and hill walking in the Black Mountains and nearby Brecon Beacons. There are ancient footpaths to follow and Wales is renowned for it castles. Shoppers can enjoy bargain hunting in the nearby towns of Brecon, Abergavenny and Hay-on-Wye. The Brecon Jazz Festival takes place in August and there are numerous county and agricultural shows throughout the summer.

MEALS: All meals are included and consist of hearty farmhouse fare. You will stop at pubs for lunch (and a tipple). Vegetarians are catered for, but please inform Myfanwy before the trip.

RIDING STUFF: The Black Mountain Ride is organized around groups of 6 experienced riders. This is a truly magnificent and stunning countryside with narrow, flower-lined lanes leading to miles and miles of unspoiled mountains and moorland. You don't have to be an expert, but you should be fit enough to spend about 6 hours in the saddle daily and be able to canter over rough ground. Good, forward going Welsh Cobs and Cob crosses are used. They are tough and made for the job. The rides are exhilarating and challenging, the pace moderate to fast with steep scrambles, sudden descents and long canters. You will be accompanied by an experienced guide, who knows the countryside, is well-versed in local history, and can show you the most enjoyable routes through the mountains. Every morning you are expected to catch your horse and get him ready for the day but, as you know, that's part of the fun and helps establish a good relationship with your horse. Rides leave around 10:30 a.m., stop for a pub lunch and return at 5:30 p.m. A back-up team transports luggage.

AUTHOR'S COMMENT: *Myfanwy's wiry Welsh Cobs and crossbred toughies are the key to unlocking some of the finest Welsh scenery. Enjoy long, fast gallops along windswept ridges in the Black Mountains, with only sheep and hawks for company. Stop for a lunch time drink at a local pub, trotting out smartly along flower-strewn lanes. Take the 50 mile ride from Llargorse to Llanthony Priory and you'll have a pilgrimage to remember.*

HIGHLIGHTS
2 to 4 day trail rides • Moderate to fast rides through mountains • Fit, spirited Welsh Cobs and Cob crosses • Stunning scenery • Small riding groups • Experienced riders able to canter over rough ground • 6 hours riding per day on extended rides • English saddles • Novices welcome on short, half and full day rides • Member: P.T.R.S.W

RHIWIAU RIDING CENTRE

BASICS: Llanfairfechan, North Wales LL33 OEH, UK
  Tel: 01248-680094 (from UK)
  Tel: (44) 1248-680094 (from US)
WHEN: Open year round.
AIRPORTS: Manchester— a 1½ hour drive to the Centre. Transfers may be arranged upon prior notice.
LOCATION: The Centre is 7 miles from Conwys;

14 miles from Llandudno on the new A55. A 1½ hour drive from Chester, Liverpool or Manchester.
PRICES: Weekly Stays: £265 ($424) per person, includes 7 nights full board and accommodations and 18 hours of riding. Weekend Rides: £95 ($152) 3 days/2 nights, per person, includes 6 hours of riding. Many other options available.

Rhiwiau overlooks the Menai Straits and the Isle of Anglesey. Situated at 600 feet, it nestles in a secluded valley in the Snowdonia National Park. Rhiwiau offers enjoyable riding and caters to every skill level. The area is one of considerable natural beauty, with its pine woods, open moorland, rolling hills and mountains. Better still, there are no roads or traffic to spoil the tranquility. Rhiwiau has been owned and operating for over 25 years under the experienced eyes of the Hill family.

CHILDREN'S PROGRAM: Except during school holiday camps, unaccompanied children must be at least 9 years old. There is no minimum age for children accompanied by an adult.

ACCOMMODATIONS: There is central heating throughout, a bar with a selection of wines, spirits and beers, a game room with table tennis, pool tables and other games. There are also 2 television lounges and a tack shop. All bedrooms have twin or bunk beds with hot and cold running water. The shower and WC are located close by.

SPECIAL ACTIVITIES: For non-riders, Rhiwiau provides an excellent base for walking or sightseeing. Castles, gardens, National Trust Houses, fishing, golf, tennis and other sports are only a few of the alternative activities available. The historic walled town of Conwys, the Victorian seaside town of Llandudno, and Caernarfon Castle are all within a 20 minute drive.

MEALS: Mrs. Hill, the owner, is well respected for her good home cooking, especially her soups, pies, cakes, Welsh lamb, and traditional British desserts, such as bread and butter pudding. Breakfast is Continental style, but a full Welsh breakfast is available to those on the B & B plan. Vegetarian and other diets can be catered for upon advance notice.

RIDING STUFF: On all extended holidays guests will be offered a combination of instruction, by BHS trained and qualified staff, in cross-country, flat work, jumping and stable management as well as trail riding. The Centre houses goats, cats, and various other farm animals and breeds some of its own horses. The horses range from pony size (11 hands) to over 16 hands high. There are a variety of breeds, including Welsh Cobs, Irish Draught crosses, and Thoroughbreds. The trails amble along, offering breathtaking views, with buzzards soaring overhead, and wild ponies grazing on the timeless mountain. The more experienced riders will have the opportunity to canter. The trail riding routes include tracks made by invading Romans 2000 years ago, a picnic ride to Aber Lake, which is situated at 1500 feet in an unspoiled upland valley. There are also local pub rides to the nearby village of Abergwygreyn.

AUTHOR'S COMMENT: *Those lucky souls who have visited Rhiwiau Riding Centre before, have retained fond memories of the experience, thanks to the friendliness of the Hill family and the excellent care given to their horses. The location too wins hands down when it comes to spectacular scenery. For overseas visitors in particular, Rhiwiau provides a splendid introduction to Wales. Mrs. Hill's cooking is well-known to both guests and locals.*

HIGHLIGHTS
Instruction on the flat and over jumps • Exciting cross-country course • Mounted games, gymkhanas, jumping or handy pony competitions • Adult pub ride • Western and Sidesaddles are available • Adult weeks and weekends by arrangement • Approved: BHS, ABRS and WTRA

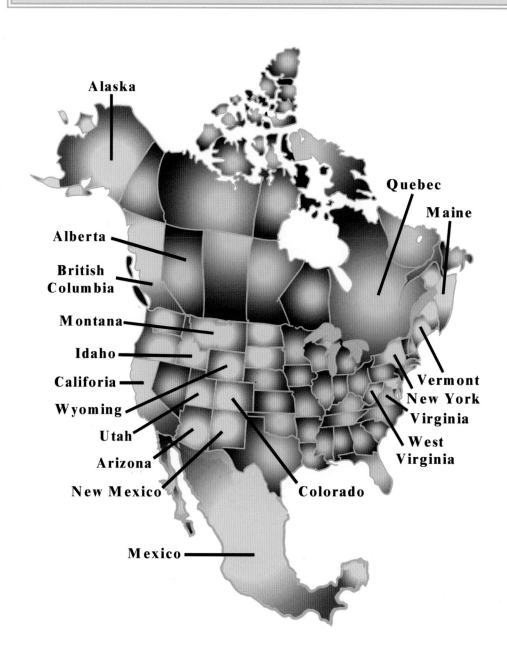

Alaska

Quebec

Maine

Alberta

British
Columbia

Montana

Idaho

California

Wyoming

Utah

Arizona

New Mexico

Colorado

Vermont
New York
Virginia

West
Virginia

Mexico

RIDING IN NORTH AMERICA

by Arthur Sacks

CANADA and MEXICO

NORTH AMERICA, ENCOMPASSING CANADA, THE UNITED STATES AND MEXICO, is an area that exhibits a diversity of riding traditions and riding holidays. The Canadian riding holiday scene offers 2 distinct riding regions, the mountainous areas of Alberta and British Columbia in western Canada, and the rolling hills and wilderness areas of French-speaking Quebec in the east. The Gaspe Peninsula Ride is a particularly attractive way to visit Quebec and, given the favorable exchange rates, a very cost effective way for riders to enjoy this part of Canada. Fall foliage rides in Quebec are spectacular and early bookings are advised. Quebec, by virtue of its principal language (French), its lifestyle and architecture, creates the feeling that you've crossed the Atlantic Ocean, certainly a more Continental atmosphere than the English-speaking areas that surround it.

The English-speaking Rocky Mountain region of Alberta, offers a variety of high mountain wilderness trips in and around the world-famous resort area of Banff and Lake Louise—a very popular and worthwhile tourist attraction—especially for those trying to capture the high mountain experience. Likewise, British Columbia boasts a great variety of riding ranches and wilderness trip outfitters in both in the coastal mountain regions as well as inland areas with more varied terrain. Associations, such as British Columbia's Dude Ranchers Association and the Alberta Wilderness Outfitters Association, are useful sources of additional information.

Ryan Schmidt, owner of Hidden Trails and partner in Ts'yl-os Park Lodge, says that Canada feels a bit freer, a bit wilder than its cousin to the south. Certainly, as you move northwards throughout Canada, you will leave paved roads and population centers behind. Like the U.S., the Canadian West shares a heritage with its indigenous people, the native tribes that still exert a visible presence in Canada. The wildlife and fishing found in western Canada are already heavily promoted for their uniqueness and abundance. Vancouver, international arrival destination for many of the British Columbia rides, is an attractive city, well-worth visiting. Calgary, the starting point for many Alberta-based trips, is host to the world famous Calgary Stampede, one of the largest Western horse shows in the world. Like the U.S., Canada has a strong English riding tradition which is not generally reflected in their holiday offerings, but can easily be observed at English riding shows. Ian Miller, a tall Canadian riding the magnificent Big Ben, was a prominent figure at international riding events for years.

Heading south into Mexico, we find a culture with a strong tradition of horsemanship, ranging all the way from an upscale Spanish riding tradition to the Mexican cowboy heritage. Sadly enough, Mexico has never flourished as a riding holiday zone of tremendous international appeal, yet the potential is there. Our 2 rides in Mexico offer great contrasts. The Banana Ride brings you in touch with the way of life still lived in rural Mexico, despite its proximity to a major coastal tourist area. The other ride, La Sierra Cavalcade, includes a visit to the world-famous Monarch Butterfly Sanctuary, where millions of these brilliantly colored butterflies converge, producing a beautiful coverlet that blankets the landscape.

There is great variety among Mexican horses. On the one hand, there are the spirited endurance-trained horses and, on the other hand, local pack animals, reflecting the peasant existence that still characterizes rural life in Mexico. Typically, pack animals are used as being better suited for transportation along Mexico's unpaved roads. In short, Mexico's rich history of horsemanship is not yet manifested in the number of riding holidays offered.

UNITED STATES

The United States is a country that offers literally thousands of riding holiday destinations, but first a word on what we do not have in the way of riding holidays. The middle part of the country is generally devoid of nationally known riding destinations, although there are numerous small B&Bs and ranches that vary from resorts to organized camping facilities with horses. For the most part, these places are located in areas that are not highly rated as desirable travel destinations. Hence states like Wisconsin, Minnesota, Michigan, Kansas, Oklahoma, Ohio and Iowa cannot compete effectively with the Rocky Mountain region, the Southwest, or the California coast. The same generally holds true for the American South, although heavily promoted as a tourist destination. However, there are some indications that coastal areas, the Carolinas in particular, will one day become popular riding holiday destinations. The Smoky Mountains do provide a small concentration of riding options which you will probably be able to locate by turning to Jim Balzotti's publications on stabling or cowboy vacations. Florida offers several riding opportunities of note, including Grand Cypress in the Orlando area, Royal Palm Tours, and several cattle ranches in northern Florida. Curiously, Kentucky, often seen by outsiders as the center of America's horse-breeding country, has not produced noteworthy riding establishments. Virginia does offer several good riding opportunities. I particularly like the Conyers House, a well-appointed B&B that serves up wonderful trail riding, fox hunting, hilltopping, and cross-country jumping. Swift Level, in West Virginia, also has an outstanding program on superior horses. Both places offer English style riding and do not cater to a Western audience. Many of the older country club resorts that serve the South also offer riding, but their programs are more often than not a mere add on and, unfortunately, the riding does not always match the overall quality of the establishments.

Nevertheless, there are numerous riding trails to be found in all of the above areas as well as in the rest of the country. Useful information on stabling your own horse and making your own arrangements for camping or sleeping out are well covered in Jim Balzotti's *U.S. Stabling Guide*, published by Balzotti Publications, Inc. The trail system in the U.S. is growing, although competition with mountain bikers (and who knows what other new trends will develop) can make "bringing your own horse" a somewhat perilous activity if not chosen and planned with care.

One further word about the U.S. riding scene, concerning English versus Western riding styles. There are many more Western style riders in America—at least as judged by the horse publications, where the largest of the Western-oriented magazines have double the subscription rate of the English-oriented journals. This however does not tell the full story. Historically, English style riders tended to belong to the upper socio-economic classes and, thus, were more likely to be able to afford the time and expense of a riding holiday. Western riders, by contrast, were often relegated to rough bunkhouses or basic camping trips. But all that is changing, the result in part of ex-President Ronald Reagan popularizing the upscale Western ranching lifestyle. Similarly, the distinctive skills of both disciplines are merging, as witnessed, for example, by the increasing attention paid to Western reining techniques, which is surely the equivalent of dressage in its emphasis on subtle control of the horse. Increasingly also, team penning, and other activities popular at Western shows, are attracting very upscale Western horse riders. Endurance racing, while still basically English in its orientation, suggests yet another way in which the 2 riding styles might be combined. It should only be a short time before Western riders discover jumping, and English riders discover reining.

EAST COAST: Maine, Vermont, New York, Virginia and West Virginia

As tennis pro, Andre Agassi once said, "image is everything." The land east of the Mississippi River is often perceived as a region of crowded *metropolii*, known more for its major cities like Boston, New York, and Washington D.C., than it's natural beauty and wilderness areas. The reality is quite different.

Maine encompasses a sparsely-populated region of low-lying mountains, lakes and pine forests. Vermont and New Hampshire are mountainous, very green, and filled with lakes, streams and rolling wooded hills. New York State is home to Adirondack Park, the largest park in the mainland United States, an area that is short on people and development, but long on natural beauty. The topography of this region has made it unsuitable for the type of large-scale agricultural development found in the Midwest, but it is a remarkably beautiful, stimulating environment in which to ride, rich in wildlife and greenery. Deer and bears populate most of the region, large numbers of moose inhabit the most northern areas, and even the coyotes and wild turkeys have returned. Pheasant, grouse, and a variety of waterfowl are abundant. Fishing in the stocked streams and lakes is excellent. Delicious wild berries dot the mountainous areas and the northern states are known for their sugar maple trees. I have had many a breakfast improved by the wild blueberries of Maine and sweet maple syrup.

The culture of the eastern rural areas, from West Virginia to Maine, is among the oldest in a young country, yet its oldest continuous family lines are often caricatured as toothless, ignorant, backcountry hillbillies. They are more generously described as stubborn for sticking to the unproductive land. It is true that in West Virginia you will ride through countryside made famous by the "Hatfields and the McCoys" whose mutual backwoods hostility became the stuff of folk myths. However, within the last 10 years, North American regional writers have increasingly returned to their roots and are describing the complex depth and richness of character found among rural people. You won't regret a peek into their history and you will find the present day locals charming—not at all like their television stereotypes. In short, you will not be shot by "Zeke," nor attacked by "Little Abner." People like Tootie and Joe Peete, proprietors of 2 very good East Coast riding establishments, will regale you with local tales. Vermont and its people will remind you of a Currier & Ives postcard reprinted from a distant past, and Maine offers great wilderness vacation land packed with legitimate "originals."

Whatever your view of the beauty or culture of the eastern United States, nobody who knows anything about riding would criticize the quality of their horses or their horsemanship. The east has led the country in the breeding and training of Thoroughbreds and Warmbloods that dominate the equestrian sports of jumping, hunting and dressage, and Morgans, a stalwart breed developed in Vermont. Until recently, East Coast riders completely dominated all of the English riding sports. However, over the last 15 years, the east has experienced a enormous growth in the popularity of Western style riding, with team penning competitions leading the way. Western and English horse shows number in the thousands and range from local pony clubs and unsophisticated backyard competitions to ranked rodeos, Grand Prix shows, and dressage events of international prominence. Polo is an increasingly popular sport, especially as "poor man's polo" becomes more popular. Fox hunting has always been a traditional pursuit, particularly in areas with strong British roots, although its gates are closing as rising insurance costs threaten affordability. That is one good reason to get yourselves to the Conyer's House in Virginia, located in the heart of one of finest and most spectacular fox hunting regions in the Lower 48. There are also many trail riding associations which sponsor up to 15 rides annually. While you might have to trailer your horse for an hour or two in the more developed suburban areas, it is not difficult to find large state parks that permit riding. There is no shortage of associations representing hundreds of breeds and styles of riding, from endurance treks to barrel racing. Finally, if there is such a thing as truth in advertising, then you should be aware that East Coast riders will experience an environment that includes rain, muddy springtime weather and cold winters as well as incredibly beautiful autumn foliage, when the changing leaves put on a magnificent color show, and balmy, sunshine-filled summers. Those of you who are planning a fall vacation should book early, because our East Coast riding

establishments tend to fill up months in advance. Riders should always bring rain gear and oint-
ments or sprays for insects and sun protection. Beyond that, common sense and the literature provided by the riding establishment you have chosen will leave you in good hands.

All of our East Coast riding establishments can arrange transfers from the nearest airport or
train station. You can also drive, and there is no shortage of rental car companies. One advantage
of renting a car is that you have increased mobility to tour the area when you are not on horseback.
As an added bonus, you can visit 1 or more major cities before or after your trip. West Virginia's
Swift Level lies near Washington D.C. and Baltimore, The Conyer's House is even closer and offers
hunting, good riding, and a pleasant atmosphere. The Bark Eater is a 5 hour drive from New York
City and our Vermont (Vermont Icelandic Horse Farm) and Maine (Speckled Mountain Ranch) rides
are reasonably close to Boston and within 8 hours of New York City. Food along the eastern
seaboard is among the best in the nation, the result of many cultures coming together. You will have
a choice of Yankee cooking and/or some Southern delights for "down-home" meals, but every part
of the east offers an entire spectrum of cosmopolitan cuisine because of its lively tourist attractions.

ROCKY MOUNTAINS: Colorado, Idaho, Montana and Wyoming

The Rocky Mountain states of Idaho, Wyoming, Montana, and Colorado with their soaring peaks, millions of acres of government-owned land, and breathtaking vistas, are a magnet for tourists from
around the world. During the summer months (June to August) Yellowstone National Park gets downright congested, and trying to book a winter holiday flight into Vail or Aspen, Colorado can be very
frustrating. It is the image of the Rocky Mountains as home to the cowboy that is the draw for equestrian folks worldwide. Horseback riding in this region also allows you to partake of the frontier spirit
in the land of buffalo and antelope. The communities that surround these riding destinations go to
great lengths to cultivate that image, often commercially. Even cowboys and cowgirls like to shop...

Generally speaking the plateaus surrounding the Rockies are situated at an elevation of 5000
feet. Many of the ranches and summer pastures are above 7500 feet, and you will routinely have
the opportunity to ride through mountain passes as high as 10,000 to 12,000 feet, often still
snow-covered in June. September can bring the first snow storms. However, except for mountain
passes, altitude by itself tells you little about the riding terrain. Mountain trails can flatten out at
10,000 feet for a mile or so, yet be steep at 7000 feet. Since steep slopes and rocky terrain will
influence, if not determine, the pace of the ride, you may wish to inquire first what you can
expect to encounter along the way. If I had to put my finger on the essence of the Rocky Mountain
riding experience, it would the sense of being a mere "mote in God's eye," surrounded by such
an awesome setting. By way of contrast, riding in eastern United States is like moving through a
series of intimate woodland sanctuaries; eastern woods comfort you with closeness, while the
Rocky Mountains seduce you with their vastness. Vastness, of course, means long hours in the
saddle, hence the Western saddle has historically prevailed over the skimpier, English version.
Although not impossible, it is sometimes difficult to track down English tack in the Rocky
Mountains. Experienced riders should inquire about bringing their own saddles.

Horseback riding in the Rockies takes many forms: cattle ranches, some offering round-ups,
camps and drives, dude or guest ranches, overnight wilderness pack trips, and fast paced rides over
the old cowboy and Pony Express trails. Some places offer a taste of each. The slower paced wilderness pack trips and dude/guest ranches are ideal for the entire family, but there are suitable cattle
drives as well. Be aware that some ranches have designated times for, or generally prefer, adults
only. Singles and couples will find that virtually every place can cater to their needs although, once
again, certain places specialize in accommodating singles. Decision-making can become compli-
cated when it comes to selecting ranches for the family. There are ranches that provide separate
activities for adults and children, while others encourage total family participation—so choose
wisely. There is a growing list too, of those places that cater especially to fit and experienced

riders, but almost all of the dude/guest ranches can accommodate every level of riding skill.

The horses used are generally reliable, hardy mountain and cattle horses, able to take a beating yet keep on ticking. They are sure-footed, able to make their way up and down steep paths and across rocky terrain. Okay, so trail horses may not be as attractive as many of the horses you find in the best of the eastern riding establishments; they are certainly less pampered. To begin with, most of the horses live outside all year long, although some ranchers do move their herds to lower ground or a warmer environment during the winter. But do not confuse the horses' rugged looks with neglect. Western horse-owners care about their horses no less then the owners of upscale hunter/jumper farms in the east. They simply have different attitudes about what a horse needs and what his function is in life. The so-called "Western" horse actually refers to many distinct breeds, and crossbreds, including the famed Quarterhorses, Pintos, Appaloosas, wild Mustangs, and more recent developments like Vermont-originated Morgans, and the Rocky Mountain Horse which, I believe, is related to both the gaited Tennessee Walker and the Missouri Fox Trotter. Gaited horses have become more popular and breeds such as the Icelandics, will surely be recognized in West someday as an ideal and very rugged horse. Historically, East Coast English style riders once viewed Western horses as akin to the old nag that pulled the rag cart with little in the way of brain power. This view prevailed until recently, especially among *afficionados* of English show events. Nowadays, as Western riding gains in reputation, we are beginning to see spotted horses in dressage and other disciplines.

A word on the wildlife: elk, antelope and deer are abundant throughout the Rockies. Bears tend to be reclusive animals, although most of the National Parks are a haven for them and they are known to behave quite brazenly. The mountain lion is more wary of human contact. Moose populate many areas of the Rocky Mountains, coyotes are all over the place, and even the wolf is being brought back, sometimes to the chagrin of local cattle and sheep farmers. Eagles and hawks also inhabit the area. Yellowstone National Park enjoys the most spectacular and viewable herds of wild animals (including buffaloes) this side of the African plains.The weather throughout the Rocky Mountains during the riding months is notoriously dry, but an occasional thunder shower can be expected. Cool mornings and even colder nights are the norm, with temperatures dropping as much as 50 degrees between afternoon highs and evening lows. Yet on a typically sunny day in July or August you will need protection from the sun and should dress in layers so as to be able to peel them off as the day grows warmer. You can trust the announcements of good trout fishing, and the hunting season, which normally begins in October,is absolutely big business.

There is an extensive list of regional and national government and private organizations that help to establish standards and insure that visitors get what they've paid for. Almost every state has its own licensing board or state organization. They will gladly provide printed information and will be happy to answer your questions.

SOUTHWEST: Arizona and New Mexico [Contributed by Russell True of White Stallion Ranch]

The Southwest is that part of the American West that has been so vividly portrayed in classic Western movies. Cowboys, Indians, communal round-ups, and the great trail drives, these are the pictures so many of us have of this unique part of our country. But it is really something else that makes this area different. Our Southwestern heritage comes from a different part of Europe. The Spanish and later their protégés, the Mexicans, originally colonized this part of the country and their influence remains dominant in many ways to this day. It is seen on the surface in the architecture, street and community names, and food. Yet these roots permeate the culture in deeper and sometimes unseen ways, in the law, the people, and the lifestyle. Once someone has been here a while they feel it, they can't always put their finger on it, but it is there and many people are drawn to it. The pace is slower, people are open and friendly, priorities are different, some would say upside down. For southern Arizona, New Mexico, and parts of Texas, this is still the way life is lived.

Visitors will enjoy the distinctive Spanish/Mexican architecture with its arches, plazas, fountains, Spanish tile roofs, and saltillo tile floors. The colors used, pink, turquoise, terra cotta, and white and red combinations, both stand out as different and blend perfectly with the landscape. The Mexican and Southwestern cuisines of the area varies by locality. Arizona, New Mexico and Texas fight over whose is the best, but all agree one of them is right. Tacos, fajitas, chimichangas, flautas, tostadas, enchiladas, and tamales are standard fare in Mexican restaurants.

The Spanish and Mexicans are not the only ones who left their marks on this region. The Native Americans indigenous to the area are central figures in its history and remain a big part of what makes the Southwest so special today. The 3 major native cultures of the area were the Anasazi, the Mogollon, and the Hohokam. They left behind the cliff dwellings of Betatakin, Canyon de Chelly, and the canal systems of the Salt River Valley. You can see echoes of their pueblo style architecture in the contemporary style called Santa Fe, named after the region where it originated. Stucco walls with tiered roof and wall lines, outlooking *vegas* (round native timbers), and flat roofs create a classic Southwestern look.

The likely descendants of the Anasazi are the Hopi, who live on 3 mesas in northeast Arizona. Carving out a life in the desert, they have an almost inexplicable ability to coax corn and other crops from land with little water. Their ability to survive is often attributed to their deep spirituality expressed though Kachinas and very elaborate ceremonies. Today visitors are able to buy their Kachinas and jewelry. Hopi jewelry is overlay silver of very high quality workmanship. It almost never has stones. Another probable descendant of the ancient pueblo tribes are the Zuni, whose jewelry is made with exquisitely inlaid stones and small polished pieces of turquoise in intricate patterns called needlepoint.

Possibly the most famous Native Americans of the area were the last to arrive, the Apache and their Athapaskan cousins, the Navajos. The Navajos are the largest tribe and have America's largest reservation in northern Arizona and New Mexico. They are known for their incredible blanket and rug making skills. A large Navajo rug can command as much as $20,000. Navajo jewelry is the most commonly found and generally has turquoise and other stones. The notorious Apaches who, under Geronimo, were the last group of Native Americans to surrender to the U. S. Government, had a giant impact on Arizona. The Apaches entered Arizona and New Mexico about the same time as the Spanish. They were a nomadic group, who depended on raiding other native tribes and later the Europeans and Mexicans who colonized the area. It was the Apaches who kept the Spanish, Mexicans, and later the ranchers from moving north of Tucson. Tucson and Tubac (60 miles south of Tucson) were *presidios* (walled cities) designed to provide protection from raiding Apaches. The Spanish were able to colonize most of New Mexico. Santa Fe, the capital of New Mexico is the oldest seat of government, founded in 1609 as a Spanish provincial capital. The Apaches maintained a significant presence in Arizona until 1870, when General George Crook subdued the Navajos and put many Apaches on reservations. This was the time when most of the ranches in the area got their start. In fact, the ranching industry exploded between 1870 and 1880. The great movie portraits of the American cowboy and the open range have created an enduring image of the American West. However, the "golden age" of ranching only lasted about 30 years (1870-1900), until barbed wire, railroads, and government involvement changed the ranchers' world.

Despite all this, if you ask a foreign visitor what comes to mind first when thinking of America, it is the cowboy. The movies of John Wayne, Alan Ladd, and others (and, more recently, Billy Crystal in *City Slickers*), have portrayed a uniquely American image of the cowboy that captures people's hearts and imaginations. Today it is possible to be a cowboy, or at least ride with some, at the many dude ranches found in this region. Southwestern dude ranches are as diverse as the people who go to them. Whenever you travel 30 minutes in any direction the terrain is likely to change and the ranches with it. From the Grand Canyon and Monument Valley to the Saguaro-studded Sonoran desert, from the forests of northern New Mexico and Arizona to the rolling grasslands of southern Arizona and the Great Plains of New Mexico—this is big land. Due to the scarcity of water, the ranches are big also.

Two long established dude ranches which began as working cattle ranches and started taking guests long ago, are Grapevine Canyon Ranch and White Stallion Ranch. The more traditional ranch, Grapevine Canyon, offers guests the opportunity to see what life is like on a Southwestern cattle ranch, at least the positive aspects. This is the real thing, but with all the comforts. Riding at Grapevine Canyon Ranch will take you to the Cochise Stronghold and the Chiricahua mountains, home to the Apaches. This is a ranch where, with good timing, guests can experience a round-up. The ranch is situated at a high elevation and is therefore able to have guests year round. White Stallion Ranch has followed the path of many other dude ranches in Arizona and added some resort style facilities and activities. Beautiful winter weather is the drawing card here. The summers are a bit too warm and the ranch closes during June, July and August. This is where High Chaparral was filmed along with countless other movies, TV programs, and commercials. The Saguaro cactus studded vistas and mountains are what brought Hollywood here.

Horses are still the central theme at dude ranches and their presence has been felt in the Southwest since the Spanish brought them over in the 1500s. Until the railroads arrived in the 1880s, horses provided all transportation. They made colonization possible and later the ranching industry viable. Horses transformed the life of the Apache. Their ability to raid and run and fight an effective guerilla war was only possible because of the horse. Even though horses are now a necessity for far fewer people, they are more numerous today than at any other time. If you haven't yet, come ride one and experience a part of our country like no other.

WEST COAST: California

Appropriately for a place that is home to Hollywood, California enjoys a rather bizarre physical environment. It has a ruggedly beautiful coastline that stretches forever, loaded with all types of attractive sea mammals along an ocean that is forbiddingly cold to swim in without wet suits, except at California's southern tip. The young Sierra Nevada mountains are every bit as fierce and beautiful as the Rocky Mountains, yet—aside from Yosemite National Park—they are not considered a *mecca* for tourists. Cities like San Francisco and Oakland, as well as much of the area to the north (such as Humboldt and Mendocino Counties), have climates that vary as much as 20 or 30 degrees within a block, depending on whether you are on the sun side or the morning fog side. As Mark Twain is commonly quoted as saying "the coldest winter I ever spent was a summer in San Francisco"—the ultimate micro-climate city. Mendocino County, where Lari Shea's wonderful rides are located, is sheer magic—no less! Donna Synder's rides are offered in the area surrounding 2 of California's largest cities. San Francisco is, to my taste (apart from New York City), the most charming and urbane city in the continental United States.

While no particular breed of horses strikes me as unique to California, it is little wonder that some of the America's best endurance riders and horses come from the state of surfboards and extreme sports. You can rest assured that California will remain a haven for any number of competitive horse events. There is, for example, an event called "ride and tie" which, I believe, is a combination of running and riding. Californians are also competing effectively in national hunter/jumper competitions. I would not be surprised if 10 years from now, riders will carry a fold up bike on their backs, adding a new twist to the multi-discipline marathons that spring eternal from the Land of Hollywood. The California climate is warmer on the whole than that of the northeastern coastal region, always drier with a brief late winter/early spring rainy season—if they are lucky. The food in Mendicino and San Francisco as well as in the Napa Valley, home to many of the major American wineries, is superb. San Francisco offers a fascinating variety of Asian cuisines in particular. Finally, there is the Sierra Nevada, among the youngest, and most spectacular mountain ranges in the world. The highest peak, Mount Whitney, is taller than any in the Rockies, younger and equally untamed. The Yosemite backwoods, where some of the pack trips take place, are home to a wide variety of wildlife, including bear and deer in abundance.

HOLIDAY ON HORSEBACK/WARNER GUIDING AND OUTFITTING

www.horseback.com

BASICS: PO Box 2280, Banff, Alberta, T02 0C0, Canada
Tel: (800) 661-8352   Tel: (403) 762-4551
Fax: (403) 762-8130
Email: warner@horseback.com
WHEN: Open May to October for riding, all year round for other activities.
AIRPORTS: Calgary Airport - a 2 hour drive by car or bus.

LOCATION: Holiday on Horseback is located in Banff National Park, 75 miles west of Calgary, home of the world-famous Calgary Stampede.
PRICE: *Lodge Rides* (2 to 6 days): $220 (£138) to $650 (£406) per person. *Wilderness Tenting Camp* (4 to 6 days): $380 (£237) to $580 (£362) per person.

Holiday on Horseback has been in operation for 36 years. With over 300 horses, they are one of North America's largest outfitters, offering everything from day rides to wilderness expeditions. They even offer wilderness learning trips, one of which is guided by a professional historian, and another guided by a naturalist, former Superintendent of Banff National Park. With over 100 starting dates, there's bound to be a program for you. The Park is located 30 miles from Lake Louise and attracts 5 million visitors per year. Local mountain peaks soar to over 9000 feet.

CHILDREN'S PROGRAMS: Children must be able to keep up with the group.

ACCOMMODATIONS: Holiday on Horseback offers a variety of trips with different levels of comfort. The lodge-based trips often make use of the upscale Sundance Lodge and a more basic Halfway cabin. Tent camps, equipped with A-frame tents and hot water basins, provide a modicum of comfort, while the expedition and instructional trips rely on 2 person portable camping tents.

SPECIAL ACTIVITIES: First time guests should visit the world-famous Lake Louise, Banff, and the surrounding majestic Canadian Rockies, a very popular tourist spot. Less than a 2 hour drive away, is the world-famous Calgary Stampede.

MEALS: Hearty Western-style breakfasts and full course dinners are sure to satisfy. Lunch is frequently a picnic eaten on the trail. Fresh baked goods and home-made salads accompany most meals.

RIDING STUFF: These trips will take you into remote areas of Banff National Park. The mountain scenery ranks, by far, as some of the best in the world. From more than 300 sturdy, sure-footed horses, a mount will be chosen especially to meet your needs and experience. The pace remains exclusively at a walk, making this an ideal ride even for novices. You will ride through meadows and streams moving from a valley low at 4500 feet to heights above the tree line at 9000 feet.

AUTHOR'S COMMENT: *Holiday on Horseback offers a quality wilderness riding experience through one of the most popular regions in the entire Rockies. Variety is the name of the game and there is something for everyone, from wilderness lodge stays to rugged, progressive camping trips.*

HIGHLIGHTS
2 to 6 day rides with lodge stays • All levels of riding skill • Ride approximately 5 hours a day • Wildlife viewing including elk, Big Horn sheep, eagles and possibly bears • Customized trips for groups • Slow pace • Hundreds of scheduled yearly riding holiday options • Riding in Banff National Park in the Canadian Rockies • Member: Alberta Outfitters Association

BIG BAR GUEST RANCH

www.bigbarranch.com

BASICS: PO Box 27, Jesmond, Clinton, British Columbia V0K 1K0, Canada
Tel/Fax: (250) 459-2333
Email: bigbar@wkpowerlink.com

WHEN: Open year round.

AIRPORTS: Vancouver International or Kamloops Airport. You can get to Clinton, British Columbia by train or Greyhound bus service.

LOCATION: Clinton is a 6 hour drive north of Vancouver.

PRICE: *Cariboo Country Horsepacking and Fraser River Raft Expeditions:* $1199 (£749) full package; $749 (£468) horseback only; $450 (£281) rafting only, 8 days/7 nights, per person, d/o. *City Slicker Ride:* $749 (£468) 6 days/5 nights, per person, d/o. *Ranch Stay:* $923(£577) 4 days/3 nights, per couple, includes all meals, accommodations and unlimited riding.

Nestled in the rolling hills of the Cariboo, surrounded by mountains and meadows, the only distractions at Big Bar Guest Ranch are the spectacular scenery, the yip-yip of coyote, the hoot of an owl, deer bounding over open meadows, Mama Bear watching over playful cubs, or the whinny of a horse. Stands of aspen and jack pine, meadows of wildflowers and lakes surround extraordinary canyons and mountain ranges above the mighty Fraser River, home of Big Horn sheep.

CHILDREN'S PROGRAM: To make this a memorable holiday for everyone, a recreational coordinator is on hand to organize activities for children of all ages.

ACCOMMODATIONS: Tillicum and Harrison Lodges, are landmarks in Cariboo cattle country, containing 15 rooms with private bathrooms, they offer warmth and comfort. Harrison Lodge is the centerpiece of the ranch, an impressive, hand-hewn log lodge, built over 60 years ago. There is a comfortable lounge with a large stone fireplace as well as a game room. There are also individual, 1 bedroom cabins dotting the hillside with lofts, fireplaces, cooking facilities, fridge, and indoor plumbing. Experience Indian living in a teepee!

SPECIAL ACTIVITIES: Enjoy nature's wonders on tranquil days, canoeing, fishing, hiking, mountain biking or relive the thrills of the "Old-Tymers" by gold panning in the Fraser River. For excitement and adventure, test your skill at paintball. Relax in the famous Fireside Lounge, game room, or star-gaze from an outdoor hot tub.

MEALS: The licensed dining room offers sumptuous ranch-style buffet meals. Enticing aromas from the BBQ waft by as you enjoy the camaraderie of newfound friends.

RIDING STUFF: The Ranch uses Western tack and offers 2 daily rides of 2 hours length and all day rides into the high country. On guided trail rides, you will encounter breathtaking views, examine old Indian carvings on cliff edges, see mountain sheep and pass rock formations that are a photographer's dream come true. There is also a live-a-day in the life of a real cowboy ride, where you will assist in a cattle drive, round-up, or other real workday tasks. Big Bar offers an extended *City Slicker* pack trip of 6 days and 5 nights over Big Bar Mountain down to the Fraser River. Offered as well is a *Cariboo Country Horsepacking and Fraser River Expedition*, a combined pack/raft trip, which combines 4 exciting days and 3 nights of horseback riding, a night at the Ranch, and 2 days rafting on the river. Evenings are spent out under the stars as riders gather around a blazing campfire to eat, socialize and relax.

AUTHOR'S COMMENT: *Big Bar is another Canadian Dream Ranch that tries very hard to offer you the best vacation you ever had. With year round facilities available, you may even wish to consider winter riding.*

HIGHLIGHTS
2 hour or all day rides • Overnight pack trips • Working cowboy rides • Buggy and hay rides • Gold panning • Canoeing • Fishing • Hiking • River rafting • Mountain biking • Paintball • Cross-country skiing • Snow-shoeing • Sleigh rides • Dog-sledding • Member: British Columbia Guest Ranch Association

CASCADE MOUNTAIN RIDE
FROM THE 49TH TO PARADISE

www.horsebackholidays.com

BASICS: International Horseback & Polo Holidays,
8034-112 B Street, Delta, British Columbia
V4C 5A7, Canada
Tel: (604) 501-1652
Fax: (604) 501-9213
Email: info@horsebackholidays.com
WHEN: Open late June to early October.

AIRPORTS: Vancouver. Transfers may be arranged.
LOCATION: Ride begins near the US- Canadian border.
PRICE: Approximately $680 (£425) 7 days/ 6 nights, per person, double occupancy, includes all land costs from the starting point at Whitworth Ranch.

Nearly 138 years ago, representatives of the British Empire in Canada decided to find a way to avoid paying the U.S. government a gold tax for consignments of the precious metal. Making their way by horse and mule from the Kootnays gold rush to the west coast, the route invariably led through portions of the United States in order to skirt the impassable mountains of British Columbia. Governor Douglas instructed Edward Dewdney of the Royal Engineers to devise a route which traveled in a direct path from east to west. The task took Edward Dewdney 3 years to complete and resulted in this famous and awe-inspiring trail that begins in Paradise Valley and crests the Cascade Mountain divide. Once called the " Mule Road to the Similkameen," the trail includes a 615 meter (nearly 2000 feet) elevation gain at some stages. There are many panoramic views of beckoning mountains and flowing rivers.

CHILDREN'S PROGRAM: Must be experienced riders, ages 14 and older.

ACCOMMODATIONS: The base camp in Paradise Valley offers luxury camping accommodations in spacious (14' x 12') sleeping tents, propane heated shower tents, and a large dining tent. While on the trail lightweight dome tents are used along with foam sleeping pads. Luggage is moved by pack mules.

SPECIAL ACTIVITIES: There is trout fishing at Nickerman Lake.

MEALS: Meals consist of typical West Coast fare, including full breakfasts and coffee to get you going in the morning. Lunch is usually served along the trail at a desirable resting place. Dinners are absolutely delicious with trout, salmon and steaks on offer.

RIDING STUFF: The Canadian outfitter conducting this trip, Jim McCrae, was instrumental in reopening parts of the trail for the British Columbia Parks Authority, and has been operating for many years in the region. His horses are sure-footed, mountain horses, strong and rugged enough to support you on difficult ascents and descents. The tack is Western. The trail covers areas where you may be subject to route alterations due to snow conditions. The climate is generally temperate. The terrain includes West Coast rainforest as well as alpine areas with pine, fir and spruce trees. Although the ride can accommodate all skill levels, advanced riders are frequently offered special opportunities to try their skills on more difficult terrain. Since the area is mountainous, the ride proceeds mostly at a walk.

AUTHOR'S COMMENT: *This ride is for people looking for that extra little bit of wilderness adventure in their lives. Maybe you will even stumble on some of the artifacts discarded by Dewdney's crew of Royal Engineers. The favorable exchange rate makes this adventure quite affordable.*

HIGHLIGHTS
Western tack • 4 to 8 hours per day in the saddle • Group size for inexperienced riders is 6 • Experienced riders may be offered different trail options • Riding through the Cascade Mountains • First time ride • Customized rides for groups of 4 or more

Photos © J. McCrae

DOUGLAS LAKE RANCH CATTLE DRIVE

www.horsebackholidays.com

BASICS: Agent: **International Horseback & Polo Holidays**, 8034-112 B Street, Delta, British Columbia V4C 5A7, Canada
Tel: (604) 501-1652   Fax: (604) 501-9213
Email: info@horsebackholidays.com
WHEN: June to September.

AIRPORTS: Vancouver/Kamloops
LOCATION: Douglas Lake Ranch is located in southern British Columbia.
PRICE: $1670 (£1043) 7 days/6 nights, per person, double occupancy, includes all riding, meals and accommodations.

Rounding-up calves and cattle, living the dream of the Old West while riding the vast open grasslands of British Colombia, this ride is well suited for experienced riders. Less experienced riders are welcome too, but you had better be in good shape to deal with long and hard hours spent in the saddle. Douglas Lake Ranch is located near the divide between British Columbia's beautiful Cariboo country and Okanangan - the former lush and green and the latter drier and flatter. After chasing cattle all day, you will be happy to rest, have meals prepared for you, while enjoying campfires and Country and Western songs performed for your entertainment by your wranglers.

CHILDREN'S PROGRAM: Children must be capable riders.

ACCOMMODATIONS: On the first and last nights you stay at Stony Lake Lodge which has 8 rooms and 15 beds. The other 4 nights will be spent at a cow camp, with separate bunkhouses, showers, and a spectacular setting reminiscent of an earlier Western Canada.

SPECIAL ACTIVITIES: There is excellent fly fishing based at Salmon and Minnie Lake Lodges. Dinner time, with its glowing campfire and cowboy singing or poetry reading is a great time to relax before retiring, while the coyotes will lull you to sleep with their soothing baying.

MEALS: The meals are typical hearty Western fare. Breakfast includes eggs, ham, bacon, spreads, breads, coffee and juices. Dinners feature steaks, salmon and fresh baked bread. Lunches are packed for the trail.

RIDING STUFF: The cattle drive occurs on rangeland that has been used for cattle for hundreds of years. You will notice the markings of cowboy crews from years gone by and many antique artifacts that ride leaders ask you not to disturb. You will be spending some long hours in the saddle, gathering and moving over 200 head of cattle from the south end of "6 Mile" to the north. The usual sequence of events entails studying maps to become familiar with the route, followed by cowboys showing you the lay of land and answering questions about the horses, tack, or other concerns. You will be getting up as early as 4:30 a.m. and be out riding by 5:00 a.m., but resting during the heat of the day. Western tack is used with Quarterhorses for 5 to 6 hours of riding per day.

AUTHOR'S COMMENT: *International Horseback & Polo Holidays has been based in British Columbia for years. Their expertise in the area has led to the selection of the Douglas Lake Ranch Cattle Drive for the excellence of the riding and the quality of the overall program. The region is beautiful with diversity that will keep you interested, between your attempts to round-up the elusive cattle.*

HIGHLIGHTS

Western tack • 5 to 6 hours riding per day • Experienced riders preferred • Riding through beautiful Nicola Valley • Abundant wildlife including black bear, coyote, cougar, eagles and ospreys • Artifacts from older cowboy crews

THREE BARS GUEST AND CATTLE RANCH

www.threebarsranch.com

BASICS: Three Bars Ranch, SS 3, Site 19-62C, Cranbrook, British Columbia, V1C 6H3, Canada
Tel: (250) 425-5230   Tel: (877) 426-5239 (Toll free from U.S. and Canada)
Fax: (250) 426-8240
Email: threebarsranch@cyberlink.bc.ca

WHEN: May 30 to September 27.

AIRPORTS: Cranbrook Airport. Free transfers to the ranch, a 15 minute drive. Alternative airports: Kalispell, Montana, Calgary, Alberta, or Spokane, Washington.

LOCATION: A 3 hour drive from Lake Louise and Banff. Rocky Mountain region of British Columbia, 20 minutes north of Cranbrook Highway 93/95.

PRICE: Low Season (May 31 to July 5, August 30 to September 27): $890 (£556) for adults; $721 (£451) for children, ages 12 and under. High Season (July 6 to August 29): $1050 (£656) for adults; $890 (£556) for children under 12. All rates 6 days/7 nights, per person, double occupancy, includes accommodations, meals, guided hiking, raft trip, and riding. The Ranch also offers 3 and 4 night programs.

Three Bars Ranch is an impressive addition to the Western guest ranch scene. It was opened to the public in 1992 by the Beckley family, which includes Jeff Beckley, a professional reining horse trainer. Jeff gives riding instructions once a week for guests who might be inclined. The principal activity at Three Bars is riding, but the ranch offers some excellent alternatives. The ranch strives to make your riding holiday a great experience.

CHILDREN'S PROGRAM: Children must be over 6 to ride or raft. The ranch program is designed so that families can participate in activities together.

ACCOMMODATIONS: Guests sleep in tastefully appointed log cabins, each with private entrance, queen beds, and full private bath. There is daily maid service. In addition there is a licensed dining room, a game room, a lounge, fireplace, library and gift shop.

SPECIAL ACTIVITIES: Apart from riding, there is an indoor pool, tennis court, good fly fishing, river rafting, archery, nearby golf, evening entertainment, and even fly fishing lessons. There are mountain bikes and skeet shooting as well as ping-pong, pool table, bocci ball, and horseshoes.

MEALS: Three Bars serves traditional ranch food including lots of fresh fruit, home baked breads and pastries. Guests eat in a comfortable dining room. Breakfast is ordered from a menu which features choices such as Belgian waffles with whipped cream and fresh mountain berries, bagels and strawberry cream cheese or ranch-sized pancakes, bacon and eggs. Lunch is served buffet-style and includes hamburger BBQs, homemade soups, deli trays, homemade buns and a salad bar. The dining room is known for its special recipes like Three Bars Ranch ribs and sun-dried tomato and red pepper chicken breast.

RIDING STUFF: Over 90 horses help fill the roster. Guests are assigned to a single horse for the week. There are 2 rides daily, 1 is a morning ride that gets you back in time for lunch and then up and at 'em once more, for some afternoon riding fun through country that ranges from mountain tops to green meadows and rushing water. After the first few days of easy riding, more accomplished riders are offered the opportunity for faster paced rides. Riding lessons are available to all guests. You might want to watch Jeff Beckley training reining horses, which is getting to be a big-time Western event. One week in June, July and September are devoted to horsemanship, with half a day of instruction and the remainder of the time available for trail riding or other ranch activities.

AUTHOR'S COMMENT: *Three Bars Ranch is an outstanding holiday destination, from its excellent riding program to its superior accommodations and food. Favorable exchange rates make this an outstanding value.*

HIGHLIGHTS
Western tack • Over 90 horses • 2 rides daily, 1 all day ride • Good wildlife viewing • Lessons offered • Large indoor riding arena • Indoor heated pool • Special horsemanship weeks • Guest capacity 40 • Tennis court • Petting zoo • Good fly fishing • River rafting • Member: DRA, BCGRA

TS'YL-OS PARK LODGE AND WILDERNESS TRIPS

www.hiddentrails.com

BASICS: Agent: **Hidden Trails**, 5396 Inverness Street, Vancouver, British Columbia V5W 3P7, Canada
Tel: (604) 323-1141   Tel: (888) 987-2457
Fax: (604) 323-1148
Email: traveler@hiddentrails.com
WHEN: June through September.
AIRPORTS: Vancouver. Air transfers to lodge included.
LOCATION: The Lodge is located 180 miles north of Vancouver on the edge of Ts'yl-os Park and the 50 mile long Chilko Lake.
PRICE: *Pioneer Express, Wild Potato Range Trip,* and *Goat Camp Trip:* $1395 (£872) 8 days/7 nights, per person, double occupancy, includes 5½ days of riding, all meals and lodging as well as flight from Vancouver to the ranch. Trips may be extended for a second week and stationary ranch vacations are also available.

Ts'yl-os Park offers great beauty, a very well planned program, and some of the fastest paced wilderness rides in North America. It is not surprising, that Hidden Trails' owners, Ryan Schmidt and partner Karen McLean, use this site as a starting point for their offerings of worldwide riding holidays. While not all of the trips require intermediate riding skill, some require riders with at least these skills who can maintain a fast paced trot and canter over considerable distances. After arrival at the lodge, riders will enjoy the many riding alternatives available. *The Pioneer Express* involves 3 nights at the ranch and 4 nights camping in vehicle supported wilderness base camps. The pace of the ride makes it suitable only for intermediate and advanced riders. *The Wild Potato Range* is a complete wilderness camping trip, that lets you experience a great variety of riding terrains and camping lakeside. On 3 of the days, pack horses will be utilized. The trip is suitable for intermediate riders. *The Goat Camp Ride*, named after the wild mountain goats residing in the area, is the slowest of the rides, but offers some of the most pristine wilderness anywhere with breathtaking vistas, and camps just below the magnificent glaciers. Although the ride occurs at a slower pace you will log some long saddle hours.

CHILDREN'S PROGRAM: Suitable for children over 12 with intermediate riding skills.

ACCOMMODATIONS: On most trips you will enjoy the first and last days at the beautiful Ts'yl-os Park Lodge, with its log cabins, individual guest rooms and teepee camp. The facilities include a jacuzzi, a large wood-burning fireplace, and great BBQ. The wilderness trips utilize pack horses and, where possible, vehicle or boat support.

SPECIAL ACTIVITIES: In addition to some exceptional fly fishing for trophy rainbow trout on the Chilko River, vacationers may opt for an extended lodge stay with canoeing, boating and hiking or a Class 5 wilderness raft trip back to Vancouver.

MEALS: Meals include typical Western ranch foods. While on the trail, delicious meals are prepared over an open fire. The wholesome food is carefully planned to provide a welcome relief for weary trail riders.

RIDING STUFF: The ranch has a strong breeding program and utilizes sure-footed, durable Arab/Quarterhorse crosses. Riders are taught the fundamentals of Western riding. Despite the mountainous terrain, there is plenty of wonderful flatland that lends itself to safe, faster riding, especially during the stationary lodge vacations. The mountain rides offer some of the most pristine wilderness in the world. No crowds, no fences, no phones, just nature as it always was.

AUTHOR'S COMMENT: *Ryan Schmidt and his partner Karen McLean, set the plate for this outstanding foray into the Canadian wilderness. The ranch serves as a more than satisfactory gateway to Hidden Trails' entire package of Canadian and worldwide rides and is a perfect place for experienced, but non-active, riders to give it a go in preparation for overseas riding.*

HIGHLIGHTS
Rides for all skill levels • Ride 4 to 7 hours a day • Good wildlife viewing including deer, elk, black bear, grizzlies, mountain goats and Big Horn Sheep • 3 to 7 day lodge stays may be arranged with some fast-paced riding • Beautiful mountain scenery in the true Canadian wilderness

GASPE PENINSULA RIDE

www.ridingtours.com

BASICS: Agent: **Equitour**, PO Box 807, Dubois, WY 82513, USA
Tel: (800) 545-0019   Tel: (307) 455-3363
Fax: (307) 455-2354   Email: equitour@wyoming.com
WHEN: May 31 to October 4. All rides begin on Sunday.
AIRPORTS: Quebec City Airport or Montreal Airport to Mont-Joli Airport.

LOCATION: The ranch is located at Mont-Joli, a 7 hour drive from Montreal and a 5 hour drive from Quebec City. There is also train and bus service.
PRICE: $795 (£497) 7 days/6 nights, per person, double occupancy, includes all meals (except Sunday night), accommodations and 5½ days of riding. Single supplement add $80 (£50).

The province of Quebec is unique in North America, with its French-speaking culture, and its old world charm. Deer, moose and a fascinating array of birds should be plentiful. Clear, swift rivers are home to the Atlantic salmon. The Atlantic Ocean can be seen from the hilltops and the area is dotted with lakes good for trout fishing. The region becomes incredibly alive with colors during the fall season. The central farm where the ride begins, enjoys a solid reputation for providing high quality riding trips at a very moderate price.

CHILDREN'S PROGRAM: Children must be experienced riders.

ACCOMMODATIONS: Guests spend 4 nights at a ranch with a huge horse barn, an enclosed riding ring, a main house and 2 new comfortable cabins. Each cabin contains 2 small bedrooms with bunk beds, a living room and a bathroom, which must be shared if both bedrooms are occupied. The other nights are spent at a charming inn and a lovely farmhouse. The hosts in each setting will make you feel right at home.

SPECIAL ACTIVITIES: Quebec City with its combination of Old and New World charm is always a delightful city to visit, a bit of France in the New World.

MEALS: Riders enjoy a hearty breakfast, an excellent picnic lunch, and fine dinners, including a 4 course dinner with wild fowl, meat and fish dishes prepared in the tradition of fine French cuisine.

RIDING STUFF: The ranch uses Quarterhorse crosses and Western tack. A limited supply of English tack is available. While the overall pace is moderate there are opportunities for long trots and canters. Riding time averages 6 hours a day. On the first day riders explore the surrounding forests, dotted with sparkling lakes. Riders rest at a picturesque waterfall on the Patchedez River, before riding to the inn for an excellent dinner and overnight stay. On the second day the group rides back to the ranch through open fields, where cattle graze, and along the White River through a beautiful maple forest. Wednesday is day with some steep riding through attractive landscape, before spending a relaxed evening enjoying spectacular views of the St. Lawrence Seaway. Thursday's activities include a long ride to the vacation town of Metis, and a 4 mile ride along the beach, where riders may discover sunning seals and ducks riding the ocean waves. The final day takes guests into the Chic-Choc Hills for a magnificent view of the surrounding area, a picnic, and the ride back to the ranch.

AUTHOR'S COMMENT: *France in the New World, beautiful countryside, and some very hard-working hosts, make this a desirable holiday. Book early if you wish to enjoy the spectacular fall color show that the rich forest land bestows.*

HIGHLIGHTS
Ride through French-speaking Quebec • Must be able to trot and canter • 5 to 6 hours a day in the saddle • Sunday to Saturday • Moderate pace • Weight limit 240 lbs. (109 kg.) (17 stone)

THE BANANA RIDE

www.horsebackholidays.com

BASICS: Agent: International Horseback & Polo Holidays, 8034-112 B Street, Delta, British Columbia V4C 5A7, Canada
Tel: (604) 501-1652
Fax: (604) 501-9213
Email: info@horsebackholidays.com

WHEN: October to March.
AIRPORTS: Puerto Vallarta
LOCATION: Yelapa
PRICE: $1200 (£750) 7 days/7 nights, per person, double occupancy, includes all meals, accommodations and riding.

Yelapa is a fishing village situated on a peninsula and is not connected to the mainland by any viable road. The area is covered by dense mountain and highland forests through which you will ride. Seemingly frozen in time by its isolation, Yelapa is reminiscent of an earlier Mexico. The village can only be approached by boat, a beautiful 45 minute sail up the Pacific Coast from Puerto Vallarta. This riding holiday has been developed and is run by Pam Arthur, an English-woman, who is a national level coach and course designer for Canada and has had the distinction of being Master of Foxhounds for 7 years. She has also served as a judge at premier equestrian events in the US and Canada. Pam has spent 17 winters in Mexico and runs a variety of ecotourism related projects, including animal care. This ride reflects her "other side," and it is not only for those with hard hats and jodhpurs. The only really formal event is the weekly Croquet Meet, where white clothing is obligatory. Temperatures range between 60° and 70° Fahrenheit.

CHILDREN'S PROGRAM: Suitable for children, ages 8 and older, provided they can ride.

ACCOMMODATIONS: There is a choice of accommodations from the upscale Casa Milagros to the family-friendly guest lodges. There is no electricity in this area and the nights are illuminated by candlelight. There are also no car fumes or automation of any kind!

SPECIAL ACTIVITIES: There is snorkelling, para-sailing, diving, kayaking, water-skiing, and dug-out punting. Friday nights are devoted to music on the beach and Saturday is croquet tournament day. The region is a dream for all types of water sports and you should plan on indulging yourself.

MEALS: Food consists of both European and Mexican fare, including breads and steaks, tamales, possole, tacos, and fresh seafood.

RIDING STUFF: The horses and mules used on the ride are small and, therefore, cannot carry persons over 6 feet (1.85 meters). Both the horses and mules come from Chacala, home of chickle, the main ingredient in a famous chewing gum. The animals are well cared for and, as you might expect, tough and usually unshod. The tack is Western style but without leather (which would mildew in this climate within a week), using rather beautiful Mexican hand-carved wooden saddles with padding. The area you will ride through is a natural paradise with highland forests, waterfalls, beaches and hills, unspoiled by commercial development. The trails are narrow and steep dictating a walking pace. You will visit Chacala, the mother village of Yelapa.

AUTHOR'S COMMENT: *This ride was selected by International Riding Holidays in part because of Pam's conscientious ecotourism orientation. Here is a chance to enjoy a Mexico that is quickly vanishing. English-women have been pioneers in the development of high quality overseas riding holidays, and Pam's offering is no exception.*

HIGHLIGHTS
Pristine environment, accessible only by boat • 3 to 6 hours per day in the saddle • Native mixed breed horses • Mule riding • 7 day holiday • Variety of water sports, including snorkelling, para-sailing, kayaking, and more

Photos © Pam Arthur

LA SIERRA CAVALCADE & MONARCH BUTTERFLY SANCTUARY

www.hiddentrails.com

BASICS: Agent: **Hidden Trails**, 5396 Inverness Street, Vancouver, British Columbia, V5W 3P7, Canada
Tel: (604) 323-1141   Tel: (888) 987-2457
Fax: (604) 323-1148
Email: travel@hiddentrails.com
WHEN: Open from October to May.
AIRPORTS: Mexico City. Transfers included.

LOCATION: A little over 2 hours drive west of Mexico City to Sierra Madre Occidental.
PRICE: $1650 (£1031) 8 days/7 nights, per person, double occupancy, includes 5½ days of riding, all inclusive from Mexico City, accommodations, meals, beverages. Single supplement add $300 (£187).

This outstanding riding holiday is led by Jose Schravesande, Mexico's leading endurance rider and trainer. Beginning with a Saturday night arrival and stay in Mexico City, you transfer to the Valle de Bravo where you will enjoy riding in the beautiful mountains of that area, at elevations from 5000 feet (1560 meters) to 11,000 feet (3437 meters). From November to March the trip includes a visit to the Monarch Butterfly Sanctuary, a large American butterfly noted for its long distance migrations and beautiful markings. The sight of millions of butterflies, creating a pageant of color, will not be easily forgotten. On Saturday, riders are transferred to Mexico City for a midday return flight.

CHILDREN'S PROGRAM: Children over the age of 12 with proven capability to ride long hours.

ACCOMMODATIONS: You will enjoy superior accommodations, with fine service and delightful meals. After your first evening in Mexico City, the entire ride emanates from a small town, typical of old Mexico, with its cobblestone streets, lively plaza and handicraft markets. All rooms have *en suite* bathrooms, and are well-appointed.

MEALS: The trip features some exceptional Mexican 4 and 5 course meals with fine wines. The food is of the highest quality, suitable for all tastes.

RIDING STUFF: The excellent horses of Jose Schravesande and his wife Lucia as well as the surrounding riding terrain make this a wonderful riding opportunity, "South of the Border." Riders will enjoy panoramic views of the Sierra Madre Occidental Mountains, riding through picturesque Mexican towns and villages, and through ecosystems that vary from mild pine forests to sub-tropical farmland with sugar cane fields and tropical forests. The brilliant tropical flowers, and exotic birds will leave you breathless. The ride is a circle tour. While the horses stay out on the trail, riders are transported back to the hotel each day by car or boat, to enjoy the comforts of the wonderful facilities. The horses will demonstrate the kind of endurance training that allows many opportunities for long canters across farmland, cattle ranches, and woodlands. There will be stream crossings as well as long uphill rides. The horses are Arabian/Spanish crosses, Quarterhorses, Trakkener, Thoroughbred and Criolla crosses.

AUTHOR'S COMMENT: *This ride is a relatively new and wonderful addition to the world of riding holidays, offering quality horses, accommodations and food. The last time I looked, those were some very important ingredients in a good riding holiday. Hidden Trails offers other riding destinations in North and South America and worldwide.*

HIGHLIGHTS
All accommodations in quality hotel with *en suite* bathrooms • 4 to 7 hours riding a day • English, Western and Mexican Charro tack • Moderate pace • Capacity 6 to 12 riders • November to March visit the world-famous Monarch Butterfly Sanctuary

GRAPEVINE CANYON RANCH INC.

www.gcranch.com

BASICS: PO Box 302, Pearce, AZ 85625, USA
 Tel: (520) 826-3185   Tel: (800) 245-9202
 Fax: (520) 826-3636
 Email: egrapevine@earthlink.net
WHEN: Open year round (closed December 1-15).

AIRPORTS: Tucson - a 90 minute drive.
LOCATION: The ranch is a 1 hour drive from the Mexican border, Tombstone and Chiricahua National Monument.
PRICE: $150 (£94) to $170 (£106) per day, per person, double occupancy.

We are all lucky that this delightful ranch is open year round, the result of a warm southern location and a cool 5000 foot altitude. Nestled in the rugged Dragoon Mountains, Grapevine supplies an excellent riding program on extremely "well-scrubbed" horses in a terrain that is uniquely Southwestern and varies considerably from the other parts of Arizona. Owner Eve Searle, who hails from Australia, has lived around the world and has created an atmosphere particularly inviting to an international clientele. Her husband, Gerry, is a man for all seasons, a great spinner of tales. You might wish to corner him and get him to discuss his stunt riding days in the famous John Ford westerns which were filmed nearby. Mexico is a 1 hour drive away, if you can ever drag yourself off this 10,000 acre spread, "smack dab" in the middle of Apache country.

CHILDREN'S PROGRAM: For insurance reasons, the ranch cannot accommodate children under 12.

ACCOMMODATIONS: Guests stay in well-appointed, widely spaced cabins or casita suites, with sundecks offering wonderful mountain views. The rooms are carpeted and include full temperature control, coffee pot, supplies, refrigerator, hair dryers, and bath robes for the hot tub.

SPECIAL ACTIVITIES: Mexico and Tombstone are certain to entertain. There are miles of hiking trails. Bass and catfish abound in a stocked pond. A heated pool, hot tub, comfortable lounge and a recreation room with pool and ping-pong tables add to the relaxing atmosphere

MEALS: All meals are served family style from a varied menu. Breakfast is cooked to order. Lunch and dinner consist of hearty, tasty meals followed by deliciously sinful home-made desserts.

RIDING STUFF: At Grapevine you can ride to weariness if you desire. In addition to the wrangler led trail riding, you can arrange for riding or horsemanship lessons. Guests usually begin the program with a 3 hour morning ride, a time to get comfortable in the saddle. After that, based upon an evaluation of your skill level, you may opt for a 2 hour morning ride and a 1 or 2 hour afternoon ride daily. All day rides are also offered on a daily basis, some involving cartage of horses and riders to different trailheads. The terrain varies from dry flat rolling hills to rugged mountain passes. Riding groups are small. Seasonal cattle round-ups are available for qualified riders. There are sunset rides June through August.

AUTHOR'S COMMENT: *Grapevine Ranch runs near to capacity year round and not without reason. The entire crew works very hard to bring you an excellent riding program, good food, and very comfortable accommodations. This is the epitome of the Western ranch experience with some hot tamales thrown in for fun!*

HIGHLIGHTS

Western tack • 60 Quarterhorses • Guest capacity 30 • Daily trail riding • All skill levels • Heated pool and hot tub • Seasonal cattle round-ups • Comfortable accommodations • Minimum stay 3 nights • Member: DRA , AZDRA

WHITE STALLION RANCH

www.wsranch.com

BASICS: 9251 W. Twin Peaks Road, Tucson, AZ 85743, USA
Tel: (520) 297-0252   Tel:(888) 977-2624
Fax: (520) 744-2786
Email: Wsranch@flash.net
WHEN: Open September 1 to May 31.
AIRPORTS: Tucson (free transfers). Phoenix is about a 1½ hour drive.

LOCATION: The ranch is located along the northern boundary of Saguaro National Park, 20 minutes from downtown Tucson.
PRICE: October 1 to December 18: $728 (£455) to $966 (£604) per week, per person, double occupancy. December 19 to May 31: $798 (£499) to $1148 (£717) per week, per person, double occupancy. Prices do not include taxes or gratuities.

Like fine wine, White Stallion Ranch has improved with age, yet still offers the quintessential Arizona riding experience. Lying on 3000 acres and sharing 2 miles of common boundary with Saguaro National Park, this is the picture postcard Arizona of high desert, tall cactus, and those funny rabbits with the big ears. White Stallion has a heated pool and hot tub, tennis courts, and full bar. Team cattle penning is also available. There is a Happy Hour at the saloon, a full range of non-riding activities, and the True family, hands-on owners, ride leaders, and gracious hosts.

CHILDREN'S PROGRAM: Young children may ride with their parents. Children 5 and older may ride their own horse. A child must be at least 8 years old to go on fast rides.

ACCOMMODATIONS: The ranch has 35 rooms in casitas with 2 to 4 rooms each. The rooms vary from cozy, economical singles to luxurious casita suites with whirlpools, 2 bathrooms, a fireplace, and more.

SPECIAL ACTIVITIES: There is a weekly rodeo on the ranch, guided hiking, cook-outs, heated pool, hot tub, bar, library room, billiards, line dancing, moonlight bonfire with a cowboy singer, and a speaker program. They even have an exotic petting zoo. Golf courses are less than 15 minutes away.

MEALS: White Stallion provides good food, including hearty ranch breakfasts, lunches and fine evening meals including steak BBQs, Indian oven dinners, and cook-outs. If you outride the food you won't even gain weight!

RIDING STUFF: The ranch maintains a fine herd of Western horses. There are as many as 4 rides daily broken down into scenic (slow), fast, desert and mountain rides. There is also an all day ride into the Saguaro National Park for the hardy and enthusiastic. Team cattle penning is popular. Be sure to try it, it's a barrel of laughs, 'specially when them little doggies get to sorting the riders! There is a weekly rodeo at the ranch (don't forget to find out which of the Trues rode the rodeo circuit). The terrain is desert sands, with long-eared rabbits and cactus high enough to hide behind. Beginners will find a thoroughly enjoyable riding program and experienced riders will appreciate the team penning and the soft forgiving desert soil.

AUTHOR'S COMMENT: *Some people are born to be great guest ranchers, it is in their blood. Check out the True family at White Stallion for a fine time in that warm and dry Arizona air. The Trues have got the business of enjoying their guests down to a science.*

HIGHLIGHTS
Western tack • Highly rated ranch • Guest capacity 75 • All skill levels • Heated pool and hot tub • Tennis courts • Full bar • Petting zoo • Member: DRA, AZDRA

ADVENTURES ON HORSEBACK

www.endurance.net/RightRider

BASICS: US Agent: **Equitour**, Box 807, Dubois, WY 82513, USA
Tel: (800) 545-0019   Tel: (307) 455-2778
Fax: (307) 455-2354
Email:equitour@wyoming.com
Website: www.ridingtours.com
Adventures on Horseback, 32628 Endeavour Way, Union City, CA 94587, USA
Tel:/Fax: (510) 487-9001
WHEN: April to October.
AIRPORTS: Oakland, San Jose, or San Francisco Airports. Car rental is necessary.

LOCATION: San Francisco Bay Area, California.

PRICE: $1650 (£1031) per person, double occupancy, includes 5 nights at a B&B, 1 night camping, 3 days of training, 1 day competition riding, breakfast and lunch daily, transportation to the event for you and your horse, and all entry and crewing assistance fees. Guests will need a vehicle to transport themselves from the airport and to and from the stables daily.

If you have some riding skill and wondered what it would be like to compete in a endurance ride on experienced horses under the guidance of a world class instructor, the opportunity is at the tip of your dialing finger. Your week at Adventures on Horseback will include 3 days of coaching on rider position, efficiency, equine balance and motion theory, training secrets, metabolic parameters, and trail strategy from Donna Synder-Smith, "the best body coach in the sport of endurance," award winner, and author of *The Complete Guide to Endurance Riding and Competition* (Macmillian 1998). Your holiday will be topped by participation in a sanctioned endurance ride on competition-experienced horses.

CHILDREN'S PROGRAM: There are no special programs for children.

ACCOMMODATIONS: Guests spend 1 night camping at the competition site. On another 5 nights you will enjoy comfortable, furnished rooms at a B&B with private bath. The B&B has a restful garden patio and is located next to an historic California Spanish mission.

SPECIAL ACTIVITIES: By arriving early you can enjoy some of the great delights of California, including San Francisco, Napa and Sonoma Counties, and an endless round of great eating experiences.

MEALS: Excellent and varied breakfasts and lunches are included every day of your stay. Since evening meals are not included in the package, you will have an opportunity to sample the wonderful foods and restaurants of the area.

RIDING STUFF: With the exception of the occasional clinic, many of us never get the opportunity to receive "world class" instruction on a personalized basis while riding trained competition horses. Many of the top trainers and riders have little time for anything but competition and the training and development of their own or a select client's horses. The rest of us may suffer as a result because great riders and horse trainers are not necessarily great instructors, nor do they necessarily want that role. Coach of 2 gold medallists in Endurance, Donna Snyder-Smith represents an exception to that rule. A born teacher, she is willing to share her knowledge, time and experience.

AUTHOR'S COMMENT: *If you think you would benefit from riding superior, athletic horses under the tuition of a world class trainer/ competitor, then this is the holiday for you. You will walk away from this experience with a newly found confidence, built on a new relationship with your equine partner. My words of wisdom on this opportunity—if you got the money and you got the time—"GRAB IT!"*

HIGHLIGHTS
Endurance saddles • Competition experienced Mustangs and Arabians • 2 riders per event • 3 days training • Participation in a 1 day endurance competition sanctioned by AERC • Weight limit 185 lbs. • Member: AERC, ARIA

McGEE CREEK PACK STATION

www.mcgee.com

BASICS: Route 1, Box 162, Mammoth Lakes, CA 93546, USA
Tel: (760) 935-4324 (Summer)
Fax/Tel: (760) 878-2207 (Fax & Winter Tel.)
Email: mcgee@gnet.com

WHEN: *High Country Wilderness Vacations*: June to September; *Ranch Vacations*: April to July and September to November; *Trail Rides*: March to May and October to November.

AIRPORTS: Mammoth Lakes (transfers included); Los Angeles Airport is a 5 hour drive; Reno Airport is a 3 hour drive.

LOCATION: McGee Creek is located 15 miles southwest of Mammoth Lakes.

PRICE: For private drop camps or trail rides the cost is determined by the number of pack animals needed to transport you to your wilderness destination. Horses and pack mules are $65 (£41) per animal, per day. Wranglers are $110 (£69) per day each. Full service trips, including Ranch Vacations, range from $150 (£94) to $180 (£112) per day, per person.

The Sierra Nevada mountain range of California, with higher peaks than the Rockies, is home to some of the most majestic wilderness areas in the United States. McGee Creek is located in the heart of this beautiful country, 15 miles from Mammoth Lakes, one of California's premier winter ski areas. On Wilderness Vacations riders travel through the John Muir Wilderness, a pristine area of the Sierra. Owners Jennifer and Lee Roeser have been in the business for more than 25 years and offer a very wide range of riding programs suitable for many interests.

ACCOMMODATIONS: Accommodations vary with the type of trip. Wilderness Vacations emphasize "light on land" travel. Medium size camp tents are provided or you can sleep under the stars. The Ranch Vacation package typically offers large tents with Montana-style walls and comfortable bedding.

SPECIAL ACTIVITIES: Hiking, fishing and swimming are always available. Off-season trail rides take you through the Alabama Hills, the location of hundreds of Western movies.

MEALS: Full service pack trips and Ranch Vacations include hearty Western fare. Fresh fruits, vegetables and meats will leave you satisfied and full. McGee's cooks have been featured in *Sunset* magazine and you can expect good food.

RIDING STUFF: McGee Creek uses ranch-bred and trained, sure-footed, reliable animals suitable for the High Sierra, including pure-bred Morgans, a horse originally bred in Vermont, as well as Tennessee mules that will feel as smooth as a big old car. Wilderness pack trips are customized for each group. Ranch Vacations take place on a working cattle ranch east of Mammoth Lakes and offer trail riding and cattle work, including round-ups, drives and cutting. The Roesers are able to offer a wide variety of riding experiences from March to November by arranging trips at different elevations as the seasons change.

AUTHOR'S COMMENT: *Having spent a good many summers traveling the backwoods of the Sierra with my 2 sons, I know how rewarding the area can be. Generally rain free in the summer months, this is an area of great beauty with backcountry that is worth exploring. Yosemite National Park is in the region. The Roesers offer High Country trips for those seeking wilderness thrills and Ranch Vacations for fit riders looking for a challenge. Mammoth Lakes is a winter ski resort and the area offers plenty of wilderness alternatives.*

HIGHLIGHTS

Western tack • Options range from spot camps to full service wilderness camps • Group size 2 to 15 • Novice to experienced • All trips are customized • Ranch style vacations (up to 40) • Member: Eastern High Sierra Pack Association

RICOCHET RIDGE RANCH

www.horse-vacation.com

BASICS: 24201 Ricochet Ridge, North Hwy. One, Fort Bragg, CA 95437, USA
Tel: (707) 964-7669   Fax: (707) 964-9669
Email: larishea@horse-vacation.com
WHEN: Open year round.
AIRPORTS: San Francisco, Oakland or Santa Rosa
LOCATION: A 2 to 3½ hour drive from the airports. We recommend that you travel Hwy. 101 to Cloverdale, then take Hwy. 128 and drive through the wine country and beautiful red-wood forests on your way to the coast.
PRICE: *Redwood and Beach Vacations:* $1750 (£1093) 7 days/6 nights, per person, double occupancy, wine with dinner, hot tubs each night, entertainment 3 nights, 2 parties, all inclusive. *North Coast Trek:* $1395 (£872) 6 days/5 nights, per person, double occupancy, dinner not included. *All Day Rides:* $195 (£122) per person, includes lunch and beverages. Special packages by request.

It is difficult to separate the magic of Mendocino County from the quality of this riding experience. First time visitors to the Bay Area eager to experience the beauty of California and who enjoy riding will find it highly rewarding to head up to Ricochet. Guests stay at local B&Bs (owner Lari Shea and her crew are happy to make arrangements), while enjoying some outrageous trail riding. On the other hand, you may wish to join one of the 8 inn to inn trips. The horses are superbly trained by Lari Shea, an award winning endurance rider, and are suitable for a variety of skill levels. The food and ambiance of Mendocino will please even the most worldly of travelers..

CHILDREN'S PROGRAM: Children accompanied by an adult are welcome.

ACCOMMODATIONS: Whether you stay nearby and enjoy riding out from the stable daily or join one of the inn to inn rides, guests stay in well appointed, charming B&Bs that are part of the unique ambiance of the area.

SPECIAL ACTIVITIES: The Mendocino Coast is world-famous for its rich variety of attractions. As a noted art center, it boasts galleries of international importance. The performing arts are also well represented with music, plays, dance, and even weekend opera. Ocean fishing, kayaking, golf, the "Skunk" steam train, and hiking will entice family members.

MEALS: The food is excellent, generally California nouveau cuisine, with fine wines available at the table. Locally grown products are used extensively and chefs are delighted to cater to individual diets with prior notice.

RIDING STUFF: The horses and riding will satisfy the most demanding purist as well as the most nervous novice. Ricochet Ridge's wranglers have a knack for producing an enjoyable riding experience for riders with a wide range of talent and experience. The horses are a mixture of Arabians, Russian Orlov crosses, Thoroughbreds, Appaloosas and Akhal Tekes. They are well trained, incredibly fit and very well tended. The tack is first class. The terrain is varied and includes beaches, coastal mountains, and redwood forest, with the heady aroma of eucalyptus thrown in for fun. Inn to inn rides vary from 1 to 6 nights.

AUTHOR'S COMMENT: *Californians already know the secret of Mendocino. European and East Coast riders who have not yet discovered it—should. During California's winter months, Lari Shea, the dynamic owner of Ricochet Ridge, often leads adventures to Africa, Australia, Fiji, India, Italy, etc.*

HIGHLIGHTS
Inn to inn riding • Stationary vacations with daily riding • Group size 2 to 20 • Novice to experienced • Australian, Western or English tack • Lessons available • Exceptional horses for all levels • Beach riding • Hot tubs available on all treks

BAR LAZY J

www.guestranches.combarlazyj

BASICS: PO Box N, Parshall, CO 80468, USA
Tel: (970) 725-3437 Tel: (800) 396-6279
Fax: (970)725-0121
Email: BarLazyJ@rkymtnhi.com
WHEN: Open May 24 to September 27.
AIRPORTS: Denver International - a 2 hour drive.

LOCATION: Bar Lazy J is located 100 miles north-west of Denver.
PRICE: $1150 (£ 719) per week, per person, double occupancy. Children's Rates: $300 (£187) to $895 (£559).

There is a lot of history at this well-run ranch which has been in operation for over 80 years. At 7500 feet, the ranch is situated in a beautiful valley. Bar Lazy J features an excellent riding program for all skill levels, a fully supervised children's program, and some excellent gold medal fishing (german brown and rainbow trout) in the Colorado River that runs past the guest cabins. Owners Jerry and Cheri Helmicki are gracious hosts who will see to your families' needs. They have created a well-rounded ranch program with evening entertainment, including sing-alongs by the campfire, Western dancing, and a staff show. There are weekly jeep rides deep into the high country, a new fleet of Diamondback cycles for mountain biking, nearby rafting, golf, and tennis.

CHILDREN'S PROGRAM: Children ages 3 to 12 may participate in a well-run program geared to keeping everyone happy and busy from 8:30 a.m. 'til noon and again from 1:00 to 5:00 p.m. The program includes riding and craft activities and is run by experienced counselors

ACCOMMODATIONS: Guests stay in cabins set along the banks of the Colorado River and are lulled to sleep by the music of its fast moving waters. The cabins accommodate from 2 to 8 people, and offer thermostatically controlled heat, nightly turn-down service, and coffee makers. Coin-operated laundry facilities are also available.

SPECIAL ACTIVITIES: In addition to the heated pool and jacuzzi, there is fishing, hiking, nearby white-water river rafting, sightseeing van trips to nearby Rocky Mountain National Park, jeep rides and mountain biking. Additionally, there is a library room and a recreation barn with a pool table, shuffleboard, ping-pong, and other games.

MEALS: All meals are served family style in an attractive log dining room. The food is Western home-style with plenty of fresh baked breads, desserts and pastries. The Helmicki family is split between meat and non-meat eaters, so they are sensitive to dietary needs or preferences, but please advise them in advance.

RIDING STUFF: Riders who haven't been on horseback for a long while, if ever, can opt for personalized riding instruction from the wranglers. There are twice a day rides at slow, medium, and fast speeds, depending on your skill level. There is also an all day ride as well as a breakfast ride. You will discover a variety of ever-changing trails among the sage-covered hills and majestic mountains of the Arapaho National Forest. You will be paired with an appropriate horse for the week to engender confidence and encourage development of a relationship with your mount.

AUTHOR'S COMMENT: *Isn't it time you piled the kids in a car, or on a plane, and took a stab at playing cowboy? Bar Lazy J offers a relaxed atmosphere where the Helmickis can nurture their most important crop—their guests.*

HIGHLIGHTS
Western tack • 60 horses • Guest capacity 38 • Daily trail riding • Sunday to Sunday stays • Extensive children's program, ages 3-12 • All skill levels • Jacuzzi • Heated pool • Pond and river fishing with optional weekly clinic • Adults-only week • Discount weeks in May, late August, and September • Member: DRA and CDGRA

DROWSY WATER RANCH

www.dude-ranch.com/drowsy_water

BASICS: PO Box 147 WRV, Granby, CO 80446, USA
Tel: (970) 725-3456   Tel: (800) 845-2292
Fax: (970) 725-3611
Email: dwrken@aol.com
WHEN: Open June 7 to September 13.
AIRPORTS: Denver International—a 2 hour drive.

LOCATION: Near Rocky Mountain National Park and Colorado River.
PRICE: $1095 (£684) per week, per person, double occupancy. Special family and children's rates. Extra charge for river rafting and pack trips.

Owners Ken and Randy Sue Fosha set the scene for a wonderful family holiday in an ideal ranch setting located near the meandering Drowsy Water Creek. The ranch is situated at an altitude of 8200 feet in a valley enclosed by aspen and pine and surrounded by spectacular high country. There are extensive children's programs and plenty of non-riding alternatives plus evening fun, all of which serve as an addition to the quality riding program. Guests arrive and depart on Sundays. There are adults-only weeks in late August and September.

CHILDREN'S PROGRAM: A range rider supervised children's program will keep the 6 to 13 year old youngsters having fun all week. Counselors entertain children 5 and younger. There is a children's rodeo on Saturdays.

ACCOMMODATIONS: Guests stay in lodge and log cabin accommodations. The living areas are large and newly refurbished in tasteful Western décor. The cabins look out over Drowsy Water Creek.

SPECIAL ACTIVITIES: In addition to a heated pool and hot tub, evening activities include square dancing, hayrides, carnival, country swing dance, and a staff show. Guests can enjoy several jeep trips as an alternative to riding or arrange for river rafting and wilderness pack trips. There are also 2 nearby golf courses.

MEALS: Breakfast is ordered from a menu. Lunch and dinner are served family style and include homemade breads, desserts, steak fries, BBQ, and other down home dishes.

RIDING STUFF: One hundred ranch-bred, raised and trained horses, including Paints, Quarterhorses and draft crosses, make up the herd for this all-Western riding program. Guests are evaluated and beginners start with riding instruction. Rides are divided into groups based on riding skill levels and there is plenty of opportunity to "graduate" to faster rides. There are morning and afternoon half day rides every day except Sunday and all day rides twice a week. There is also a breakfast ride. You may wish to arrange for an overnight wilderness camping trip. It is truly a unique experience to sleep out in the wild, and these professional outfitters always help to produce a truly enjoyable experience. The riding trails cover magnificent high country where you may observe abundant wildlife including deer and elk.

AUTHOR'S COMMENT: *This ranch provides a charming family environment while maintaining quality and an authentic Western ranching experience. Located 1½ miles from any paved road on 600 acres, Drowsy Water's owners and staff will give you the kind of family vacation that makes the kids yell "More Drowsy Water Ranch, Ma!"*

HIGHLIGHTS

Western tack • 100 horses • Guest capacity 60 • Daily trail riding • Sunday to Sunday stays • Extensive children's programs for infants to age 14 • All skill levels • Hot tub • Heated pool • Licensed wilderness outfitters • Pond, river and lake fishing • Big game hunting camp, mid-October to November (License #277) • Member: DRA, CDGRA

RAWAH GUEST RANCH

www.coloradovacations.com/duderanch/rawah/ranch

BASICS: Glendevey, CO Route, 11447 N CR 103, Jelm, WY 82063, USA
Winter address: 1612 Adriel Circle, Fort Collins, CO 80524   Tel:(800) 820-3152 (year round)
Tel: (970) 435-5715 (Summer)
Fax: (970) 435-5705 (Summer)
Tel: (970) 484-8288 (Winter)
Fax: (970) 407-0818 (Winter)
Email: rawah@compuserve.com

WHEN: Mid-June through September.
AIRPORTS: Denver International (150 miles) or Laramie (60 miles). Transfers from Laramie included.
LOCATION: The ranch is 75 miles west of Fort Collins, 60 miles southwest of Laramie.
PRICE: $1250 (£781) to $1435 (£897) per week, per person, double occupancy. All inclusive plus 3.65% state tax

The problem with Rawah Ranch is one of "too much to do, so little time." There is too much good riding, too much wildlife, too many snow-peaked mountains, too much fun for the kids, and too much good food. Shucks! At 8400 feet, situated next to the 76,000 acre Rawah Wilderness, you will be surrounded by beauty, while being offered an excellent and multi-optioned program in a very friendly family atmosphere. Owners Pete and Ardy Kunz and John and Tracey Zirzow make it happen just the way you want it.

CHILDREN'S PROGRAM: Rawah welcomes children 6 and over, old enough to really get out and enjoy a ranch experience including riding, fishing, hiking, a recreation room with lots of fun stuff and always-ready snacks and drinks. Children love the freedom to have their own fun, secure in the knowledge that their parents are nearby to share their activities.

ACCOMMODATIONS: Guests sleep in 1 or 2 bedroom log cabins with private bath, fireplace, porch and sitting area, or comfortable log lodge rooms with private bath. Each bedroom accommodates 2 guests.

SPECIAL ACTIVITIES: Excursions to Laramie, Rocky Mountain National Park, Steamboat Springs, Cheyenne Frontier Days week in July, and rafting on the nearby Cache la Poudre River. There is a variety of nightly stuff including Western entertainment, square dancing, talks by local geologists and campfires.

MEALS: If Rawah Ranch doesn't overwhelm you with all its options and beauty, then their food will surely "do you in." Cowboy-sized meals for hungry riders include steaks and chicken grilled over aspen, plenty of fresh greens and fruit, home baked breads and "dare you to put on weight" desserts.

RIDING STUFF: You will be assigned your own ranch-owned and trained horse for your stay. Riding options are plentiful and cannot be exhausted in less than 2 weeks. There are 2 distinct types of riding terrain that varies from alpine pine and aspen forests to sage covered hills and top-of- the-world views that will keep you in awe ... when the moose and antelope aren't stealing your attention! We won't list all the different types of rides you can enjoy because, whatever your riding needs, they will be taken care of in small wrangler-led groups. Unlimited complimentary lessons are encouraged for anyone who feels so inclined. The wrangler to guest ratio is superb.

AUTHOR'S COMMENT: *Rawah is a solid, well-rounded ranch destination with a "we are here to satisfy" riding program. Kids 6 and older have a great time. Rawah offers an adults-only program in September, followed by big game hunting season. Sunday arrivals are followed all too quickly by sad Sunday departures and you are on your way home. Darn!*

HIGHLIGHTS

Western tack • Well trained, sure-footed mountain horses • Guest capacity 32 • Varied and exciting trail riding • All skill levels • Hot tub • Excellent fly fishing (complimentary instruction) • Abundant wildlife • Sunday to Sunday stays • Member: DRA, CDGRA

SYLVAN DALE GUEST RANCH

www.sylvandale.com

BASICS: 2939 NCR, 31 D, Loveland, CO 80538, USA
  Tel: (970) 667-3915 Fax: (970) 635-9336
  Email: ranch@sylvandale.com
WHEN: Mid-June through August (full program dude ranch). Sylvan Dale also operates during the off-season as a B&B and retreat.
AIRPORTS: Denver International. Van service to Loveland is available at the airport. Free transfers from Loveland.

LOCATION: The ranch is located 55 miles northwest of Denver.
PRICE: $838 (£524) 7days/6 nights, per person, double occupancy, includes all meals, accommodations, and gratuities. Discounted children's rates are available. The basic riding package adds $225 (£141) per person, but you have the option of choosing á la carte riding opportunities for less.

Sylvan Dale has been operating as a ranch since the 1920s and it has benefitted from the diligent care of the Jessup family since the 1940s. During the summer months the Jessups provide a cordial family atmosphere at their working cattle ranch which also offers a host of alternative activities, including first-class fly fishing with instruction by licensed guides, overnight pack trips, 2 tennis courts, white-water rafting, an outdoor heated pool, and nightly entertainment. Only an hour from Denver, with the Big Thompson River ambling through the property loaded with trout for hungry anglers, Sylvan Dale offers plenty of activities for riders and non-riders alike.

CHILDREN'S PROGRAM: Youngsters, ages 5 to 12, are offered a supervised program during part of the day which includes horsemanship lessons, nature hikes, tubing, gardening and ranch chores. Child-care is available for younger children at additional cost.

ACCOMMODATIONS: Guests sleep in comfortable, 1 and 2 bedroom cabins with private baths, adjacent sitting area, and outside decks. The sweetheart cabins have fireplaces. There are additional accommodations in the original lodge. The 2 guest houses are suitable for larger families. All units are nicely decorated in country/antique style. A new facility, "The Heritage," completed in 1998, provides pleasant surroundings for social gatherings and games.

SPECIAL ACTIVITIES: In addition to riding, there is first-class fly fishing with instruction by licensed guides, overnight pack trips, tennis, white-water rafting, horseshoes and softball games, an outdoor heated pool, game room, Western dancing, horse-drawn hayrides, cook-outs, nature hikes, and live entertainment, including a Native American presentation. Van tours to Rocky Mountain National Park are also available.

MEALS: Fresh vegetables and fruits, healthy breads and, less healthy, but delicious, cherry pies, and other goodies, make up the ranch fare. Guests eat in either the antique dining room, on the porch overlooking Big Thompson River, or by the grill. How do those cowboys stay so thin?

RIDING STUFF: The many riding options include 1, 2, and 3 hour rides, breakfast rides, overnight pack trips, cattle drives (from late June to early July), team penning, and instruction. If you plan to ride alot, choose the full riding package (available to riders over 13), which includes a breakfast ride, 5 group riding lessons and a lesson on horsemanship, an overnight pack trip, and a gymkhana, plus up to 6 additional hours of riding. Riders must qualify for overnight pack trips, cattle drives, and team penning. The horses are ranch-raised, registered Quarterhorses.

AUTHOR'S COMMENT: *Sylvan Dale is a well-rounded working cattle and horse farm that is also a guest ranch. Catering to more than riders with plenty of alternate activities and very convenient to Denver, Sylvan Dale is the place to nurture your inner cowboy.*

HIGHLIGHTS
Western tack • Guest capacity 60 • Daily trail riding • Sunday to Saturday ranch holidays • Special children's program • All skill levels • Optional clinics in horsemanship • Excellent fly fishing • Tennis • Cattle drive week • Adults-only week • Member: CDGRA

WILDERNESS TRAILS RANCH

www.wildernesstrails.com

BASICS: 23486 County Road 501, Bayfield, CO 81122, USA (May 1-October 1)
1766 County Road 302, Durango, CO 81301, USA (Winter)
Tel: (970) 247-0722 (Summer)   Tel:(800) 527-2624
Fax: (970) 247-1006
Email: ctinfo@wildernesstrails.com
WHEN: May 31 to October 10.

AIRPORTS: La Plata Airport, Durango. Albuquerque is a 4½ hour drive.
LOCATION: The Ranch is a 1 hour drive from Durango or Bayfield.
PRICE: $1550 (£969) per week, per person, double occupancy, includes gratuities. Lower seasonal and children's rates available.

For nearly 30 years, Jan and Gene Roberts, certified riding instructors, have been offering up their own brand of a wonderful ranch stay suitable for the entire family. Their riding program provides quality instruction by certified instructors in addition to trail riding activities. The ranch has separate programs for different age groups. Located near Lake Vallecito, surrounded by the snow-capped San Juan Mountains, Wilderness Trails Ranch provides an ideal setting for a quality family vacation. *A Blend of the Past and the Present.*

CHILDREN'S PROGRAM: There are 3 children's programs. Pony Express (ages 3 to 5): Children are introduced to horses under close supervision and are allowed individual rides if appropriate. Other activities include crafts, tracking, fire starting, survival skills, archery, gold-panning, swimming and games. Saddle Tramps (ages 6 to 11): Children ride daily on their own assigned horses, they learn wildcraft, i.e., tracking, fire starting, survival skills, and can participate in gold panning, archery, and more. The Posse (ages 12 to 17): These youngsters are offered horseback riding with instruction, water-skiing, hiking, swimming, fishing, and other fun stuff.

ACCOMMODATIONS: Guests sleep in 2 bedroom log cabins with private baths. Some units have Jacuzzi tubs, gas fireplaces, and cathedral ceilings. They are suitable for families of 3, 4 or 5. There are also 3 bedroom cabin suites with 3 baths, woodstove and refrigerator. All cabins have coffee makers and fluffy bathrobes are available in cabin suites.

SPECIAL ACTIVITIES: There is a 72 foot heated pool, scenic 4 wheel drive trip, a trip to Anasazi dwellings, hiking, rafting, horse-drawn hayrides, water skiing on Lake Vallecito, and good fishing.There is nightly entertainment, sing-alongs, and Western dancing.

MEALS: Wilderness Trails provides made-to-order breakfasts, lunch, and dinner buffets, individually served meals, and cook-outs with lots of home baked breads and decadent desserts. Service varies from grill your own steaks to elegant candlelit dinners.

RIDING STUFF: The riding program takes center stage at this ranch and encourages enjoyment of the horse as a source of companionship, not just a means of transport. Gene and Jan are both ARICP certified riding instructors. Along with their qualified staff of wranglers, they provide a safe, enjoyable riding experience. You can choose from half to all day rides, and there are also optional (extra cost) overnight wilderness trips. Guests ride in small groups, divided according to ability. Riders can jog and canter or lope after instruction. Many of the horses have been raised on the ranch, assuring sturdy, sure-footed horses, suited to mountain riding. It's great fun to visit the foals too!! The surrounding area includes the Piedra Wilderness Area and the San Juan National Forest. There is an exciting, ranch-based cattle round-up for intermediate and advanced riders in early October.

AUTHOR'S COMMENT: *It's a family affair at Wilderness Trails Ranch. The Roberts and their grown children, Randy, Lance, Erika and Sasha, share their passion for the natural environment, good horses, riding, and providing their guests with a quality holiday.*

HIGHLIGHTS

Western tack • Guest capacity 46 • Located near Lake Vallecito • Abundant trail riding • Optional instructions in riding and horsemanship • Optional overnight wilderness trip • Excellent children's and teen programs • Hot tub • 72 foot heated pool • 2 fishing ponds on property • Sunday to Sunday stays • Cattle round-up in September • Adults-only program in September • Member: DRA and CDGRA, Licensed Outfitter #661

WIT'S END

http://ranchweb.com/witsend/glance.htm

BASICS: 254 C.R.500, CT, Bayfield, CO 81122, USA
   Tel: (970) 884-4113   Fax: (970) 884-3261
   Tel: (602) 263-0000 (Winter)
   Fax: (602) 234-0298 (Winter)
   Email: weranch@aol.com
WHEN: May 1 to October 20. Special groups year round.

AIRPORTS: La Plata Airport, Durango
LOCATION: A 1 hour drive from Durango.
PRICE: $1900 (£1190) to $2200 (£1375) per week, per person, double occupancy. Lower rates for children and nannies.

Owners Jim and Lynn Custer will welcome you to their award-winning ranch, rated among the top ranches in the lower 48. The 12,000 to 14,000 foot peaks of the rugged San Juan Mountains and 2 million acres of national forest and wilderness will surround you. The magnificent, 125 year old, fully restored, central eating and recreational lodge offers a full bar with crystal mirrors from the 1836 Crystal Palace of London. Deer, elk, bald eagles, and waterfowl abound.

CHILDREN'S PROGRAM: There are separate, counselor supervised programs for pre-teens and 12-17 year olds. On 1 night the kids camp and eat out under the supervision of the counselors. On nights reserved for fine dining, counselors host the youngsters' meal, allowing adults to enjoy a romantic or quiet dinner. There are special eating and riding activities planned for the entire family as well as various children's recreational programs, including a riding program.

ACCOMMODATIONS: The main ranch consists of 35 cabins, including 54 private bedrooms with a capacity of 220 people in a family setting. Conference groups may take advantage of additional cabins off-site. Cabins come equipped with down comforters, balloon drapes, berber carpeting, stone fireplaces, full kitchens, well-appointed rooms and porches.

SPECIAL ACTIVITIES: There is a 52 foot heated pool, scenic 4 wheel drive trips, fishing, and tennis.

MEALS: Breakfasts are a family meal served in either the dining room or on the deck. Lunch and dinner options include splitting into adult only groups and youngster groups or family groups. There are cookouts 3 evenings a week. The evening dining experience varies from Western cookouts to elegant, full service meals.

RIDING STUFF: Yes folks, Wit's End has a delightful riding program with more than 100 ranch-owned horses. There are extensive riding trails for twice a day, morning breakfast, and all day rides. Optional wilderness pack trips, arena riding, and lessons are available. (Private lessons at additional cost.) The horses don't work on Saturday (Horse Union Rules). You are usually assigned a horse for the duration of your stay, but assignments may be switched if desired or necessary. All riding groups are wrangler led, restricted to 6 people per wrangler, and paced according to ability and desire. For those of you who dare, comfortable wilderness pack trips will offer you and your entire family a rare opportunity to enjoy a very beautiful natural setting at 10,000 to 13,000 feet under the guidance of licensed wilderness outfitters.

AUTHOR'S COMMENT: *Owner Jim Custer is a gracious man who is honored to be the recipient of a whole host of good ratings from Mobil, Reeds, and many more. Wit's End is an excellent destination for family vacations, corporate retreats, and anybody who wants to enjoy the Rocky Mountains in comfort and style.*

HIGHLIGHTS

Beautiful guest cabins • Guest capacity 220 • Abundant trail riding • Weekly and seasonal cattle drives • Wilderness trips • Full children's programs • Hot tubs • 52 foot heated pool • Fly fishing (ponds, river, lake) • Lake swimming, boating, water sports • Tennis • Mountain biking • Mountain motor tours • Corporate retreats • Member: Colorado Outfitters and Guide Association, Licensed Outfitter #1004

SMALL CATTLE

www.awetrips.com

BASICS: Agent: **American Wilderness Experience**, 2820-A Wilderness Place, Boulder, CO 80301 USA
Tel: (800) 444-0099   Tel: (303) 444-2622
Fax:(303) 444-3999
Email: awedave@aol.com

WHEN: Open June through October.
AIRPORTS: Idaho Falls is a 1 hour drive.
Transfers are included.
LOCATION: Small Cattle is located 120 miles from Jackson Hole and 170 miles from Sun Valley.
PRICE: $1000 (£625) 5 days/ 4 nights, per person.

Join world-renowned rodeo champion Butch Small, one of the best saddle bronc riders in history, on a ranch that began operations around 1866. Nestled between the Bitterroot and Grand Teton Mountains, the lifestyle on this ranch hasn't changed much in 100 years - good food, evening cowboy entertainment around the campfire and some long hours in the saddle. You will have the opportunity to visit historic Native American campsites and pioneer homesteads as you move cattle amidst the abundant wildlife along the Continental Divide. There is a rodeo arena on the property where you can watch the cowboys buck horses. The spring cattle round-up is suitable for beginners, while the fall round-up in steep mountains is better suited for experienced riders.

CHILDREN'S PROGRAM: Recommended minimum age is 12.

ACCOMMODATIONS: The main lodge, where all meals and entertainment are provided, is a large, hand-hewn log structure. The lodge features Coleman lanterns for lighting, a full kitchen with a cooking range and refrigerator, a wood-burning stove, comfortable couches and a sundeck complete with barbecue and smoker. There are also rustic cabins equipped with propane heaters and either double or bunk beds not far from the lodge. Teepee tents are available during the summer. There is a shower house with 2 separate bathrooms, each featuring a shower, sinks and flush toilet.

MEALS: From juicy sizzling steaks to elk fajitas, you will find the food tasty and filling, served family style to crew and guests. A sack lunch is provided on the trail.

RIDING STUFF: Welcome to the real world of cowboys and become a part of the crew. The quality of the working cattle horses is reflected by the custom-made Slickrock saddles and bits the ranch uses. Days will be spent in the saddle helping to find strays, sort them out, ride the fence, haul salt. Be prepared for the unexpected. Ability and interest will divide the group, with chores determined by the needs of the ranch. You will see plenty of elk, moose, deer, eagles and hawks depending on the season. On a typical day, you are in the saddle at daybreak and back in camp by mid-afternoon, spending an average of 6 to 8 hours on horseback. The ranch sits at approximately 7000 feet and the terrain is largely open meadows and treeless hills, but the higher elevations on the Continental Divide are forested. Cattle operations are offered every day at the ranch. There is also a spring round-up and a fall round-up.

AUTHOR'S COMMENT: *Host, Butch Small, is a legend in the world of saddle bronc riders, having qualified 13 times in the sport's premier championship event, the National Finals Rodeo. Riding with him at this "genuine item" cattle ranch is bound to be an experience that you will long remember.*

HIGHLIGHTS

Western tack • 28 horses • 7 guest limit • Long days in the saddle • Intermediate to advanced riding skills • Abundant wildlife including elk, deer, moose, hawks and eagles • Minimum stay 5 days • Weight limit 200 lbs. (91 kg.) (14 stone) • Beginners may join in if they are fit

"Don't Fence Me In." © *David R. Stoecklein*

SPECKLED MOUNTAIN RANCH

BASICS: RR2, Box 717, Bethel, Maine 04217, USA
   Tel/Fax: (207) 836-2908
WHEN: Open year round; May to October for riding
   holidays.
AIRPORTS: Portland, Maine
LOCATION: A 2 hour drive west of Portland; a 3½
   hour drive northwest of Boston.
PRICE: *Riding Retreats:* $300 (£187) 2 days/2 nights, per person, double occupancy, includes 5 meals, and 2 rides (2 to 3½ hours each). Additional days may be added for $100 (£63) per day for a riding companion, or $60 (£38) per day for non-riding companions sharing the same room with all meals included. *B&B:* $60 (£38) per night, double occupancy. Single supplement add $15 (£9).

Nestled in the foothills of Maine's Speckled Mountain, the Ranch is owned and operated by a knowledgeable, hard-working horse professional, Leo Joost. It is a lovely year round escape, with a guest capacity of 6. Speckled Mountain Ranch is a beautiful property, surrounded by lush mountain greenery in season. It is an ideal location for nature lovers, mountain bikers, and other outdoor enthusiasts. The riding packages can accommodate advanced riders as well as novices with a desire to learn. The Ranch also offers romantic evening carriage rides and tours with picnic lunch in the White Mountain National Forest. Speckled Mountain Ranch is also a perfect location for winter sports, including cross-country and downhill skiing and, if conditions are right, spirited winter horseback rides through powered snow.

CHILDREN'S PROGRAM: During the month of July, Speckled Mountain functions as an overnight camp for children, ages 12 to 15, who already possess intermediate or advanced riding skills. Group size in limited to 5, so there is plenty of individualized attention. Camp activities include carriage driving lessons.

ACCOMMODATIONS: The farmhouse is sunny, spacious, and smoke-free. There are 3 rooms with queen and double-sized beds and 2½ shared bathrooms.

SPECIAL ACTIVITIES: In addition to the various non-riding sports activities that are available, guests can visit nearby historic Bethel, Mount Washington. There are also golf courses and llama trekking, dog-sledding, and *skjoring* opportunities.

MEALS: Breakfast is a hearty meal and includes coffee, pancakes, homemade breads and other delicious goodies. The Ranch uses produce from their own organically-grown garden crops whenever possible. The food is healthy and wholesome.

RIDING STUFF: The 2 to 5 day riding packages are designed for groups of 2 to 5. Advanced riders who can comfortably handle a horse at all gaits over varied terrain will enjoy galloping up the Miles Notch Trail, crossing Pleasant River, and jumping a log or two along the way. Riding and horsemanship instruction is offered for less experienced riders who are serious about learning. The typical riding day involves 2 to 3½ hours in the saddle. You will be encouraged to groom, and tack up your horse. Leo may be persuaded to offer some carriage driving lessons if you ask. There are many miles of good riding trails that wind through mountains, along streams, and down dirt roads, offering beautiful views. The adult camp offers week-long sessions focusing on cross-country riding and carriage driving singles and pairs.

AUTHOR'S COMMENT: *Speckled Mountain is a small, intimate B&B with great riding and driving programs, a beautiful location, and a comfortable farm house. Leo is a serious horse lover, living his dream, and willing to share it with you. The country needs more places like this and East Coast riders will surely find Speckled Mountain Ranch to be an ideal place to ride and drive.*

HIGHLIGHT
English tack • Haflingers, Morgans, Hungarian Warmbloods, Friesans, and Quarterhorses • Ride capacity 4 • Children's summer riding camp in July • All skill levels • Adult riding camp • Weight limit 190 lbs. (87 kg.) (13.6 stone) • Full winter sports program, including downhill skiing at nearby Sunday River Ski Valley • Good widelife viewing, including moose, deer and, possibly, bear

FLYNN RANCH VACATIONS

www.workingranchvacations.com

BASICS: 674 Flynn Lane, Townsend, MT 59644, USA
Tel: (406) 266-3534   Tel: (406) 949-3612
Fax: (406) 266-5306
Email: ted@workingranchvacations.com
WHEN: Open May through September.

AIRPORTS: Helena, Bozeman - a 40 minute drive. Transfers are included.
LOCATION: Midway between Glacier and Yellowstone National Parks, 45 minutes from Bozeman and Helena.
PRICE: $875 (£546) per week, per person.

The Flynn Ranch began marching toward its present day status as a 15,000 acre, 700 head cattle ranch in 1875—just 70 years after Lewis and Clark explored the Missouri River Valley. Four guests a week are invited to join the activities at a spread where cattle remain the principal focus. The riding can be demanding and Ted Flynn, a 5th generation rancher, suggests that the type of riding experience the ranch offers is best enjoyed by people with at least intermediate riding skills and the ability to log some long hard hours in the saddle. This ranch is a true gem for those lucky riders who still have a nose for the genuine item.

CHILDREN'S PROGRAM: Children under 12 cannot participate in the adult riding program, but can join a modified riding program designed to impart basic riding skills.

ACCOMMODATIONS: Guests enjoy the early 1900s vintage ranch house with all modern amenities, sleeping in private rooms with shared bath or shower facilities. During the summer months, you may sleep overnight in cabins or teepees on cattle drives and round-ups.

SPECIAL ACTIVITIES: Fly fishing for wild trout, including lessons and equipment. The Big Belt Mountains are home to large herds of deer and elk and photo opportunities abound.

MEALS: Breakfast and evening meals are served family style at either the ranch house or one of the mountain cabins. Lunch is almost always a picnic style meal served wherever the work takes you. Special dietary requirements can be accommodated.

RIDING STUFF: Riding is a daily activity, weather permitting, and is organized around the needs of the cattle ranch which include checking fences, moving cattle, hauling salt, looking for strays, etc. The typical riding day is at least 2 to 4 hours and moving herds from one place to another can increase saddle time to 8 to 10 hours. Usually guests and horses are driven 15 to 25 miles through beautiful mountain scenery to get to where the cattle are pastured during the summer. Guests seem to get a tremendous pleasure out of riding the open spaces as well as herding cattle, an activity that has sent this rider into a smiling frenzy.

AUTHOR'S COMMENT: *Flynn Ranch will give you a chance to work the knots of civilized living out of your head. It is an ideal place for good riders who are fit enough to log long hours in the saddle and love it. The rituals of cattle farming will sing their sweet nothings and soon you will be a happy and willing cowboy/cowgirl riding the range in search of your next adventure, which may well turn out to be a be another week at the Flynn Ranch!*

HIGHLIGHTS

Western tack • 15 ranch horses • Guest limit 4 • Long hours in the saddle • Intermediate riding skills required • Abundant wildlife • Fly fishing • Comfortable accommodations • Minimum stay 1 week • Member: Montana Outfitters & Guides Association

HARGRAVE CATTLE RANCH

www.hargraveranch.com

BASICS: 300 Thompson River, Marion, MT 59925, USA

Tel: (406) 858-2284   Fax: (406) 858-2444

Email: hargrave@digisys.net

WHEN: Open year round.

AIRPORTS: Kalispell, Montana (48 miles from ranch).

LOCATION: Northwestern Montana

PRICE: $1050 (£656) to $1620 (£1013) per week, per person, double occupancy, depending on type of accommodation chosen. Children's rates from $990 (£619) to $1050 (£656) per week, per child.

While providing a seemingly endless round of opportunities to ride, rope, see the high country, or enjoy a host of other non-riding activities, Hargrave Cattle and Guest Ranch offers a relaxed atmosphere that allows guests to choose their own way. As ranch owner Ellen Hargrave recently commented, "You may join with the cowboys in spring branding, summer herd riding, and fall round-up, or just sit back on the wide veranda." Although Hargrave is a working ranch, guests can decide what they want to do each day—ride or just kick back and relax. It's not a contest, it's a holiday!

CHILDREN'S PROGRAM: There are special wranglers for the children and plenty of fun activities, including horsemanship lessons, rope swings over the lake, or a camp-out. The program runs from July to August 20th.

ACCOMMODATIONS: Guests may choose between the ranch headquarters with its antique-filled bedrooms, tastefully styled cabins, or the new, very luxurious, lodge. A terry cloth robe is left on your bed and there are coffee fixings for those early morning wake-me-ups.

SPECIAL ACTIVITIES: There are many alternative activities including, 4 wheel drive trips to remote areas, fishing, weekly camp-outs, and, on Fridays, trips to Glacier National Park. During winter, cross-country skiing is available.

MEALS: Grandma's at it again! This time, geared to current tastes. A platter of fresh fruit is offered with your sourdough hotcakes, steamed vegetables with your prime rib, and fresh homemade breads and desserts with every meal. Food is served family style in a stylish oak floored dining room with windows overlooking the meadow.

RIDING STUFF: Hargrave Cattle Ranch offers the chance to ride as hard and long or as little as you like. Guests can help gather the remuda at dawn, ride out to check and sort newborn calves in the spring or herd cows onto the Ranch's 84,000 acres of grazing pasture. Cattle are pastured throughout the vast mountain valley over the summer and guests can help to gather the herd and drive them back to the home valley in the fall. Learn to rope from those who do it for a living. There is also trail riding to the top of the ridge, where 3 mountain ranges fade into the distance. The horses are basic cattle and trail horses, and the tack is Western.

AUTHOR'S COMMENT: *Owners Ellen and Leo Hargrave are experienced and charming hosts, and it is no surprise that their guests return year after year. This is one of those places that make you want to chuck it all in favor of a life more closely tied to the rhythms and joys of the land.*

HIGHLIGHTS

Western tack • Guest capacity 18 • Unlimited riding • Licensed outfitters • Wilderness pack trips • Children's program in July and August • All skill levels • 84,000 acre ranch • "Women's Week" and "Singles Week" • Excellent fly fishing on 2 miles of private trout stream • Day trips to Glacier National Park • Fall round-ups • Skeet shooting • Winter cross-country skiing • Member: DRA and MTDRA

LAZY K BAR RANCH

www.mcn.net/~kirby/lazykbar.htm.

BASICS: PO Box 550, Big Timber, MT 59011, USA
Tel: (406) 537-4404   Fax: (406) 537-4593
Email: kirby@mcn.net.
WHEN: June 23 through Labor Day.
AIRPORTS: Bozeman or Billings, Montana. Transfers
are $100 per trip, certain restrictions apply.
LOCATION: Southern Montana, 85 miles northeast
of Bozeman; 100 miles west of Billings.
PRICE: Cabin, without bath: $715 (£447); Cabin,
with bath: $920 (£575) to $995 (£622) 7 days/7
nights, per person, double occupancy, all
inclusive except gratuities. Single rates slightly
higher. References required. Guests may begin
their 7 day stay on any day other than Sunday.

Lazy K Bar Ranch has been in hands of the Van Cleve family since 1880 and has been hosting riders for 76 summers. With 16 hand-hewn log cabins, and a classic old log lodge, Lazy K Bar Ranch is a journey to the West that Was. The ranch consists of 22,000 deeded acres, where raising Quarterhorses, beef and pork are the principal ranch activities – aside from catering to their guests of course! Elevations on the ranch range from 5500 feet (1719 meters) to 11,000 feet (3475 meters), offering spectacular views. The program is laid back and flexible.

CHILDREN'S PROGRAM: There is a special wrangler who plans and supervises activities and rides for children ages 6 to 12. Children under 6 not permitted.

ACCOMMODATIONS: There are 16 hand-hewn log cabins from 1 to 4 bedrooms, with and without living rooms. All but 2 of the cabins have private baths. Each cabin has a fireplace or wood-burning stove; they are individually appointed, with magnificent views of the mountains that surround the ranch. Guests may make use of the ranch laundry service or do their own wash in the coin-operated laundry.

SPECIAL ACTIVITIES: There is swimming and fly fishing. Lazy K Bar Ranch prides itself on its laid back atmosphere, breaking the mold only with a Saturday night square dance. There are also 2 special campfire meals. Special excursions to Yellowstone Park, Native American reservations, or a Hutterite colony may be arranged for a small additional charge.

MEALS: Ranch food is generally supplied from the ranch itself, including meats, milk, cheese, and butter. Children eat at the "Kids' Table" with their wrangler. All meals are served family style and you may expect plenty of good food, including fresh baked breads and pastries.

RIDING STUFF: There are morning, afternoon, and all day rides, using Western tack and ranch-raised Quarterhorses. Some amount of cattle and ranch work is available at different times of the year. Riding is generally at a walk or jog through high alpine country in the Crazy Mountains, which reach to the sky at over 11,000 feet (3475 meters). Guests choose their own schedule and there is plenty of time to enjoy alternate activities. Lazy K Bar Ranch has a very loyal following and we recommend making your reservations as early as possible.

AUTHOR'S COMMENT: *Owner-operators Barbara Van Cleve, Tack Van Cleve, Barbie Van Cleve and Carol Van Cleve Kirby manage this historic ranch and keep it running smoothly, although with very few programmed activities. The Van Cleves were pioneers in the world of guest ranches and they have surely mastered the art of providing a winning formula for their guests. One special note, the Hutterite colony mentioned under Special Activities is a fascinating American "utopian community," with a life-style similar to that of the Amish, but also reminiscent of other radical utopian groups like the Shakers and the famed Amana community in Iowa.*

HIGHLIGHTS
Western tack • Ranch bred horses • 35 guest limit • Unlimited riding • Cattle work • Fly fishing • Comfortable accommodations • 7 night stays • Swimming pool • Rodeos • Extensive and unusual library • Ranch store • Piano and billiard table in main lodge • Member: MRVA , DRA

LONESOME SPUR GUEST RANCH

www.cruising-america.com/lonespur.html

BASICS: RR 1, Box 1160, Bridger, MT 59014, USA
   Tel/Fax: (406) 662-3460
   Email: wschwend@wto.net
WHEN: Open April 15 to November 1.
AIRPORTS: Billings, Montana (Logan International) or Cody, Wyoming. Transfers included.

LOCATION: The ranch is located 45 miles south of Billings; 50 miles north of Cody, in Clarks Fork Valley, between Beartooth and Pryor Mountains.
PRICE: $1078 (£673) per week, per adult; $756 (£472) per week, per child under 10. Price includes all taxes, gratuities and transfers.

Lonesome Spur is a 5th generation working cattle ranch lying in the Clarks Fork Valley, overlooking the Clarks Fork of the Yellowstone River, situated between Pryor and Beartooth Mountains. Lonesome Spur, located on 36,000 acres, is a cow-calf operation managed on horseback. Riding is available for all skill levels. Whitetail and mule deer are abundant, as are coyotes, red fox, and the occasional elk. Guests also will get to see some dramatic sunrises and sunsets. Lonesome Spur Ranch is the model for the homestead of Tom Booker's grandparents described in the popular novel *The Horse Whisperer* by Nicholas Evan (now a motion picture). The personalities of owners Lonnie and Darlene are reflected by characters (Frank and Diane) in the book and their names also appear in the book.

CHILDREN'S PROGRAMS: There are no organized children's programs, but kids are welcome to participate in the ranch and riding activities as their abilities allow.

ACCOMMODATIONS: Accommodations offered include 2 log cabins, a new bunk house with 2 private rooms, bath and living area, 2 decorated Indian teepees, a large lodge house with a loft, kitchen, eating area, recreation area and 2 decks, plus 2 guest rooms in the main house.

SPECIAL ACTIVITIES: Viewing the Pryor Wild Horse Range, touring the Buffalo Bill Historical Center and Old West Trail Town, reliving the Battle of Little Big Horn, experiencing the scenic Beartooth Highway, conquering white water on a rafting trip down the Yellowstone River, or enjoying a relaxing float trip down Clarks Fork, a real "whoop em up" rodeo, team penning, games on horseback, and fishing provide alternatives to regular ranch activities.

MEALS: All meals are served family style and consist of satisfying ranch food including beef stews, sausage and biscuits, BBQ ribs and fresh baked goods daily. Special dietary concerns can be catered to upon advance notice.

RIDING STUFF: The horses are your basic mountain crossbreds, suitable for the terrain and cattle work. Everyone receives basic riding and safety advice. No one will be allowed or expected to do anything he or she is not capable of or comfortable accomplishing on horseback. Guests are given the opportunity to ride with the cowboys trailing the cattle to summer and fall pastures, checking fence lines, rotating pastures during the summer months, searching for strays and collecting bulls. Extracurricular riding includes high country scenery, Native American pictographs, team penning, games on horseback, and some roping. Weather (heat and rain) play a role in determining the number of hours you will spend on horseback during your stay. The more experienced riders are often asked to help out with the extensive riding involved in tending cattle in this rugged country. A local Pony Express reenactment group, the "Outlaw Gang," invites some of the guests to ride with them in reenactments throughout the summer.

AUTHOR'S COMMENT: *Fiction and reality meet at this 5th generation ranch—a crossroads between the West that Was and the West that Is.*

HIGHLIGHTS

Fifth generation family ranch • Western tack • All skill levels • Riding and horsemanship instruction • Guest limit 6 to 10 • Hiking • Wagon rides • Native American pictographs • Abundant wildlife • Fishing

MONTANA EQUESTRIAN TOURS— SWAN VALLEY WILDERNESS RIDE

www.seeleyswanpathfinder.com/pfbusiness/mtequestriantours/horse

BASICS: PO Box 1280, Swan Valley, MT 59826, USA
Tel: (406) 754-2900
Tel: (800) 484-5757, Ext. 0096
Fax: (406) 754-2966
Email: cnd2900@montana.com
WHEN: Mid-June to mid-September.

AIRPORTS: Missoula or Kalispell. Transfers can be arranged.
LOCATION: Less than a 3 hour drive from Glacier National Park; a 7 hour drive from Yellowstone.
PRICE: $1045 (£653) to $1395 (£871) per person, double occupancy. No credit cards.

The discovery of this new riding opportunity was a very pleasant surprise. Swan Valley Wilderness Ride represents a new hybrid type ride south of the Canadian border. A true Western mountain wilderness riding trip, it offers plenty of opportunity for safe but faster paces while enjoying nightly stays at upscale log cabins, wilderness inns, and lodges. In addition to the regularly scheduled trips, small groups may opt for customized excursions. One week per season is set aside to cater to the specific needs of children and families. This is the closest thing to an inn-to-inn ride the Wild West has ever seen and suggests the development of a new international style of riding holiday in cowboy and cowgirl country.

CHILDREN'S PROGRAM: One week per season is set aside to cater to children and families.

ACCOMMODATIONS: Nightly lodging provided by select, elegant B&B lodges. Each facility is charmingly appointed, most with private baths, and provide a welcome place to relax and enjoy a pleasant dinner after a long day's ride.

SPECIAL ACTIVITIES: Local old-timers around warm campfires with panoramic views share cowboy poetry and valley history. You will get a chance to enjoy some swimming or at least getting wet. A hot tub will greet your weary bones at your last night's lodging.

MEALS: Elegant, hearty and nutritious Continental fare are accompanied by fine wines. Vegetarian alternatives are available. Picnic meals are served for lunch during 90 minute riding breaks at scenic locations along the trail.

RIDING STUFF: The herd consists of 20 well-trained, sure-footed horses, selected for sensible behavior, but always eager to move out. Riders enjoy 4 days of 6 hour rides, covering 17 to 25 miles with a 90 minute mid-day lunch break. Accompanying wranglers maintain radio communications with facility based support staff. Riders should be comfortable on extended trots and canters. On some days you will be transported to trail heads to meet the horses. The trails consist mainly of abandoned logging roads covered by grassy pathways. Lakes, waterfalls, deer, elk, bear, the occasional moose or eagle, and plenty of those magnificent panoramic views the West seems to manufacture, will certainly entertain you on your ride.

AUTHOR'S COMMENT: *It is my feeling that this unique riding opportunity will enjoy some very healthy booking and we recommend that you act accordingly. This is an ideal ride for singles, couples and small groups who like some zip in their ride along with sophisticated creature comforts. Glacier and Yellowstone National Parks are both nearby (at least by Montana standards, a state without a speed limit on most roads) and provide a bonus for those of you who have not yet experienced these magnificent*

HIGHLIGHTS

Nightly lodging in elegant B&Bs • Great Bear Expedition 6 days/5 nights includes 4 days of 20 miles a day riding with many opportunities for trots and cantering • Group size 4-10 • Weight limit 250 lbs. (113 kg.) • Not for beginner riders • Customized family trips • Western, English or Australian tack available

DOUBLE E GUEST RANCH

www.doubleEranch.com

BASICS: PO Box 280, Gila, NM 88038, USA
Tel/Fax: (505) 535-2048
Email: doubleE@wnmc.net
WHEN: February through November.
AIRPORTS: Albuquerque to Silver City. Transfers from Silver City included.

LOCATION: A 30 minute drive northwest of Silver City; a 5 hour drive from Phoenix, El Paso or Albuquerque.
PRICE: $950 (£594) 7days/6 nights, per person, double occupancy. Special family and group rates.

Colorado natives Debbie and Alan Eggleston picked this rugged but beautiful piece of land as the ideal place to set their life's ambition in motion. The Double E is spread out over 30,000 acres, which includes privately protected Native American archeological sites as well as their own herd of Rocky Mountain Big Horned Sheep. The great Gila National Forest and Wilderness, home to deer, bear, turkey, mountain lion and many varieties of migratory birds, provides the backdrop for a unique experience. The limited number of guests allows the Egglestons to develop a very personalized approach to riding and general ranch fun.

CHILDREN'S PROGRAM: Children accompanied by families are welcome at the ranch. Children under 5 are not permitted to ride off ranch premises.

ACCOMMODATIONS: Guests stay in either a 4 bedroom, rustic guest house with 2 full baths, kitchen, and down comforters, or in the new 2 bedroom guest house. Only 1 related group per house.

SPECIAL ACTIVITIES: Historic sites in nearby Silver City, Gila cliff dwellings, Native American ruins on the ranch, gold panning and fishing or boating on Lake Roberts supply guests with plenty of alternatives.

MEALS: Double E serves the kind of bountiful, delicious meals that used to be cooked when time was not a consideration. Hungry ranchers will appreciate the homemade biscuits, breads, pies, and cakes that are served with each meal. Picnic lunches are prepared for all day rides.

RIDING STUFF: There is no pre-set riding program. Each guest will work out an individual routine of riding tailored to his or her particular desires and experience. Basic skill lessons are offered to initiate novices into the joys of riding. Experienced riders will be offered a wide range of trails based on ability and interest. The terrain varies from beautiful canyon bottoms with a creek at 4500 feet to rugged 'up and down riding' at 7000 feet. Trails are made—not followed, and with the huge Gila Forest (3.3 million acres) and the pristine Gila Wilderness available, you couldn't exhaust the riding possibilities in a year. Experienced riders are welcome to participate in ranch and cattle work as the need arises.

AUTHOR'S COMMENT: *Double E is located in an area of the Southwest that is rich in Native American ruins and artifacts. The Gila Wilderness reflects an unspoiled beauty— yours to enjoy in a very private setting that allows maximum freedom while catering to your needs as a guest and rider. So come and discover what made Alan and Debbie leave Colorado to pioneer in one of America's last great wilderness areas.*

HIGHLIGHTS

Working cattle, horse and buffalo ranch in Gila Wilderness • 7 days/ 6 nights packaged stays • Ranch capacity 12 • Family oriented holidays • Western tack • More than 30 ranch horses • Trail riding • Cattle work • Hiking • Gold panning • Privately protected Native American ruins and archaeological sites • Abundant wildlife

HARTLEY RANCH

www.duderanch.org/hartley or www.guestranches.com/hartley

BASICS: HCR 73, Box 55, Roy, NM 87743, USA
   Tel: (800) 687-3833   Tel:(505) 673-2244
   Fax: (505) 673-2216
   Email: rhart@etsc.net
WHEN: April through mid-October.
AIRPORTS: Albuquerque International–less than a
   4 hour drive. Transportation provided.

LOCATION: The ranch is 25 miles southwest
   of Roy; 220 miles northeast of Albuquerque;
   and 160 miles northeast of Santa Fe.
PRICE: Adults: $900 (£562); Children (ages 2–16):
   $800 (£500) 6 days/5 nights, per person, dou-
   ble occupancy, all inclusive.

Hartley Guest Ranch, located in breathtaking northeastern New Mexico ("Land of Enchantment") is a family owned and operated working cattle ranch that has been in the Hartley family since the 1940s. The ranch encompasses more than 25,000 acres of private land, with elevations of 4800 to 6000 feet. There are mesas and red rock canyons with 200 miles of trails winding through forests of juniper, oak, and ponderosa pine. Guests come to enjoy meeting the Hartley family and to participate in all the various ranch activities, which include: branding, searching for strays, round-ups and driving the cattle. The ranch is secluded and there are less than a dozen guests per week, so everyone gets very personal attention from the family.

CHILDREN'S PROGRAM: Children over 5 are welcome, those 9 and older do the best. Parents are encouraged to accompany their young children on rides.

ACCOMMODATIONS: There is a 6 bedroom guest house, most with private bath and queen-size beds, One of them has a king-size bed and a Jacuzzi. There is a shared kitchen for snacking and morning coffee (with a refrigerator full of soft drinks and juices) and comfortable living and dining rooms for reading and playing board games. Laundry facilities are available.

SPECIAL ACTIVITIES: You can visit ancient Native American sites, see dinosaur tracks and unusual geological formations including the impressive red rock canyons that surround the ranch. Exhilarating white-water rafting trips and day trips to Santa Fe and Taos add to the alternatives. Try fishing for bass, catfish and perch in stocked ponds, enjoy a hike (guided or not), relax in the hot tub or join in a game of basketball or volleyball and be sure to keep an eye out for deer, roadrunner, coyote, mountain lion and bear.

MEALS: The food is generous and home cooked including breads and desserts made at the ranch. The meals are served family style. There are picnic lunches on days when you are out on the range, working the cattle. Guests join the Hartley family at all meals.

RIDING STUFF: All riders are given a short orientation, horses are selected and, after determining your level of competence, a wrangler will suggest an appropriate group of riders. The amount and type of cattle work varies with the season, and ranges from serious cattle round-ups and flanking (throw and hold down calves) to vaccinating or ear tagging. You can ride as much or as little as you like and are free to just watch or join in the work. Since the cattle are pastured over the breadth of the ranch, cattle work will often involve some lengthy riding.

AUTHOR'S COMMENT: *Fun riding, that can be as challenging as you can safely handle, a friendly, warm family atmosphere, with your hosts treating you as friends. Add 25,000 acres of spectacular landscape and you are sure to become a cowboy or cowgirl. The Hartleys were recently featured on ESPN's* Men's Journal *and included in* Sunset *magazine's "Western Roundup of 50 Great Dude Ranches."*

HIGHLIGHTS:
So You Should Have a Cowboy? horseback riding • 200 miles of trails • Guest capacity 10 • Cattle drives, round-ups, branding • Working cattle ranch • Camp-outs • Rafting trips • Day trips to Taos and Santa Fe • Hot tub • Member: DRA and New Mexico Cattlegrowers Association

N BAR RANCH

www.dallypostn_dar

BASICS: N Bar Ranch, Outlaw Land & Cattle Co.
PO Box 409, Reserve, NM 87830, USA
Tel/Fax: (800) 616-0434
Tel: 505-533-6253   Fax: 505-533-6355
Email: Ranchfun@aol.com
WHEN: May 1 to October 30 (approximate dates).
AIRPORTS: Albuquerque, (transfers included).

LOCATION: Southern New Mexico, near Gila
National Forest, a 4½ hour drive from
Albuquerque.
PRICE: $850 (£531) 7 days/6 nights, per person,
includes all meals, accommodations, riding
and transfers. Special group discount rates.

N Bar Ranch offers an unlimited riding program that will take you through some of the oldest wilderness area in the U.S. N Bar's main headquarters are at 8000 feet (2439 meters) with surrounding peaks producing a climate of cool nights and warm, but moderate, summer temperatures. Ranching and riding during the cooler, spring and fall months are concentrated at lower elevations of 5000 feet (1563 meters) extending the season of ideal riding weather. N Bar is a genuine working cattle and horse ranch in western New Mexico's mountains, extending to 78,000 acres (125 square miles). Elk, bear, deer, Bighorn sheep, and javalina inhabit the region. The Ranch caters to people who want to ride hard, and don't require fancy trappings.

CHILDREN'S PROGRAM: There is no special program for children. Children under the age of 13 are not permitted unless by special arrangement with a large group.

ACCOMMODATIONS: Guests stay in 7 rustic cabins or 2 wood-paneled wall tents, each with 2 beds, a table with kerosene lamp, wool rugs and a small wood-burning stove. The tents are watertight with plenty of headroom, screen doors and a window. There is a shower room with lots of hot water just in case you aren't one of those dust free riders.

SPECIAL ACTIVITIES: You can always find a place to fish or swim, or enjoy the hot tub.

MEALS: Hearty ranch food consisting of "homegrown" meat, and vegetables from the garden. There is a big breakfast, and dinner provides an opportunity to relax and enjoy some fine food.

RIDING STUFF: The horses are bred and raised on the farm. Tack is Western. The riding program is varied, and organized around a central activity. There are 3 pack trips annually in the magnificent Gila wilderness, passing over the Middle Fork of the Gila river nearly 100 times, taking in rushing waterfalls, stopping for a swim, enjoying the abundant wildlife and maybe passing a hot spring or two. The trips occur in June, July and August. *Posse Week* is offered 3 times a year. These are all out fun weeks, the guests choosing whether to join the long arm of the law and become a part of the posse or become one of the bad guys who can rob and pilfer with abandon. Bad guys or chasing posse may hang out at one of 2 outlying cow camps, with comfortable beds and good feed. The outlaws have the chance to win a free week by successfully capturing all the gold. It's a very hard riding week of fun, with laser weapons or paint guns. On non-posse weeks, a one-day game may break out if guests are willing. There are 9 spring and fall round-up weeks, and 6 ranch work weeks. Team penning is also available. Wow.

AUTHOR'S COMMENT: *Okay, so you want to ride your heart out. This is one of the places that will let you do just that, served up in a spectacular wilderness area. My question for you is, "Do you feel lucky?" Are you going to be the one to win that pot of gold, or will you let those lawmen take you down?*

HIGHLIGHTS
Spring round-ups • Fall Round-Ups • Unlimited riding • Wilderness pack trips into Gila Wilderness • Fun and games at Posse Week • Good wildlife viewing • Hot tub

BARK EATER INN

www.tvenet.com/barkeater

BASICS: PO Box 39-CT, Alstead Hill Road, Keene, NY 12942, USA
Tel: (518) 576-2221
Fax: (518) 576-2071
Email: barkeater@tvenet.com
WHEN: Open all year.
AIRPORTS: Albany Airport. Transfers may be arranged.

LOCATION: Bark Eater is located 10 minutes from Lake Placid; 5 hours from NYC
PRICE: Summer Riding Program: $925(£578) 5 days/4 nights, per couple, includes 5 breakfasts, 4 dinners, 2 hours of riding per day. Additional riding: $10 (£6.25) per hour. For polo, add $100 (£62) per day, includes horses, instruction, stick and ball, mallets, etc.

Country inns can be charming or sterile and this one owes much of its charm to its rascally owner, Joe Pete Wilson, an ex-winter Olympian and world competitor in numerous winter sports. Located just minutes from the Winter Olympic Village at Lake Placid and connected to its complex of cross-country trails, Bark Eater is an ideal getaway from big city living. The property is located on the Wilson's family farm, nestled in the Adirondack Mountains, and offers good trail riding as well as a polo field on which you can learn the fundamentals of the game.

CHILDREN'S PROGRAM: There is no special children's program, but children old enough to entertain themselves with a variety of outdoor sports will enjoy the place.

ACCOMMODATIONS: Guests sleep in comfortably furnished rooms, most with private baths, located in either the main inn house or in one of the surrounding buildings. There are comfortable, well-appointed sitting rooms in the main house, good reading material, and coffee is always available.

SPECIAL ACTIVITIES: The Inn is only 10 minutes from Lake Placid, home to 2 Winter Olympics and there is plenty to do in the area. A visit to town is always fun, although you may want to guard your shopping dollars from the store owners who manage to offer everything you ever wanted or needed and more. Don't miss the Olympic jump site, it will take your breath away and you don't have to go on it!!

MEALS: If you leave the Bark Eater hungry or dissatisfied with the food, especially the former, drive immediately to the Bronx Zoo and demand entrance to the elephant house, you must be an elephant. Plentiful and good, that's what the Inn's fine cooking is all about.

RIDING STUFF: The trail riding in this area lends itself to a nice pace for qualified riders. You will be riding over countryside suitable for an Olympic cross-country ski course, meaning that the trails are soft and rolling, ideal for riding. There are miles of dirt roads and you will be pleasantly surprised by the riding opportunities. Joe Pete has tack rooms full of English and Western tack from which to choose. Special family polo clinics at very reasonable prices may be arranged—why not give it a try?

AUTHOR'S COMMENT: *I was pleasantly surprised by what I discovered at the Bark Eater, a rascally owner, who kept me smiling, nice accommodations, horses and more horses with great trails in some very beautiful countryside. I would have loved the place if they hadn't tried so hard to get me fat! Owner, Joe Pete and his sister, Marge Lamay, are among the best this country has to offer. Trained Olympic athletes with a love of the outdoors and horses, they deliver a great riding experience with humor and a touch of irreverence.*

HIGHLIGHTS
All skill levels • Great trail riding • Special instructional polo package • Ideal family ride • Charming country inn • English or Western tack • Excellent cross-country winter skiing, minutes from Olympic Trail Complex • Guest capacity 35 • All types of winter sports

VERMONT ICELANDIC HORSE FARM

www.rotunda.madriver.com/icehorse

BASICS: PO Box 577, Waitsfield, VT 05673, USA
Tel: (802) 496-7141
Fax: (802) 496-5390
Email: horses@madriver.com
WHEN: Open all year for riding; May 1 to November 1 for inn to inn season.

AIRPORTS: Burlington and Rutland. Transfers may be arranged for $65 (£41).
LOCATION: A 50 minute drive from Burlington; a 1 hour drive from Rutland.
PRICE: $185 (£116) to $225 (£141) per day, per person, double occupancy. Rates vary with season.

Deep in the heart of central Vermont's Green Mountains, riders will find a unique opportunity to ride the famous Icelandic horses on 2 to 6 day treks. Icelandic horses may be short in stature at only 13 to 14.2 hands, but they are exceptionally sturdy and can easily transport a 250 lb. person on extended, fast paced rides through the mountains! Add to their strength and stamina their unique gaits which place the rider comfortably in the English style saddle while providing plenty of zip over long stretches, and you will discover a "must do" horse experience. The Icelandic gait requires less effort from the rider than the posting trot associated with English riding styles and is kinder to less experienced riders. This breed, the product of 1000 years of selected breeding, is a remarkable creature which has redefined our understanding of horses.

CHILDREN'S PROGRAM: Children under 10 must have riding experience and those over 10 should have some.

ACCOMMODATIONS: Guests sleep in charming New England style country inns. Most have private baths. The inns of New England are well-appointed, reflecting careful attention to detail and the history of the area.

SPECIAL ACTIVITIES: There are opportunities for fishing, swimming, hot tubs and massage at various inns. Fall foliage rides offer spectacular colors. Ben and Jerry's world famous factory, Sugarbush Ski Resort, and the charming town of Waitsfield round out some of the possibilities.

MEALS: Meals are designed for hungry riders. Breakfast is a 3 course gourmet meal, lunch is picnic style and dinner is elegant. The settings for breakfast and dinner are the charming inns of New England.

RIDING STUFF: Riders spend 5 to 6 hours in the saddle on the hilly terrain that is characteristic of Mad River Valley. Almost all groups end up doing some walking, mostly tolting (the name given to the smooth 4 beat gait of Icelandics) and a bit of cantering. The scenery is lush and green in these well-watered mountains. You will pass through meadows, streams and rich forested land. Temperatures in all but the winter months are warm during the day and cool in the evening. Experienced guides vary the trip according to each group's riding skills. These horses provide a very good workout for the rider given the pace they maintain and you will be glad to enjoy the charms of a New England inn at day's end. Luggage is transported by vehicle.

AUTHOR'S COMMENT: *If you are an experienced rider and haven't yet enjoyed these horses—do it! If you love horses and haven't experienced this amazing breed—do it! The horses combined with the charm of New England inns makes one feel as if moving through a Currier and Ives Christmas poster in the winter, a brilliant color show in the fall, and an enchanted land of greenery during the spring and summer. New England is a perfect setting for this ride and brave souls should consider accepting the challenge of winter riding.*

HIGHLIGHTS

30 Icelandic horses • 2 to 6 day inn to inn rides • Group size 4-8 • Ideal family ride • Charming country inns • Half and full day rides all year • Riders up to 250 lbs. (114 kg.) (17.8 stone) • Helmets are supplied

SWIFT LEVEL

http://wvweb.com/www/swift_level

BASICS: RR2, Box 296, Lewisburg, WV 24901, USA
  Tel: (304) 645-1155
  Fax: (304) 647- 5212
  Email: swiftlevel@inetone.net
WHEN: April 1 – November 15.
AIRPORTS: Greenbrier Valley Airport (15 minutes by car, rentals available at airport). Nonstop US Air From LaGuardia (NYC).
LOCATION: A 4 to 5 hour drive from Washington,

D.C., Charlotte, NC, Columbus, OH. Amtrak stop at White Sulphur Springs (a 20 minute drive).
PRICE: Main house accommodations with full day ride and all meals: $200 (£125) per day, per person double occupancy, plus 6% tax and 15% gratuities. There are 4 private cabins suitable for families and groups at lower rates. Riding program is optional.

Swift Level is located in the beautiful Greenbrier Valley, nestled in the Allegheny Mountains. This 150 acre farm was built in 1820 and the main house is listed on the National Register of Historic Places. The property operates as a guest facility as well as a horse farm and provides one of the very best riding programs in the East. Its owner, Tootie O'Flaherty, and her staff create a gracious atmosphere where you can enjoy a riding or non-riding holiday. Groups are welcome and should call to arrange a personalized program.

CHILDREN'S PROGRAM: There are no special children's programs, although children are very welcome.

ACCOMMODATIONS: There are 2 well-appointed guest rooms with private bath in the main house, and 4 cabins, with décor ranging from country elegant to rustic, that offer self-catering opportunities.

SPECIAL ACTIVITIES: Non-riders will enjoy the property and nearby white-water rafting, canoeing, mountain biking, hiking, fishing, and caving. Lewisburg is only 3 miles from Swift Level and is the hub for cultural events, theatres, restaurants, and cafés.

MEALS: Breakfast is provided for main house guests, and breakfast provisions are available for guests staying at the cabins. Guests should check with the main house to see if dinner

will be served. Alternatively, guests will find an excellent variety of restaurants in Lewisburg.

RIDING STUFF: Swift Level uses Thoroughbred crosses, trained to move at an extended trot. The horses are balanced, well cared for and of the highest quality. Tootie is a superior horsewoman, attentive to detail and knowledgeable, with the keen eye of a trainer. Daily rides offered include a 2 hour, half day and full day ride (with a picnic lunch) and will take riders through open areas, woods, and mountains. All rides are guided. Riding instructors are encouraged to bring their own groups and accompany them on the rides. In addition to the Swift Level based rides, there are 3 to 5 day point to point rides where guests stay in secluded lodges or country B&Bs. If you are planning to capture the beauty of a fall ride, please book early, as others are sure to have had the same idea.

AUTHOR'S COMMENT: *Swift Level is located in a beautiful region of the United States. The riding is excellent, the terrain superb, the accommodations charming, and the property delightful. International visitors and those of you not familiar with the region will be astonished by the luscious green that characterizes this delightful area of the country. Only a 4 hour drive from the nation's capital. Come on down, y'all!*

HIGHLIGHTS

Daily inn based riding • 2 hour, half day, full day rides • 3 to 5 day point to point rides • Optional "in house" therapeutic massage • Full health club facilities, steam, sauna, hot tub, etc. only 5 minutes away • Corporate retreat center • Wide variety of nearby sporting activities including mountain biking, white-water rafting, hiking, canoeing, caving and fishing

Purple Glow, 1994, pastel/litho, 12" x 23¾"

Good Grazing Land, 1994, pastel/paper, 11" x 33"

Story Sky, 1994, pastel/paper, 7½" x 40"

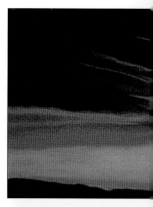

Incoming Storm, 1994, pastel/paper, 7½" x 40"

Collection of the artist.

WYOMING VIEWS
Pastels by Nancy Ungar

BITTERROOT RANCH

www.ridingtours.com

BASICS: Route 66, Box 807, Dubois, WY 82513, USA
  Tel: (307) 455-2778   Tel: (800) 545-0019
  Fax: (307) 455-2354
  Email: equitour@wyoming.com
WHEN: Open May through October.
AIRPORTS: Riverton or Jackson. Transfers can be arranged.
LOCATION: The Ranch is located 100 miles east of Jackson; 80 miles from Riverton; only a few hours drive from Yellowstone National Park.

PRICE: Low Season (May 24-Jun 28): $1062 (£664); Children's Rate (ages 4-15): $795 (£497); High Season (June 28-September 30): $1250 (£781); Children's Rate (ages 4-15): $937 (£586). Prices are per week, per person, d/o and include lodgings, all meals, and daily riding (except Sundays). There is a 15% Service Charge which covers all taxes and gratuities. Single supplement add $280 (£175).

Mel and Bayard Fox, owners of Equitour (one of the premier equestrian vacation agencies in the world) view this outstanding ranch as a gateway to their exciting domestic and international riding programs. The ranch lies 16 miles from the highway in a remote valley surrounded by snow-peaked mountains and national forest land. Bitterroot offers excellent food, good accommodations, and an opportunity to experience some of the most spirited riding in the country. The ranch is distinguished by its international atmosphere with staff and guests from around the world and offers a diversified riding program, including pack trips, cattle drives, and teaching clinics.

CHILDREN'S PROGRAM: There are no special children's programs.

ACCOMMODATIONS: There is room for 29 guests in semi-detached and detached heated log cabins, comfortably furnished, with full bath. Many have wood-burning stoves.

SPECIAL ACTIVITIES: Bitterroot offers stocked ponds, good stream fishing and provides equipment. Bayard Fox is an avid fisherman and you can rely on his advice. There is a brief hunting season during the autumn. You may wish to enjoy the hot tub before taking advantage of the pleasures afforded by a comfortable video room, library, pool room, reception area and porch. Yellowstone and Grand Teton National Parks are nearby and worth the trip.

MEALS: All meals are served family style. The meals present a sophisticated international cuisine, with pre-dinner *hors d'oeuvres* topped off by complimentary wine. There are always options available and special diets will be catered to upon advance notice.

RIDING STUFF: Riding is a twice a day affair, except for Sundays. The horses are very well cared for, super fit and agile. Riders are divided into as many as 4 groups per ride, depending on ability and desire. Bitterroot offers even the most advanced riders an opportunity to enjoy some spirited riding. The terrain varies from wooded mountain pine forests to sagebrush covered rolling hills with spectacular Western vistas. You will ride over different trails every day. There are 2 group lessons per week. Each session is videotaped and reviewed at night. There is a weekly team cattle sorting session and twice a year cattle drives. Overnight and extended wilderness trips can be arranged. Every ride ends with a delightful plunge in a stream to cool the horses before dismounting—a wonderful Wyoming way to finish every ride. In addition to the 130 riding horses, the ranch has 30 brood mares and they breed Arab and Percheron/Arab horses.

AUTHOR'S COMMENT: *A friendly farm atmosphere with strolling peacocks and assorted farm animals, wonderful food and an exciting riding program. All the natural beauty of the West plus an international ambiance make this a perfect introduction to Equitour's worldwide riding program. Bitterroot is the perfect place for experienced riders to enjoy some vigorous riding as a prelude to an international vacation that features long hours in the saddle*

HIGHLIGHTS
English and Western tack • Horse breeding farm • 3 horses per guest • Wilderness pack trips • Twice a year cattle drives and round-ups • Weekly team cattle sorting contests • Fly fishing • Individual log cabins • Minimum stay 1 week • Approved by the British Horse Society

HIGH ISLAND RANCH

www.GORP.com/HIGHISLAND

BASICS: PO Box 71, Hamilton Dome, WY 82427, USA

Tel: (307) 867-2374   Fax: (307) 867-2314

Email: HIGHLS1994@aol.com

WHEN: Open May through September.

AIRPORTS: Cody is the nearest airport. There is a $35 (£22) charge, per person for roundtrip transfers to and from the Ranch.

LOCATION: High Island Ranch is a 1 hour drive southeast of Cody, Wyoming.

PRICE: *Branding and Round-Up Weeks:* $995 (£621) 7 days/6 nights, per person. *Authentic Cattle Drives:* $1250 (£781) 7 days/6 nights, per person. *Prairie to High Mountain Round-Up:* $1050 (£656) 7 days, 6 nights, per person. *Trout Fishing and High Mountain Riding Adventure:* $1250 (£781) 7 days/6 nights, per person. *1800s Period Cattle Drive:* $1550 (£969) 7 days/6 nights, per person. Prices do not include gratuities or state taxes.

High Island Ranch, under the able management of Frank and Karen Robbins and family, is a 45,000 acre spread that encompasses extensive prairie land at 6000 feet as well as the Owl Creek Mountains at 9000 feet. Riding hard, cattle drives, and round-ups are part of the extensive program that runs from the end of May to September. There are 14 weeks of programs, some suitable for children. Three weeks are devoted to a combination of trout fishing and high mountain riding in which children can participate.

CHILDREN'S PROGRAM: Children 12 and up are welcome for early June branding and round-ups, as well as a variety of other rides. Certain age restrictions and discounts are applicable on different trips.

ACCOMMODATIONS: Guests sleep part of the time in a comfortable lodge with a large den, dining room, and private sleeping rooms. There is a large shower house with 2 private toilets. At the higher mountain camps, accommodations are provided in wall tents, a lodge, or a cabin. There are showers and outhouses at these camps.

SPECIAL ACTIVITIES: Nighttime brings some good country music around the campfire.

MEALS: The morning meal includes fresh brewed coffee, bacon, eggs and hot-cakes. On the trail, meals are prepared over a campfire. The food is hearty Western fare including beef, chicken, fresh fish and fruit, freshly baked breads and desserts.

RIDING STUFF: High Island Ranch offers the quintessential cowboy riding experience. The horses are reliable, sure-footed cattle horses, familiar with the area and the job at hand. The riding will leave you happy but tired, as ranching in Wyoming requires lots of leg power to carry you over the 45,000 acre range that the cattle call home. There is abundant wildlife, deer, elk and antelope abound, some spectacular sites such as the Washakie Needles (12,800 feet), and plenty of riding. By offering week-long programs that emphasize different aspects of cattle ranching, the Robbins supply the real thing in a series of diverse packages, including an 1800s Period Cattle Drive, replete with music and food from that era.

AUTHOR'S COMMENT: *High Island Ranch is in a wonderful location for some spirited riding. Frank Robbins will work you hard in the saddle, offering an opportunity to truly test your skills, improve them, and come back for more. You are likely to form a pretty good team with your fellow riders, working together to keep the cattle in line and yourselves proudly in the saddle.*

HIGHLIGHTS

Western tack • Large cattle ranch • 1800s Cattle Drive Weeks , Cattle Round-Up and Branding weeks • High Mountain fast riding adventure • Guest capacity 25 • Trout fishing • Member: Wyoming Dude Ranchers Association

LAZY L & B RANCH

www.guestranches.com/lazyl&b

BASICS: 1072 East Fork Road, Dubois, WY
82513, USA
Tel: (307) 455-2839   Tel: (800) 453-9488
Fax: (307) 455-2634
WHEN: June 1 to mid-September.
AIRPORTS: Riverton or Jackson.

LOCATION: The ranch is located 100 miles east of Jackson; 80 miles from Riverton; a 1½ hour drive from Yellowstone and Grand Teton National Parks.
PRICE: $1000 (£625) 7days/6 nights, per person, double occupancy.

The Lazy L & B Ranch, located miles from the main highway, lies in the idyllic Wind River valley, surrounded by national forest land and the snow-covered Absaroka Mountains. The charm and experience of owners Lee and Bob Naylon set the tone for a superior riding holiday. Their emphasis on offering a safe and enjoyable riding experience for everyone is delivered with zest. Lazy L & B is an ideal family vacation destination.

CHILDREN'S PROGRAM: There is an excellent children's riding program, a petting zoo, hayrides, and a cook-out for the youngsters. Children over 5 may join the riding program. Wranglers will lead younger children around the corrals.

ACCOMMODATIONS: Up to 35 guests sleep in various sized cabins, with full baths, refrigerators, porches and heaters. Most of the cabins are log built and provide wonderful views of Wind River and the horse pastures. There is a very comfortable and stylish lounge in the main lodge.

SPECIAL ACTIVITIES: A solar heated swimming pool, a hot tub and fishing conspire to help you relax. Once a week guests are invited to shoot at the rifle range. Yellowstone and Grand Teton National Parks are nearby. Weekly square dances in Dubois and visits to nearby attractions round out a full program.

MEALS: All meals are served family style. Fresh baked breads and desserts accompany most meals. There are also cook-outs and BBQs. The ranch will cater to special diets upon request.

RIDING STUFF: Sunday's arriving guests are encouraged to visit the corrals, where abilities and comfort levels are assessed. Riders are then divided into small groups and enjoy a 1½ hour introductory ride in the valley. You are encouraged to become involved in saddling, bridling, and general care of the horses as well as learning the do's and don'ts of safe riding. The ranch advocates interaction between rider and horse, which not only teaches horsemanship, but also builds confidence. Following the introductory program on Sunday, there are 2 to 3 hour morning and afternoon rides on Monday, a half day ride on Tuesday, and all day rides on Wednesday and Thursday. The program is always adjusted to your individual needs. There are horse games or gymkannas on Friday afternoons. The terrain is very varied which allows qualified riders to safely strut their stuff. You could ride the area daily for a month and experience different trails and terrain on each ride.

AUTHOR'S COMMENT: *The varied terrain of open meadows, green river bottoms, alpine forests and the surrounding mountains and hills creates ample opportunities for trotting and loping. Concern for safety and emphasis on horsemanship means that most riders will leave with increased skills and knowledge. Lazy L & B offers an ideal ranch vacation with a challenging and safe riding program.*

HIGHLIGHTS
Western tack • 70 mountain horses • Excellent children's program • Sunday to Saturday • Extensive trail riding daily • Horse games on Friday afternoons • Adult weeks in September • Wilderness trips at Bear Basin Wilderness Camp (see separate entry for more detail) • Member: DRA, WY DRA

LAZY L & B's BEAR BASIN WILDERNESS CAMP

www.guestranches.com/lazyl&b

BASICS: 1072 East Fork Road, Dubois, WY 82513, USA
Tel: (307) 455-2839   Tel: (800) 453-9488
Fax: (307) 455-2634
WHEN: July and August for pack trips. Hunting trips available in October.
AIRPORTS: Riverton or Jackson.

LOCATION: The ranch is located 100 miles east of Jackson; 80 miles from Riverton; and a ½ hour drive from Yellowstone and Grand Teton National Parks.
PRICE: $200 (£125) per day, per person, double occupancy.

Lazy L & B owners Lee and Bob Naylon and family see this genuine wilderness camp, located in the vast Washakie Wilderness, as a wonderful opportunity for up to 8 people to have a true wilderness experience returning to a comfortable base camp at day's end. The wilderness camp is to a ranch, as a rural farm is to a major metropolis, serene and natural. When the excitement of finding yourself in a new environment dissipates, you will quickly begin to enjoy a peaceful relaxation, in tune with your surroundings. The riding is superb. This is a perfect way for a family to enjoy the wilderness without the discomforts of backpacking.

CHILDREN'S PROGRAM: Children over 7, capable of riding 4 to 5 hours a day are welcome.

ACCOMMODATIONS: Guests sleep in comfortable stand-up wall tents, with cots and pads supplied. There is a cook tent as well as a dining tent for those who don't opt for eating 'round the old campfire. Your luggage is moved for you by pack animals from the main ranch in the East Fork Valley.

SPECIAL ACTIVITIES: Lay back at the camp, enjoy some great fishing over at Bear Creek, observe the wildlife, and soak up the beauties of nature.

MEALS: Breakfast and dinner are prepared by the camp cook and you can rest assured that the food won't remind you of the freeze-dried rations that so often accompany wilderness camping.

RIDING STUFF: The sure-footed, mountain horses will not only carry you to and from your camp, but will also take you out for some leisurely mountain rides deep in the wilderness area, exploring the timbered canyons and high mountain passes up to 11,000 feet. In addition to the views, you will catch more than occasional glimpses of the diverse wildlife that thrives in the Rocky Mountains—deer, elk, moose, occasional bear, soaring eagles and hawks.

AUTHOR'S COMMENT: *This is a perfect way for any small group to bond through the shared experience of being mere specks in the wonder of it all, while avoiding many of the discomforts of wilderness living. Big comfortable tents, beautiful surroundings, horses to ride, and people to serve you—a taste of that Great Green Pasture where the deer and the antelope roam.*

HIGHLIGHTS:
Western tack • Excellent fishing • 4 to 6 day wilderness pack trips • Abundant wildlife viewing • Guest limit 8 • Comfortable wilderness tents • Can extend ranch vacations at Lazy L & B • Member: DRA, WY DRA, Wyoming Outfitters Association

LOZIER'S BOX "R" RANCH

www.boxr.com

BASICS: Box 1000-WWRV, Cora, WY 82925, USA
   Tel: (307) 367-4868   Tel: (800) 822-8466
   Fax: (307) 367-6260   Email: info@boxr.com
WHEN: May 24 to September 13.
AIRPORTS: Jackson Hole. Transfers included.
LOCATION: A 1 hour drive southeast from Jackson;
a 2 hour drive from Yellowstone and Grand Teton National Parks.
PRICE: Rates vary with program. Ranch Stay: $995 (£621) 7 days/ 7 nights, per person, double occupancy during July and August, when special activities for the family are scheduled.

For more than 100 years, Lozier's Box "R" Ranch has been a working cattle/horse ranch, the only private land to border Wyoming's wilderness. Today, 5th generation Loziers get to show you their stuff, which includes one of the more varied riding programs in the American West. Cattle drives, ranch stays, wilderness pack trips and spot and drop trips offer an array of quality options hosted by a very experienced ranching family. Put it all on beautiful ranch land, surrounded by the vast, 840,000 acre Bridger Wilderness, and what can you say but "Here I come!"

CHILDREN'S PROGRAM: Children 8 to 16 are welcome during the family ranching periods in July and August when there are special planned activities for the entire family.

ACCOMMODATIONS: Up to 20 guests stay in 1 to 3 room cabins that vary from comfortable to plush, all with private baths. Some of the rooms adjoin the entertainment center and others have a family room with large fireplace. On the Lonesome Dove Cattle Drives, round-ups, and ranch stay/pack trip combos, guests may stay at a wilderness camp.

SPECIAL ACTIVITIES: Yellowstone Park, a true national treasure, is about a 2 hour drive. You can always grab your gear and go fishing, provided you're big enough and strong enough to reel in those Wyoming fish!

MEALS: All meals are served family style in the ranch dining room. Substantial portions, fresh breads and pastries, international cuisine and Western beefsteak, chicken, ham and trout combine to ensure your dining pleasure.

RIDING STUFF: The ranch uses more than 100 horses and mules for its riding program. Guests are each assigned to a personal horse for the duration of their stay and are encouraged to catch, bridle and saddle their horses daily—a positive way to build a relationship with your horse. All guests participate in a basic orientation program (to check horsemanship as well as the ability to mount, dismount, trot and canter) as a prerequisite to the tougher rides off-ranch. Instruction is available to help bring guests up to safe riding standards. Riding activity varies from trail riding to cattle work. There is unlimited riding and qualified riders will find plenty of freedom and suitable terrain to quicken their pace and enjoy some whoopin' and hollerin'. Elevations vary from 7500 to 11,000 feet and the typography moves from meadow bottoms and aspen hillsides to timberline granite peaks.

AUTHOR'S COMMENT: *The Box "R" provides lots of options for singles, couples and families and is designed to accommodate a wide range of riding skills and experience. How to decide what's best for you? Give them a call, study their brochures and away you go to one of Wyoming's most extensive riding programs. The ranch is attractively situated near the Bridger National Forest, which offers a majestic environment to explore.*

HIGHLIGHTS

Western tack • Adults-Only and Family Weeks planned • Spring 3 and 4 day programs (May 24 to June 7) • 3 Lonesome Dove Cattle Drives, 7 nights; June 7, 14 & 21 • Ranch stays and ranch stay/pack trip combos, June 28 to August 30 • 2 fall cattle round-ups, August 30 to Sept.13 • 3 to 10 day wilderness pack trips • Spot pack trips and gear drops • Fishing • Member: DRA, Wyoming Outfitters Association

RENEGADE RIDES

www.renegaderides.com

BASICS: HC30, Box 15, Ten Sleep, WY 82442, USA
Tel: (888) 307-2689   Tel: (307) 366-2689
Fax: (307) 366-2605
Email: belinda@renegaderides.com
WHEN: May to October.
AIRPORTS: Worland. Transfers included.
LOCATION: Rides begin in north central Wyoming among the foothills of Big Horn Mountain

near the town of Ten Sleep, 120 miles from Cody.
PRICE: Weekly Rates: $1350 (£844) 8 days/7 nights, per person, double occupancy. *Wagon Train Ride*: $400 (£250) 5 days/4 nights, per person, double occupancy. *Cattle/Sheep Drives*: $1350 (£844) 7 or 8 days/6 or 7 nights, per person, double occupancy.

Belinda Daugherty, owner and head wrangler at Renegade Rides has been in the business for over 22 years, and is now enjoying the opportunity (along with co-owner, Bernie Weiss) to create programs that offer exciting riding on sure-footed, well-trained horses. Each of the 5 point to point rides afford plenty of opportunity for very spirited, but safe, riding for those who are willing and able. The early and late season cattle drives as well as the July 1-4 wagon train ride to Ten Sleep Rodeo are family oriented and are designed to accommodate riding groups with a mix of skills and experience.

CHILDREN'S PROGRAMS: Children over 8 are welcome on the slower paced wagon train ride and cattle drives with family members. On the harder rides they must be over 13, accompanied by an adult, and demonstrate good riding skills.

ACCOMMODATIONS: On the first night, guests sleep in a cattle ranch bunkhouse. Hot showers are available and couples may opt for private tents. On all point to point rides, guests sleep in large stand-up teepee tents, with comfortable foam pads and sleeping bags (rentals available). If water is available, a shower trailer will be set-up.

SPECIAL ACTIVITIES: The Warpath Ride includes special activities at day's end including a presentation on Native American warrior skills such as spear throwing, arrowhead making, and black powder shooting.

MEALS: You won't go hungry on a Renegade Ride. Breakfasts are the kind of hardy meals that cowboys need to fuel a day on horseback. Lunch is eaten during planned trail breaks and is packed for your ride along with snacks. Dinner is served around the campfire. The food, including vegetarian options upon request, is prepared by experienced camp cooks. Menus include steak and potatoes, chicken parmesan, broccoli and cheese casserole, Indian tacos, and fresh salads with every meal.

RIDING STUFF: Renegade Rides offers the opportunity to enjoy vigorous, hard riding, improve your horsemanship, and experience the real Wild West. The horses are well-trained and carefully matched to each rider's ability. You are encouraged to get to know your horse prior to the trip. While many of the rides move at a fairly fast pace, the safety of both horse and rider is a paramount consideration. Most Renegade Rides are tailored to the intermediate horseperson, meaning that you should be comfortable riding at a trot, posting, and galloping in the forward seat over uneven terrain. Participants must be fit and able to spend from 5 to 8 hours in the saddle each day. Experienced wranglers determine the pace based on the skill levels of the riders in each group. The cattle drives and Ten Sleep Wagon Train welcome beginners and children as well as more experienced riders.

AUTHOR'S COMMENT: *The "B&Bs," Bernie and Belinda, have put together an exciting new riding program, ideal for those of you who are looking for some spirited riding and a true wilderness experience. Early and late season cattle drives, plus the mid-season wagon train designed for families, rounds out the programs on offer. Some of the rides have already booked up, so get your dialing fingers to the phone.*

HIGHLIGHTS
Western tack • 5 point to point rides: The Warpath, Oregon Trail/Pony Express, Eagles Eye, Hole-In-The-Wall, Red Rocks to Big Horn Mountain • Riding experience necessary • Cattle/Sheep Drives (no experience necessary) • Special family trip: Ten Sleep Rodeo Horse and Wagon Train • Abundant wildlife, antelope, deer, elk and eagles • All rides vehicle supported • Group capacity 12

VEE BAR GUEST RANCH

www.vee-bar.com

BASICS: 2091 State Highway, 130, Department A, Laramie, WY 82070, USA
Tel (800) 483-3277   Tel: (307) 745-7036
Fax: (307) 745-7433
Email: veebar@lariat.org
WHEN: Open all year.
AIRPORTS: Laramie. Complimentary transfers from the airport.
LOCATION: A 20 minute drive west of Laramie; a 3 hour drive northwest of Denver.
PRICE: Summer Program (June 13 to September 5): $1447 (£904) 7 days/6 nights, per person, double occupancy, or $675 (£421) 4 days/3 nights, per person, double occupancy, (plus 8% tax), all gratuities included. Each additional person per cabin: $700 (£437). Winter B&B: $100 (£62) per cabin, per night, includes breakfast, hot tub, and private fishing.

Cozily nestled among the working cattle ranches of Centennial Valley, in the shadows of the beautiful Snowy Range Mountains, lies the Vee Bar Guest Ranch. This 100 year old landmark has served as a cattle ranch, a buffalo ranch, a stagecoach stop, and a boys' school, and is currently operated as a guest ranch during the summer and a B&B in the winter. The Vee Bar is owned by Jim "Lefty" Cole and his son Kelly Cole. They maintain an easy-going atmosphere that is ideal for families interested not only in riding, but also fishing, river tubing, cook-outs, cattle work, nightly entertainment, and a friendly comfortable lifestyle.

CHILDREN'S PROGRAMS: Children over the age of 6 may participate in riding activities at wrangler discretion. There is no special children's program.

ACCOMMODATIONS: The cozy comfortable cabins and riverside suites have gas operated or wood-burning stoves, just right for relaxing with a good book, daydreaming or visiting with friends. The great room and new riverside suites were built with recycled logs from the late 1800s. The suites have full bath, washer and dryer, a small refrigerator and a coffee maker. Decks overlook the Little Laramie River.

SPECIAL ACTIVITIES: There is hiking, great fishing, and river tubing for those who want even more outdoor activity. Evening activities vary from narrated slide shows and storytellers to country dance lessons and bluegrass fiddlers. The ranch has its own liquor license and saloon that doubles as a recreation room with a pool table and other games.

MEALS: The historic main lodge is headquarters for one of the most important ranch activities— eating! Hearty ranch cooking is supplemented with fresh fruit, homemade bread and the ever-full cookie jar. The ranch chef will be happy to cater to special dietary needs upon prior notice.

RIDING STUFF: Guests arrive on Sundays for the week long ride. (Those opting for a shorter stay can begin on Wednesdays or Sundays.) On the first morning, guests are assigned a horse for their stay and are taken on an orientation ride, to ensure that horses and riders are properly suited to each other. There is also an afternoon ride and the same again on Tuesday. Wednesday offers an all day ride. On Thursday, after your morning ride and some lunch, you will move on out to an overnight camp-out at Deerwood, a 5000 acre cattle ranch owned by Jim "Lefty" Cole. After a range breakfast, guests hunker down on horseback to do some serious cattle work before returning to the Vee Bar. Gymkhanas (games on horseback) are played on Friday afternoons. The morning and afternoon rides are about 2 hours each and the all day ride is 6 hours. Guests will be divided into groups according to experience on horseback. Groups typically consist of about 5 riding guests and 1 wrangler. This is pretty nice territory for some fast riding, if you are experienced.

AUTHOR'S COMMENT: *A good friend of mine, "Cowboy Ron," who takes about 5 riding holidays annually, raved about Vee Bar. Coming from him, that's no small praise. The ranch offers very good riding, easy access, superior accommodations, and the type of friendly staff you look for in a ranch vacation.*

HIGHLIGHTS
Western tack • Guest capacity 38 • Private cabins • Hot tub • Fishing • Trap shooting • Overnight camp-out at cattle ranch followed by cattle work the next morning • Nightly entertainment

WESTERN ENCOUNTER

www.horseriders.com

BASICS: 24 Birchfield Lane, Lander, WY 82520, USA
Tel/ Fax: (307) 332- 5434
Tel: (800) 572-1230
Email: dashley@wyoming.com
WHEN: Mid-May to mid-September.
AIRPORTS: Riverton, WY. Transfers included.

LOCATION: A 3 hour drive from Jackson Hole, Yellowstone and Cody.
PRICE: Wild Horse/Mountain and Pony Express: $1295 (£809); Outlaw Trail: $1345 (£840); Cattle Drive: $1575 (£984). All prices are per week, per person.

Your hosts, Skip and Vivian Ashley, offer 4 point to point riding and camping adventures that are among the best known and appreciated riding opportunities in the United States, and for good reason. These rides combine the chance to enjoy Western wilderness scenery along with safe, spirited riding. Each trail is a part of Western folklore, such as The Outlaw Trail, Butch Cassidy and the Sundance Kid's 'Hole in the Wall Gang' country. A second ride covers the old Oregon Trail used by Pony Express Riders. Ride among the herds of wild mustangs on the Wild Horse/Mountain Ride. Partake in an authentic Wyoming cattle drive. All rides offer good opportunities for galloping. The creature comforts and food supported by vehicles are 5 levels above the typical wilderness trip.

CHILDREN'S PROGRAM: Limited to children with demonstrated riding ability

ACCOMMODATIONS: On the first and last nights, guests stay at Lander's Pronghorn Lodge. Once you hit the trail, riders sleep in comfortable 8' x 8' tents, using sleeping bags (rentals available) and thick cushioned foam pads. Hot showers and toilet facilities are provided. Riders do not change camps daily. Luggage and provisions are moved by motor vehicle.

MEALS: Western Encounter provides superior cuisine for your stay in town as well as on the trail, including wine with dinner. Special diets will be accommodated, but please notify at time of booking. We assure you the quality food provided does not resemble the cowboy meal in "Blazing Saddles"—a difference that hungry riders welcome.

RIDING STUFF: Western tack is used and you may bring your own saddle. The sure-footed, well-behaved horses are trained for endurance. You will be riding a minimum of 5 hours a day with opportunity for varying pace determined by the guest riders working with Skip and the wranglers. That same rider/wrangler interaction also determines routes and distance. All riders will need fitness and experience to accommodate the hours and vigors of riding. Skip will exert his considerable expertise to help riders achieve a comfortable rhythm. The Cattle Drives are part of the Wyoming cattle ranchers' late spring gathering, branding, castrating, ear tagging and doctoring of calves before moving them little doggies higher up to the enriched summer pastures. Only 12 guests are permitted on these trips.

AUTHOR'S COMMENT: *Skip, Wyoming-raised, is soft spoken and half Cherokee, while Vivian hails from the last true American Wilderness, New York City. But don't try to push her out of Wyoming, 'cause it ain't going to work. Great, energetic, experienced hosts, good planning and well-behaved endurance horses make this a can't miss "American riding experience." All trips begin and end on Saturday. The season lasts 16 weeks.*

HIGHLIGHTS

Western tack • 4 different point to point rides including Outlaw Trail, Pony Express/Oregon Trail Ride, Wild Horse/Mountain Ride and Cattle Drives • Riding experience is necessary

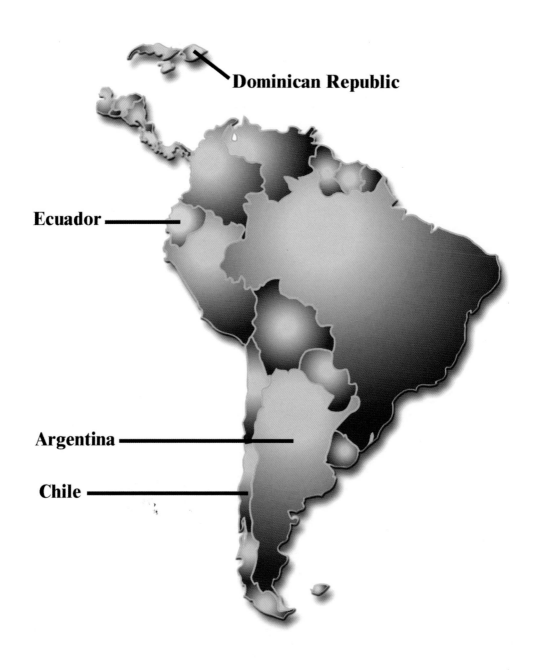

Dominican Republic

Ecuador

Argentina

Chile

SOUTH AND CENTRAL AMERICA AND THE CARIBBEAN

by Arthur Sacks

THE CARIBBEAN HAS A RICH HISTORY of riding imported from the colonial powers that occupied many of the islands until relatively recently. Jamaica has racing and polo as well as numerous places to enjoy day riding, even though the quality of the horses tends to be rather uneven, ranging from fine Thoroughbred mounts to basic, small, thin island crossbreds. Cuba is the next area to be opened to riding holidays. The UK's In the Saddle, Anne Mariage from Cheval d'Aventure, and Rafael Belmonte of Cabalgar Rutas Altenativas all feature riding treks in Cuba. Eastern Trekking offers riding holidays on St. Maarten and other Caribbean destinations. The Dominican Republic, offers several riding opportunities, including a trekking-type tour offered by Cheval d'Aventure. Casa de Campo, in the Dominican Republic, is a world class resort, which maintains and breeds one of the largest polo herds in the world. In addition polo, Casa has a good training program in classical English events such as jumping. They also maintain a large herd of horses on their private farm at Higueral for extensive and spirited trail riding. With golf, shooting, tennis, and miles of beaches, Casa de Campo provides a sportsman's holiday in a resort setting.

Central America offers many riding opportunities, most of which are best described as a combination of riding holiday and adventure trip, often including rafting, swimming, and/or hiking. Costa Rica and Belize in particular are featured by many of the equestrian agencies listed in this book. Belize is English-speaking, and both countries are extremely gracious to their visitors.

South America has a rich tradition of horsemanship imported from Spain and, to a lesser degree, by the Germans who have established communities there. Brazil will soon be a new riding destination and Equitour, USA is planning to launch a new ride there. Venezuela offers beach-riding holidays, and is featured by several equestrian agencies. However, securing direct information can be difficult as neither country has an organized means of responding to inquiries. Ecuador has several distinct riding destinations, mostly confined to the higher mountain areas. Ecuadorian outfitters offer good accommodations, willing horses, and a chance to explore a fascinating culture that combines their indigenous Indian heritage with a strong Spanish influence.

Many of the equestrian agencies on both sides of the Atlantic feature rides in South and Central America. Peru, Chile and Argentina each have their share of high mountain adventures, and Hidden Trails offers a ranch vacation in Columbia. Argentina certainly stands out as one of the premier riding environments in the world. There are many celebrated *estancias* that feature polo, a sport at which the Argentineans excel. In addition to high mountain adventures and polo, Argentina and the surrounding countries have a rich tradition of cattle farming and cowboy riding *á la* the *gaucho* tradition, and there are many opportunities to experience any or all of these riding activities. Although, if you don't speak Spanish, the information might be difficult to come by.

In many ways South and Central America remain untapped locations for a great variety of riding holidays and we expect to see a significant increase in offerings from this region within the next decade. Brazil, with its diversity of cultures and varied topography, seems like a particularly attractive holiday destination, ready to explode on the riding world. Since the seasons in South America are opposite to those in the Northern Hemisphere, you can enjoy riding holidays year round. We expect to greatly expand our Central and South American offerings in the third edition of this book.

CASA DE CAMPO

www.casadcampo.com

BASICS: Casa de Campo, La Romana, Dominican
Republic
Tel: (809) 523-3333 Fax: (809) 523-8394
(Property)
US Reservations Agent: **Premier World Marketing**
Tel: (800) 877-3643   Tel: (305) 856-5405
Fax: (305) 858-4677
Email: res@prmwldmktg.com
WHEN: Open year round.

AIRPORTS: Casa de Campo/La Romana - a 5 minute
drive; Santo Domingo - a 90 minute drive.
LOCATION: Dominican Republic
PRICE: Seasonal variations. Multiple inclusive
packages range from $163 (£102) per day,
per person, double occupancy (low season)
to $222 (£139) per day, per person, double
occupancy (high season).

Guests fly into La Romana Airport, 5 minutes from Casa de Campo. The resort offers world class comfort, food, sports of every type, an attractive ambiance, a recreated 16th century Mediterranean village, lots of shops, restaurants, ideal island weather, and a friendly gracious staff. There are 2 Pete Dye-designed golf courses, 1 of them ranked among the top 100 courses in the world. The tennis center offers ball boys to chase down errant shots and professional instruction. There are a variety of restaurants to choose from on the inclusive or European plans and nightly activities including a nightclub and disco.

CHILDREN'S PROGRAM: There is an extensive supervised program for children ages 3-12 and baby-sitting services for the tiny ones. These programs can keep your children engaged from early morning till bedtime if you choose.

ACCOMMODATIONS: Guests either stay in oversized, well-appointed "casita rooms" in the central area, or in 2, 3 or 4 bedroom villas, each with private bath, kitchen and a spacious living area. Some villas come with private pools as well as maid and butler service.

SPECIAL ACTIVITIES: There are many tourist attractions that may be arranged at the central reservation desk including deep sea fishing, boating trips on the Chavon river, and shopping expeditions

MEALS: For lunch and dinner guests enjoy a choice of restaurants located on this 7000 acre resort which vary from the formal elegance of international cuisine to fun food places. Breakfast includes a daily omelet buffet, fresh fruit, juice bar, home made breads and more.

RIDING STUFF: The 40 to 50 island trail horses are rotated from farms at Higueral. There are 1, 2 and 3 hour trail rides twice a day. Typically, 1 wrangler is provided for every 5 or 6 riders. Private wrangler service may be arranged. Western and English tack are available. Special rides for experienced riders can be arranged. Helmets and long pants or jodhpurs are mandatory. There are pony rides for children. A dozen jumpers, certified instructors, and a quality jumping ring that is home to international competitions, offer guests an opportunity to improve their riding and jumping skills. Casa de Campo has a world class reputation for polo. Alina Carta, a top Palm Beach polo player, leads the program. There are 3 playing fields, the largest herd of polo ponies in the world, grooms and stables. Equipment and instruction for every level is available and guests may hire ponies for stick and ball and compete against each other.

AUTHOR'S COMMENT: *This is one of the few luxury resorts that has a well-rounded and enjoyable riding program. Casa de Campo provides the solution to the problem of divided family sporting interests. Located on an island that enjoys terrific weather for riding, golf, swimming, boating and vacationing year round, it is an ideal resort for families or groups.*

HIGHLIGHTS

Five star resort • 2 world class golf courses • World class shooting center • 13 tennis courts • Private beaches • Capacity 1500 • Trail riding packages • Jumping and riding lessons by certified trainers • Polo center • Polo lessons

ESTANCIA HUECHAHUE TREK

www.ridingtours.com/argentina.htm

BASICS: Agent: **Equitour,** PO Box 807, Dubois, WY 82513, USA
Tel: (800) 545-0019   Tel: (307) 455-3363
Fax: (307) 455-2354
Email: equitor@wyoming.com
WHEN: November through April.
AIRPORTS: Buenos Aires (international) to San Martin de los Andes or Bariloche Airports.

LOCATION: Northern Patagonia. The main ranch, Estancia Huechahue, is about 120 miles from Bariloche and 45 miles northeast of San Martin. Free transfers from San Martin.
PRICE: $220 (£138) per night, per person, double occupancy, includes all accommodations, meals and riding. Flexible dates.

Patagonia is a land of beautiful geological formations. Lanin Volcano, at 13,000 feet (4060 meters), is visible from the ranch. The Estancia, where the trips begin and end, is a 15,000 acre ranch run by Englishwoman, Jane Williams, who offers high quality treks and ranch stays. The riding at the ranch can be vigorous or slow while, on pack trips, the pace and riding are determined by the group's skill level.

CHILDREN'S PROGRAM: There is no special program for children.

ACCOMMODATIONS: The accommodations at the main ranch are comfortable and tasteful. There is a private guest house, with 3 twin-bedded rooms and *en suite* bathrooms. Additional accommodations are available in the main house. On pack trips through the Andes, 2 person tents are utilized and are set-up by camp staff.

SPECIAL ACTIVITIES: There is a tennis court near the main house on the ranch. The near-by River Alumine is good for swimming, fishing, and floating trips. This is a good area to hike, visit ancient Indian burial caves, and the fishing is world-famous.

MEALS: Meals tend to be large and bountiful. Lunch and dinner are served with a variety of fruits and vegetables, many of which are grown on the *estancia*. Lunch is frequently an *asado* or Argentine BBQ, utilizing the world-renowned Argentine beef. Dinner is a late meal, never served before 9:00 p.m. On extended pack trips there is a crew to cook and set-up camp. Vegetarian meals are available with some advance notice.

RIDING STUFF: The horses are Criollo crosses. A stay at the *estancia* includes riding through an Indian reservation, possibly spending a day floating down the River Alumine, participating in moderately-paced rides, and experiencing herds of red deer, guanaco, and rhea. Riders may even have the opportunity to visit condor nesting places. Guests may also participate in a camping trek, involving 3 or 4 nights of camping, with a stay at the ranch before and after the trip. Ride to thermal springs for a swim, travel through dense forests with bamboo thickets, above the tree line at Cera Malo Ranch, and through indigenous Monkey Puzzle Tree forests, and more.

AUTHOR'S COMMENT: *Argentina is a land with a rich tradition of horsemanship, ranging from working gauchos to world-class polo players. The land is rich and unpopulated, offering spectacular landscapes and varied trail riding opportunities.*

HIGHLIGHTS
Working *estancia* • From novices to experienced riders • Ranch stays • Areas of great beauty • Extended pack trips in Lanin National Park (in the Andes Mountains) • Group size on pack trips 4 to 12 • Spectacular bird viewing opportunities

THE PATAGONIA EXPERIENCE

www.hiddentrails.com

BASICS: Agent: **Hidden Trails**, 5396 Inverness Street, Vancouver, British Columbia V5W 3P7, Canada
Tel: (604) 323-1141   Tel: (888) 987-2457
Fax: (604) 323-1148
Email: vacations@hiddentrails.com

WHEN: December to March.

AIRPORTS: Santiago, Chile /Puerto Montt or Buenos Aires/Bariloche

LOCATION: Southern Chilean and Argentinian Andes and Patagonia.

PRICE: *Cassidy & Sundance Kid* (Chile and Argentina): $2345 (£1465) 11 days/10 nights, per person, includes meals and 5 days of riding. Airfare from Santiago to Puerto Montt is about $200 (£125). *Gaucho Trails in the Andes* (Chile): from $2595 (£1622): 14 days/13 nights, per person, includes 9 days of riding. *Patagonia Trail* (Argentina): $1775 (£1109) 12 days/11 nights, per person. Rates vary slightly depending on the accommodations chosen and there is an additional single supplement. Local air transfers not included.

About 100 years ago, the notorious outlaw duo Butch Cassidy and the Sundance Kid, drove their cattle across the Patagonia wilderness from Argentina to Chile. Their route over the Andes, once named the "Cochamo Road," now known as the Gaucho Trail, had been used by local Indians, Jesuit priests, and traders centuries before. *Gauchos* still run their herds across the mountain pass today. Clark Stede, an internationally known outdoor specialist, rides this trail on horseback with experienced *gauchos* and adventure travelers in small, well-equipped teams. Any traveler, beginner or experienced rider, who is fit and ready to work in a team can join one of the last true adventures in the Patagonia region of Chile and Argentina. Each of the 3 riding opportunities offers its own unique emphasis and you should ask Hidden Trails about the details.

CHILDREN'S PROGRAM: These rides are not suitable for children.

ACCOMMODATIONS: All trips involve a combination of hotels and camping. Gaucho Trail offers cabins or tents, while Cassidy & Sundance Kid offers 3 nights at a hotel, 2 at inns, 4 camping, and 1 night in the bunkhouse. The Patagonia Trail in Argentina offers 9 nights of camping and 2 in hotels.

MEALS: Large US style breakfasts, lunches on the trail, and dinners which typically offer lamb and salmon cooked over the campfire.

RIDING STUFF: The rides follow the rugged terrain that Butch Cassidy and Sundance rode over during the 4½ years they spent hiding-out in Argentina and Chile. These rides provide all of the excitement of the Andes as well as the spectacular beauty of Patagonia, which is located at the southern tip of the Andes. Non-riding partners in adventure are welcome on the Gaucho Trail and they will enjoy rafting, hiking and boating. Rugged peaks, mountain passes and the pampas of Patagonia, will supply you with opportunities to view wildlife, including puma and condor, ford rivers, enjoy waterfalls, all part of a true wilderness adventure that is exceptionally well-organized, yet flexible enough to ensure safe encounters with the unexpected.

AUTHOR'S COMMENT: *Hidden Trails, an agency that offers rides around the world and throughout Central and South America, sponsors this fantastic riding opportunity in Patagonia. The 3 ride combination should prove as attractive to riding purists as it is to adventure seekers, even those for whom riding is not the principal interest.*

HIGHLIGHTS
Riding in the Andes in Argentina and/or Chile • 5 to 6 hours riding a day • English tack • Skill level varies with ride • Ride the Gaucho Trail and visit the hide-outs of outlaws Butch Cassidy and the Sundance Kid • Inland boating trip across the Andes from Argentina and back to Chile • Rafting trip

TORRES DEL PAINE

www.inthesaddle.com

BASICS: Agent: **In the Saddle,** Laurel Cottage, Ramsdell, Tadley, Hampshire, RG26 5SH, UK
Tel: 01256-851-665   Fax: 01256-851-667 (from UK)
Tel: (44) 1256-851-665
Fax: (44) 1256-851-667 (from US)
Email: rides@inthesaddle. com

WHEN: September through March. There are 11 scheduled dates.

AIRPORTS: Santaigo, Chile to Punta Arenas. Transfers from Punta Arenas included.

LOCATION: Torres del Paine National Park in southern Chile.

PRICE: *Wilderness Camping Trip:* £1280 ($2048) 10 days/9 nights, per person. *Wilderness Rides* (local accommodations): £1530 ($2448)10 days/9 nights, per person. Prices include 7 days of riding, accommodations, meals, wine, and equipment, except sleeping bags. Airfare, accommodations and meals during the first night in Punta Arenas are not included. Singles must be willing to share accommodations.

Spectacular views, well-planned expeditions, glaciers, penguins, condors, and good horses are all found in this gem of Chile's National Park system. Torres del Paine National Park encompasses 243,000 hectares of solitary beauty and wild landscape lying to the extreme south of Chile, on the edge of the Patagonia icecap. The Park, created in 1959, was subsequently declared a Briosphere Reserve by UNESCO in 1978. It takes its name from a Teheulche Indian word meaning "blue," the color of the area's many lakes, which contain glaciers and icebergs. The Park is surounded by huge, craggy mountains, including Cuernos del Paine (Pain Horns) and the famous Torres (Towers).

CHILDREN'S PROGRAM: The rides are suitable only for teenageers 16 and older, if accompanied by parents.

ACCOMMODATIONS: On the Wilderness Camping Ride you will sleep in spacious "3 person" tents with 2 guests per tent. All equipment is supplied apart from sleeping bags, which you may hire. On the Wilderness Ride using local accommodations, you will stay in *refugios*, which provide basic accommodations, up to 3 in a room. There is, however, a plentiful supply of hot water and good food. The last night on both rides is spent at historic *estancia*, Hosteria Lazo, in comfortable cabins with spectacular views of nearby Laguna Verde.

SPECIAL ACTIVITIES: You will visit a penguin colony and, if you wish to extend your trip, the area offers exciting fishing, hiking and kayaking expeditions.

MEALS: All meals and wine are included on the camping part of your trip, while at Hosteria Lazo, dinner is included, but not wines or spirits.

RIDING STUFF: The horses are bred locally and vary in size from 14 to 16 hands high. They are strong, sure-footed, responsive, and safe. Western-style saddles are covered with sheepskin to improve your comfort. Luggage is transported for you. The terrain is varied, offering good opportunities to gallop. Occasionally, you will need to dismount in order to cross a steep pass or narrow bridge. You need to be competent at all gaits. The horses spend a great deal of each day doing the "*gaucho*-gait," which resembles a long-strided sitting trot. Group size is limited to a maximum of 8, and a minimum of 4. The 2 rides cover similar terrain and, in fact, end at the same location. The riding will be across open valleys and plains, where distant mountains and glaciers look surreal, set against the contrasting green of the open valleys. Wildlife viewing will include guanaco herds, penguins, and the magnificent condors. Glaciers and icebergs will be seen while on horseback.

AUTHOR'S COMMENT: *Chile, why not? It's warm when the UK and US are cold. Another one of the incredible riding opportunities that is both adventure and ride. The warmest winter you ever spent, might be in Chile this year!*

HIGHLIGHTS
Riding through Torres del Paine • Visiting glaciers on horseback • Western-style riding • Gaited horses • 5 to 7 hours in the saddle per day • Good galloping opportunities • English-speaking guides • "Do the *Gaucho*-Gait"

ANDEAN MOUNTAIN RIDE

www.ridingtours.com/ecuador.htm

BASICS: Agent: **Equitour**, PO Box 807, Dubois, WY 82513, USA
Tel: (800) 545-0019   Tel: (307) 455-3363
Fax: (307) 455-2354
Email: equitour@wyoming.com
WHEN: Year round

AIRPORTS: Quito International.
LOCATION: The inn is about a 2 hours northeast of Quito, near Octavalo
PRICE: $1650 (£1030) 8 days/7 nights, per person, double occupancy, includes 4½ days of riding. Single supplement add $100 (£61).

The culture of the native people, who were among the first to inhabit Ecuador, still predominates in this area of the Northern Andes. The location of the Hacienda Zuleta allows you to ride amidst distinctive landscapes, including snow-capped peaks, waterfalls, valleys, and mountain lakes. The Hacienda offers quality accommodations and excellent horses, well trained to accommodate riders with a variety of skill levels, starting with advanced beginners. The year round temperatures are between 60° to 75° Fahrenheit (10° to 25° Centigrade) during the day. Nights are generally cooler and each season offers its own enticements.

CHILDREN'S PROGRAMS: Children must be experienced trail riders and accompanied by an adult.

ACCOMMODATIONS: The first and last nights are spent in Quito, the capitol of Ecuador, a delightful city founded in 1534. Guests enjoy a small charming hotel with en suite bathrooms, cable television, and telephone. The 5 nights of the riding program are spent at a small 8 room country hacienda, located on a 4,000 acre estate, 2 hours northeast of Quito. The estate was built in 1691 and is now owned by the descendants of former Ecuadorian President, Galo Plaza. The bedrooms are tastefully decorated and have shared bathrooms. There is also a comfortable living room with a fireplace for relaxing in the evening.

SPECIAL ACTIVITIES: There are opportunities to explore Quito with a guided tour and spend some time in the world-famous Indian market at Octavalo.

MEALS: Most of the produce, trout, and beef is grown on the 4,000 acre farm. Meals are eaten together in a warm friendly atmosphere. Lunch is served on the trail during riding days. Alcoholic beverages are included with meals.

RIDING STUFF: Four and a half days will be devoted to riding, 4 to 6 hours a day. The pace is fairly slow due to the terrain in the Andes Mountains, but there are good opportunities for cantering on soft grassy meadows. Riders should be comfortable at the walk, trot, on short canters, and be able to ride up and down steep hills. There is a weight limit of 200 lbs. (91 kg.) (14 stone). The horses are Andalusian and Thoroughbred crosses bred on location at Hacienda Zuleta. The tack is South American, a style similar to Western with a deep seat. Riders will experience the paramo, the tree line at 11,000 feet, archeological sites built by the Caranquis to honor their gods and departed, and a trek to a volcano.

AUTHOR'S COMMENT: *Ecuador is a country that has not yet experienced the tourist boom. It is one of the last frontiers in a world that wants a different experience with each ride. This ride allows you to capture the beauty of the Andes and the colorful people who live there, as well as the cultural and geological diversity of the region.*

HIGHLIGHTS
Western tack • Ancient buildings and sites • Riding the High Andes • Visits to world-famous Octavalo Indian markets • Comfortable inn accommodations at a hacienda • Moderate riding pace • Friendly family atmosphere

WHO CAN HELP?

TRAVEL AGENCIES

Here is a most valued list, the list of equestrian travel agencies, with special attention paid to those who kindly joined our efforts. These are the boys and girls, in big people's bodies, who work hard in offices assisting you in your choice of riding holidays, in order that they may enjoy what you enjoy. Theirs is a labor born of love. Are they reliable, are they good? The competition is fierce, slackers disappear, they are the crème de la crème, the connoisors of work-a-day riding holiday industry. Are they for you? You will only know if you contact them review their literature and log some time on the phone.

By agency location:

ASIA:
INTERNATIONAL HOLIDAYS & POLO HOIDAYS
D 383, Defence Colony, New Delhi 110024, India
Tel: (091) 11-4624879   Fax: (091) 11-4616137
Email: inder.tigers@aworld.net.
Web: www.horsebackholidays.com

(*See* **North America**)—Agency cover the world, with riding and polo holidays.

AUSTRALIA:
EQUITREK:AUSTRALIA
Club Equitrek, 5 King Rd., Ingleside NSW 2101, Australia
Tel: (61) 2-9913-9408   Mobile: (61) 018-444-117
Fax: (61) 2-9970-6303 (International)
Tel: (02) 9913-9408 (from Australia)
Email: nelly@equitrek.com.au
Web: www.equitrek.com.au
Specialists in Australia and New Zealand

EUROPE:
France
CHEVAL d'AVENTURE
Mas du Pommier, 07590 Cellier-du-Luc, France
Tel: (33) 466-466273   Fax: (33) 466-466209
Email: cheval.daventure@wanadoo.fr
Web: www.person.wanadoo.fr/cheval.daventure
Offers holidays around the world

EQUITOUR: PERIGRINE *
41 South Parade, Summertown, Oxford, England, OX2 7JP
Tel: 01865 511642 (UK); 011 44 1865 511642 (US)
Fax: 01865 512583 (UK); 011 44 1865 512583 (US)
Email: 106357.1754@compuserve.com
Extensive world offerings.

IN THE SADDLE
Laurel Cottage, Ramsdell, Tadley, Hampshire, England, RG26 5SH
Tel: 01256 851 665 (UK); 011 44 1256 851 665. (US)
Fax: 01256 851 667 (UK); 011 44 1256 851 667 (US)
Email: rides@inthesaddle.
Website: www.inthesaddle.com
Extensive world offerings.

INNTRAVEL
Hovingham, York, England, Y06 4JZ
Tel: 01653 628811 (UK); 011 44 1653 628811 (US)
Fax: 01653 628741 (UK); 011 44 1653 628741 (US)
Email: inntravel@inntravel.co.uk
Extensive riding holidays in Western Europe.

RIDE WORLD WIDE
58 Fentiman Road, London, England, SW8 1LF
Tel: 0171 735 1144 (UK); 011 44 171 735 1144 (US)
Fax: 0171 735 3179 (UK); 011 44 171 735 3179 (US)
E-mail: RideWW@aol.com
Offers worldwide riding holidays.

Other UK Equestrian agencies:

AMERICA ROUND-UP (North American ranching experts)
Oxenways, Membury,
Axminster, Devon, EX13 7JR
Tel: 01404 881777 (UK); 011 44 1404 881777 (US);
Fax: 01404 881778 (UK); 011 44 1404 881778 (US);

---

*Equitour is a common name for equestrian agencies and they are generally not related and operate as independent agencies as is the case with those mentioned here.

CAMPFIRE CLASSIC ADVENTURES
31 Grosvenor Road, Shaftesbury, Wilts SP7 8DP
Tel: 01747 855558 (UK); 011 44 1747 855558 (US)
Fax: 01747 855058 (UK); 011 44 1747 85558 (US)
Email: kiff@campfire.co.uk

FOXCROFT TRAVEL
245 Ratcliffe Road,
Sileby, Loughborough, England, LE12 7PY
Tel: 01509 813252 (UK); 011 44 1509 813252 (US)
Fax: 01509 814707 (UK); 011 44 1509 814707

J&C VOYAGEURS
Buckridges, Sutton Courtnay, Abingdon, Oxon,
0X14 4AW
Tel: 01235 848747 (UK); 011 441-235-848-747 (US)
Fax: 01235 848840 (UK); 011-441-235-848840
Email: jcvoyageurs@compuserve.com

RANCH AMERICA (North American ranching
experts)
Suite 2a, Horseshoe Business Park,
Upper Lye Lane, Bricket Wood,Hertfordshire, AL2 3TA
Tel: 01923 671831/2 (UK); 011 44 1923 671831/2 (US)
Fax: 01923 671833 (UK); 011 44 1923 671833 (US)
Email: ranch.america@ virgin.net
Website: http://www.ranchamerica.co.uk

RANCH RIDER (North American ranching experts)
The Coach House, Brand Lane,
Woodhouse Loughborough, LE12 8TY
Tel: 01509 239950 (UK); 011 44 1509 239950 (US)
Fax: 01509 239960 (UK); 011 44 1509 239960 (US)

NORTH AMERICA:

AMERICAN WILDERNESS EXPERIENCE
2820 A-Wilderness Place, Boulder, CO 80301
Tel: (303) 444-2622 Fax: (303) 444-3999
Email: awedave@aol.come
Website: www.awetrips.com

Offers adventure holidays throughout the
Americas, including riding and combination
adventure trips.

**CROSS COUNTRY INTERNATIONAL
EQUESTRIAN VACATIONS**
PO Box 1170, Millbrook, NY 12545
Tel: (914) 677-7000   Tel: 800-828-8768 (toll free
North and South America) Fax: 914-677-6077
Email: xcintl@aol.com
Web address: www.equestrianvacations.com

Covers Europe and some holidays in US.

EASTERN TREKKING ASSOCIATES
2574 Nicky Lane, Alexandria, VA 22311-1312
Tel: (703) 845-9366   Tel: (423) 933-0219
Fax: (703) 379-4059

Web Address: www.horsevacations.com
Email: susaneak@erols.com

Offers worldwide alternatives.

EQUITOUR*
PO Box 807, Dubois, Wyoming, 82513
Tel: 307-445-3363   Fax: 307-455-2354   Tel: 800-
545-0019 (Outside of Wy. –US toll free)
Email: equitour@wyoming.com
Web: http://www.ridingtours.com

Offers a worldwide menu of rides.

HIDDEN TRAILS
5936 Inverness St., Vancouver V5W 3P7, Canada
Tel: (604) 323-1141 or Tel: (888) 9-TRAILS   Fax:
(604) 323-1148
Email: vacations@hiddentrails.com
Web: http://hiddentrails.com

Offers a worldwide menu of rides.

INTERNATIONAL RIDING & POLO HOLIDAYS
8034-112 B Street, Delta, British Columiba V4G
5A7, Canada
Tel: (604) 501-1652   Fax: (604) 501-9213
Email: info@horsebackholidays.com
Web: www.horsebackholidays.com

Offers a worldwide menu of rides.

RIDING VACATIONS, INC.
P. O. Box 502
2575 North Medina Line Road
Richfield, OH 44286
Tel: (216) 659-6007

Specializes in equestrian vacations in North
America.

TOURIST BOARDS

National and regional tourist boards perform a
wealth of services for their nations tourist trade.
While the desire to please might be equal, there is a
degree of unevenness in terms of the literature, or
knowledge they may possess about riding holidays.
Some countries have extensive information on riding holidays, other's none. Some have their equestrian publications translated into friendly languages, others do not.
    If you are completely stymied on the official
level, do what politicians and others have learned to
do, up the ante, increase the pressure and call the
embassies of the respective countries. This process
while necessarily slower than the tourists board, can
yield, if you can endure, some very productive
results. Rather than burden you with long lists, we

suggest you consult your telephone directories, or operator assistance. Please note that the tourist boards often have toll free numbers in North America.

PUBLICATIONS

Many of the equestrian magazines publish articles on riding holidays and should be utilized by readers who wish to keep up to date or even study the ads on riding holidays. The following publishers have published books on riding holidays:

Jim Balzotti's Best Horseback Vacations and **US Stabling Guide** by Jim Balzotti
Balzotti Publications, 5 Barker St., Pembroke, MA, Tel: 800-829-0715

Saddle Up! By Ute Haker and **Ranch Vacations** by Gene Kilgore
John Muir Publications, PO Box 613, Santa Fe, New Mexico 87504

Farm, Ranch & Country Vacations in America, by Pat Dickerman, Adventure Guides Inc., 7550 East McDonald Drive, Scottsdale AZ 85250, US.

And also note:
The Good Holiday Cottage Guide, Swallow Press, PO Box 21, Hertford, Herts, SG 14 2DD, Tel: 01438-869489 or visit internet at:
www.abeeydes.co.uk/cottageguide.

Many riders, including many from the overseas, looking for accommodation to tie with riding could well turn to numerous self-catering holiday homes now availlable through England, Scotland, Wales and Ireland. Joint author John Ruler knows many through his work as a researcher for the guide, now in it's 18th year. Based entirely on first-hand inspection, the properties listed include many close to riding centers, especially in popular tourist areas. We are pleased to recommend the guide to readers as a useful tool for those seeking self-catering accommodation, handy if you want to relax in the comfort of "your own home" after a long day's riding.

Whole Horse Catalog—Steven Price, Fireside Publications/Simon & Schuster—Widely available in bookstores, revised edition scheduled for release. Fascinating book on the complete guide to owning, maintaining and enjoying horses, with expert advice on stabling, equestrian activities, shoeing, health, tack selecting a horse, apparel and there is even a chapter on riding holidays.

ASSOCIATIONS

Nearly all of these organizations can send you literature, either for free or at a nominal charge. Our web site at www.ridingholidays will offer a more extensive list for interested readers who have assess to the web.

EUROPE:
Austria:
O.N.T.E.:Geise Bergstrasse 26, 35/512 A, 1110 Vienna, Austria

France:
Delegacion Nationale Au Tourisme
30 Avenue d'Iena 75116 Paris, France

Finland:
Finish Horse Riding Association
Radiokatu 20, 0093 SLU
Helsinki, Finland
Tel: (358) 9-3481-2315

Italy:
A.N.T.E. (Associazione nazionale per il Turismo Equestre)
Via de Ponte di Castel Giubilco, 27/a 00188 Rome, Italy

Norway
Norwegian Equestrian Federation
Hayger Skolevel 1, 1351 Rud, Norway

Hest I turistnearing (Horses in tourism)
Fjellritter 2935, Beitostolen, Norway

Switzerland:
Swiss Association for Equestrian Sports
(Schweiz.Verband fuer Pfedesport):
Papiermuehle 40, 3014 Bern, Switzerland

Association Suisse de Randonnee Equestre
Case Postale 67, 1001 Lausane

United Kingdom:
Association of British Riding Schools
Queens Chambers, 38-40 Queen St., Penzance, Cornwall, England TR18 4BH
Tel: 01763 369440   Fax: 01736 351390
Web: www.abrs.org.uk

British Horse Society:
Stoneleigh Deer Park, Kenilworth, Warwickshire, England CV8 2XZ
Tel: 01203-690676   Fax: 01926-707743
Email: bookshop@bha.org.uk
Web: www.bha.org.uk

British Horse Society/Trekking & Riding Society of Scotland
Boreland, Fearnan, Aberfeldy, Perthshire, Scotland PH15 2PG
Tel: 01887-830274   Fax: 01232-240960

Wales Trekking & Riding Association
Depart. PO 01, Cardiff CF 12XN (UK), Standby House, 9 Nevill Street
Abergavenny Monmouthshire, Wales NP7 5AA (UK)
Tel: 01222 457766

NORTH AMERICAN:
Canada:
Alberta Outfitters Association:
PO Box 6267, Hinton, Alberta, T7V 1X6

British Columbia Guest Ranch Association
PO Box 4501, Williams Lake, B.C., V2G 1V8, Canada
(800) 663-6000

United States:
Arizona Dude Ranchers Association
PO Box 603, Cortaro, AZ 85652
Tel:

Colorado Dude and Guest Ranch Association
PO Box 300, Tabernash, CO 80478-0300
Tel: 970-887-3128   Fax: 970-887-3212
Email: 103104.1071@compuserve.com
Web address: www.@spout.entertain.com

Colorado Outfitter's Association
PO Box 440021
Aurora, CO 80044
Tel: 303-368-4731

Dude Ranchers Associations
PO Box 471-H, 471-H, LaPorte, CO 80535
Tel: (970) 223-8440   Fax; 970-223-0201
Email: 102,403.1624@compuserve.com
Web: www.duderanchorg.

Montana Outfitter's and Guides Association
PO Box 1248, Helena, MT 59624
Tel: 406-449-3578   Fax: 406-443-2439
Email: moga@niitco.net
Web: www.recworld.com

Wyoming Dude Rancher's Association
PO Box 618, Dubois, WY 82513
Tel: 307-455-2584   Fax: 307-455-2634
Email: motivations@wyoming.com
Web: www.wilderwest.com/wyoming/wdrassoc/duderanch

Wyoming Outfitters and Guide Association
PO Box 2284, Cody, WY 82414
Tel: 307-527-7453
Email: woa@wave.park.wy.us
Web: www.wyoga.org

INDEX OF RIDES

Adventures on Horseback, California, 280

African Horseback Safaris, Botswana, 26

Albion Rides, England, 232

Alcainca Dressage Program, Portugal, 214

Allie Cross Equestrian Centre, Ireland, 192

Altai and Arkhangai Trips, Mongolia, 78

Andaluz Adventure, Spain, 220

Andean Ride, Ecuador, 376

Aravalli Hills, India, 64

Argyll Trail Ride, Scotland, 236

Banana Ride, Mexico, 268

Bark Eater Inn, New York, 328

Bar Lazy J, Colorado, 286

Big Bar Guest Ranch, Canada, 254

Bitterroot Ranch, Wyoming, 340

Blue Coast/Mira Atlantic/Trail to the End of the World, Portugal, 216

Brush Gully Guest House, Australia, 94

Cabalgar Rutas Alternativas, Spain, 224

Cappadocia Tour, Turkey, 86

Casa de Campo, Dominican Republic, 368

Cascade Ride, Canada, 256

Castles Ride, Austria, 158

Clip Clop Horse Treks, Australia, 108

Connemara and Coast Trails, Ireland, 194

Corbett's Trails and Times, India, 62

D & P Equestrian Enterprises, England, 234

Double E Guest Ranch, New Mexico, 320

Douglas Lake Ranch Cattle Drive, Canada, 258

Drowsy Water Ranch, Colorado, 288

Drumgooland House & Equestrian Centre, Ireland, 198

Ellesmere Riding Centre, Wales, 240

El Rancho Horse Holidays, Ltd., Ireland, 200

Equus Horse Safaris, South Africa, 44

Eric Pele: "The Art of Horsepersonship" at Brookvale Farm, Ireland, 204

Estancia Huechahue Trek, Argentina, 370

Explorers' Ride, Austria, 160

Finca el Moro – Riding the Borders of Extremadurra, Spain, 226

Finnair Riding Tours, Finland, 164

Flynn Ranch Vacations, Montana, 310

Gaspe Peninsula Ride, Canada, 266

Grapevine Canyon Ranch, Arizona, 272

Hadoti Ride, India, 66

Hargrave Cattle Ranch, Montana, 312

Hartley Ranch, New Mexico, 322

Haurida Skogs Hast Safari, Sweden, 230

Hayfield Riding Centre, Scotland, 238

Heart of Provence, France, 180

Heart of Tuscany, Italy, 212
High Island Ranch, Wyoming, 344
Holiday on Horseback/Warner
    Guiding and Outfitting, Canada, 252
Horizon Horse Adventures at Triple B,
    South Africa, 46
Horseback Safaris on Lewa Downs,
    Kenya, 28
Horse Holiday Farm, Ireland, 206
Horse Riding in Bhutan/Chitwan
    National Park in Nepal, Bhutan/Nepal,
    60
Horse Trek Australia, Australia, 110
Hurunui Horse Treks, New Zealand, 124

Icelandic Riding Tours, Iceland, 182

Kelly's Bushranging Adventures,
    Australia, 96
Khancoban Trail Rides, Australia, 98

La Sierra Cavalcade & Monarch
    Butterfly Sanctuary, Mexico, 270
Lazy K Ranch, Montana, 314
Lazy L&B Ranch, Wyoming, 346
Lazy L&B's Bear Basin Wilderness
    Camp, Wyoming, 350
Le Moulin du Chemin, France, 174
Lonesome Spur Guest Ranch, Montana,
    316
Lozier's Box "R" Ranch, Wyoming, 352

Malvarina Trail Ride, Italy, 210
Mavuradonna Wilderness, Zimbabwe,
    48
McGee Creek Pack Station, California,
    282
Millamolong Station, Australia, 100
Montana Equestrian Tours, Montana,
    318
Mudinina Horse Trekking Centre,
    France, 176

Namib Desert Trails, Namibia, 42
N Bar Ranch, New Mexico, 324
New Zealand Backcountry Saddle
    Expeditions, New Zealand, 128
Nyika Horse Safaris, Malawi, 40
North River Treks, New Zealand, 118

Offbeat Safaris Africa Limited, Kenya, 30

Pakiri Beach Horse Rides, New Zealand,
    120
Pakistani Journeys, Pakistan, 84
Patagonia Experience, Chile, 372
Pub Crawls on Horseback, Australia, 106
Pushkar Fair Ride, India, 72
Pyrenees Mountain Ride, France, 178

Rawah Guest Ranch, Colorado, 290
Renegade Rides, Wyoming, 354
Ricochet Ridge Ranch, California, 284
Rhiwiau Riding Centre, Wales, 242
Riding with the Nihangs and Into the
    Himalaya, India, 68
Russian Adventure, Russia, 218

Safaris Unlimited Africa Ltd., Kenya, 34
Shalivan Stables, India, 74
Sierra Nevada: The Contraviesa and
    Alpujarra Rides, Spain, 228
Small Cattle, Idaho, 306
South Bohemia Ride, Austria/Czech
    Republic, 162
Southern Oasis and High Atlas Valley,
    Morocco, 38
Speckled Mountain Ranch, Maine, 308
Swift Level, West Virginia, 334
Sylvan Dale Guest Ranch, Colorado, 292

Te Urewara Adventures of New
    Zealand, New Zealand, 122
Three Bars Guest and Cattle Ranch,
    Canada, 260
Torres del Paine, Chile, 374
Ts'yl-os Park Lodge and Wilderness
    Trips, Canada, 262
2000 Olympic Rides, Australia, 102

Valley of the Mustang Ride, Nepal, 80
Vee Bar Guest Ranch, Wyoming, 358
Vermont Icelandic Horse Farm,
    Vermont, 332

Western Encounter, Wyoming. 362
White Stallion Ranch, Arizona, 276
Wilderness Trails Ranch, Colorado, 294
Wit's End, Colorado, 298